D1520598

RETURNING TO IRIGARAY

SUNY series in Gender Theory

Tina Chanter, editor

RETURNING TO

IRIGARAY

*Feminist Philosophy, Politics, and
the Question of Unity*

EDITED BY

MARIA C. CIMITILE
ELAINE P. MILLER

STATE UNIVERSITY OF NEW YORK PRESS

Published by
STATE UNIVERSITY OF NEW YORK PRESS,
Albany

© 2007 State University of New York

For information, address State University of New York Press
194 Washington Avenue, Suite 305, Albany, NY 12210-2384

Production, Laurie Searl
Marketing, Anne M. Valentine

Returning to Irigaray : feminist philosophy, politics, and the question of unity / edited by
   Maria C. Cimitile, Elaine P. Miller
      p. cm. — (SUNY series in gender theory)
   Includes bibliographical references and index.
   ISBN-13: 978-0-7914-6919-4 (hardcover : alk. paper)
   ISBN-10: 0-7914-6919-0 (hardcover : alk. paper)
   ISBN-13: 978-0-7914-6920-0 (pbk. : alk. paper)
   ISBN-10: 0-7914-6920-4 (pbk. : alk. paper)
   1. Irigaray, Luce. 2. Feminist theory. I. Cimitile, Maria, 1967– II. Miller, Elaine P.,
1962– III. Series.

B2430.I74R48 2006
194—dc22

2005037171

10 9 8 7 6 5 4 3 2 1

CONTENTS

ACKNOWLEDGMENTS

Margaret Whitford's essay "Irigaray and the Culture of Narcissism" and Penelope Deutscher's essay "*Between East and West* and the Politics of 'Cultural *Ingénuité*': Irigaray on Cultural Difference" appeared previously in *Theory, Culture and Society*, vol. 20, no. 3 (June 2003). We thank the editors and the authors for permission to reprint the essays here.

The editors wish to express their gratitude to Sara McNamara, J. P. Baertson, and Jim Fox for their invaluable help in completing this project. Sara's meticulous bibliography provides an important resource for those who are looking for a complete account of Irigaray's published work in all languages. Her work represents many hours of rigorous and careful research. J. P. Baertson made certain the details of the many differently formatted manuscripts were brought into a consistent format. Jim Fox provided invaluable help with difficult formatting and word processing problems. We also thank Jane Bunker and Katy Leonard of SUNY Press for their patience, good sense, and advocacy in all the stages of this project. A special thanks to Tina Chanter for her encouragement and support at the start and throughout the process of the project.

In addition, Elaine Miller thanks Ferit, Sofi, and Leyla Güven, the last of whom shortly after birth had to share the attention of her mother with a fussy manuscript. Their support and appreciation made even the most difficult of tasks bearable.

Maria Cimitile thanks her friends and family for their support and encouragement, with special thanks to Jacqueline Scott, Kim Pesenti, Jim Fox, Judy Whipps, Allen Whipps, Coeli Fitzpatrick, Michael DeWilde, Dorothy Berg, and Sheila Grant for the advice, faith, and laughter they provided.

INTRODUCTION

Elaine P. Miller and Maria C. Cimitile

It has been ten years since the publication of *Engaging With Irigaray*. Since that time, three special issues of journals have been devoted to Irigaray's later writings, but there has been no book-length project that addresses the question that has been raised tangentially by both of these, namely whether Irigaray's corpus of writings, viewed as a whole, manifests a unity in her own sense of an ongoing open-ended dialogue that respects difference. This volume seeks to address that question and to consider the latest changes in the relational climate of Irigaray scholarship and its critics. Whereas Irigaray's earliest writings gave rise to a flurry of charges of essentialism, the question that dominated the 1998 special issue of *diacritics* on Irigaray's "middle" (post-1984) writings was what exactly she meant when referring to sexual difference as the question that determines our age. Today, the critique of Irigaray seems most focused on the shift in style and subject in her latest, most specifically political and "applied" writings that, at least at first glance, contrast sharply with everything she wrote before. And so our focus in this volume is on the unity of Irigaray's corpus—not its completion—if only in the sense of, as one of the authors in this volume argues, an impossible yet-to-come.

Recent Irigaray scholarship often makes reference to the shift in thematic focus, tone, and style of Irigaray's latest writings from her earlier, arguably more poetic and more textual philosophical commentary to a purportedly more overtly political, "applied" philosophy that "spells out" a message. This reference, however, rarely goes beyond what is seen as a nod to the obvious. This book considers whether

1

there has been a radical conceptual "turn" in Irigaray's thought in addition to the apparent stylistic shift, and, if so, what the implications of such a shift may be. Similar to the language used to describe Heidegger's *Kehre*, some Irigaray scholars seem implicitly to refer to an Irigaray I of texts such as *Speculum of the Other Woman*, *This Sex Which Is Not One*, and *Elemental Passions*, on the one hand, and an Irigaray II of texts such as *I Love to You*, *Thinking the Difference*, and *Je, tu, nous*, on the other, with *The Ethics of Sexual Difference*, published in 1984, marking a kind of turning point, both chronologically and thematically and in terms of the kind of critique that Irigaray began to receive even from her most sympathetic readers.[1]

The interesting question to emerge from this debate is not so much a final answer as to whether or not Irigaray has made a conceptual "turn," but rather what is at stake in arguing for or against this continuity, or for or against one style or focus of philosophical inquiry or another. How one interprets these issues of continuity and style reveals as much about current philosophical concerns as it does about Irigaray's thought. This question already arose in brief in a *diacritics* special issue on Irigaray in 1998, but it was eclipsed by the discussion of the role and meaning of sexual difference in Irigaray. Our hope is to continue to stimulate and to further develop a debate regarding this question by collecting a variety of philosophical positions in a more extensive forum.

In interviews with Brena Niorelli and Ida Dominijanni, Irigaray insists on the continuity between *The Forgetting of Air in Martin Heidegger* and *I Love to You* in particular (Irigaray 2000 [1998][2], 129–41).[3] Irigaray's point is that, in spite of the chronological span between the original publication of the two works and, as the interviewer points out, despite even the seeming "significant difference" in the depiction of the relationship between man and woman, there is a "bridge" to be built between conceptions of intersubjectivity in the two works and, by extension, between the styles and foci of the two works (Irigaray 2000 [1998], 129). The bridge is arguably emblematic of the thematic and stylistic connections between her earlier and later writings. Interestingly, Irigaray also often describes the symbolics of the couple as a "bridge" and writes that "[t]he alliance between man and woman becomes . . . a bridge between nature and culture, a bridge which has yet to be built" (Irigaray 2001 [1994], 84).

The reconsideration of Irigaray's later work as different from yet not opposed to her earlier style and focus calls into question a whole series of oppositional structures. Perhaps one of the most salient of these structures is the oppositions between nature and culture, followed by the oppositions between the ideal and the real, the academy and politics, and intellectual analysis and practical application. Irigaray's method of challenging binary oppositions points us to her larger strategy of opening a place for change and difference, emphasizing spaces of ontological dynamism, rather than static totalizing concepts.

What would it mean to read Irigaray's later work not as a break from her earlier writings, but with this notion of the bridge as a means of bringing the more critical and speculative work into the context of the political? We are interested in considering whether one could read the earlier work's style of transformative mimesis as a prelude to the affirmative politics of Irigaray's later work, and whether the effort to take the symbolic and bring it into the realm of the civic succeeds or fails. One focus of discussion that we hoped would arise out of this consideration is whether the conjunction of two styles and foci can be seen as a unified project, as Irigaray herself appears to contend, or whether there is nevertheless a marked break, as many Irigaray commentators assume. As Carolyn Burke writes, perhaps "Irigaray's message is best served when both aspects of her style are present and engaged in dialogue with each other—and with the reader" (Burke et al. 1994, 257). We explicitly extend this dialogue to the consideration of questions of the intersection of theory and practice and the relationship between author and commentator, in particular the feminist commentator.

Irigaray herself has fairly recently argued for a conception of both theory and practice, based on the "tradition of India," that is ever open, never fully achieved (Irigaray 2002 [1999], 21), and extends this to a model of dialogue. We assert here that this can be taken as a prototype for feminist commentary with Irigaray herself. What Irigaray calls "an engendering preceded by an exchange of breath and of words" (Irigaray 2002 [1999], 52) aligns the breathing practices of yoga with nonappropriative dialogue that does not attempt to reduce the other to the same, a dialogue that might engender something new through its encounter with difference. The practitioner of yoga attempts to free herself from excessive attachment to any one theme or thought, not by berating herself when she slips back into a familiar theme or train of thought, but by observing the thought and letting it go, allowing for a new awareness to arise without trying to control its contours. As Irigaray notes, this is only accomplished in interaction with a spiritual guide, that is, in dialogue, and there is no specified goal at the outset, nor a place where any one outcome is definitively achieved. There is always room for further growth, in particular that which would overcome static dualisms, such as that between mind and body, through breath, as we will elaborate on further.

Yet for us commentators, asserting such an open-endedness is not in itself a satisfactory substitute for articulating the trajectory of a thinker, in particular because, as Penelope Deutscher notes, "among the most interesting aspects of Irigaray's corpus is the elaborate secondary literature it has provoked" (Deutscher 1998, 170). In accord with this statement, this volume seeks to bring out the subtleties of the responsibility of the feminist commentator in particular. Margaret Whitford contrasts interpretations of Irigaray that either "immobilize or energize" and argues that "it is more valuable to choose the dynamic interpretation, rather than imprisoning Irigaray in the limitations of her own perspective" (Whitford 1991, 6). Indeed, according to Whitford, "the important thing is to engage with Irigaray *in order to go beyond her*" (ibid.). We agree with this claim and contend that the strength of Irigaray scholarship lies in the fact that it can engage with Irigaray's texts in a manner that pushes interpretation beyond the relationship of disciple to master, and thus has the potential to exemplify feminist theory at its best, a practice that Irigaray herself developed.

We therefore gather papers here that critically analyze Irigaray's later thought with recourse to her earlier work, both on its own terms and in terms of the tradition that it seeks to deconstruct and transform. Our contention is that although the shifts in Irigaray's later works may be more immediately striking to readers than their continuities, as scholars of Irigaray's thought we cannot read these writings out of context, but must foster a dialogue around the question of just *how* the political focus of Irigaray's recent thought emerges. In these analyses the volume as a whole reflects on the implications of the unity or apparent disjunction of Irigaray's earlier and later thought. In particular, we have considered themes that have become prevalent in Irigaray's later texts such as intersubjectivity, feminine subjectivity, civil identity, democracy, community, and non-Western traditions. In engaging with Irigaray's later texts we seek to balance emerging and established Irigaray scholars in order to consider the tenability and implications of the temporal, stylistic, and political distinction that has been drawn in Irigaray.

We reopen here a question that was posed but not elaborated upon in the special issue on Irigaray of *diacritics*. Editors Pheng Cheah and Elizabeth Grosz address the question of the continuity of Irigaray's corpus and note with disappointment the fact that Irigaray's later work has been largely dismissed, though some of her earlier writings have earned a place in the canons of philosophy and feminist and literary theory:

> Most commentators regard her as primarily a thinker of sub-jectivity, identity, sexuality, and desire, and rarely consider her as a political theorist or an analyst of social and cultural life. Thus, even the most sympathetic readers have tended to extract the social and political implications of her work from her earlier and primarily psychoanalytic texts, which are then taken as so emblematic of her work that her later writings are rarely read, let alone discussed. . . . Consequently, *Speculum of the Other Woman* and *This Sex Which Is Not One* have effec-tively functioned as synechdoches of her entire oeuvre. (Cheah and Grosz 1998, 5–6)

As Cheah and Grosz note, these texts are clearly groundbreaking and enduringly important works of feminist theory, but they do not rep-resent the breadth of Irigaray's work, which has undergone numerous self-reflective transformations and changes of emphasis over the thirty-some years she has been publishing. Irigaray's work continues to reach a relatively narrow audience, mostly in academic and literary con-texts, despite the fact that she is now addressing herself broadly to issues in the social sciences and politics in addition to philosophy.

Philosophy itself, we might add, takes Irigaray's work insuffi-ciently seriously despite her many important readings of philosophy, which have had an irreversible effect on the way in which we con-sider certain texts. Hegel and Plato, to name only two, will never be the same since Irigaray turned her critical eye on them. Yet, it is in her later work that Irigaray attempts to address a perennial critique of philosophy, its inability to leave the "ivory tower" and concretely transform what it critiques. It is perhaps telling that in attempting to do precisely this, Irigaray has lost many of her previous interlocutors.

Illustrative of the debate among commentators is the consider-ation and often consternation regarding Irigaray's discussion of sexual difference. The special issue of *diacritics* somewhat narrowly focuses on the theme of sexual difference, because Irigaray's emphasis on this theme in the early 1980s effectively dominated discussion of her work at this time. As the editors note, the focus on the duality of sexual difference caused great consternation among readers who had rejected the essentialism critique and who associated Irigaray with a celebration of multiplicity, both of sexuality and desire and of identity or subjectivity. Naturally associated with this worry was a more specific and serious concern, that Irigaray's new focus on sexual difference implied not only a reduction of her conception of identity but a distinct privileging of heterosexuality. Although the editors contest this interpretation, both Judith Butler and Drucilla Cornell, whose interview forms the centerpiece of the issue, argue that Irigaray's more recent work has become increasingly conservative, in particular that the emphasis on sexual difference both preserves that traditional assumption that heterosexuality is the sexual norm and contributes to a homogenization and reduction of sexual, racial, and class politics.

In part, the present volume responds to this debate by looking at how the question of sexual difference has unfolded in a wealth of different directions in Irigaray's work in the years since this special issue appeared. The essays in this volume focus on the areas of nature and technology, social and political theory and praxis, ethics, psychoanalysis, and phenomenology. Sexual difference both continues to delineate Irigaray's concerns, in that her call for sexuate rights reflects her belief in the primacy of the question of sexual difference for our age, but has also been complicated by Irigaray's interest in non-Western traditions and "third" elements beyond the duality of male and female. The volume includes essays that argue for the continuity of Irigaray's early and late writings, as well as sharply critical essays that carry on the theme of disappointment in the turn that Irigaray seems to have made.

Ultimately, Cornell and Butler's discomfort seems to arise in large part from Irigaray's claim, in *The Ethics of Sexual Difference*, that "according to Heidegger, each age has one issue to think through, and one only. Sexual difference is probably the issue in our time which could be our 'salvation' if we thought it through" (Irigaray 1993 [1984], 5). Cornell associates this line with a Heideggerean move of "turning sexual difference into a way of thinking about the truth of Being in a particular historical era" (Cheah and Grosz 1998, 32). No wonder Irigaray is thought to have made a *Kehre*! If sexual difference is thought not as a quasi-Heideggerian epoch of Being, but rather in its full range of symbolic, cultural, and political effects, it can perhaps be disentangled from the enormous baggage even a superficial linkage with the late Heidegger can entail. Indeed, in the 2002 work *The Way of Love,* her most recent work to be published in English, Irigaray explicitly states the need to go beyond the historical reflection of Heidegger, moving from the house of language toward being with the other in her difference (Irigaray 2002, 70–71).

Irigaray's "sensible transcendental" can be seen as an attempt to overcome a sharp distinction between the ideal and the real, such that the ideal might be instantiated in the real. The ideal is not to come from the outside in order to shape the real, but to be instantiated within the real, albeit not in a Hegelian sublation. Seen in this light, the early work of mimesis is, in Grosz's words, "an attempt to generate an anomaly that produces a new future . . . the breakdown from inside the system that allows that system itself to generate a future that isn't containable by that system" (Cheah and Grosz 1998, 40). Mimesis thus would link directly to cultural and social and political, not merely philosophical, transformation. When we reflect upon the mimetic strategy that Irigaray employs in her early work, we recognize its deconstructive use in uncovering the phallocratic assumptions grounding philosophical projects. In addition, we argue that in the very act of destruction, a creation is also occurring. Irigaray creates a space for a new cultural, social, and political moment. Irigaray's mimesis in her early work is transformative *both* philosophically and politically in the sense that it opens up possibilities that will only come to fruition in her later work.

Indeed, the politics of Irigaray's later work can be seen as the "other side of the mirror" of her early strategy of mimesis as a phenomenological method of deconstructing the canon and exposing both the ways in which woman has been philosophically erased and positive possibilities for transformation. Irigaray has indirectly addressed this concern in works published since 1998, especially in her taking up of the themes of breath as a figure for unity in difference and of the love of the other that retains the other's difference. Using the practice of yoga as a primary metaphor, Irigaray shows that the concept of breath can mediate across East and West as well as fundamental philosophical binaries: body and soul, real and ideal, practice and theory. In *Between East and West* Irigaray also addresses the implication that sexual difference seems to take precedence over all other kinds of difference with reference to race and culture. Whereas before it seemed that Irigaray was subordinating racial and cultural differences, just as differences in sexual identity, to sexual difference, she attempts to rectify this problem, although arguably problematically, through the concepts of *mixité* and respect for all forms of alterity.

This volume seeks to cover the incredible breadth of Irigaray's thinking, from psychoanalysis to phenomenology to social and political theory, and their relationship. Although we are thinking about turnings, we do so in order to overcome this kind of dichotomous categorization. We want to avoid the *distraction* caused by overfocusing on a division or a turning in a thinker's work, such as we have seen happen within Heidegger commentary. Thus, "returning" to Irigaray involves not only a temporal or spatial return, but also a focus on the idea of a "turn" in Irigaray as a return to themes that have concerned her all along. Most of the essays in this collection argue against the interpretation of a turn in Irigaray as a radical break. Although taking up different themes in her work, most of our contributors agree that it is important not to read any of Irigaray's writings in isolation from the others. If there is a theme that these diverse articles all share, it is perhaps relationality. Relationality in difference and the necessity of reading in context is at the center of all these essays—in the themes of intersubjectivity, sexual difference, and dialogue.

The idea of relationality as the interaction between two is already familiar to readers of Irigaray. But, in her latest work, Irigaray seems to gesture toward a way beyond the two, or a way that engages the two in such a way as to allow for a multiplicity or at least a third that would not simply be an extension of or sublation into a monolithic one. The discussion of relationality in Irigaray can often be reductive, either limiting her dialogue to only one other thinker or restricting her method to negation or appropriation. With the discussion of the third, Irigaray puts positive interaction at the center of her concern.

For example, in *The Way of Love*, Irigaray defines herself most explicitly against Heidegger in her reflection on being, world, and temporality, yet part of her critique is to show Heidegger's unwitting complicity with Hegel and other thinkers he himself critiques. The purpose of this critique is not simply dismissal, however, but leads into a discussion of positive possibilities to emerge from this engagement. Here, a critique of Hegel, in particular his conception of recognition as the basis for intersubjectivity and ethics, which Irigaray has often argued reduces the other to the same, is layered with an engagement with Heidegger:

If the Being standing in front of me forgets the other's difference, then I am not confronted with the singularity of my own representation and with what it implies for my looking. If what stays in-front-of is only a same unthought as such, I can turn back to my network of interrelations inside of one and the same world. . . . I return to myself unchanged in a closed History or world. . . . My ideal image is then deferred into the beyond, into God, which guides my steps toward the different, toward difference, without having any possibility of experiencing it. . . . The relation between those who are same and different weaves a groundless ground. It corresponds neither to the abyss nor to nothingness but results from an act of grounding which does not end in any ground. The ground is not equivalent then to a multiplicity of interweavings where man already stays and where he dwells—where he is both safeguarded and enclosed. (Irigaray 2002, 71–72)

The passage interweaves critiques of two thinkers and reflects a critique of Hegel that Heidegger draws on, yet it is turned against what is seen as a blind spot in Heidegger himself. Irigaray targets Heidegger's discussion of dwelling as a kind of withdrawal from, rather than an active engagement with, the world. Irigaray's response is complex and not merely negative. Rather, it provides the opening for a new engagement both with oneself and the other:

The meaning of "identity" is then modified insofar as it is no longer determined by the same understood as an equivalence between two terms—be they "thinking" and "Being." It is rather the difference between two terms—man and woman—that brings each one back to oneself thanks to the construction of a temporality in which relation to the same does not take root in a tautology but in a becoming. The same, from then on, is not appraised as similitude, but as a fidelity to oneself compelled by the care of the human, particularly as care of the other. (Irigaray 2002, 81–82)

What interests us about Irigaray's engagement with Hegel and Heidegger here is not merely her conceptual interaction with their thought, but also her ability to perform a new methodology for us. In the very act of engaging with Hegel and Heidegger she reflects the trajectory of her own thought over time, the move from the deconstructive project to the constitution of identity and inter-subjectivity, and ultimately politics. As readers, we cannot understand this last moment in her thought without having experienced her earlier engagement with the philosophical canon.

Respect and care for alterity relates to a dynamic temporality that holds possibility, rather than a cherishing of already constituted being, to be the most important human good. This possibility again is linked to dialogue and relationality that is never ascertained in advance:

> In order to pass from the past to the future, a releasing all hold is indispensable, a letting be. Rather than a diving into the depths, why not envision it as the uncovering, the unveil-ing of a still closed sky. . . . The dialogue between two living subjects opens and closes again at each moment the question of what Being is. (Irigaray 2002, 83)

The desire to foreclose the possibility of a self-enclosed oneness leads Irigaray, in a move that surprises, given her almost exclusive emphasis on twoness heretofore, to claim that "the real exists as at least three: a real corresponding to the masculine subject, a real corresponding to the feminine subject, and a real corresponding to their relation" (Irigaray 2002, 111). This three has implications beyond the realm of sexual difference, and many of the essays collected here explore the question of duality and its overcoming.

Gail Schwab's essay "Reading Irigaray (and Her Readers) in the Twenty-First Century," with which this collection opens, offers us an expansive chronological perspective within which we can situate in-dividual issues within Irigaray scholarship. Schwab's historical over-view opens the way to viewing Irigaray's corpus as consistently addressing the female generic—from contesting its predetermination within the economy of the same to a psychoanalytic account of othering. Irigaray's highly contested claim that all difference begins in sexual difference is contextualized as Schwab shows Irigaray's intellec-tual trajectory to be dialogical, that is, a conversation with historical, cultural, and philosophical forces. In particular, Schwab speaks to the criticisms of Irigaray's claim of the primacy of sexual difference and argues that Irigaray does not conflate sexual difference and hetero-sexism. Drawing on textual sources that are often overlooked, she shows the female-male relationship to be one of ontological necessity in terms of the psychoanalytic necessity of the other, and not simply constitutive of sexual identity. Schwab writes:

> The choice to live separately, apart from men and exclusively among women, is itself a choice that foregrounds the existence of the two genders. It can effectively fulfill a generic identity, and define a community, but nonetheless owes a debt to sexual difference—not to heterosexuality, but sexual difference, which, again, is not dyadic, not about heterosexual couples, or couples at all, but about, in the words of Liz Grosz, "the right of the other to have its other." (Schwab, "Reading Irigaray and Her Readers in the Twenty-First Century," 42)

Krzysztof Ziarek reads the third as a kind of energy in his essay "A New Economy of Relations," showing Irigaray's analysis to be a kind of transformed Heideggerian meditation on temporality and technology:

> While the two kinds of energy, vital and cultural, become locked into the dialectics of production, a dialectics underpinned by the subject-object metaphysics, the third energy Irigaray alludes to breaks free of the nature-culture divide. It is neither natural (biological, physiological, sexual) nor cultural (intellectual, spiritual, technological, etc.). This "new" or "alternative" energy does not submit itself to manufacturing, creation, or production of objects and goods; in other words, it is not convertible into either production or consumption, and, as such, it does not operate in terms of the technological, and now, informational, economy of relations. (Ziarek, "A New Economy of Relations," 62)

Ziarek's essay explores the implications of Irigaray's latest work, work that espouses a new relation to the other based on the recognition of the enabling invisibility of difference. Irigaray argues that difference cannot be made visible, for to do so would render difference into sameness through appropriation, but that the invisible energy of "letting-be" suggests an alternative to this economy of the same. Ziarek takes Irigaray's claim about alterity and shows how it might suggest an alternative to the hegemony of late capitalist culture manifest as the consumerist Information Age, what he calls, expanding on Heidegger's critique of technicity, the "info-technical economy of relations." Ziarek's essay demonstrates the connection between the transformation of Being into discrete units of quantifiable data and the economy of visibility. Irigaray's new energy of enabling attempts to transcend the dialectic of visibility through the actual recognition of difference. Following this reading, Ziarek gives a critique of the hegemony of the economy of visibility and its conception of the human being as primarily a productive agent as well as a strategy for fighting contemporary culture's movement toward quantification as knowledge. He shows how Irigaray redraws the relationship between visibility and invisibility that has been constitutive of the "Western metaphysical optics of being," and reconceives the human being as the one who has the ability to open up invisibility rather than make being visible and knowable. This reading helps us to conceptualize Irigaray's corpus as a continuum that begins with her phenomenological critique of the metaphysics of presence and continues in her positive positing of an economy outside simple dualism.

Ann Murphy's essay "Beyond Performativity and Against 'Identification': Gender and Technology in Irigaray" takes a different stance on Irigaray's critique of technology. Murphy argues that Irigaray's misgivings with reference to technology lead her to a dismissal of discourses of androgyny and performativity in gender identification, both of which Murphy reads as misguided attempts to attain a status of equality for women, doomed insofar as they are complicit with misogynist cultural norms. Reading Irigaray's critique of technology as a "technophobia," Murphy finds a dangerous tendency within Irigaray's concurrent reluctance to valorize narratives of transgenderism and transsexuality that might align with the attempt to normalize or naturalize experience on phenomenological grounds. She thus sees Irigaray as having moved beyond the subversive parody of the natural that she performed in her early work, but, troublingly, having become invested in categories she once insisted lay well beyond the grasp of discourse, namely the anchorage of sexual difference in biological nature. Murphy argues that Irigaray's later work forgets the growing impossibility of discerning between nature and technology. She writes:

> At its most hyperbolic, and arguably its most ominous, Irigaray's investment in nature is accomplished as an appeal to a discourse that is at best dismissive and at worst hostile towards certain gender narratives. . . . To privilege the natural and even

morphological differences between men and women in a way that justifies the pejorative and even vitriolic treatment of the contemporary discourse on gender identification is to come dangerously close to exemplifying the dismissive and phobic manner in which some have navigated the philosophical discourses on transgenderism and transsexuality. (Murphy, "Beyond Performativity and Against 'Identification': Gender and Technology in Irigaray," 88–89)

Elaine Miller's essay "Reconsidering Irigaray's Aesthetics" also grapples with Irigaray's conceptualization of nature, this time with reference to aesthetics. Irigaray's aesthetics have been called uncharacteristically conservative by commentators, and it has been suggested that what makes Irigaray's contribution to aesthetics valuable concerns the integration of theory and aesthetic praxis rather than her discussion of actual art or artists. Miller expands on the immanent analysis of Irigaray's writings that directly concern art by contextualizing them within her larger philosophical corpus, arguing in particular that Irigaray's conception of nature, which has always been a contentious topic of discussion among commentators, can be illuminated by examining it in relation to her aesthetics. Supplementing both the psychoanalytic and the biological readings of Irigaray's discussion of nature with an analysis of Irigaray's engagement with German Idealism and Marx, Miller shows how "nature" is a highly complex concept for Irigaray, one which ultimately has important implications for aesthetics. In particular, Miller reads Irigaray's discussion of the beauty of nature with and against that of Hegel and Adorno. Adorno writes that natural beauty as a concept only arose in the early bourgeois period out of the historical progress of art, and the purportedly pure representation of nature in art occludes this historical emergence. Artworks that represent nature merely repeat the gesture of industry, relegating nature to raw materials. The beauty of nature can thus only be represented in art nonrepresentationally. Miller argues that "nature" functions in a similarly destabilizing way in Irigaray:

Irigaray argues that sexual difference, as the fundamental polarity in nature, is an immediate delineating force that must be preserved and addressed in all theorizing about nature or spirit (human activities). "Nature" functions similarly in Irigaray's writings to the way in which Adorno describes it, as

> a cipher for that which resists the overarching contemporary
> economy of instrumental reason and calculative exchange
> value, or, as Irigaray might rather put it, of the male symbolic
> order. . . . For both thinkers, the beauty of nature represents a
> resistance to the colonizing power of a specific mode of think-
> ing, that thinking that reduces alterity to something to be
> reworked and consumed. . . . [Beautiful art] keeps this promise
> of the beauty of nature by distorting the lens that purports to
> reflect reality back faithfully but in doing so reduces the other
> to the same. (Miller, "Reconsidering Irigaray's Aesthetics,"
> 105–106)

Irigaray's writings on art can thus also provide a miniparadigm for her
readers of the shift in Irigaray's writings from a primarily critical and
deconstructive stance to the attempt to show what it might mean to
construct positive, ideal representations of women's identity.

Kelly Oliver, too, addresses the theme of Irigaray's relation to
Hegel, albeit with respect to ethics and politics, in her essay on the
transformation of Irigaray's concept of vision from her earlier critique
of the priority of vision in the Western tradition to her reconceptualization, in the later works, of vision as a loving look. In "Vision,
Recognition, and a Passion for the Elements," Oliver traces Irigaray's
transformed concept of vision and its connection to intersubjectivity
through her engagement with Merleau-Ponty and Levinas. In particular, Oliver argues that Irigaray's new theory of carnal vision, that is, a
vision of touch, can be connected to her attention to the elemental in
a way that might ground her more recent thoughts on intersubjectivity.
The loving look is a vision before vision, as Oliver writes,

> . . . a tactile look that does not pry or gaze, but caresses in the
> flow of irrigation and irradiances. This look that sees without
> seeing, this look that touches the unseen substrate of the visible,
> seems to be an immersion in the ebb and flow of the moving
> elements that give birth to and nourish sensation and therefore
> thought, vision, and visions. A loving look becomes the inau-
> guration of "subjectivity" without subjects. (Oliver, "Vision,
> Recognition, and a Passion for the Elements," 128–129)

Mediated by the elemental, in particular by air, the gaze cannot capture or objectify the other. Oliver guides the reader in understanding

Irigaray's later thought, which attempts to build the possibility of a new ethic of recognition. If we are to take Irigaray's ethic seriously, we must understand this recognition of difference as beyond the Hegelian master-slave dialectic, a recognition that ultimately subsumes the Other into the One.

Penelope Deutscher's essay "*Between East and West* and the Politics of 'Cultural *Ingénuité*': Irigaray on Cultural Difference" addresses contemporary concerns about the inadequate treatment of race and cultural difference in Irigaray's writings. Deutscher first takes up the problematic by making a comparison between Irigaray and Simone de Beauvoir's tendency to generalize issues of racial difference. In the context of French intellectual discussions of the mid-twentieth century, including those of Fanon, Sartre, Cesaire, and Senghor, Beauvoir is unique in not taking up the politics of *négritude*, nor even a concomitant politics of *féminitude*. Deutscher draws out the parallels between these works of the 1940s and '50s that Beauvoir neglected, on the one hand, and Irigaray's recent discussion of cultural difference, on the other. Although the two thinkers' positions on equality versus sexual difference are clearly divergent, they share a blind spot with reference to race. While both tend to generalize differences of race, Irigaray's inattention to voices of cultural difference is more problematic, in Deutscher's view, given her treatment of sexual difference, which one might think would serve as a model for analysis of cultural difference. Deutscher draws on Irigaray's recent *Entre Orient et Occident* to demonstrate Irigaray's failure to treat cultural difference attentively and with the same philosophical rigor that she applied to sexual difference. With regard to cultural difference and Irigaray's embrace of yoga and other non-Western ideas, Deutscher argues even more strongly that Irigaray might well be reifying the very structures of the economy of the same that she deconstructs with regard to sexual difference, such that the East is idealized as a mere mirror for the West, without a space for its own voice to emerge.

Deutscher's essay brings these questions to bear on Irigaray's work with regard to cultural difference in general, and race in particular, issues that Irigaray herself raises yet, in Deutscher's view, fails to adequately address, especially given the insights that Irigaray's earlier writing on sexual difference have provided. Deutscher writes:

> The question Irigaray takes up in her recent politics is how to live with the (culturally different) other. Is cultural difference

just a matter of learning new means of living with difference?
As Irigaray asked of sexual difference, what about fostering
the conditions for new formations of difference? What if
Western culture has been founded on the exclusion of
the possibility of such formations? The conditions for the
invention of new formations of difference might be as important as a politics of recognition of and living with difference. (Deutscher, "*Between East and West* and the Politics
of 'Cultural *Ingénuité*': Irigaray on Cultural Difference,"
143–144)

Nevertheless, Deutscher sees a possible productive line of critique aris-
ing from Irigaray's earlier writings that can be brought to bear on problematic depictions of race and cultural difference, even Irigaray's own.

Debra Bergoffen extends the idea of an economy beyond simple
dualism, which Ziarek claims can be found in the figure of the third
and Murphy believes Irigaray has overlooked, to argue that it provides
the foundation of a new ethics for Irigaray. In "Irigaray's Couples,"
Bergoffen takes on that most disconcerting aspect of Irigaray's remarks—that sexual difference grounds all other difference. On the
basis of this remark, Irigaray has been accused of hetereosexism, as we
have seen, and her later philosophical project has been called into
question. Bergoffen offers an analysis of Irigaray's writings as pointing
us toward the placental economy as a means of overturning the patriarchal psychoanalytic, historic, and political instantiation of sexual
difference. The placental relation interrupts the patriarchal reading of
ego development, whether through the Freudian oedipal moment and
the Lacanian law of the phallus or through the assumptions of biology
or cultural myths. Bergoffen argues that Irigaray dismantles the dichotomous thought inherent to the discourse of autonomy and provides a new conceptualization of ethics based in the community.
Bergoffen writes:

What was identified in the placental economy as the hope of
the ethical relationship and analyzed in the mother-daughter
couple as the promise of individuated identity, is now considered from the perspective of the we of the community and the
limits of subjectivity. Moving from the almost ethical to the
ethical, and from the ethical to the political, the question
now becomes: What sort of identity will/can ground a social

order where the boundaries of the self are protected and the difference(s) of the other(s) is respected? (Bergoffen, "Irigaray's Couples," 164)

However, Bergoffen goes on to critique Irigaray's own suppositions regarding the primacy of the couple, that is of the two, borrowing Irigaray's own analysis to further the political end of disrupting patriarchy's stronghold on ethical determinations.

Emily Zakin's essay "Between Two: Civil Identity and the Sexed Subject of Democracy" asks parallel questions of Irigaray's shift toward a focus on democracy and establishing civil rights for women. Irigaray seems in her recent work to be affirming the possibility of answering the questions of "what woman is and what she wants," questions she repeatedly challenged in her earlier works. In answering the questions of women's identity and desire, Irigaray seems to go against her earlier critique of a masculine politics of desire. Zakin argues that Irigaray's later work elaborates on and strengthens her earlier critique while also offering a promising relation between democracy, sexed subjectivity, and civil identity. She shows that Irigaray has consistently refused to abandon the psychoanalytic insight that subjectivity emerges in relation to parental others and is thus sexed from the beginning, and that her interest remains in seeing how reconceiving how sexual difference might illuminate our understanding of the relation between nature and the civil, opening up new political possibilities that defy the hegemony of what Zakin calls "totalitarian democracy," in which egalitarianism works toward the disappearance of women. Democracy proper should ensure the space of the "in-between" in order to avoid the collapse of civic neutrality into masculine subjectivity, and the only way this is possible is to ensure that women emerge as citizens in their own right and with their own rights. Zakin emphasizes that sexual difference implies an acceptance of loss and lack rather than a plentitude of stable identity. Thus, the theme of sexual difference develops themes articulated in Irigaray's early work, albeit with a new, increasingly political significance. In her rethinking of the conceptual bases of democracy, Irigaray does not recuperate themes that she had earlier dismantled, Zakin argues, but instead explores their concrete political possibilities. She writes:

Irigaray is thus attempting, with the idea of sexuate rights, to introduce the feminine into politics, and the body into language,

in a way that does not simply position the feminine as the
outside, the limit, the subversion of the political. It would
thus be mistaken to assume that the idea of a feminine universal must imply a reversion to content over form, status
instead of rights, substance rather than subject, to a closed
concept of the feminine. By demanding rights as women and
not as persons, Irigaray is not basing political claims on an
essential or substantive identity, but on the formation of universality itself. In this way, she aims precisely to give form to
a feminine subject. (Zakin, "Between Two: Civil Identity and
the Sexed Subject of Democracy," 194)

Margaret Whitford also addresses the psychoanalytical import of
Irigaray's later writings. In "Irigaray and the Culture of Narcissism,"
drawing on the main variants of theories of narcissism, and emphasizing the work of Melanie Klein and the post-Kleinians, Whitford demonstrates the connections between Irigaray's critique of Western
civilization and her other related critiques. To the untrained reader,
Whitford argues, Irigaray's discussion of the female imaginary and
symbolic may seem abstract, isolated from the contemporary urgent
need for a critique and transformation of phallocentricism, colonialism, racism, or classism. Against this interpretation, Whitford shows
that Irigaray's work of the 1980s and '90s can be contextualized within
post-Freudian psychoanalytic work that moves away from an exclusive focus on the Oedipus complex, castration, and the role of the
phallus (the Lacanian context) into other models of the psyche.
Whitford's analysis reconstructs for the reader how the process of the
psychic derailment into narcissism, which prohibits full maturation of
the self and causes projective identification, is taken up by Irigaray on
a cultural level such that the feminine other becomes the repository
for the masculine projective fantasy of omnipotence, both rendering
the feminine invisible and subsuming her into the economy of the
same (though she is discussing an entire culture, not individual subjects). The essay is careful to avoid easy comparisons or conflations of
Irigaray and Klein's work, but instead gives the reader an understanding of the psychoanalytic grounding of Irigaray's political claims, in
particular Irigaray's abiding concern with the problem of cultural
narcissism. Whitford calls Irigaray's diagnosis of narcissism "phenomenological," leading Irigaray to distance herself from strict psychoanalytic theory even while she makes use of its resources and techniques.

Characterizing narcissism as, in part, the inability to give up the fantasy of omnipotence, Whitford shows that Irigaray focuses on the fantasies of Western culture in general, in particular its hostility to anything new or other and its resistance to fundamental change. In refusing to acknowledge its debt to the mother-woman and, by extension, to nature or to the rest of the world, Western culture manifests a desire to destroy what it cannot possess. Irigaray's work oscillates, Whitford argues, between a critique of the narcissistic hatred of otherness and its cultural effects, and a quest for non-narcissistic models. Whitford states in conclusion:

> To suppose that [Irigaray's] work concerns (white Western) women only would be to miss in a quite significant way the implications of her oeuvre, which—on my reading—is far from being a marginal analysis. On the contrary it is structurally similar to some of the major currents of social and political critique of the post-war period. (Whitford, "Irigaray and the Culture of Narcissism," 219–220)

Catherine Peebles's essay "Knowing the Other: Ethics and the Future of Psychoanalysis" also engages with the critique that Irigaray's recent thought has strayed from its earlier critical engagement with psychoanalysis. Addressing Penelope Deutscher's suggestion in 1998 that Jacques Derrida's work is now more productive for a feminist rethinking of ethics and psychoanalysis than is Irigaray's, Peebles argues that Irigaray's later work reflects a transformed rather than a discarded perspective on psychoanalysis. Peebles individually addresses the criticisms that Irigaray seems to now believe that the other can be stably identified and known, and the related claim that, for Irigaray, narcissism seems to be a completely successful subordination of other to the self. Both claims imply that Irigaray's thought has "fallen into sameness," or that she assumes that "cultural cannibalism" succeeds. This overemphasis on identity originates out of Irigaray's vision of two sexes, which it reinforces. Peebles complicates this reading of identity and narcissism through a reading of Irigaray's use of recognition and sexuate identity as destabilized through the notion of gender as being both of oneself and more than oneself, both external to the self and to be created by the self. Peebles concludes that insofar as Irigaray's thought continues to mark sexual difference as the site for the creation of ethics, psychoanalysis *must* continue to be operative in her thought, even if it is a psychoanalysis that is "yet to come." Thus, the positions of Irigaray and Derrida have a certain proximity rather than diverging in their focus:

> What Irigaray and Derrida share, via their respective empha-
> ses on incompletion and alterity, is an emphasis on the yet to
> be, the impossible, as a site of possibility and of creation. The
> important difference, of course, is Irigaray's almost exclusive
> focus on sexual difference as an ontological category, and as
> a privileged category when it comes to conceiving ethics. While
> it is true that her more recent works do not spend as much
> time as the earlier ones on what psychoanalytic thought might
> or ought to contribute to her ethics of sexual difference, it is
> nevertheless the case that in marking sexual difference off as
> *the* site for the creation of ethics, her work necessarily sup-
> poses the possibility of psychoanalysis, or a psychoanalysis to
> come, as a primary locus for ethical interrogations, because it
> is, by definition, and like no other field of knowledge, prima-
> rily concerned with elaborating the significance of sexual
> difference. (Peebles, "Knowing the Other: Ethics and the Fu-
> ture of Psychoanalysis," 237–238)

Sara Heinämaa's "On Luce Irigaray's Phenomenology: Between the Feminine Body and Its Other" returns to the question of the meaning of Irigaray's claim that sexual difference grounds all differ-ence. Heinämaa also addresses another common critique of Irigaray's work by feminist commentators: how can woman be a subject in philosophy and speak in her works, given Irigaray's own argument that, historically, philosophy excludes woman as subject (and women philosophers from the canon), and/or that philosophy defines itself in opposition to the feminine? Irigaray has been criticized for seeming to reject the philosophical canon in her early work, only to affirm it in her later work. Heinämaa argues that while it might appear that Irigaray takes contradictory positions on the role of women and the feminine within philosophy in her early and late work, in fact Irigaray's corpus is continuous in its position on this issue. By showing that Irigaray's early work is a critique of modern philosophy rather than of the entirety of Western philosophy, Heinämaa offers an alternative to the view that Irigaray's early work totalizes and rejects philosophy, and thus shows Irigaray's corpus to be logically consistent. Heinämaa draws on Irigaray's statements from the 1980s and '90s to make the claim that Irigaray's work *in toto* is "to think through and, to work for, the constitution of the 'feminine identity.' " Heinämaa shows Irigaray's adaptation of Husserl's phenomenological account of the relation between intersubjectivity and objectivity to articulate an intersubjectivity of differently sexed bodies:

> The critical side of her argument is that our notions of intersubjectivity are restricted by our inability to think beyond one kind of bodily subject, or even to recognize this subject as of one kind. What we call inter-subjective is actually just relations between bodies of one kind and their diverse versions. . . . by thinking through the sexual difference, in its bodily concreteness, we can arrive at the recognition of two different kinds of corporeal subjects. And this recognition serves as a basis for a true understanding of intersubjectivity, between "at least two." (Heinämaa, "On Luce Irigaray's Phenomenology: Between the Feminine Body and Its Other," 251)

Maria Cimitile's essay "Irigaray in Dialogue with Heidegger," like Heinämma's, argues for a continuity of Irigaray's work. Her essay follows the trajectory of Irigaray's philosophical relationship with Heidegger from *Speculum* to *The Forgetting of Air in Martin Heidegger*, to *The Way of Love*. Cimitile argues that Irigaray leads the reader through a layering of theoretical positions into a new feminist politics that can be illuminated through her dialogue with Heidegger that evolves over time. An engagement with language is at the heart of Irigaray's analysis of the power structures of thought and relations between men and women. While Irigaray has learned much from Heidegger, especially in the uncovering of hidden elements that undergird what is present before us, in particular the privileging of one of two binary oppositions, Cimitile argues that Irigaray is not simply educated or influenced by Heidegger. Rather, we must understand Irigaray's dialogue with Heidegger as projecting the very movement of her thought. The sense of relationality that emerges in *The Way of Love* reflects the discourse between the two thinkers:

> While it is easy to read Irigaray's latest work on Heidegger with an atomistic perspective, and thus as a dismissal or overcoming of Heidegger's thought, to do so does not

provide the means for a full understanding of what Irigaray
offers us in her latest work, the importance of which lies
not only in the text, but in the movement of thinking that
has brought this text to us. (Cimitile, "Irigaray in Dialogue
with Heidegger," 270)

In the course of her essay, Penelope Deutscher returns to the
early critique of Irigaray as essentializing woman, showing that this
criticism rests on the misconception that Irigaray's notion of feminine
identity prescribes a subjective reality, when in fact she offers a hypothetical response to an excluded possibility. As Schwab also notes in
her essay, many who offer this misconceived critique had not accounted for the whole of Irigaray's writings, even to all those available
at the time that the critique was leveled in the late-1980s and early-
1990s, but relied almost solely on translations of *Speculum* and *This
Sex Which Is Not One*. One of the benefits of a second movement of
Irigaray scholarship, which goes beyond the important work of bringing Irigaray's work to the attention of Anglo-American readers, is the
added knowledge and hindsight that her later work opens up new
questions on just such an issue as essentialism, an issue which one
could argue has been a defining issue for Anglo-American feminism
given the intersection of feminist activism and feminist theory in the
twentieth century. The material conditions of women's lives from the
early suffragist movement up until the 1970s and '80s, and still today,
make it difficult to accept a theory of difference without worries of a
backlash against the call for women's equality. Yet, Irigaray's latest
work offers a real attempt to suggest an alternative to simple calls for
economic parity and equal political representation that do not address
the complexity of women's needs in systems whose very structure
ensures that such measures alone will not guarantee them a true
political existence. Ultimately, this volume does not seek to argue for
the viability of any of Irigaray's particular views, but rather to explore
the richness of her thought, which can only be fully appreciated by
considering her work in its full context, taking into consideration the
unity of her early and later writings. In so doing, we hope also to
provide a paradigm of feminist scholarship, scholarship that at its best
should be open to turning and returning to a thinker to allow her to
explore the full range of her theoretical possibilities and to respond to
her critics.

NOTES

1. This is not to imply that Irigaray's relationship to Heidegger is the primary lens through which to view her work, nor that it is invested in the hermeneutical project—the term "turn" and the reference to Heidegger are used analogically and structurally, not to imply content.

2. Throughout this volume, works by Irigaray will be referenced in author date form, with the publication of the English translation first and the original publication date in brackets, in order to give readers an immediate sense of the chronology of Irigaray's writings, which often were published in translation much later, or in some rare cases earlier, than their original version.

3. Although the former was published in France in 1981, its translation came out relatively late in English and, as a result, it is often mistakenly classified with the "later" Irigaray in Anglo-American scholarship.

WORKS CITED

Burke, Carolyn, Naomi Schor, and Margaret Whitford. 1994. *Engaging with Irigaray*. New York: Columbia University Press.

Cheah, Pheng, and Elizabeth Grosz, eds. 1998. *diacritics* 28:1 (Spring).

———. 1998. "Of Being-Two: Introduction." *diacritics* 28:1 (Spring), 2–18.

———. 1998. "The Future of Sexual Difference: An Interview with Judith Butler and Drucilla Cornell." *diacritics* 28:1 (Spring), 19–42.

Deutscher, Penelope. 1998. Review of *I Love to You* by Luce Irigaray. *Hypatia* 13:2 (Winter): 170–74.

Irigaray, Luce. 1993. *An Ethics of Sexual Difference*. Translated by Carolyn Burke and Gillian C. Gill. Ithaca, N.Y.: Cornell University Press.

———. 2000. *Why Different? A Culture of Two Subjects* (with Sylvère Lotringer). Translated by Camille Collins, Peter Carravetta, Ben Meyers, Heidi Bostic, and Stephen Pluháček. New York: Semiotext(e).

———. 2001. *To Be Two*. Translated by Monique M. Rhodes and Marco F. Cocito-Monoc. New York: Routledge.

———. 2002. *Between East and West: From Singularity to Community*. Translated by Stephen Pluháček. New York: Columbia University Press.

———. 2002. *The Way of Love*. Translated by Heidi Bostic and Stephen Pluháček. New York: Continuum.

Whitford, Margaret. 1991. *Philosophy in the Feminine*. New York: Routledge.

READING IRIGARAY (AND HER READERS)
IN THE TWENTY-FIRST CENTURY

Gail Schwab

ON RETURNING TO IRIGARAY

When Maria Cimitile and Elaine Miller contacted me about contributing to the new anthology, *Returning to Irigaray: Feminist Philosophy, Politics, and the Question of Unity*, I gave their proposed title some thought before committing to the project. Minus the subtitle, it reminded me grammatically, structurally, of the title of the 1994 Carolyn Burke, Naomi Schor, Margaret Whitford anthology, *Engaging with Irigaray*.[1] Was it a conscious, or unconscious, reference perhaps to what is still the only major book-length collection of essays on Irigaray's work? In either case, it pointed up the timeliness of publishing a new collection, since 1994 was ten years ago, and since Irigaray has continued to write with almost uncanny energy. But what would it mean to "return to Irigaray?" Since my translation of *Parler n'est jamais neutre* had only just come out, I felt no special need for a return. Perhaps it was even time to move on, away from, or beyond, Irigaray. However, as I put aside *To Speak Is Never Neutral* (Irigaray, 2002 [1985]), took up Irigaray's other books once again, and became more involved with the "late writings"—specifically the ones that came out after *I Love to You* (Irigaray, 1996 [1992])—I was once again caught up in the hypnotic rhythms of Irigaray's language, and in the intensity of her vision. It seems I had returned to Irigaray . . .

In the Prospectus sent to contributors to the new Irigaray volume, editors Cimitile and Miller recommended specifically that we try to address the question of "what it would mean to read Irigaray's later work, not as a break from her earlier writings, but as a means of bringing the more critical and speculative work into the context of the political," and that we "consider whether one could read the earlier work's style of transformative mimesis as a prelude to the affirmative politics of her later work, and whether the effort to take the symbolic and bring it into the realm of the civic succeeds or fails" (Cimitile and Miller, Prospectus for *Returning to Irigaray*). *Engaging with Irigaray*, in which various readers explored Irigaray's "early and late writings," as well as their reception since the 1970s by both francophone and anglophone audiences, even as they attempted to leave old misconceptions about Irigaray behind and break new ground in Irigaray studies, once again came to mind. It would seem that the sheer mass of Irigaray's work, which is encyclopedic at the same time that it is protean and impossible to totalize or even summarize, invites these sorts of periodic stock-takings, reassessments, and reorientations. Since another of the issues contributors to the *Returning to Irigaray* project were asked to think about was "the intersection between theory and practice," I was also reminded of the Spring 1998 special issue of *diacritics*,[2] edited by Pheng Cheah and Liz Grosz, which addressed the general question of the future of the concept of sexual difference through a close look back at Irigaray's work, assessing its political and practical value for the future.

So—would, or should, a return to Irigaray cover the familiar territory already explored in *Engaging with Irigaray*, and in the Spring 1998 issue of *diacritics*, or should it be a journey to another place and time? To come back to my own case, the relationship between Irigaray's early and late writings, as well as questions of theory and practice, are precisely the issues I have already tried to address, and more than once, in writing about Irigaray's books. The history of these questions is in some ways the history of my own "engagement" with Irigaray. So perhaps for me, "returning to Irigaray," and exploring the relationships among her texts, would also mean reading back through what I had said, or thought I had said, about Irigaray in the past, thinking about the relationship between that and what certain others had written, as well as the relationship between all of the above and the more recent works, and then asking myself about the future—that is, where it might be appropriate to go from here, with Irigaray, or without her . . .

DIALOGUE AND STYLE

Back in 1991, I published an article called "Irigarayan Dialogism: Play and Powerplay" in a collection entitled *Feminism, Bakhtin and the Dialogic*.[3] In large part, it was a reading of one essay from *To Speak Is Never Neutral*, "In Science, is the Subject Sexed?" (Irigaray 2002 [1985], 247–58), together with the title essay from *An Ethics of Sexual Difference*, "An Ethics of Sexual Difference" (Irigaray 1993 [1984], 116–29). In addition to emphasizing the concretely political and social agenda articulated in the former text in particular, the article focused on the differences of tone and style between, on the one hand, texts like *Speculum* (Irigaray 1985 [1974]) and "When Our Lips Speak Together" (Irigaray 1985 [1977], 205–18), and, on the other hand, *To Speak* and the *Ethics*, texts that I at the time considered Irigaray's "late writings." It already asked the question of whether Irigaray had changed direction, and whether the later essays marked a clear break from the earlier work, and it then went on to answer that question in the negative, attempting to reconcile the perceived differences in tone and style as a function of dialogism, that cornerstone of the linguistic philosophy of Mikhail Bakhtin. I analyzed Irigaray's mimeticism as a dialogic strategy[4] and found dialogism in all of Irigaray's work, in both the early, and in what were in 1991, the "late" writings. "Transformative mimesis" for me was dialogue, and Irigaray herself a philosopher profoundly, inextricably, engaged in dialogue with the Other.

"Irigarayan Dialogism" never attracted much attention from readers of Irigaray. It is entirely probable, if ironic, that Bakhtin's name tended to discourage a certain type of feminist dialogue from the outset; readers of *Rabelais and His World*[5] have always had a difficult time trying to recuperate Bakhtin for feminism, although I, along with many others,[6] still think his paradigms can be useful tools. In all fairness both to Bakhtin and to those who find him misogynous, I should also state that one of the reasons for the lack of response to my article was perhaps that the article itself was insufficiently developed and would have required both more theoretical breadth and more detailed analysis to be completely compelling—although I am not now disavowing the fundamental idea of Irigarayan dialogism—on the contrary—as I shall try to make clear below. Perhaps another reason had to do with timing. In the late 1980s/very early 1990s, even though *Amante marine* (1981), *Passions élémentaires* (1982), *L'Oubli de l'air chez Martin Heidegger* (1983), *Ethique de la différence sexuelle* (1984), *Parler n'est jamais neutre* (1985), and *Sexes et parentés* (1987) had all been published in French for some time, they had not been translated, and only *Speculum* and *This Sex Which Is Not One* were generally known to the anglophone public. Non-francophones were not reading the more recent books and could not yet be especially interested in whether Irigaray had changed or not. The question had not yet really come up for most readers. Lack of linguistic access, however, does not explain the problem completely, nor does it explain the vastly more interesting and important problem of why, when the other books did come out in English, readers' attention did not seem to shift much in their direction.

In 1991, most of those who were reading Irigaray at all remained focused on *Speculum* and *This Sex*, and it would seem that this is still very much the case. It is symptomatic that an early essay from *This Sex*, "Women on the Market," has managed to find its way onto the syllabus of the Honors course in the Humanities in my institution, independently of any special effort on my part, whereas it is fairly unlikely that a later piece by Irigaray would appear, unless I personally became involved in the establishment of the curriculum. To bring in another example, perhaps an even more telling illustration of this phenomenon is a scroll through "Nate's list" on Amazon.com—a list of the supposedly *sine qua non* texts in postmodernist philosophy for today's undergraduate, a list compiled by the mythical "Nate"—theoretically an undergraduate interested in philosophy. On Nate's list one finds the names and works of the "great" males one would expect to find there—Nietzsche, Heidegger, Lyotard, Foucault, Baudrillard, et al. One also finds the name of Julia Kristeva, whose work is evaluated very positively by Nate. The only text by Irigaray that made the list (poor Irigaray) is *This Sex Which Is Not One*, a book Nate characterizes as "French feminism at its silliest"—albeit a "classic." In the introduction to the aforementioned special Spring 1998 issue of *diacritics*, editors Cheah and Grosz discuss this blind spot where Irigaray is concerned and note that even the most sympathetic readers have tended to extract the social and political implications of her work from her earlier and primarily psychoanalytic texts, which are then taken as so emblematic of her work that her later writings are rarely read, let alone discussed. *Speculum of the Other Woman* and *This Sex Which Is Not One* have effectively functioned as synedoches of her entire oeuvre.[7]

It is true that one of the most thrilling, if not the most thrilling, aspect of Irigaray's work is her style—in particular that infamous "transformative mimesis" that so shocked and intrigued readers when *Speculum* first came out.[8] The thrust of Irigaray's work was in her brilliant critique, in its irony and elegance, and that was what readers reacted to—either in the positive or in the negative. While many Anglo-American feminists took her as the negative "essentialist" model[9] against which they defined themselves, and wanted to define feminism, many others saw both her technique and her intimate and complex relationship to the Western philosophical tradition, as positive models, something they themselves wanted to imitate.[10] In the special issue of *diacritics*, Cheah and Grosz interview Judith Butler and Drucilla Cornell on the subject of the "Future of Sexual Difference," and Butler very candidly discusses her own reaction to *Speculum*:

> Her engagement with philosophy was a curious mixture of both loyalty and aggression. And it became very interesting to me when I started thinking about her whole practice of critical mimesis . . . and I read *Speculum* again and again, frightened by its anger, compelled by the closeness of the reading, confused by the mimeticism of the text. Was she enslaved[11] to these texts, was she displacing them radically, was she perhaps in the bind of being in both positions at the same time? And I realized that . . . the feminine . . . for her . . . had something to do with this strange practice of reading . . . That struck me as a feminist critical practice, a critical practice that I could learn from . . .[12]

It is revealing that Butler, who so aptly characterizes the relationship between Irigaray and her philosophers as a "curious mixture of loyalty and aggression," or even, as she puts it a few lines further on in the interview, "a certain masochistic-sadistic engagement,"[13] responds in the negative when questioned by Pheng Cheah about whether her own relationship to Irigaray's texts is a relationship of love, clarifying that she is "probably too frightened," and doesn't "engage them that closely, probably because [she finds] it frightening to be in that particular knot."[14] What comes across during the whole interview is an intense ambivalence; on the one hand there is Butler's intellectual sense of fairness, her desire to do justice to the importance of Irigaray's work and to the influence it has had on her own thought; on the other hand, one perceives Butler's need to distance herself and even eventually to impose certain totalizing readings on Irigaray's texts, particularly the later texts.[15]

With respect to whether Irigaray changed style, tone, and direction between the early texts published (in French) in the 1970s, and those published (in French) in the mid- to late-1980s, both Butler and Cornell are fairly unequivocal in asserting that they believe she had, and that the shift in tactics or change in tone even represented a kind of betrayal of the promises of *Speculum*, or indeed of feminism itself.[16] Both critics clearly situate the break from the early work at the moment of the *Ethics of Sexual Difference*, a book that comes to represent a rupture, or a moment of fundamental discontinuity in Irigaray's work. It is in the *Ethics* that, Butler claims, Irigaray's relationship to the philosophers becomes less aggressive and "more loving."[17] I do not disagree that there are significant differences in tone between the *Ethics* and the earlier works; trying to come to terms with those differences back in 1991, I wrote that the *Ethics of Sexual Difference* "is an unsettling work on first reading . . . Irigaray seems almost too methodical, almost anti-Irigarayan . . . Her seminars . . . are more didactic and professorial, more serious in tone and more traditional . . ."[18] "The exchange [with the philosophers] tends to be less contentious . . ."[19] As I tried to point out in the article, the *Ethics of Sexual Difference* came out of a specific historical and personal context for Irigaray, who had been ignominiously expelled from the French university system after the publication of *Speculum*. That experience was a public humiliation extremely difficult to overcome emotionally, and it had the practical effect of depriving Irigaray of students, of a live audience, so to speak, and of living partners to engage in dialogue, as well as of a means of propagating her work in an arena more personalized than publishing. When in 1982 she was named to the Jan Tinbergen endowed chair at the Erasmus University in Rotterdam, and delivered the series of lectures that was to become the *Ethics of Sexual Difference*, she felt both honored and vindicated, and something of those feelings can be discerned in the book. In a passage I quoted in French in "Irigarayan Dialogism," where she conceptualizes herself and her historical, social, and philosophical position in Rotterdam, she [writes]: "Coming to Rotterdam to teach philosophy represents something rather special. An adventure of thought, an adventure of discovery, or rediscovery, in a country that has offered a haven to several philosophers. Offered them tolerance and encouragement in their work. Outside of any dogmatic passion. [In most cases.]"

(Irigaray 1993 [1984], 116). And she proudly adds, "I shall not fail that history."[20]

I wrote in 1991 that Irigaray was placing herself into a "certain history. She [was] carrying on a tradition and [was] aware of it. The texts written by those other philosophers in Holland are an integral part of Irigaray's project. In the same way that Freud was *in* "The Blind Spot," Descartes [and] Spinoza . . . are *in* the *Ethics of Sexual Difference*. Their words are Irigaray's. Her words are theirs."[21] Differences in tone and style could be accounted for dialogically, given that "Irigaray engages at once with more distant partners in her philosophers [who had been welcomed by Holland in the past], and with more intimate ones in her students . . ."[22]

Carolyn Burke has also characterized the *Ethics* as dialogic, and dialogic in a different mode from *Speculum*. She analyzes the (only) slightly more traditional scholarly apparatus of the *Ethics*, showing how Irigaray's use of spacing, nonindentation, and italics, a usage she calls "differently eccentric," and "somewhat less discomforting than that set up by her earlier practice of weaving her own voice in and out of others' texts,"[23] illustrates the "*entre-deux*"[24] of her relationship to her philosophical interlocutors, and goes on to demonstrate that Irigaray herself has explained the style of the *Ethics* as a "double style: a style of loving relationships, [and] a style of thought, of exegesis, of writing. The two are consciously or unconsciously linked, with a more immediately corporeal and affective side in one case, a more socially developed side in the other."[25] It is the more "socially developed side" that becomes increasingly important in the texts of the late-1980s and '90s that follow the *Ethics*.[26]

It is frequently forgotten—or ignored—that Irigaray is a trained social scientist who began her professional career as a psychologist and psycho-linguist. Her initial research, first published in various French journals, notably the journal *Langages*, was in linguistics,[27] and in psycho-linguistics. She worked first on establishing an appropriate investigative methodology[28] and then on the construction of models of linguistic performance for pathological populations in whom the linguistic function had been significantly impaired by senility, aphasia, or schizophrenia.[29] With this extensive empirical research behind her, she then went on to publish *Speculum* and to explore the more theoretical problems of female subjectivity with which her work has traditionally been associated. I have made the claim elsewhere that it was,[30] at least in part, the violent opposition to her theoretical works that inspired her to return to her earlier linguistic research and to apply the methodology developed there to her feminist theory, a particularly appropriate move given that the work done with senile dementia, aphasia, and schizophrenia patients had already revealed certain gender differences in language use. As I wrote back in 1998, when Irigaray "encountered resistance to the ideas that language as we know it is men's language and not women's language, that men and women have different relationships to language, that they use language differently, she understood that she would have to demonstrate their validity, and was well prepared to do so,"[31] using her early research as a methodological base.

The later "technical" (Carolyn Burke's adjective) studies from the 1980s and '90s—*To Speak Is Never Neutral*; *Je tu nous*; *Sexes, Genders, and Languages* (Irigaray 1990, translation unpublished); and so on—are thus an integral part of the Irigarayan oeuvre.[32] They can almost be thought of as a swing of the pendulum away from the theory and philosophy of *Speculum* and *This Sex Which Is Not One* back toward the social scientific orientation of the late 1960s and very early 1970s. The importance of both the earlier and the later social scientific work can also be very clearly seen in *I Love to You* (Irigaray 1996 [1992]), which followed *Sexes, Genders, and Languages*, and which can in some ways be read as a transitional work, a work relying heavily on the empirical linguistic research, but nonetheless highly philosophical, and combining both her "poetico-philosophical" and her "empirical-social-scientific" styles. In at least two of her most recent works, *To Be Two* (Irigaray 2000 [1994]) and *The Way of Love* (Irigaray 2002), her philosophic arguments continue to be grounded in her linguistic research (which she continues to pursue[33]), and yet both texts are generally conceived as poetic "dialogues"[34] with some of Irigaray's traditional, as well as with some totally new, philosophic interlocutors—notably Jean-Paul Sartre, with whom, and with whose French existentialism, she had never previously engaged.[35]

If little-known early works like the book *Le Langage des déments* (Irigaray 1973, no translation), in which Irigaray reports on her linguistic research with senile dementia, aphasia, and schizophrenia patients, are included in the Irigarayan corpus, it is far easier to understand why Irigaray has never ceased to affirm that her oeuvre is of a piece, why she refuses to see her "technical studies" as some sort of aberration, or departure, from her "real work," and why she insists that the later social scientific work is a continuation of the work of *Speculum* and *This Sex Which Is Not One*, which thus deserve no special place apart from the rest. In an essay entitled "The Question of the Other," published in *Democracy Begins Between Two* (Irigaray 2000 [1994], 121–41), Irigaray narrativizes what she conceives as the continuity of her work from *Speculum* onwards, maintaining that, for her, it has always been about the creation of a culture of two subjects. In "The Question of the Other," she seems to conceive of her work in three phases that flow organically one from the other, and to illustrate this, she structures the essay in three parts entitled: 1) "The Other: Woman," 2) "The Mediations Needed by the Feminine Subject," and 3) "The Other: Man."

In the first part, "The Other: Woman," Irigaray discusses the early critiques of (especially) Freud and Plato in *Speculum*, emphasizing how they pointed out the fallacies, omissions, unquestioned assumptions, and blind spots in our "monosubjective, monosexual, patriarchal and phallocratic philosophy and culture" (Irigaray 2000 [1994], 130), in order *"to free the two from the one* [Irigaray's emphasis], the two from the many, the other from the same, and to do this in a horizontal way by suspending the authority of the One: of man, of the father, of the leader, of the one god, of the unique truth, etc." (Irigaray 2000 [1994], 129). The second part, "The Mediations Needed by the Feminine Subject," makes the claim that the next step, already begun in *Speculum*, and carried on in *This Sex Which Is Not One*; *Sexes and Genealogies*; *Thinking the Difference*; and *Je, tu, nous*, was a logical follow-up to that critique—that is, defining "the characteristics of the feminine subject, characteristics which are indispensable to her affirmation as such, to avoid falling back into a lack of differentiation or into subjection to a singular subject" (Irigaray 2000 [1994], 130–31). The final section of the essay, "The Other: Man," demonstrates how the elaboration of a feminine subjectivity leads inevitably back to the question of the other, asking "how could the feminine subject . . . cultivate sharing with the other without becoming alienated?" (Irigaray 2000 [1994],137). Irigaray conceives of *I Love to You* and *To Be Two* as efforts at finding answers to that question. *The Way of Love* had not yet been written in 1994 when "The Question of the Other" was written, but it is clearly the continuation of the work begun in *I Love to You* and *To Be Two*.

HETEROSEXISM AND/OR SEXUAL DIFFERENCE

When assessing the relationship between the early and the late writings, even for those who are prepared to accept the idea of the underlying continuity of style and intent of Irigaray's project, a problem remains. Certain readers, like Drucilla Cornell in the interview in *diacritics*, have read Irigaray's later work as a regression, an effort to reinscribe "conservatism on the deepest level of her understanding of sexual difference."[36] Cornell and Judith Butler both pinpoint the *Ethics* as the moment when a blatant heterosexism comes in to vitiate Irigaray's project. Butler maintains that

> a certain heterosexual notion of ethical exchange emerged in *An Ethics of Sexual Difference* . . . The intense overt heterosexuality of *An Ethics of Sexual Difference* and indeed of the sexuate rights discourse, which is all about mom and motherhood and not at all about postfamily arrangements or alternative family arrangements, not only brought to the fore a kind of presumptive heterosexuality, but actually made heterosexuality into the privileged locus of ethics, as if heterosexual relations, because they putatively crossed this alterity, which is the alterity of sexual difference, were somehow more ethical, more other-directed, less narcissistic than anything else. It was, in some sense, compelling men out of what she used to call their *hom(m)osexualité* into this encounter with alterity . . . and what would emerge from that exchange would be a certain kind of heterosexual love which would come to capture the domain of the ethical.[37]

Certain of these criticisms, the less important ones, are based on misreadings or incomplete readings; sexuate rights, for example, are not really about "mom and motherhood," in the sense that Butler understands them here. Irigaray does insist that mothers (those who have chosen maternity under the sexuate right to voluntary maternity that she demands) need special state protection for their children. This, however, in no way reinstates the patriarchal family, and, in fact, can be read as requiring that society recognize its responsibilities when it comes to nurturing and educating the next generation.[38] Drucilla Cornell herself points out the appropriateness of Irigaray's legal analyses to the French legal system, claiming that she has always "read her as programmatically serious about sexuate rights, and seeing them as realizable. Such rights are certainly inconsistent with the way the law [read here 'the American legal system'] operates now, but it is not inconsistent with the concept of the French legal system."[39]

Nevertheless, the charge of heterosexism is a serious one, and it has at least occurred to many readers to wonder at the new focus on the heterosexual couple that emerges at the time of the *Ethics*. I was not unaware of this new focus back in 1991 when I wrote "Irigarayan Dialogism," but did not choose to deal with it at that time and focused on more formalistic issues instead. Others have found ways of reading Irigaray that do not limit her thought to a monolithic presumptive heterosexuality. In the *diacritics* interview, Cheah and Grosz themselves offer subtler alternatives to this reading, many of which had already been articulated by Grosz in "The Hetero and the Homo: The Sexual Ethics of Luce Irigaray,"[40] an article published in *Engaging with Irigaray*. Although it would be inappropriate to reproduce the whole of her argument here, it is useful to recall, with Grosz, that Irigaray was at one time seen to be the advocate of a radical "presumptive" lesbianism.[41] Grosz cautions readers against such presumptions, pointing out that Irigaray maintains a critical distance from all existing types of sexual relations under patriarchy,[42] and insisting that all current sexualities—hetero-, homo-, or lesbian—"represent the primacy of a sexuality conceived in phallic terms," but that "there still remains the possibility of both heterosexual and homosexual relations based on an acceptance of women's pleasure."[43] In other words, the future of all sexual relations beyond phallocentrism remains a completely open question. Far from being presumed, heterosexuality *as we currently conceive it* might not even exist in a world where sexual difference had actually emerged from the economy of the same. And this would, of course, also hold true for homosexualities *as currently conceived.*[44]

Margaret Whitford has proffered another reading of the supposed "discontinuity" that marks Irigaray's shift to an emphasis on relations between women and men, coming to the conclusion that "there *is* a continuity" in her work.[45] Whitford sees the new focus as Irigaray's response to the fundamental ambiguity of feminist politics,[46] as an attempt to overcome some of the divisiveness and social conflicts occasioned by feminism's emphasis on the deconstruction and destruction of patriarchy:

> By this I mean that she has moved from the stress on *un*binding, or *un*doing (e.g., undoing patriarchal structures) to a stress on binding (e.g., constructing new forms of sociality). What has been described as the "philosophical terrorism" of

Speculum has given way to an apparently more law-abiding
concern with citizenship and rights, in which the central
political concept is love between the sexes.[47]

Irigaray recognizes, of course, that love between the sexes, as
currently practiced, is no unadulterated source of social harmony, and
she has repeatedly insisted that, as Whitford puts it, "this is because
it remains primitive, 'uncivilized,' unsublimated, a purely private affair, when it should be a civil and social recognition of two generic
identities."[48] In her more recent works, this idea has become almost
a mantra. I focused extensively on this issue in an article published in
Metaphilosophy back in 1996, entitled "Women and Law in Irigarayan
Theory."[49] For Irigaray, instituting sexuate rights is all about shifting
the focus of the law away from the subject-object relation—that is,
away from regulating the relations between persons and property, and
toward establishing a civil and social basis for relations between persons, relations that have remained unthought, mired in a supposedly
"natural" immediacy, which is not natural at all, but corresponds rather
to a nature perverted by the power structures of patriarchy, particularly those within the patriarchal family. Irigaray insists that if we do
not bring the eros in operation between men and women out of this
pseudonature and into culture, we put ourselves at the mercy of its
violence and destructive force.[50]

Nevertheless, the question still remains—why focus so heavily
on the relations between men and women, as opposed to intrageneric
relations? Especially given that such a focus gives rise to the kinds of
concerns expressed by Judith Butler in the *diacritics* interview, that
"heterosexual love comes to capture the domain of the ethical,"[51] and
that "what she [Irigaray] has done has completely obliterated the way
in which an ethically enabling difference exists in homosexual love."[52]
Even Grosz, who, it seems, would caution against any move that
would ontologize homosexual love, recognizes that one thing Irigaray
does not make clear is whether the encounter between two subjects
of the same sex "contains the same potential for immense creativity"
as encounters between differently sexed partners, and she notes that
"this omission has provoked justified anxiety on the part of gay and
lesbian theorists for its refusal to accord a place to gay and lesbian
relations, as it were, beyond the phallus."[53]

At this moment, there seem to be no simple and straightforward
answers to these questions; however, I will now attempt to address a

series of issues that can perhaps be taken together to form the beginnings of a response. It might be useful to begin by returning to an article entitled "Sexual Difference as Model: An Ethics for the Global Future," published in the special issue of *diacritics*,[54] where I argued that Irigaray, who had always been very much outside mainstream political and academic feminism herself, saw very clearly that the monologic voice of white Western feminists of equality did not speak for all women globally. The postmodernist fragmentation of identities, due to recognition of the importance of differences of race, class, ethnicity, nationality, age, sexual orientation, body configuration, health status, and so on, logically led her to seek a principle that would be universally operative—that of sexual difference. In the article, I tried to analyze the dense philosophical arguments in support of the universality of sexual difference that Irigaray develops specifically in *I Love to You* and to demonstrate that sexual difference is not about heterosexuality, or about sexual object choice at all. It would be beyond the scope of this article to reproduce that analysis here; it would, however, be useful to remind us briefly how sexual difference can be thought as universal, and universally practical for social change. Pheng Cheah puts it succinctly during the course of the interview with Judith Butler and Drucilla Cornell:

> She seems to be saying, "we may not all be mothers and fathers, but all of us have been children once. And until the cloning of humans is successful, in order for us to be born, in order for us to *be*, there must be two sexes or at least the genetic material from two sexes." At any rate, this is the trace of the other in us, the constitutive trace of sexual alterity. The argument is not phrased in terms of sexual preferences at all . . . [55]

Although the universal principle of sexual difference is not about sexual orientation, either hetero- or homo-, it does become, for Irigaray, a philosophically useful tool for thinking about the ethics of relationships between women and men, an ethics that—I think few would disagree here—is in serious need of development on a planetary scale. Quite apart from the so often disastrous emotional and/or erotic relations between men and women, their professional, civil, and familial—what Irigaray calls genealogical—relationships are difficult to say the least, and violently conflictual at worst. This is not to suggest that woman-to-woman and/or man-to-man relations do not exhibit many of the same sorts of problems, but rather pragmatically to recognize that if we are to make a difference we must start somewhere. I believe that it is Irigaray's position that if relations between men and women were to be cultivated, "civilized" as Whitford says, brought out of their supposed "naturalness" into civil society, then relations among women and relations among men would necessarily change as well.

In addition, it also seems clear that, at least when Irigaray first began to focus on the relations between women and men, a feminist strategy was also in operation. In the above-mentioned article in *diacritics*, I discussed Irigaray's ongoing concerns about women's futures, given that young women of the current generation were in general not especially aware of the feminist accomplishments of their elders, tended to take them for granted, and even resented any implication that they themselves should join together with the older generation to work for freedom for women.[56] One reason for the conflicts inherent in this particular aspect of the intergenerational woman-to-woman relationship was, as Irigaray saw it, younger women's attachment to men, and the perception on their part that they were being asked by their feminist elder sisters and mothers to give them up, or at least to behave in ways that would jeopardize their relationships with them. Irigaray became aware that, in order to respond to the concerns of young women, she would need to think about relationships between women and men and to theorize their potentiality outside of the economy of the same, and she began to do so, unfortunately to the consternation of some of her readers.

However, once she had begun, it seems to have become clear to her that she had opened up an entirely new field, one heretofore almost totally unexplored in the history of Western philosophy, and infinitely rich in possibilities: the theoretical elaboration of ethical relations between women and men—and by that I do not mean the same old love-hate story of man and his female complement that we have been telling ourselves and each other for eons—but rather future relations in sexual difference, a *new* story of two different subjects coming together, yet remaining separate in the recognition of, and respect for, the limits of their own identities. The excitement she feels about telling this story, about creating it, bringing it into being through her work, can be felt in the passion and poetry of her latest philosophical works: *I Love to You; To Be Two;* and *The Way of Love.*

It should also be noted that her relationship with the Italian politician and member of the European Parliament, Renzo Imbeni, is extremely important in this context.[57] Irigaray acknowledges the centrality of their relationship to her thinking about relations between men and women, and names him quite openly in more than one place in her work. She discusses in some detail, in an article entitled "Towards a Citizenship in the European Union," published in *Democracy Begins Between Two* (Irigaray 2000 [1994], 60–94), their collaboration on a proposed code that was to have instituted citizenship in the new European Union whose constitution was in the process of being written. The draft defined the civil identities of male and female citizens and the respective rights and duties incumbent upon them as citizens of Europe.[58] The proposal, by the way, did not receive support from the Parliament. In some ways, however, the fate of this one specific proposal is actually less important than the Imbeni/Irigaray collaboration itself. The way they succeeded in working together, and their mutual commitment to respect each other's differences in identity (as two individuals who differ not only in gender, but also in ethnicity, language, politics, and profession), as well as in opinion (Imbeni was a strong advocate for equal rights when they began working together on this project, while Irigaray, obviously, was the advocate for sexuate rights and sexual difference), come to represent a model for the future of fruitful collaborative efforts between a woman and a man. The limits and the respect for each other that they maintain in the public, civic aspect of their relationship carry over into what I will call their "mythical," or literary, relationship. Renzo Imbeni is *in* Irigaray's books as addressee and interlocutor. He represents the (male) other of sexual difference her writings seek.[59]

Does all of this then inevitably mean that Irigaray's work is presumptively heterosexual, heterosexist? Does a focus on the ethical potential of one sort of relationship in sexual difference necessarily indicate the poverty of other sorts of relationships in sexual difference? I believe that we need to be careful and nuanced in our assessment here and recognize that there are complexities at work in Irigaray's philosophy. I would like to turn briefly to a recent text that has not yet received much attention from readers, *To Be Two*, and try to analyze certain of these complexities. As the title indicates, *To Be Two* is a book about relationships—and not exclusively about relationships between human beings, since the poetic hymns of the prologue and the epilogue also celebrate relationships to the elements— earth, air, water, and sun—and to the trees, flowers, and birds that live with and depend upon them. However, it is principally human relationships that are the focus of the essays in between prologue and epilogue.

The second essay of the collection, entitled "Daughter and Woman" (Irigaray 2001 [1994], 30–39), deals with Sartre's analysis of the relation to the other; Irigaray takes Sartre to task for neglecting the "subject's history and its impact on the present encounter with the other, with others" (Irigaray 2001 [1994], 30). In Sartrean existentialism, the physical body of the individual, whose pre-oedipal, prelinguistic past is ignored, or erased, amounts to no more than a material body of pure "factuality" or "facticity"—that is, Sartre's *en-soi*, or "pre-given," "a thing without intention," and this, according to Irigaray, is what results in the infamous Sartrean "Hell is other people." (Irigaray 2001 [1994], 31). Irigaray takes issue with this erasure of past individual experience and insists upon the always ethical nature of the subject's initial relationship with the maternal other (or, to use the more politically correct language, with the primary caretaker, since a gender switch here would not invalidate the point Irigaray is trying to make):

> in fact, intention exists both on the part of the mother towards the girl or boy, and on the part of the child towards the mother. Thus, the affectionate gaze of the mother towards the body of her son or of her daughter, as well as their attention towards the mother, is forgotten in Sartre's thought. (Irigaray 2001 [1994], 31)

Failing to acknowledge that "the body is inhabited by a consciousness which begins with its first relationship with the parental other, with the mother in particular" (Irigaray 2001 [1994], 31), Western thought and Western civilization, here typified in Sartre's philosophy, have reduced human beings to abstract entities in the economy of the same, all identical and interchangeable. If the relationship with the other resembles hell, the cause could be precisely this abstract consciousness which dominates, alienates, and erases the child in us. We are no longer animated by love, by language, by intentions; each of us is a nothing of existence . . . (Irigaray 2001 [1994], 32). As Irigaray herself says:

> As abstract "nothings of existence," we find ourselves incapable of dealing with the other, of relating to the other, except

vertically in genealogy, or in religion, or horizontally in the unthought, uncultivated experience of sexual desire. (Irigaray 2001 [1994], 36–37)

In order to overcome this impasse, which she sees as the disaster of contemporary culture, Irigaray maintains that subjective history must be cultivated at both the individual and the social levels. She further makes the claim that it is impossible *not* to recognize that the mother's prelinguistic (and this could now perhaps even be extended back to the intrauterine stage, given current technologies) relationship to her daughter is different from the one she experiences with her son, thus making that first relationship a sexuate relationship, one that will eventually develop into separate generic identities for the male child and the female child. An intention is pre-given in my body, a for-itself is inscribed in it: relationships with my gender and with the other gender are inscribed as different ones. My body is not, therefore, a simple "facticity;" it is a relationship-with: with me, with my gender, with the other gender (Irigaray 2001 [1994], 33).

Up to this point, perhaps, there may not be that much here that goes far beyond her arguments in *I Love to You* (except the engagement with Sartre), although her discussion of the pre-oedipal relation to the mother does hark back to, and develop further, issues she had not focused much on since *La croyance même* and *Je, tu, nous,*[60] and it also looks forward to all the work she is currently doing with children and on children's education.[61] However, there is a section of "Daughter and Woman" that, as I read it, specifically addresses the question of the perceived heterosexism of Irigarayan sexual difference, making a serious effort to include relations between persons of the same gender, and the homosexual love relation, within the ethics of sexual difference. It has always been my sense that this had been implied from the start, and that it is possible to read all discussion of the ethics of sexual difference openly, avoiding heterosexuality as the exclusive model. In "Daughter and Woman," however, Irigaray is explicitly *inclusive*. After grounding sexual difference in the first relationship with the parental other as "an identity in which the relationship to the other is inscribed in the pre-given of my body," Irigaray discusses subsequent experiences of the relation to the other as the "fulfillment of the self as body . . . as a destination inscribed in the properties of my body," and although she does emphasize that "it is above all to the other gender as other that I am destined," she also specifies quite clearly that "this other can be of my gender or of another . . ." (Irigaray 2001 [1994], 34).

She then goes on to clarify what she means by this:

> Certainly, I can decide to become woman while suspending the empirical relationship with the other gender—on account of historical impossibility, for example—but I can neither deny nor fail to take into consideration, in my becoming, the relationship with the other gender which goes with belonging to my own. To be woman necessarily involves . . . to be in relationship with man, at least ontologically. . . . (Irigaray 2001 [1994], 34)

Although generically, to be woman requires a relation to the other man, just as to be man requires a relation to the other woman, becoming woman at the level of the individual is not dependent upon a heterosexual love object choice—that is, an "empirical" relationship with a man. In other words, it would seem that the concerns expressed by Judith Butler in the *diacritics* interview are being addressed here by Irigaray: "the ethically enabling difference" (from the other) has not been "obliterated" from homosexual love,[62] and heterosexual love has not "captured the domain of the ethical" relation to the other.[63] The pre-given relation to the other inscribed in identity *can be* fulfilled in a relationship with an other of my own gender. Homosexual love is thus very much within the scope of sexual difference, which is always already in operation at the generic level. Irigaray discusses what she calls a "utopia of our age": a woman gives birth to a woman, and they live in a community of women separated from the other part of the world. A woman in such a situation should consider her identity as woman as an identity in relationship with the other gender, at least in so far as it is her intention to fulfill her own gender (Irigaray 2001 [1994], 34).

The choice to live separately, apart from men and exclusively among women, is itself a choice that foregrounds the existence of the two genders. It can effectively fulfill a generic identity, and define a community, but nonetheless owes a debt to sexual difference—not to heterosexuality, but sexual difference, which, again, is not dyadic, not about heterosexual couples, or couples at all, but about, in the words of Liz Grosz, "the right of the other to have its other."[64]

Finally, I would note here that it is a typical Irigarayan move to address questions that have come up regarding her ideas in this way—

that is, by incorporating a discussion of the issues into a text that does not specifically, or single-mindedly, address those particular questions. Aware of the concerns that her work has raised among homosexuals and lesbians, she integrates an attempt at a response into a text dealing with the fundamental importance of the relationship to the other, allowing that the relationship with an other of one's own gender is ethically creative and fulfilling. This might seem at first glance to be an off-handed way to deal with questions and criticisms, but I would argue, rather, that it is dialogic.

ONGOING DIALOGUES

The whole of Irigaray's oeuvre is an encounter. At times, this encounter is feisty and even conflictual, at other times, thoughtful and creative, and at still others, intense and passionate. Never is her text limited, closed off, autistic or solipsistic. Insisting on the importance of the relationship to the other in Irigaray's work, I wrote back in 1991,

> No other feminist writer is so profoundly dialogic as Irigaray. Her theoretical stance has always been that of a respondent or a questioner. She engages another in dialogue, reacts to the other, interacts . . . She never totalizes her ideas into a conclusion which could then be read as "Irigaray's final word.". Irigaray herself underlines the specifically relational character of her thought when she claims that what she really wants and intends to do is "*faire la noce avec les philosophes.*" Jane Gallop has boldly translated Irigaray's "*faire la noce*" as "have an orgy with the philosophers," and the French expression does indeed imply those excesses of food, drink, and sex that orgies involve. Irigaray and her philosophers are going to comingle and interpenetrate . . . They're going to have an orgy—and the end result will be an enrichment of each by the other . . . Difference is not to be bred out, but sought out and maintained.[65]

In conclusion then, I would like to turn to a text published over ten years later, in 2002, by the Edinburgh University Press—*Dialogues: Luce Irigaray Presents International, Intercultural, and Intergenerational Dialogues Around Her Work*. In a short piece entitled, very appropriately for my purposes, "Poetic Nuptials," Judith Still, one of the editors of the volume, takes up once again the problem of the possible

English translations of *"faire la noce."* Still begins by discussing multiple relationships to/in textuality.

> Poetic nuptials . . . can take place between text and reader or
> translator; they can take place within the text, between ele-
> ments of the text; they can be a mode of intertextual relation-
> ship—the way in which the text stages its relationship with
> other texts . . . Poetic nuptials would take place *as if* between
> (at least) two subjects, and lead us on to consider inter-
> subjective relations in general. . . . (Irigaray 2002, 7)

Irigaray's text, Still maintains, is a place where all of these different
types of poetic nuptials take place. It is a text that is "searching"
(Irigaray 2002, 8), seeking a relation to its readers, "readers who will
reciprocate. Not readers who are already identical to themselves, not
readers who are to be subjugated or who will seek to subjugate [it], but
readers who will respond to the gift of the text" (Irigaray 2002, 8).
    Reading as nuptials, or better yet, as orgy, can have its rewards.
In an essay entitled "Reading Irigaray in the Nineties," to which the
title of this essay owes a rather large debt, Margaret Whitford has
written that "Irigaray's complexity is such that it is probably not
possible—and certainly not desirable—to provide the definitive account of her work . . . Interpretations may either operate a restrictive
closure or, more productively, engage with Irigaray and open up the
possibility of using her work as a feminist resource."[66] Readers prepared to take on an "intertextual relationship" with Irigaray, and
commit to the nuptials, or to the orgy, will leave themselves open,
and allow that her text remain open, untotalized, seeking, connecting, and moving on. At the beginning of this essay I wondered, rhe-
torically, if it were time to "move beyond" Irigaray. I now wonder if
this is possible. It seems that when we attempt to leave Irigaray behind, we find that it is she who has moved on, that she is no longer
where we left her, or thought we left her, but rather, having read,
listened, thought, embraced, and created, she is already elsewhere. I
find I am grateful that the party is not yet over . . .

NOTES

    1. *Engaging with Irigaray*, ed. Carolyn Burke, Naomi Schor, and Mar-
garet Whitford (New York: Columbia University Press, 1994).

2. *Irigaray and the Political Future of Sexual Difference*, ed. Pheng Cheah and Elizabeth Grosz, *diacritics* 28:1 (Spring 1998).

3. Gail Schwab, "Irigarayan Dialogism: Play and Powerplay," in *Feminism, Bakhtin and the Dialogic*, ed. Dale M. Bauer and Susan Jaret McKinstry (Albany, N.Y.: SUNY Press, 1991), 57–72.

4. For presentations of/on Bakhtin's linguistics and philosophy see, for example, Katarina Clark and Michael Holquist, *Mikhail Bakhtin* (Cambridge: Harvard University Press, 1984); M. M. Bakhtin, *Rabelais and His World* (Bloomington, Ind.: Indiana University Press, 1984); M. M. Bakhtin, *The Dialogic Imagination*, ed. Micahel Holquist, trans. Caryl Emerson and Michael Holquist (Austin: University of Texas Press, 1981); *Bakhtin: Essays and Dialogues on His Work*, ed. Gary Saul Morson (Chicago: University of Chicago Press, 1981).

5. Bakhtin, *Rabelais and His World*, ibid.

6. See, for example, Hannah Rockwell, "An 'Other' Burlesque: Feminine Bodies and Irigaray's Performing Textuality," *Body and Society* 2:1 (March 1996): 65–89; and Elizabeth Hirsh, "Back in Analysis: How to Do Things with Irigaray," in Burke et al., see 300–302, in particular.

7. Cheah and Grosz, "Of Being-Two: Introduction," 5–6.

8. Carolyn Burke writes that "by 1985, when *Speculum* and *This Sex Which Is Not One* appeared in English, roughly a decade after their original publication, even readers who had responded enthusiastically to their massive rethinking of the conditions of theory-making found it hard to take an interest in the 'new,' as yet untranslated Irigaray—the one who was writing about the elements, angels, and female spirituality . . . What, they asked, has become of the savagely witty thinker who deconstructed Freud and Lacan, who practiced Derridean turns on the (non)articulation of sexual difference?" (Carolyn Burke, "Translation Modified: Irigaray in English," in Burke et al., 249–50.)

9. For a summary and analysis of the essentialism debate see Naomi Schor, "Previous Engagements: The Receptions of Irigaray;" Margaret Whitford, "Reading Irigaray in the Nineties," Carolyn Burke, "Irigaray Through the Looking Glass;" and Naomi Schor, "This Essentialism Which Is Not One: Coming to Grips with Irigaray," in Burke et al., 3–78.

10. In a book review of Tina Chanter's *Ethics of Eros: Irigaray's Rewriting of the Philosophers* (New York: Routledge, 1995), published in the journal *Metaphilosophy* in 1996, Liz Grosz analyzes this Irigarayan affect, claiming that "Irigaray's writings entail an eros—hers are among the most powerful and moving erotic writings within the history of Western philosophy . . . One cannot be moved by it, one cannot feel it, respond to it or produce it in oneself from an exterior position. Her writings are a mode of seduction" (Elizabeth Grosz, "Ethics, Eros and Irigaray," *Metaphilosophy* 27:1–2 [January/April 1996]; 254–55). Irigaray was, and still is, sexy; in 1985, certainly, she was the "hottest" read in philosophy or French.

11. It is worth mentioning here that Irigaray herself actually uses the word "slave" when discussing mimesis, or mimicry. She expresses some bewilderment with regard to the ongoing admiration and/or controversy her early style continues to inspire, claiming that it was merely one strategy among many: "The use of mimicry on my part was very strategic and selective. I do not understand very well why it encounters such success . . . I have suggested that mimicry could serve in a strategic way as a joke to overcome a past status, but certainly not as a new way of becoming woman. Mimicry is a behavior of a slave . . ." (Luce Irigaray, *Luce Irigaray Presents International, Intercultural, Intergenerational Dialogues Around Her Work*, [Edinburgh, 2002], 115).

12. Cheah and Grosz, "The Future of Sexual Difference: An Interview with Judith Butler and Drucilla Cornell," 19.

13. Ibid., 20.

14. Ibid.

15. Butler and Cornell both, in fact, seem to experience a fair amount of "anxiety of influence" with respect to Irigaray, which is, of course, interesting in light of Irigaray's own thinking about the difficulties and tensions involved in intergenerational woman-to-woman relations.

16. In response to a comment made by Liz Grosz that Irigaray really does not "deal with texts that deal with homosexuality, hardly at all," Butler responds, "That's fine, but then let's put her in heterosexual studies rather than in feminism" (Cheah and Grosz, "Interview," 30).

17. Ibid.

18. Schwab, "Irigarayan Dialogism," 61.

19. Ibid., 62.

20. Ibid., 63. Just to clarify—when I wrote "Irigarayan Dialogism," I quoted Irigaray's text in the French. Here I replace the French with Carolyn Burke and Gillian C. Gill's English translation and add the final sentence, which I had left out initially, back in, in brackets.

21. Ibid.

22. Ibid., 61–2.

23. Burke, "Translation Modified," 254.

24. Ibid., 255.

25. Ibid., 257.

26. Carolyn Burke writes that in "*Parler n'est jamais neutre, Sexes et parentés, Le Temps de la différence, Je, tu, nous*, and *Sexes et genres à travers les langues* . . . the analysis of the formal structures of discourse is carried out at the expense of what seemed her most radical endeavor, her gestures toward a different style or styles. The enigmatic tone of her earlier prose has given way to a prophetic voice, one that spells out its vision rather than trying to enact it . . ." (Ibid.).

27. In 1967, Irigaray and her research partner, Jean Dubois, published a seminal article that became the basis for much of her subsequent linguistic

investigations (Luce Irigaray and Jean Dubois, "Approche expérimental des problèmes intéressant la production de la phrase noyau et ses constitutants immédiats," *Langages* 3, 90–125).

28. See Ibid.

29. Irigaray's first book, *Le Langage des déments* (Paris: Mouton, 1973) reports on this research into the languages of aphasia, dementia, and schizophrenia. In addition, some of this work, initially published in journals, was republished in *To Speak Is Never Neutral.* Readers who would just need a summary and an analysis of Irigaray's empirical linguistic research might consult an article I published in 1998. See Gail Schwab, "The French Connection: Luce Irigaray and International Research on Language and Gender," in *Untying the Tongue,* ed. Linda Longmire and Lisa Merrill (Westport: Greenwood, 1998), 13–24.

30. Schwab, 17

31. Ibid.

32. Thus, what looks like a rupture, or a break, in Irigaray's work is not really one. In reference to the works where Irigaray reports on and analyzes her empirical linguistic research, Burke notes that "however technical these studies seem, they can be read in the broader context of her overall program, since—as she says again and again in the recent books—Irigaray believes that women will only attain full subject status when the female gender is revalorized: because grammar is coded on the basis of social realities, sexual liberation can come about only through radical shifts and changes in language" (Burke, "Translation Modified, 259).

33. See, for example, Luce Irigaray, *Le Partage de la Parole* (Oxford: Legenda, 2001), trans. Luce Irigaray, *Key Writings* (London: Continuum, 2004).

34. I use the word "dialogue" here in the Bakhtinian sense that I have tried to clarify above.

35. Except, briefly and respectfully, in a discussion of her relationship to Simone de Beauvoir. See Luce Irigaray, "A Personal Note: Equal or Different," *Je, tu, nous,* 1993 (1990), 9–14.

36. Cheah and Grosz, "Interview," 32.

37. Ibid., 27–8.

38. For a detailed discussion and analysis of Irigaray's concept of sexuate rights that also deals with Drucilla Cornell's position, see Gail Schwab, "Women and the Law in Irigarayan Theory," *Metaphilosophy* 27:1–2 (January/April 1996), 146–77.

39. Cheah and Grosz, "Interview," 26.

40. Elizabeth Grosz, "The Hetero and the Homo: The Sexual Ethics of Luce Irigaray," in Burke, et al., 335–50.

41. Ibid., 335. Margaret Whitford also discusses Irigaray's past association with lesbian separatism and situates a "turning point" in her career at the point where she dissociated herself from a politics of sexual object choice—

presumably the moment of the *Ethics of Sexual Difference*, although Whitford does not make this explicit in this context. Margaret Whitford, "Reading Irigaray in the Nineties," in Burke et al., see 27.

42. Grosz, "The Hetero and the Homo," 335.

43. Ibid., 348.

44. Grosz rearticulates her position in the *diacritics* interview, maintaining, despite Butler's claim that it is her own (Grosz's) invention—"the Liz Grosz-Pheng Cheah supplement to Irigaray"—that Irigaray's work authorizes a reading wherein we interpret what "Irigaray is asking as . . . : 'what would other relations of sexuality be like if and when there was a recognition of the existence of more than one sex?' What changes would there be to homosexuality, to love between women, between men, to sexual love of all kinds, if this recognition were possible?" (Cheah and Grosz, "Interview," 28–9.)

45. Margaret Whitford, "Irigaray, Utopia and the Death Drive," in Burke et al., 395.

46. Whitford writes that "there is some evidence to suggest that Irigaray considered the triumphal moment of feminism and its celebration of relations between women as too dangerous; relations between women became too readily fusional and evoked the murderousness of the primitive and unsymbolized feelings for the mother. Not to mention men's counterviolence in response. This violence needs to be bound in a symbolic way. The dangers in feminism, as Irigaray sees them, lie in a politics that is heedless of the functioning of the patriarchal death drive. Such a politics risks an escalation of violence that leaves the sacrificial foundation untouched. I would suggest that Irigaray sees it as one of her tasks to work toward a new symbolization. In her attempt to rewrite a founding myth for the new era, she wants to bind the death drive with eros" (Ibid., 394).

47. Ibid., 381.

48. Ibid., 394.

49. Schwab, "Women and Law in Irigarayan Theory."

50. Irigaray continues to insist upon the critical importance of this issue for the future of the planet. She comes back to it most recently in "*Le Partage de la Parole*," for example.

51. Cheah and Grosz, "Interview," 27–8.

52. Ibid., 28.

53. Grosz, "The Hetero and the Homo," 348.

54. Gail Schwab, "Sexual Difference as Model: An Ethics for the Global Future," *diacritics* 28:1 (Spring 1998), 76–92.

55. Cheah and Grosz, "Interview," 28.

56. Schwab, "Sexual Difference as Model," 76–8.

57. I would like to make clear from the beginning that I have no knowledge of the nature of the personal relationship between Luce Irigaray and Renzo Imbeni, or if indeed there is one. It would be inappropriate and irrelevant for me to discuss it if I did know. I know only what can be read

in her books, in which he plays an important part. I therefore characterize their relationship as both "public" and "civic," and "mythical" and "literary."

58. Irigaray lays out the politics of this failure in the essay, indicating also that she would like to continue the fight, and that she has hope for the future.

59. See the Prologue to *I Love to You* for a particularly developed representation of the role of Renzo Imbeni as expressly acknowledged literary interlocutor of Luce Irigaray. It is also worth reminding ourselves that the book is dedicated to him.

60. See in particular *La Croyance même* (Paris: Galilee, 1983), also published as "Belief Itself" in *Sexes and Genealogies* (Irigaray 1993 [1987], 23–53), and "On the Maternal Order," in *Je, tu, nous* (Irigaray 1993 [1990], 37–44). For a detailed discussion of the developmental aspect of subjectivity and the preoedipal relation to the mother see Gail Schwab, "Mother's Body, Father's Tongue," in Burke et al., 351–78.

61. See *Le Partage de la Parole*, for example.

62. Cheah and Grosz, "Interview," 28.

63. Ibid., 27–8.

64. Ibid., 26.

65. Schwab, "Irigarayan Dialogism," 59–60. The reference to Jane Gallop can be found in Jane Gallop, "The Father's Seduction," *The Daughter's Seduction* (Ithaca, N.Y.: Cornell University Press, 1982), 78.

66. Margaret Whitford, "Reading Irigaray in the Nineties," 15.

WORKS CITED

Bauer, Dale M. and Susan Jaret McKinstry, eds. 1991. *Feminism, Bakhtin, and the Dialogic*. Albany, N.Y.: State University of New York Press.

Burke, Carolyn, Naomi Schor, and Margaret Whitford, eds. 1994. *Engaging With Irigaray*. New York: Columbia University Press.

Chanter, Tina. 1995. *Ethics of Eros: Irigaray's Rewriting of the Philosophers*. New York and London: Routledge.

Cheah, Pheng, and Elizabeth Grosz, eds. 1998. *diacritics* 28:1 (Spring).

Irigaray, Luce. 1985 [1974]. *Speculum of the Other Woman*. Translated by Gillian C. Gill. Ithaca, N.Y.: Cornell University Press.

———. 1985 [1977]. *This Sex Which Is Not One*. Translated by Catherine Porter. Ithaca, N.Y.: Cornell University Press.

———. 1993 [1984]. *An Ethics of Sexual Difference*. Translated by Carolyn Burke and Gillian C. Gill. Ithaca, N.Y.: Cornell University Press.

———. 1993 [1987]. *Sexes and Genealogies*. Translated by Gillian C. Gill. New York: Columbia University Press.

———. 1993 [1990]. *Je, tu, nous*. Translated by Alison Martin. New York and London: Routledge.

————. [1990]. *Sexes, Genders, and Languages*. Translated by Gail Schwab and Katherine Stephenson. Unpublished.

————. 1996 [1992]. *I Love to You*. Translated by Alison Martin. New York and London: Routledge.

————. 2001 [1997]. *Essere due*. Bologna: Bollati Boringhieri. 1994. Translated by Luce Irigaray as *Etre Deux*. Paris: Grasset. Translated from the Italian into English as *To Be Two* by Monique M. Rhodes and Marco F. Cocito-Monoc. New York: Routledge.

————. 2001. *Le Partage de la Parole*. Oxford: Legenda. Translated as "Sharing Words" by Gail Schwab in *Key Writings*. London: Continuum, forthcoming.

————. 2002 [1985]. *To Speak Is Never Neutral*. Translated by Gail Schwab. London and New York: Continuum.

————. 2002 [1994]. *Democracy Begins Between Two*. Translated by Kirsteen Anderson. London: Athlone.

————. 2002. *Dialogues: Luce Irigaray Presents International, Intercultural, Intergenerational Dialogues Around Her Work*. Edinburgh: Edinburgh University Press.

————. 2002. *The Way of Love*. Translated from the unpublished French manuscript by Heidi Bostic and Stephen Pluháček. London and New York: Continuum.

Longmire, Linda, and Lisa Merrill, eds. 1998. *Untying the Tongue*. Westport, Conn.: Greenwood Press.

Rockwell, Hannah. "An 'Other' Burlesque: Feminine Bodies and Irigaray's Performing Textuality." *Body and Society* 2:1 (March 1996): 65–89.

Wallace, Kathleen and Marjorie Cantor Miller, guest eds. January/April 1996. *Metaphilosophy* 27:1–2.

A NEW ECONOMY OF RELATIONS

Krzysztof Ziarek

INTRODUCTION

Economy seems to be on everyone's mind these days, whether it be in the times of a crisis or a downturn, as is the case at the moment that I am writing this essay, or during an economic boom. Hardly an hour seems to go by without market updates or economic news, whose frequency, importance, and scope appear to grow in proportion to the rapid advances in information and telecommunication technologies. At the same time, however, such statements about the prominence of economy and the proliferating "news" about its performance appear as commonplace as they are true, which reflects the degree to which economic and technological developments have come to shape the rhythm of everyday life, not just in the minds of economic and financial specialists but, it seems, also for an average citizen. On the level of cultural representation, market reports punctuate existence with the ups and downs of the indexes, whose uneven pulse provides the modern measure of human existence in terms of the techno-economic activity, almost to the point of overshadowing any other concerns. This preeminence given to economy indicates the extent to which social practice has come to be determined in terms of the increasingly technological operations of consumption and production. The iconic function that Dow Jones, for instance, plays in the contemporary "media" consciousness of the day-to-day reality is more than a matter of popular representations of the increased dependence of modern life on economic rhythms, a metaphor for the economic and technological advance of globalization—it also reflects a more complex and formative relation between the techno-economic indicators and the constitution of experience at the beginning of the twenty-first century. It bespeaks a progressively pervasive foreshortening and compression of experience into information, which takes the form of headlines and economic data, in which catchy, "information-loaded," phrases and readily comprehensible numbers serve as the shorthand for what appears to constitute the "essence" of contemporary being.

To approach this problem from a slightly different angle, one could say that the attention given in today's society to economy in its strict sense of production and consumption reflects a deeper determination of the overall "economy" of social relations in terms of technicity and its latest incarnation, information. By the technicity of modern relations I understand here the growing ease with which reality becomes pliable as information, and thus readily foreshortened to what appears to be its intrinsically techno-informational core, as, for example, is the case with the human genome. That being in its different manifestations is technical in the sense proposed above means that it appears as predetermined in its essence for extraction or abstraction into information, and, as such, remains predisposed and readily available for storage, processing, and even reprogramming. This intrinsic predisposition toward availability, manipulation, and processing, so characteristic of what we call today the information age, was described by Heidegger as the *Gestell*, as the enframing determinative of the essence of modern technology. In the context of the information age, the notion of the *Gestell* can be rethought to reflect the current situation in which all that is, including various relations constitutive of our daily existence and multiple operations of the contemporary world, is "framed," or encoded, as information; that is, it can be posited (*stellen*), produced (*herstellen*), represented (*vorstellen*), ordered (*bestellen*), and processed as information. That information is the key to contemporary reality means also that reality appears, in its very essence, to be an informational code. To put it differently, the real is literally ciphered as information, that is, it is numerical, a cipher transformable into an information byte, characterized by its predisposition to being stored, processed, and reprogrammed. It is in this specific sense that the measure of contemporary reality is technical, or better yet, info-technical, which indicates that, in its fundamental character, reality comes to be revealed as an informational matrix.

The information age signals, thus, the unprecedented degree of the transparency of the informational makeup of contemporary reality, a thorough visibility of being as information. If, as I indicate in the initial, short section of this essay, Heidegger's critique of technicity makes it possible to see the economy of relations today in terms of their intensifying manifestation and availability as information, Irigaray's recent work on (in)visibility and the energy of "letting be" suggests an alternative to this info-technical economy of relations. This different economy of relations would be predicated on what she describes as the energy of invisibility, associated with a refashioned relation to alterity. Rethinking the other's difference beyond the optics of negation, Irigaray finds in the invisibility that marks the other's alterity a source of transformative energy. Developing a new culture of this energy of invisibility would entail an elaboration of an unfamiliar ethics of letting be, that is, of an economy of relations based not just on production but, rather, on the energy of transformation released by the other's difference, on the potentiality brought into existence by the "invisible" alterity of the other. This economy of letting be has become forgotten in the modern techno-informational economy of production and consumption, which is based on visibility and availability, and values primarily making and power. What I try to show in sections II and III is that Irigaray's insistence on cultivating the distinctive energy of invisibility can be seen not simply as a supplement to the dominant economy of production but as a critique of the techno-productionist makeup of modern relations.

I

Etymologically, the word "economy" describes the rules of ordering, organizing, and maintaining a household. "Economy" thus indicates the system of the various correlated practices of production and consumption constitutive of the economic activity today, but, when thought in broad terms, it refers also to the order or the organization of a house. And the house in question here is, to allude to Heidegger, the house of being, comprising a complex, historically evolving system of relations and operations which organize and transform ontological, economic, political, and cultural relations. What is clear at the beginning of the twenty-first century is that the language of this house is techno-economic: it is the language which formats reality as information, thus precipitating its calculability and opening it to multiple and complex operations of processing. To put it in the context of Heidegger's reflection on the history of metaphysics and its technological determinations of being, the essence of being today is information, and its primary characteristic is its availability: everything is constituted as a standing reserve of information, which means that it becomes readily convertible into data and is thus at once rendered pliant and processable. Revealed in its "true" texture as information, reality, from its material components to its human energies and desires, becomes instantly and throughly available. For example, musical sampling, so characteristic of recent developments in popular, noise-based, and even some classical music, shows not only that music can be manipulated but that it is, in essence, manipulable sound. Ekkhard Ehlers impressive CD *Betrieb*,[1] composed from the samplings of the music of Ives and Schoenberg, is a creation based on the principle of transformative reprogramming, as it weaves sampled sounds into loops and repetitive patterns. This creation becomes possible only when the "reality" of music is disclosed as consisting of sound bytes, of digitizable information, which, with appropriate technological equipment, can be processed and resequenced into a new musical form. In sum, Ehlers's creation is not only an example of creative musical transformation, but an indicator that music has become, or has come to be revealed, like other sectors of culture, and even more broadly reality in general, as reprogrammable in its essence.

This disclosure of reality as information means that cultural, political, and social relations are undergoing a similar process of informatization. While not only economic but also cultural and political relations are described nowadays in terms of production and consumption, these very notions, that is, production and consumption, appear to have an informational structure or texture today. Both political campaigns and cultural products have become a matter of properly construed informational content. Cultural products and relations, including works of art, are not only a matter of consumption and production, but also work as information. The relations through which artworks are produced and which they themselves in turn construct with regard to the "consuming" public have informational structure. To be discernible, to become an "object" of public discussion, what artworks (are supposed to) evoke in the audience has to be compressible into a marketing statement, into a book blurb or a film synopsis, susceptible in its very structure to infinite repetition and reprocessing for the benefit of dissemination—and, of course, anticipated profit. The merit of works is calculable in terms of the number of copies or tickets sold, or reflected in the number of awards, which count precisely because they help to increase sales. When works resist such categorizations, when they are not translatable into information or go further and call into question the hegemonic "informational standard" of reality, they become classified as obscure, difficult, or elitist, and thus disqualified to the margins of existence. At issue here, in addition to the often discussed commercialization of art and culture, is a deeper "informating" of modern reality, which underlies and makes possible such phenomena as commercialization and mass culture. Informating here describes the prevalent formating of reality with its constitutive relations in(to) the terms of information. In (post)modernity, reality is of the order of information, which means that the economy of relations constitutive of such reality is informational. Thus, today we have not only the rapidly expanding information economy, with the Internet and telecommunications industries as its flagships, but, on a more fundamental level, the economy of information, in which beings and relations come to be constituted as or formatted into information. To be real today is to be convertible into and processable as information, since the metaphysical "proof" of existence is info-technical.

This "informating" of contemporary being is epitomized in the project of Virtual Reality (VR), in which reality would be manufactured and regulated as a master computer program. The fascination with the idea of a technological facility capable of producing an alternative, fully controllable, reality reveals a deep-seated desire for mastery, mastery that would culminate in the ability to (re)produce a reality as a matter of total transparency and complete manipulability, where possibilities, accidents, and even contingencies would be programmed in advance. In short, what would be experienced as unpredictable would in fact be, within the informational spectrum of being, as it were, perfectly envisioned, manipulable, and reprogrammable. After all, isn't everything information? In a way, VR is the latest technological incarnation of the long-standing dream of comprehending reality to the utmost degree, a form of comprehension that would allow for the full transparency of everything precisely to the extent to which it can all be rendered manifest as information. Such manifestness of all that is, that is, of reality as such, would be tantamount to making this reality not simply knowable but, and perhaps more important, controllable and programmable in its very essence. VR appears thus to be an offshoot of the dream of power over the real, in which power, comprehension, and manipulation become thoroughly technological and informational in character. The fascination with VR, which is clearly part of its commercial appeal as both a source of entertainment and a facility of telematic manipulation, can be traced back to the prevalent intoxication with power, in which power operates as technological manipulation, as the super ability to (re)program what happens and also what could happen. Such a techno-informational approach to reality is not just warranted but also induced by the fact that reality itself has become disclosed as informational in essence, as a kind of an information code or a computer program.

A critical part of this informational economy of modern relations is played by capital. Contemporary capital has been clearly aided in its current expansion by information and telecommunication technologies, and not just by the development and incorporation of new technologies and devices, but, more importantly, by the inclusion and growth of information *as* capital. Whether such information capital is financial, consumer, or technological, information as capital, combined with the rapid growth of telecommunications industry and the Internet, has revolutionized, as common knowledge—read: media— would have it, the way business is done. But even more important for understanding what has been described here as the informational economy of relations is the fact that capital itself has become informational in nature. Capital today works like information, its human, material, and, more recently, immaterial resources have the structure of availability redolent of information: all is open to seemingly infinite processing and reproduction. And not just open; in fact, all that exists appears to be constituted into a form of availability, into an existence that has an informational structure, in principle open to manipulation and reprogramming. Capital is as information-based as the reality from which it arises and which it actively produces and shapes through the processes of manufacturing and consumption.

To approach capital in this way, namely as a historical manner of revealing being, it is necessary to rethink capital beyond the subject-object dialectic. In *Kapital und Technik: Marx und Heidegger*, Michael Eldred undertakes such a postmetaphysical rethinking of capital, in which, modeling his thought on Heidegger's understanding of the essence of technology as the enframing (*die Gestell*), he proposes to conceive of the essence of capital as the "win" (*das Gewinnst*).[2] *Das Gewinnst* describes the event of truth in which being discloses itself in terms of value, profit, competition, and so on—everything exists insofar as it is capable of being assigned value and used for potential profit. Seen in this way, capital is a historical revealing in which all that exists becomes disclosed as susceptible in its essence to being (re)produced, valued, and profited from. Capital is thus rethought as an event in which being and beings are engaged specifically with a view to their potentiality for production and profit. As a result, other potentialities are either covered over or subjected to the overpowering draw of the "win." In this context, Eldred suggests that Heidegger's thought of *die Gestell* has to be supplemented with the figure of *das Gewinnst* in order to account for the double play of technology and capital in the modern world, a play that engages reality in terms of conceptualization, grasping, and representation, all reflected in another term Eldred introduces, *der Gegriff*.

While Heidegger does not venture explicitly into the analysis of either economy or capital, his notion of the enframing does not simply specify the powers operating in technology, as Eldred's argument seems to imply, but delineates a certain general economy of relations, according to which all that exists does so only to the extent to which it is always "challenged" to be available for technological fashioning, that is, enframed and posited (*stellen*) as part of the overall reserve of resources, available for production (*herstellen*) and ordering (*bestellen*). This economy is a certain technics precisely because it defines existence as the potentiality to be measured, calculated, produced, or manipulated. Technicity here means that beings are constantly challenged to coincide with their technological calculus, and if they do not fit it or exceed its criteria of measurement, their "reality" is called into question. As a result, today, beings, events, and relations come to be characterized in terms of their intrinsic availability as "information," always close to hand, ready to be instantly processed, computed, or stored as data. If capital reveals being as the potentiality for production, value, and profit, then what makes possible the operations and growth of capital is the underlying technicity of being engaged, brought out, and amplified by the enframing, which renders being into a resource, that is, lays it open in terms of its open-ended availability for. . . . There would be no capital without a prior "capitalization" of being, that is, without the disclosure of being as the potentiality for production and profit, the potentiality linked to the general constitution of being in modernity in terms of being available, amenable, even more, intrinsically disposed, to technological remaking. While capital grounds and powers economic activity, it does so to the extent that it itself functions as part of a deeper info-technical disposition of relations in modernity. And it is because this technic economy of relations engages and mobilizes being as, in its essence, available for technological refashioning, that capital historically comes into existence and determines economic relations in their narrow sense of production and consumption. Hence, the very idea of production, and its corollary, consumption, is grounded in availability, and today, specifically in the availability of beings and relations as information. In historical terms, it is the rapid intensification of economic activity associated with the information and telecommunications industries that has made visible the underlying disclosure of being in its potentiality as information. The analysis of capital in the age of information becomes therefore even more important, provided it sharpens our attention to its own grounding in the fluid "info-technicity" of modern relations, which determines the shape of social praxis today.

II

In her most recent texts and lectures, Luce Irigaray continuously emphasizes the necessity of a new culture or economy of energy, one that is missing from the technological civilization of the West. Irigaray associates this energy with a different understanding of the relation to the other, in which the other's alterity is not a source of trauma but an enabling difference which contributes both to one's becoming and to the transformation of relations with others. While Irigaray does not explicitly develop the implications that this new economy of energy might have for the techno-informational character of relations in the information age, the terms "culture" and "economy," which she repeatedly employs, suggest an important connection between the energy she writes about and the informational economy of relations sketched in the first part of this essay. To formulate this link more explicitly, we have to understand what kind of energy and economy of relations is at stake in Irigaray's thought and, above all, to flesh out how her refashioning of the relation to alterity can evolve a disposition of forces and relations alternative to the dominant techno-informational paradigm of being in modernity. My suggestion here is that the enabling energy Irigaray associates with the difference marked by otherness is not simply supplementary to production and technology, but makes possible a recasting of the technic dynamics of relating constitutive of contemporary social praxis.

Irigaray introduces the idea of a new economy of energy in order to supplement her conception of the working of the negative, necessary to the critical reformulation of the relations to others in the context of sexual and gender differences: "And if, in my book *I Love to You*, I explain that, to recognize the other as other, I must use negativity with respect to myself—and in another way to the other— to this new dialectical process I have to add a culture of energy that the occidental tradition lacks" (Irigaray 2001 [2000], 15).[3] What Irigaray acknowledges here is that the (dialectical) workings of negativity, while indispensable to the opening of a difference or an otherness within the self, and, dialectically, within the other, does not capture the "positive" energy of the encounter. Negativity makes it possible to reconstitute the subject, and the other, as intrinsically open to difference, but it does not account for the transformative potential which Irigaray ascribes to otherness. For the "culture" or the "economy" of the energy Irigaray describes in "Being Two, How Many Eyes Have We?" (Irigaray 2001 [2000]) does not operate in terms of negation or positing. Part of the difference and the alternative character of this economy comes from the fact that it does not explain itself in either positive or negative terms, that, in short, it eschews, or better, transcends and transforms, the dialectical operations of difference.

To suggest how the dialectical negativity of difference needs to be supplemented with a new culture of energy, Irigaray redraws the relationship between visibility and invisibility constitutive of the Western metaphysical optics of being. In a move to substantially recast the understanding of the human, Irigaray complicates the dialectics of the visible and the invisible, on which the ideas of knowing, difference, and otherness are based. Thus, a characteristic mark of being human is, for Irigaray, not the capacity for making visible and knowable, but, on the contrary, the ability to open up invisibility: "What distinguishes a human being from other living beings rather is his ability to create invisibility more than to make appear, to render visible" (Irigaray 2001 [2000], 13 E). When the human being is traditionally defined in terms of the capacity to see and to know, that is, in terms of a certain reading of *logos*, then, within the dialectics of the visible and the invisible, the visible becomes the positive term, to be extracted and won from the "negativity" of the invisible. The faculty of sight thus becomes tantamount to the ability to translate the invisible into the visible, to bring the unknown into the horizon of intelligibility. Irigaray's revision consists in recasting invisibility as a source of a different seeing: the invisible is not a lack in seeing, not a failure of the human sight to appropriate what presents itself negatively to it, that is, as absent from the field of the visible or lacking in clarity, but a potential for transformation in the very parameters of visibility.

It is this transformation in the very optics of being that opens up the possibility of a new culture of invisibility, which dramatically revises the signification of alterity: ". . . the invisibility of the other is no longer felt as a lack of seeing but as an invisible source of seeing. To contemplate the invisibility of the other gives or gives us again life . . ." (Irigaray 2001 [2000], 21 E). What becomes transformed in this flip between the visible and the invisible are the parameters of seeing, the optics within which otherness and difference signify. Thus, what is also modified in the same gesture is the very modality in which the other's difference, his or her invisibility, signifies. To "see" the invisibility in the other, that is, the other's alterity, either as a lack of seeing or as a lack in being, is to always already operate within a metaphysics of visibility which associates positivity (seeing, knowledge, order) with the idea of the visible, with the movement of appropriating and forming the invisible into visibility, whether we think here of rendering something knowable or fashioning something in the process of production. Thus, the very term "lack" reveals the economy which regulates relations within the optics of visibility: it is an economy which consists in making appear, in rendering visible, and thus, to echo Heidegger here, in procuring or making available: for knowledge, manipulation, production, mastery, and so on. Within this economy, invisibility signifies negatively, that is, as a lack or a gap which needs to be either redeemed or covered over, either appropriated and rendered visible or marginalized and excluded. Invisibility functions here as a disturbance or a threat to the stability of the economy of the visible, a disruption which has to be mended, woven back into the texture of visibility. The dominant economy of visibility assures that all the resources for growth and development are associated with the terms of visibility, that is, that only what explains itself in terms of the visible, what can itself be seen and known, merits the potential for change. Logically, what resists visibility or fails to manifest itself within the parameters dictated by the optics of the visible, becomes an obstacle in the expanding field of visibility and knowledge.

Irigaray reverses this relation by investing invisibility with the energy of enabling and transformation. As she emphatically states, "the invisibility of the other gives or gives us again life" (Irigaray 2001 [2000], 21E). Life and becoming are associated here not with the steady increase in visibility, with the progressive rendering of being into a "visible" and available resource, but with a radical requalification of invisibility. As a result, it is the invisible that becomes the source of another energy, the third ground, as Irigaray calls it, namely, the ground of transformation and becoming. She calls invisibility the third ground in order to differentiate it from the two modalities of energy, vital and cultural, in terms of which the dialectics of visibility operates. "To succeed in transforming one's vital energy and one's cultural energy into a free energy, available, not already determined nor finalized, would be for me the characteristic of a human being" (Irigaray 2001 [2000], 17 E). To be human thus means to be capable of the third kind of energy, an energy without ends or finality which supplements the physiologically, materially-based vital energy and the intellectual, cultural energy of the spirit. Irigaray invokes breath as the figure for this third energy, because it is breath that ensures the junction of body and soul, the material and the spiritual (Irigaray 2001 [2000], 19 E), and suggests that the disappearance or lack of importance of this kind of energy in Western culture is related to the dominance of one gender, with "the other one being constrained to conform to so called universal norms or forms" (Irigaray 2001 [2000], 17 E). Thus, the new economy Irigaray suggests in her writings would be one of breath, where breath constitutes "the third ground" from which human beings become: "The breath, as vital or spiritual matter of a human being, corresponds to this third ground from which we can appear as humans and relate between us" (Irigaray 2001 [2000], 20 E).

It is particularly important to develop here three points implied in this "revision" of invisibility. First, the energy associated with the other's invisibility is irreducible either to vitality or to cultural sublimations, which means also that human becoming cannot be defined and circumscribed exclusively in terms of vitality and production, or, in other words, nature and culture: "Becoming human in part has been perceived so, the part which concerns the transformation of vital energy. But the end or the means proposed for this process was to transform vital energy—in particular sexual energy—by submitting it to a defined culture, by manufacturing objects corresponding to this culture. It would consist as it were in going from one determination to another, from one submission to another" (Irigaray 2001 [2000], 16/17 E). The third energy is not a matter of submitting "natural" energy to "cultural" controls, in other words, to the operations of sublimation. Instead, this third energy calls into question and revises the understanding of human beings through the binary model of natural and cultural processes of development. I will return later to the very important question of the implications of this new economy of energy for the model of production. Let me just suggest here briefly that, while the two kinds of energy, vital and cultural, become locked into the dialectics of production, a dialectics underpinned by the subject-object metaphysics, the third energy Irigaray alludes to breaks free of the nature-culture divide. It is neither natural (biological, physiological, sexual) nor cultural (intellectual, spiritual, technological, etc.). This "new" or "alternative" energy does not submit itself to manufacturing, creation, or production of objects and goods; in other words, it is not convertible into either production or consumption, and, as such, it does not operate in terms of the technological, and now, informational, economy of relations.

Second, the revision of the optics of visibility and invisibility cannot be confined to the relation to the human other. In addition to pertaining to the question of the other's invisibility, the culture of breath concerns the invisibility and otherness manifest in the world, or, to put it even more strongly, it pertains to invisibility that manifests itself *as* the world's becoming. The invisibility at issue here can be linked to the Heideggerian problematic of the event, that is, to the manner in which the manifestation of being and time always already involves a withdrawal and a restraint. This withdrawal, however, is not a lack or an absence, and, as Heidegger remarks on several occasions, it is not a matter of the failure of human faculties, of "a lack of seeing" in other words. On the contrary, the withdrawal intrinsic to the unfolding of the event is, as "Letter on Humanism" or "On Time and Being" make evident, a clearing and a giving, an enabling of time and being, that is, an enabling of beings in their temporality and historicity. What the event enables, or gives, is the coming into being and the becoming of all that is, that is, the finite and historical occurring of the world. The implication here is that the economy of energy Irigaray has in mind has to register precisely this enabling withdrawal of the event in its broadly ontological scope, and thus to become much more attentive to the temporality and historicity which are, as it were, the operative modality of the enabling energy she brings to our attention.

Third, the new visibility involves an important rethinking of the ethical relation, and, quite literally, of the ethical rhetoric which has become so pivotal to recent philosophical, cultural, and literary discussions. For Irigaray, the breath which conjoins body and soul, matter and spirit, "the living and the properly human" is also "necessary for entering into presence of a human as human, more necessary than language and in a different way" (Irigaray 2001 [2000], 19 E). The new culture of breath, the energy associated with enabling and transformation is the very condition of the openness to the other, and thus of ethics. What is striking about this formulation is that ethics is no longer "simply" a matter of the acculturation of the natural, vital energies, of submitting to an ethical culture—though "simply" clearly does here an injustice to the complexity of this junction between nature and culture. Just as the economy of energy Irigaray has in mind spans and yet extends beyond the nature-culture doublet, so ethics too is not a question of morality and of a moral culture, but involves a transformative openness enabled and energized by the encounter with difference. As such, it involves the relation with other humans but also, more broadly, the manner of being or dwelling in the world, an alternative ethos which this new economy of energy implies. This implied other way of dwelling makes stark the disappearance of ethics, or better, of the ethos, of otherness in the info-technical economy of relations, where everything becomes a matter of rendering available as information. The proliferating conferences on business ethics are only an ironic reminder of that very disappearance.

In this context it is interesting to bring into conversation Irigaray's thought with Levinas's understanding of the relation to the other. The Levinasian notion of the ethical relation to the other is based on a prohibition of killing the other, who, exceeding the world of the subject, disturbs and disquiets it. The other is an excess for Levinas, an excess which the subject tries to bring under control, even resorting to a symbolical or a literal killing of the other. Yet, the other always remains an excess, an opening or an exposition, which cannot be made to conform to the parameters of subjectivity, truth, or representation. Levinas's work presents a whole spectrum of the significations of the other's alterity, from the double negation of "you shall not kill" to the sense that the other's difference is a call that makes possible an ethical comportment, a welcoming of otherness. Above all, the other in Levinas marks an obsession, a becoming hostage, an inescapable responsibility, or a weight that opens the space for ethical action, and signifies as, at the same time, a prohibition and a call: a prohibition to kill or hurt and a call to act and help. In an interesting modification, Irigaray sees the invisibility characteristic of the other, the mark of the other's excess, as primarily enabling. Referring to her analysis of Hegel and negativity in *I Love to You*, Irigaray clearly insists on the importance of negativity in the recognition of the other as other. However, she also makes clear that to respect and offer hospitality to the other's invisibility, the dialectical process of what she describes as taking the negative upon oneself has to be supplemented with a new culture of energy, which "sees" in invisibility an enabling energy, a relation that makes possible seeing, perhaps even seeing otherwise (Irigaray 2001 [2000], 15 E). While remaining in a way very close to Levinas, Irigaray gives ethics a different inflection: it is not a prohibition or a call that comes from the other but, first and foremost, an enabling, a giving of life, a giving of a new visibility. Both Levinas and Irigaray use the trope of breath as pivotal to their reconceptualization of the relation to the other. However, for Levinas, breath is as much inspiration as it is obsession; what it inspires, literally breathes into the subject, is the ethical trace, a trace of responsibility and obsession, even of being taken hostage. For Irigaray, on the other hand, breath indicates a breath of possibilities, a becoming. It is a potentiality for transformation, for a different visibility of the world, a breath of fresh air, as it were. Without doubt Levinas and Irigaray are concerned with the same issue of radically revising the parameters of the encounter with the other in order to expose the ethical signification of alterity, but this issue is manifested in their text in quite different tonalities. As Ewa Plonowska Ziarek suggests, Levinas excludes sexual relations from the sphere of ethics, while Irigaray makes them the very source of her reformulation of ethics into an ethics of sexual difference.[4] But this distinction marks itself just as prominently in their respective rhetorics. Levinas's thought of radical alterity is cast predominantly in what might be regarded as "masculine" terms: obsession, hostage, responsibility. Irigaray's language, on the other hand, places the emphasis on the potentiality unfolding from the other's difference, so that the other's invisibility does not only ex-posit the subject but, primarily, enables both the one and the other to become, to "be two." Alterity is thus expressed through a feminine rhetoric, which foregrounds change, potential, and a new economy of sexual relations.

   Irigaray's thought reverses the optics of the relation to the other in such a way that the other's invisibility, instead of disturbing the subject—whether that disturbance/excess is construed, as happens in different discourses, as lack, prohibition, or demand, becomes immaterial here—inaugurates a new economy of relations. It is only when this third ground of human relations, as Irigaray calls it, is forgotten or covered over that invisibility acquires the "negative" connotations of a lack in seeing. What comes from the other, that is, from the other's invisibility, is, for Irigaray, primarily a flow of energy, which gives a new visibility to the world: no longer the visibility of an I, a visibility that is "mine," but a visibility that is "between us." This visibility sheds all pretensions to totalization or complete transparency, as it is based, in principle, on a sharing of mutual invisibility. It is not vectored toward the centrality of the subject but, instead, extended toward and continuously transformed by the energy of invisibility. The other's invisibility no longer signifies lack, absence, or fault in seeing but, on the contrary, the energy of the unexpected and the new. Such a visibility "between us" is not only capable of but in fact predicated on change; its parameters are not transparency and mastery but the enabling of transformation. In short, what the other's invisibility allows is a different visibility of the world and of the others we encounter within it.

This enabling of a new optics is critical here and needs to be developed beyond Irigaray's remarks. In this new visibility, which the other's invisibility gives to the world, what changes is precisely the signification of the other's alterity: this alterity is no longer either lack or excess, nor the ambiguous play of the two, nor perhaps even a trace. For Irigaray, the other is certainly not a traumatic wounding of the subject but, instead, a giving and an enabling of difference. The scenario called into question here is a familiar one in which the other shocks or traumatizes the visibility of the world in which I exist, thus forcing or calling on the subject to revise this optics. Irigaray departs substantially from this dominant vision of otherness, suggesting instead that the other's difference initially offers a new way of looking, a new light, as Irigaray puts it, so that, one might say, everything appears in a different light. If, in the first scenario, at issue is the generosity of the subject, in Irigaray's case, it is the generosity intrinsic in, and opening from, the other's invisibility. In this specific sense, the other for Irigaray is less a trace taken as the mark of the erasure of an absence than a radical alterity figured as the generosity of a new energy and visibility, a transformative energy precisely because it remains "invisible" in terms of the dominant economies of visibility.

III

Irigaray's sense of a new economy of energy signifies a crucial shift from trauma, wounding, and lack conceived as the originary parameters of the relation to the other, constitutive of the predominant "culture" of the other's invisibility. For this "traumatic" signification of alterity is operative precisely only within the visibility and the culture that come into question in her writings and become transformed by the generosity of the other's invisibility. To the extent to which our culture is dominated and generated by images, by an obsession with making visible, presentable, and measurable, the other's invisibility is a gift, a gift of transformative energy. One can either remain within the culture of visibility, the culture dominated by images and information, and thus, predictably, see the other's invisibility as a trauma or a wound in the reigning pan-spectrum of visibility, or one can "welcome" the energy that comes from this invisibility and direct it toward opening a new economy of relations, toward seeing the world and others as always unknown. This is also why Irigaray insists on the necessity of supplementing the dialectics of negativity with the economy of enabling, since it is not enough to either arrest the dialectic in the negative or to keep negativity continuously in play as the index of transformation. For a new culture of energy to emerge, it will not suffice to see the other differently through the changed perspective of the negative already operating within the subject, a negative taken upon oneself, even though such negative plays a pivotal role in undoing the dominant representations of otherness. Instead, the other has to acquire a different signification, a different visibility, so to speak, in which invisibility becomes a gift of energy, a giving and an enabling akin perhaps to the sense in which Heidegger's *Ereignis* gives time and being. This gift of energy, when it begins to flow within the reciprocity of relations, can transform the optics and the economy of those relations. In this act, also, the modality of how one relates to the world and to others becomes decisively transformed: it is now cast in the middle voice, more a matter of enabling than of power, production, or manipulation. This new way of looking "will be more contemplative, passive as well as active, capable of discovering an other or a world always unknown" (Irigaray 2001 [2000], 23 E). Given in the middle voice, both passive and active, this visibility offers the world in a new mode, through a new economy of energy and relations.

Irigaray suggests that "this generation of an invisible light is perhaps most fertile in sexual difference. Escaping the physiological or cultural imperatives of genealogy, it is kept up by the desire and the respect for the other as other" (Irigaray 2001 [2000], 22 E). Respect for alterity becomes here a transformative relation, which, while determined by material and cultural genealogy, that is, by both embodiment and constant cultural shaping of identity, is neither constrained nor limited by it. Within a respectful and desirous relation to the other, the other's difference and invisibility enable both one's becoming and the becoming of one's relation to the other beyond what is made possible by material and cultural genealogies. The other's invisibility takes the becoming beyond the horizon of genealogy and inheritance, and to such a degree that it surprises and revises their parameters. It is even capable of changing the very optics in which the encounter itself takes place. In this gesture, Irigaray makes the relation to the other, especially the other in sexual difference, into an event which enables becoming and transformation. It is the other's difference which introduces the potentiality for change and becoming, and this potentiality is a truly radical one, since, and Irigaray is explicit on this point, the enabling potential which opens from the other's difference makes possible escaping the imperatives of one's genealogy. If one is not stuck in one's heritage, in one's continuing and evolving determination by culture and social praxis, one owes this possibility to the other's difference, as well as to what one's own difference offers for the other. This reciprocal enabling eschews closing in upon itself or forming a totality (of the relation). This is the case because enabling does not incorporate or contain the other within the relation, nor does it render the other into the support for one's emerging new form of the self. Rather, the dynamic of such a reciprocal enabling through difference takes the form of one's becoming *through* the other, which is coupled with the other's becoming through the one, where this reciprocal becoming is continuously inflected by the other's enabling difference as much as, at the same time, it itself too enables the other to become and change. And since such a reciprocal becoming evolves a new visibility, it avoids folding the relation upon itself and instead opens it outward, unfolding and radiating a new economy of relations.

It is important to recognize the possibilities which this short essay by Irigaray opens for a pivotal revision of the very notions of seeing and visibility. The title suggests the possibility of developing a new eyesight, a seeing that is neither one's nor the other's but, instead, transpires as a seeing "between us" and thus enables a revision of the seeing/knowing doublet fundamental to the historical development of Western/European cultures. Talking about eyes, looking, seeing, visibility, and invisibility, Irigaray recodes these terms, progressively taking them away from the association with knowledge, representation, and possession. Seeing here ceases to be a matter of rendering something visible and thus making it available for grasping, representing, knowing, and, subsequently, also for manipulating and (re)producing. Instead, seeing opens up difference and releases the energy of transformation, which affects and alters the parameters of visibility themselves. As a consequence, seeing no longer has here the value of presence, of rendering something present and thus of grasping and knowing it as existing and present in its very presence. Rather, seeing unfolds in an ecstatic temporality, always ahead of itself, futural in its outlook, so to speak, which means that such a seeing is a matter of transformation and becoming. To see the other's invisibility is to become transformed through the other's difference, to be given entrance into a new economy of relating to the other. If previously seeing concerned grasping and knowing, now it involves, or better evolves, becoming and transforming, where becoming transpires without ends or objectives, and becomes enabled by the relational energy of difference. In the end, this reading of Irigaray's essay performs a transformation of seeing itself: from the pivotal role it has played in systematizing the conceptuality of knowledge and representation to a new paradoxical seeing of invisibility, whose importance lies not in an ability to "see" and thus to grasp (Hegel's *Begriff*, Eldred's *Gegriff*), but in its enabling potentiality. Simplifying the issue, one could say that the critical difference here lies between visibility as grasping and (in)visibility as the energy of enabling and becoming.

To the extent that Western history is underpinned by a fundamental connection between visibility and knowledge, on the one hand, and production and manipulation, on the other, this revision of visibility evolved out of Irigaray's conception of a seeing between us touches directly on the problematic of the technological economy of relations in modernity. The link between seeing/knowing and labor/manipulation points to the fundamental technicity of relations that lies at the basis of Western civilization and increasingly pervades its cultural and social practices. In the information age, visibility is circumscribed, sustained, and fed by the potential of transforming everything into information. This informational capacity means that what is in truth seen of things, beings, and relations today, and what is thus real about them, is primarily what becomes visible of their existence in terms of information. This informational visibility dominant in the age of spectacles, images, and virtual reality reflects the extent to which the modality of relating characteristic of modernity has been determined by the growing, often in leaps and bounds, capacity for rendering available for perceptual, intellectual, and manipulative grasp. One could sum up the contemporary stage in this developing capacity for rendering visible and graspable in the following way: to be visible today means to be available as information. And, as such, information, to enter into a web of relations operating in the modality of an informational relay: fluid, expandable, growing and changing from within. Even though the informational networks have this inbuilt capacity for flexibility, unexpected links, and creative rewiring, their operation is predicated on the "solid" and "inflexible" translatability of being into information. Underneath the contemporary rhetorical "glitz" of flexibility, multiplicity, and fluidity works the overpowering and manipulative drive toward the total transparency and convertibility of what is in terms of information. In short, the age of information, seen in terms of its metaphysical underpinnings, even if it keeps proclaiming itself as absolutely scientific and free of metaphysics, is based on a thorough visibility of everything as information, which opens the door to an unprecedented capacity for grasping and manipulation. Energies, forces, and relations become visible as their informational "content" and thus are rendered available for rapidly intensifying manipulative power. Paradoxically, the obverse side of this intensifying complexity of modern reality is the unprecedented uniformity of everything as information, information translatable into sequences of zeros and ones. On the one hand, we have the growing sophistication and dizzying complexity of the culture of images, virtual reality, financial capital, and telematics, and, on the other, the corresponding disappearance of invisibility, which gives room to the growing uniformity and transparency of reality as processable information.

There is an important difference between transformation as processing and transformation as the enabling of becoming, and Irigaray's conception of the three energies provides a way to explain the difference. Transformation as processing is characteristic of the subsumption of vital energy into culture, that is, into the energy of labor, production, manipulation, and so on. This transmutation of vital energy into cultural energy reveals beings, events, and relations in terms of their availability as resources in the operations of modern technicity. These two energies work in terms of visibility, forming a historical process of the intensifying degree of visibility, which, at the present moment, operates in terms of the visibility of being as information. By contrast, transformation as enabling has to do with the third type of energy, with the energy of invisibility, that is, with the "invisible" manifestation of the giving and the enabling which unfolds from the spaces of otherness and difference, and, as it were, energizes the potential of becoming. The transformation in the first case has to do with the augmented ability to make appear, to render visible and available, while, in the second case, it evolves into a new economy of energy flowing from the spaces of invisibility. In the first type of transformation, invisibility is an obstacle to be overcome on the road to a better and more comprehensive visibility. It is not surprising, therefore, that invisibility becomes progressively erased or excluded from the info-technical economy of availability and assigned to the space of unreality, fantasy, and pseudomystery. The second kind of transformation, the ethical becoming par excellence for Irigaray, draws its energy from the invisible, the other, and the different, and becomes impeded precisely by the exclusion or representation of difference characteristic of the economy of availability.

Recently, Irigaray entitled one of her publications *The Age of Breath*,[5] (Irigaray [1999] 2004), which, perhaps with a good deal of irony, indicates that the new economy of energy she had begun to outline can be understood as an alternative to the informational and technological culture of today, namely, to the information age. Yet this Irigarayan economy of relations remains doubly invisible today: in addition to its intrinsic invisibility, it is covered over by the specular, metaphysical—in spite of all affirmations to the contrary—culture of images, by the ever more flexible operations of capital, and, finally, by the informational constitution of being. What these different and complex systems of relations which subtend social and cultural practices at the beginning of the twenty-first century have in common is their technical facility of rendering what is into something that becomes characterized, in its essence, as intrinsically available. It is available to be seen and known, to be manipulated and (re)produced, capitalized and consumed, and finally, to be transmitted and stored as information. All these operations are different, and without doubt result in the production and proliferation of differences, in hybrid cultures and a multicultural world. Yet, these differences remain, to return to Irigaray, the differences of the visible, or, in other words, differences within the overall technicity of modern relations. What this means is that, in spite of the growing pluralization, these differences fail to provide the energy to evolve a different sense of visibility.

They certainly have plenty of energy that gets channeled into the technological and informational operations of capital today, operations which are characterized by the rapidly increasing facility of manipulation, or of processing, in the informational parlance, which constitutes the new lingua franca of today. The info-technical economy of relations operates in terms of the various modalities of processing and transformative manipulation, which extend their gamut from the old fashioned "use" of resources, to financial capital, telecommunications, and genetic engineering. The complexity and differential character of such operations notwithstanding, it is information processing that becomes emblematic of what I have called the info-technical economy of relations because it bespeaks the facility to render something as information and thus to gain the ability to manipulate and control it.

The new economy of relations suggested in the title of this essay points to a significantly different modality of relations, one based, so to speak, on the invisibility as information. But this "invisibility" as information does not imply a lack of seeing, that is, it does not mark a failure of the powerful modern informational grasp of being to bring something within its purview and make it meaningful (as information). Rather, the invisibility as information is a source of a new, noninformational seeing, and the potential for a different modality of relations implied in this revised visibility. These relations are characterized by becoming and transformation, as differentiated from relations of availability, processing, or manipulation, characteristic of the info-technical economy of forces. The critical distinction here is between processing and manipulation—both tributaries of the dominant economy of production—on the one hand, and letting be, on the other, that is, between the potentiality for (re)production and profit, and the enabling of the new. The "old" economy, which today parades in the new images of the information age, is essentially a productionist metaphysics of being, in which all that is becomes revealed as available for the ever intensifying and differentiating processes of production. To the extent that it facilitates the manipulation of being in all its facets to an unprecedented degree, information is simply the contemporary, and at present the most efficient, vehicle for the intensifying technicity of relations, a new chapter in the continuing "romance" with being in terms of production and manipulation. Perhaps more than that, it marks the culmination of the history of being as the history of production/manipulation.

What remains to be thought in this context is the specific sense of the enabling that "energizes" the alternative economy of relations suggested above. Most importantly, this enabling differs from production and its workings have to be distinguished from the operations of rendering material available or manipulable. It gives without becoming part of the economy of information, it enables without producing, and operates in a manner that is neither passive nor active, strictly speaking. Elsewhere I explored this sense of enabling in terms of Heidegger's distinction between *lassen* and *machen*, that is, between letting which enables and making which produces.[6] Irigaray, too, makes this critical distinction between making and letting be in *The Way of Love*: "Submitting raw material to a making often amounts to causing it to vanish in an end imposed from outside rather than letting its properties appear." (Irigaray 2002, 117).[7] Thus, letting be allows what is to emerge as what it indeed is, while making, by disregarding and disrespecting otherness, fashions material into an end. For Irigaray, the distinction making/letting be, the title of one of the sections in *The Way of Love*, becomes pivotal to both self-recognition and respect for the other: "To accept not to make, in favor of letting be, is a gesture required for turning back to the ground of oneself and for recognizing the other as other" (Irigaray 2002, 123). It would be a mistake to assume that Irigaray disparages or underestimates the importance of making and production, for making, as she remarks several times, is indispensable to human development. Rather, what Irigaray wants to question is the predominance of making over letting be, which has led to a certain inability to let be and, more important, to the prevalent disregard for letting be, misunderstood as a symptom of powerlessness and inaction.[8] She suggests that, since "The blossoming of man requires, in fact, a making and a letting be" (Irigaray 2002, 124), making and letting be need to be kept distinct, without, however, being conceived as opposites. The opposites of making and action are inaction and passivity, while letting be, by contrast, involves a transformation which is, strictly speaking, neither an act—always a "product" of a subject or an agency—nor passive acceptance/resignation. Therefore, the crucial question that arises in this context is "why has man, throughout History, privileged making?" (Irigaray 2002, 123). Though Irigaray does not answer the question, one could venture here a Nietzschean-Heideggerian answer: making has been privileged because of its implication in power. Making, production, and technology have become intertwined in history to evolve into a complex operations of power, which have, as their goal, understood here in a nonteleological and nonintentional manner, a continuing over-powering, that is, an intensification of power into an overpower, as Heidegger puts it in *Besinnung*.[9] Within this economy of power/production, making and letting be become cast as the mutually exclusive poles of power/action and powerlessness/inaction.

The problem that faces us is that the economy of relations based on making has become so successful that the critical distinction be-tween enabling/letting, on the one hand, and making/producing, on the other, is invisible today. We either "see" enabling as a form of making, as indistinguishable from creation and production, or do not see it at all, that is, we inscribe enabling into the overall economy of making or, alternatively, exclude it from it. We can either see en-abling as active, that is, as a genre of making, or as passive, that is, as not acting at all, as not doing anything. Either view distorts en-abling, fashioning it back into making and action or disqualifying it as passivity and inaction. What we fail to see is precisely the "invis-ibility" within the specific informational visibility of being in which we live today, of the energy of enabling. This is even more the case because the standard of visibility, the proof of being real, so to speak, and thus the guarantee of becoming useful, is the convertibility into and the availability as information. And if we insist on the different modality in which enabling works, we risk being accused of seeing something that is not there, that carries no information, and, is, there-fore, not real—at best, a subjective impression, at worst, a dangerous illusion which entails the risk of "blinding" us to the social and po-litical realities of the world, realities which can, apparently, be tackled only in terms of power, that is, through (re)making and action. But this is only if we foreclose the possibility of seeing, thinking, and thus also acting, differently, if we remain unquestioningly within the "blind-ing" visibility of the image-oriented culture of the information age. For the invisibility, and thus the difference, at stake here is more than just a distinction between terms, or between two types of rhetoric— it is a critical differentiation in the modality of relating, a different way of being-in-the-world. This difference needs to be let back into our language, and into our thinking and acting, so that it enables a different visibility, a visibility that unfolds from the invisible rather than from the visible. And, as Irigaray suggests, it needs to be cultured into a new economy of relations.

NOTES

1. Ekkhard Ehlers, *Betrieb*, Mille Plateaux.

2. Michel Eldred, *Kapital und Technik: Marx und Heidegger* (Dettelbach: J. H. Roll, 2000), 78.

3. Luce Irigaray, "Being Two, How Many Eyes Have We?" (Rüsselsheim: Christel Göttert Verlag, 2000), 15 E. The essay appears in a quadri-lingual edition: French, Italian, German, and English. The quotations and page references come from the English version.

4. Ewa Plonowska Ziarek, *An Ethics of Dissensus: Postmodernism, Feminism, and the Politics of Radical Democracy* (Stanford, Calif.: Stanford University Press, 2001); see the section "The Ethical Passions of Emmanuel Levinas" from chapter 2, "Ethical Responsibility, Eros, and the Politics of Race and Rights," 48–62 , and the section "Labor of Love, Labor of the Negative: An Ethical Model of Erotic Relations" from chapter 5, entitled "Labor of the Negative: The Impossible Ethics of Sexual Difference and the Politics of Radical Democracy," 163–72.

5. Luce Irigaray, *Die Zeit des Atems* (Rüsselsheim: Christel Göttert Verlag, 1999).

6. For a more substantial discussion of the distinction between *machen* and *lassen* see my essay "Art as Forcework," *Existentia* 11 (2001) 3–4: 355–71.

7. Luce Irigaray, *The Way of Love*, trans. Heidi Bostic and Stephen Pluháček (London and New York: Continuum, 2002), 117.

8. This remark echoes Heidegger's claim in "The Question Concerning Technology" that technicity, as the dominant mode of revealing, conceals and, thus, effectively excludes poiesis as an alternative modality of revealing. *Basic Writings*, ed. David Farrell Krell (San Francisco: HarperCollins, 1977, 1993).

9. Martin Heidegger, *Besinnung, Gesamtausgabe*, vol. 69 (Frankfurt am Main: Vittorio Klosterman, 1997); see, for example, 16–29 and 187–96.

WORKS CITED

Ehlers, Ekkhard. 2000. *Betrieb*. Original sound recording made by Mille Plateaux.

Eldred, Michael. 2000. *Kapital und Technik: Marx und Heidegger*. Dettelbach: J. H. Roll.

Heidegger, Martin. 1977. "The Question Concerning Technology." In *Basic Writings*. Edited by David Farrell Krell. San Francisco: HarperCollins.

———. 1997. *Besinnung Gesamtausgabe*, vol. 69. Edited by Friedrich-Wilhelm Von Hermann. Frankfurt am Main: Vittorio Klosterman.

Irigaray, Luce. 1999. *Die Zeit des Atems*. Rüsselsheim: Christel Göttert Verlag.

————. 2001 [2000]. "Being Two, How Many Eyes Have We?" Translated by Luce Irigaray with Catherine Busson, Jim Mooney, Heidi Bostic, and Stephen Pluháček. Rüsselsheim: Christel Göttert Verlag.
————. 2002. *The Way of Love*. Translated by Heidi Bostic and Stephen Pluháček. London: Continuum.
Ziarek, Ewa. 2001. *An Ethics of Dissensus: Postmodernism, Feminism, and the Politics of Radical Democracy*. Stanford, Calif.: Stanford University Press.
Ziarek, Krzysztof. 2001. "Art as Forcework," *Existentia* 11, 3–4: 355–71.

BEYOND PERFORMATIVITY

AND AGAINST 'IDENTIFICATION':

GENDER AND TECHNOLOGY IN IRIGARAY

Ann V. Murphy

In what follows, the bind between sexual difference and nature in the work of Luce Irigaray will be interrogated, specifically in reference to the manner in which her understanding of nature, and her attendant hesitations regarding technology, lead in her later work to the forthright dismissal of discourses on androgyny, the neuter, performativity, and gender identification. The pernicious tone that characterizes Irigaray's critique of these discourses is worrisome insofar as it targets figures that are central in contemporary theory on sexuality, and queer theory in particular. Indeed, the alarmist tenor with which Irigaray approaches this discourse is a marked characteristic of her later thought, where Irigaray becomes increasingly concerned with the ways in which the notion of the neuter or the strategy of androgyny is bound to the increasing hegemony of an ever more technocratic society.

In an age of technocratic imperialism, Irigaray mourns the exploitation of the feminine and the natural as they are suppressed beneath the cloak of calculative and technocratic reason. She reads both the figure of the neuter and the practice of androgyny as doomed attempts to attain a status of equality for women, doomed insofar as they are already complicit with misogynist cultural norms that render the specificity of the feminine invisible.

Irigaray calls into question the efficacy of feminist strategies mired in the drive for equality, but in so doing, she vilifies and devalues discourses that have given voice to marginalized and oppressed sexual identities. To be fair, Irigaray notes on more than one occasion that she "is not advocating a return to a more repressive, moralizing, conception of sexuality. On the contrary," she claims "what we need is to work out an art of the sexual, a sexed culture" (Irigaray 1993 [1987], 3). Yet, while her appeal to nature is neither regressive nor essentialist in its announced intent, one might wonder if this mood affects her later writing regardless.

While the early part of this essay is dedicated to the exploration of the ways in which nature and the feminine are bound in Irigaray's work, and in particular the importance of this bond in her critique of Heidegger, the latter part of the essay is critical of Irigaray's naturalism. If Irigaray is compelled to critique Heidegger on the grounds that he has failed to consider that fundamental materiality that subtends his own criticism of metaphysics, in her later works, Irigaray herself fails to consider what has been subject to erasure in her own metaphysics of sexual difference. In other words, Irigaray's spiteful treatment of the discourses on gender identification, androgyny, and the neuter is enabled by the problematic primacy that Irigaray affords sexual morphology as a consequence of its status as a natural given.

Irigaray's reticence in the face of the hypertechnical tendencies of modern society may indeed be legitimate, but when this reticence is employed in the dismissive manner that it is, some worrisome consequences come to light. Moreover, Irigaray's technophobia complicates the manner in which she can be located in the landscape of contemporary feminist theory, a landscape that has now shifted to accommodate narratives of transgenderism and transsexuality, which at the very least, complicate the model of sexual difference with which Irigaray is working. Finally, Irigaray's indictment of technology provokes concern regarding the viability of the figure of sexual difference on a landscape where the boundaries between nature and culture have become quite radically blurred.

Irigaray's position regarding Heidegger, particularly in *The Forgetting of Air*, 1999 [1983], is of central importance in understanding Irigaray's thought on nature and technology. Indeed, *Forgetting* is important in that it marks a tension between what, in her earlier work, was a mimetic engagement with nature, and what will become, after the publication of *Forgetting*, an increasingly (and problematically so) descriptive and speculative relation to the natural. While this essay does not seek to offer a definitive resolution to debates concerning the coherence or lack thereof in Irigaray's line of thought, it does aspire to address the consequences of the shift in methodology, and to at least partially problematize her own contention that her more recent forays into the realm of law, for instance, are consistent with her earlier approach to sexual difference. This is in no way to suggest that there are not important respects in which Irigaray's work maintains consistent themes—this much seems doubtless given her sustained interest in sexual difference and its cultural reverberations— but it is to dispute the claim that the methodological shift does not entail important political consequences. For these reasons, it is legitimate to take seriously the space that *Forgetting* holds in relation to the others in the Irigarayan corpus.

Irigaray herself has emphasized the continuity that the text bears in relation to her later work,[1] but *Forgetting* is most frequently grouped with her earlier writings and thought of as a close cousin to the earlier *Marine Lover*, 1991 [1980]. Given that it is usually Irigaray's early work that is identified with her mimetic methodology, *Forgetting*'s occupation of the precipice between her earlier mimetic writings and her more recent work is worthy of note. Few philosophers are as closely identified with their method as Irigaray. For this reason, her movement in the last decade into more "concrete" venues—and the consonant transgression of her earlier methodology—has justifiably become an important locus of recent Irigaray scholarship.

A GENEALOGY OF 'NATURE' IN IRIGARAY

Irigaray's interest in nature is an abiding one, in part due to her understanding of the way in which nature and the feminine are bound through their mutual oppression, erasure, and predation within the confines of a masculinist society. If the early Irigaray is compelled to speak of the feminine as the unrepresentable, the culturally invisible, "a more or less obliging prop for the enactment of man's fantasies," she is equally as inclined to view the figure of nature in this manner as well (Irigaray 1985 [1977], 25).

However, when the arc of Irigaray's work is traced through the lens of her philosophy of nature, the differences between the politics that emerge from her early and later work becomes lucid. More precisely, when the figure of nature is no longer approached through mimetic ideology and poetic language, and when it is instead employed within the confines of a prescriptive and applied political theory, there are some worrisome consequences that come to light. When the bond between women and nature ceases to be accomplished through mimesis, and when it is instead employed in the service of prescription, the reified nature of this bond becomes problematic not only insofar as it appears to concretize and homogenize the feminine as a category, but also insofar as this link reifies the connection between women and nature, a link that bears investigation. The two are bound in Irigaray's philosophy though their mutual predation by a masculine symbolic, which is itself reliant upon an exploitative ontology that renders some things (i.e., man, culture, etc.) intelligible only as others are made to serve as the unintelligible and invisible ground of this intelligibility.

Still and always, Irigaray has professed that sexual difference is the most "universal" and important question to be addressed, and her justification of the privileging of sexual difference over and above race, class, religion, and so on, cannot proceed *without* reference to nature. Thus, the investigation of the figure of nature in Irigaray is particularly urgent, as it is specifically in reference to the "natural" and "universal" status of sexual difference that Irigaray feels entitled to privilege this difference over others. She defends the privileging of sexual difference with explicit reference to its status as a "natural given":

> Without doubt, the most appropriate context for the universal is sexual difference. Indeed, this content is both real and universal. Sexual difference is an immediate natural given and it is a real and irreducible component of the universal. The whole of human kind is composed of women and men and of nothing else. The problem of race is, in fact, a secondary problem . . . and the same goes for other cultural diversities—religious, economic, and political ones. (Irigaray 1996 [1992], 47)

Within the confines of this naturalism, race, religious affiliation, economic status, and political considerations become subordinate. Given the centrality of the bind between nature and the feminine in Irigaray's body of work, it is worth pausing to consider the ways in which she understands the two to be connected.

Irigaray's interest in the material or natural traffic that subtends the symbolic order has informed her project from the start. She claims, in a number of places, that the trafficking and exploitation of women and nature alike is so fundamental to our cultural order that "there is no way to interpret it except within this horizon" (Irigaray 1985 [1977], 171). This contention would seem to commit Irigaray to the claim that whatever "nature" is, it is something concealed beneath a multitude of misogynist cultural insignia and hence impossible to recognize in itself.[2] Nature remains impossible to conceive beyond the purview of our libidinal or symbolic traffic; nature/woman/the material has never emerged or been thought in other than a warped, veiled, and reduced manner. Instrumental and technocratic reason, and the attendant economy of calculative exchange, demands that nature remain the unthought and unnamed figure that encapsulates all that is othered by this economy.

In *This Sex Which Is Not One*, the bond between nature and the feminine is investigated on Marxist terrain—particularly in the essays "Women on the Market" and "Commodities Amongst Themselves"—where society and culture are rendered as the consequence of the traffic in women and figures of femininity—a trafficking governed by the incest taboo (Irigaray 1985 [1977], 170/167). It is none other than women's bodies—their consumption, circulation, and privation—that make cultural life possible, although insofar as women's bodies serve as the infrastructure for this economy, they must remain invisible as such.

The circulation of women among men is thus at the origin of society, and this circulation is itself enabled by man's appropriation of nature, his transformation of it according to his own criteria, and the reduction of natural matter to man's practical activity (Irigaray 1985 [1977], 184). One requisite consequence of this appropriation is that women become objects that emblematize relations among men. For Irigaray, this objectification is accomplished in three ways. As mother, virgin, and prostitute—roles that have been imposed upon them—women enable the production of a cultural symbolic though they fail to reap the privileges of this symbolic trafficking, forbidden, as they are, to attain the privileges of subjectivity.

Hence, the cultural imaginary is said to be governed by an economy of "semblance," where relations of material and natural reproduction are masked by symbolic and imaginary structures—structures that render natural life invisible (Irigaray 1985 [1977], 171/168). This trafficking in women subtends the construction of a hom(m)osexual economy that remains prohibited in practice—unacceptable—and hence must be projected upon the bodies of women, which come to serve as "an alibi for the smooth workings of man with himself" (Irigaray 1985 [1977], 172/168). It is for this reason that Irigaray might argue that women's bodies are rendered as commodities whose circulation and exchange generate the cultural (masculine) symbolic, thus illuminating not simply the commodification of women, but the association of feminine matter and natural matter within the margins of such an economy.

Irigaray's thinking in this regard is sustained in her critique of Heidegger in *The Forgetting of Air*. Although her infamous stylistic strategies—namely the mimicry and pastiche that became familiar in *Speculum* and the *Marine Lover*—are here employed in her negotiations with Heidegger, the book is not itself as mimetic as these earlier texts. However, remembering *Marine Lover*, there is much in *Forgetting* that is familiar. One sees, for instance, a sustained discussion of the gift and of a mourning that must refuse its true object. Just as she attributed Nietzsche's "abyssal forgetfulness" to his deep contempt for his own nostaligia for the mother (Irigaray 1991 [1980], 24), Irigaray notes that Heidegger's depiction of Being as a gift, or propriation, affectively elides and hence forgets that "prior to the gift of appropriation there is the gift of she who offers herself for this move"—a materiality that is at once infinitely close and infinitely far from the representation of Being that it enables (Irigaray 1999 [1983], 136). The materiality that enables Heidegger's wonder, like the "other landscapes" that have been subjected to Nietzschean neglect, is the feminine, the maternal, the natural. For Irigaray, our current metaphysics implies a hatred of nature, an abhorrence of the natural, a desire on man's part to distance himself from this primal ground, unable to repay the debt that he owes to the mother who founds his social order despite her invisibility within it (Irigaray 1999 [1983], 75).

Though *Forgetting* may not readily qualify as a mimetic work, this is not to say that Irigaray's engagement with Heidegger is not aptly characterized as an internal critique in an important sense; as Tina Chanter has argued,[3] Irigaray's interrogation of sexual difference could only have been raised in a post-Heideggerian climate. Indeed, the Heideggerian legacy is inscribed at the heart of Irigaray's project. Whereas Irigaray aspires to return to the maternal feminine that has been barred entry to language and culture even while she serves as its ground, Heidegger advocated a return to the question of Being in order to illuminate the unthought ground of Western metaphysics. Still, Irigaray insists that Heidegger remains well within the confines of the very metaphysics he seeks to escape. One symptom of this confinement, according to Irigaray, is Heidegger's refusal to acknowledge the material, the elemental, that is air. "The elementality of *physis*—air, water, earth, fire—is always already reduced to nothingness in and by his own element: his language. An ecstasis relative to his natural environment that keeps him exiled from his first homeland" (Irigaray 1999 [1983], 74). Irigaray's formulation of language as the *element* of men, and hence of man's formalization of nature, is indicative of her concern to reveal the exclusions—the forgetfulness—that subtend "the house of Being." As she will later write, in *I Love to You*:

> Without sexual difference, there would be no life on earth. It is the manifestation of and the condition for the production and reproduction of life. Air and sexual difference may be the two dimensions vital for/to life. Not taking them into account would be a deadly business. (Irigaray 1996 [1992], 37)

For Irigaray, Heidegger surely traffics in this "deadly business," forgetful as he is of the elementality that enables one's being in language.

While Irigaray follows Heidegger as he implores us to think differently—indeed meditatively—about our role as the guardians of Being, and while she will likewise whole-heartedly assent to his claim that there is some danger to be associated with the widespread expansion of technological thinking, she insists that Heidegger remains implicated in the very same architectonic he seeks to critique. For while Heidegger does explore the forgotten ground upon which Western metaphysics has been predicated—an interrogation that will lead him to explore ontological difference and ultimately to posit Being as this ground—Irigaray construes the Heideggerian endeavor as another instance of matricide, the dispossession and subjection of women and nature alike, as they are mutually condemned to serve as the invisible and unacknowledged ground for Being. Hence, Irigaray names the materiality of air as that which serves as Being's constitutive outside and makes possible Being's very emergence, an emergence enabled by an ontology that is created to erase and obscure an originary debt to the mother.[4] Irigaray posits, beneath calculative and technical language, a "maternal saying" whose expressions remain unexamined and invisible, having been subjected to the technical imperatives of phallogocentrism (Irigaray 1999 [1983], 141/127). This maternal saying would be a speech that "would not have a care for itself," a speech "that would not desire to be seen"—a speech that offered the possibility for exchange and not brute assimilation, not propriation, a speech that had no care for recognition (Irigaray 1999 [1983], 143/128).

Indeed, air allows itself to be forgotten to the extent that it refuses capture by perception and knowledge, despite its being irreducibly constitutive of the whole. To acknowledge the air that was displaced for the sake of Heidegger's own metaphysics would be to acknowledge the debt to the mother, to nature, to materiality. For Irigaray, it is the acknowledgement of this debt alone that would truly imply the ruin of metaphysics, and in the absence of this acknowledgement, Heidegger's own proclamation of metaphysics' end is little but a ruse.

TECHNOLOGY IN IRIGARAY AND HEIDEGGER

In spite of Irigaray's criticism of Heidegger, there is an abiding proximity between the two concerning their thoughts on technology. Heidegger describes technology as a "way of revealing," a bringing-forth, an occasioning, presencing, or unconcealing.[5] Rendered thus, technology is neither a mere means to an end, nor an instrumental essence, nor our fate, but rather a way in which "the growing things of nature . . . come at any given time to their appearance" (Heidegger BW, 317). *Techne*, as a manner of revealing, somehow transcends the confines of brute manufacturing. For this reason, Heidegger claims that *techne* is also applicable to the activity of the artist—"it is something poetic" (Heidegger BW, 318). Despite this rendering of *techne*, which wrests it free from total subsumption by the calculative thinking of instrumental rationality, Heidegger cautions that, in our era, modern technology has ceased to be poetic. Thus, while *techne* was first rendered as a bringing-forth or way of revealing—one that was not necessarily technical in an instrumental sense, and indeed equally as apt to describe poetic presencing—Heidegger ultimately concludes that modern technology has lapsed into an instrumental and calculative presencing, which demands of nature that it be suppressed in the name of human interest. Nature is thus rendered as standing reserve, energy that has been transformed, distributed, and stored according to our needs (Heidegger BW, 322). So profound is this technical mode of presencing that it ceases to even conceive of nature as an object; rather, nature is prereflectively rendered as that which is on hand for our exploitation.[6] Modern technology thus transcends the *objectifica-*

tion of nature in an exploitation of the natural that is much more profound. The object that was nature "disappears into the objectlessness of standing reserve" (Heidegger BW, 324).[7]

The proximity between Irigaray and Heidegger on this point is striking, as both note that it is not the objectification of nature that is so alarming, but its reduction to pure reserve, beyond objectification, quite literally out of sight, subordinated to the demands of utility. It is an oppression and devaluation that defies representation:

> For hatred can be recalled but not remembered. It remains, insists, consists: in oblivion. Void, spacing, gap, border, boundary, it orders representation, it shelters, frames, and aids it without being expressed or presented in representation. The dwelling of man is not built without hatred of nature; that is why it must ensure the safekeeping of nature, and of man. (Irigaray 1999 [1983], 75)

In arguing thus, Irigaray aligns herself with Heidegger to the degree that she insists on the manner in which technocratic society subordinates nature not through brute objectification, as this would imply its representation as such, but through the simultaneous and unrepresented devaluation and maintenance of the figure of nature as that which is on hand for exploitation.

Irigaray follows Heidegger in the assertion that the technological enframing of the world brings with it an undeniable danger, namely the danger that all beings will be enclosed in this calculative enframing, inducing a foreclosure of other types of revealing and thinking. This dimension of the Heideggerian agenda is quite amenable to her own. Yet, while Irigaray finds that Heidegger's analysis is true to the extent that it explores the dangers of this expansionist thinking, she will want to locate the ground of technological thinking at a different level than does Heidegger (Irigaray 1999 [1983], 86). Hence Irigaray's claim that while Heidegger may indeed have aimed at the ground that was lost in metaphysics and yet preserved therein. She insists that his understanding of technology remains indebted to a metaphysics that forgets the materiality of air, a materiality that unknowably subtends his understanding of nature.

Irigaray's charge here is surely well-founded. Heidegger's conception of nature is already—apart from its subsumption into the technical—marked by a *logos* that elides an even more primal materiality

(Irigaray 1999 [1983], 87). In short, Heidegger's project cannot accommodate Irigaray's attempt to think the Other of her discourse—
whether this is nature or woman—as wholly other, an absolute alterity
in the Levinasian sense.[8] Thus, the masculine formalization of nature
must proceed by a double masking: first of nature itself and then of its
own status as artifice. Should it fail to succeed in the latter of these
two concealments, it would be exposed for what it is—a very delib-
erate obliteration.[9]

Taking seriously Heiddeger's claim that technology is not wholly
"demonic," but also mysterious, it is clear that for Heidegger, the
essence of technology is importantly ambiguous. While the peril of
enframing bears the threat that all revealing will be a calculative
ordering, it also bears, as part of its essence, the promise that we
might be called to ever more primal experiences of the truth. For
Heidegger, technology bears both terror and hope.

This ambivalence in Heidegger's exploration of technology is of
notable import. Technology is not marked by this ambiguity for Irigaray,
and her discussions of it are far less tempered and far more fraught
with alarm and peril. While clearly in sympathy with Heidegger's
analysis of *techne* as a mode of presencing that had become, in the age
of modern technology, an imperative to order nature and to render it
as standing reserve, Irigaray will excavate no saving power from the
technological viewpoint. Thus, the importantly ambiguous nature of
technology for Heidegger is ignored by Irigaray, who sees no promise
at all in its proliferation, only the repetition and multiplication of acts
of matricide and appropriation that conceal not only their own violence, but the very visibility and being of their victims. The ambivalence that characterizes Heidegger's account of technology, namely
the thought that technology inspires both terror and hope, is altogether abandoned by Irigaray. It is here that Irigaray and Heidegger
part ways. Of further interest is the fact that Irigaray's categorical
denunciation of the modern world's technocratic tendencies lends
itself to the ridicule of sexual identities that she considers to be somehow complicit in a type of technocratic imperialism.

AGAINST 'IDENTIFICATION':
GENDER AND TECHNOLOGY IN IRIGARAY

Bracketing, for the moment, queries concerning the efficacy or feasi-
bility of a framework that seems categorically distrustful of technol-

ogy, it nonetheless is obvious that Irigaray's thoroughgoing dismissal of technology motivates some worrisome condemnations, for instance her rather pernicious treatment of women who have children without male partners, or who utilize artificial methods of fertilization (Irigaray 1993 [1990]). Admittedly, Irigaray's alarm is motivated by her view that such practices are a symptom of the compulsion that women feel to mother—a compulsion that she understands as unjust and oppressive—but her comments cannot be wrested free of considerations of the manner in which Irigaray's thinking is bound to a traditional and conservative understanding of nature and artifice. Women who mother nontraditionally, she argues, have been seduced by the ideal of independence, but, in their embrace of these identities, risk "the further loss of female identity" (Irigaray 1993 [1990], 133). Such strategies, she insists, only end up recuperating the notion that women can only be defined in relation to men, as the logic involved amounts to thinking oneself *without* the male other and not thinking *about* oneself (Irigaray 1993 [1990], 133). Indeed, Irigaray even goes so far as to enumerate the ways in which the male presence remains in artificial procreation in order to argue that women who utilize methods such as these are in fact in bad faith. When Irigaray asks, "test-tube mothers, surrogate mothers, men engendering futuristically, what next?" one must pause to consider what assumptions motivate such a query (Irigaray 1993 [1990], 135). It is not that Irigaray's reticence in the face of the hypertechnical tendencies of modern culture is in itself problematic, but when technology is repeatedly and explicitly linked— as it is—to Irigaray's pernicious dismissal of the neuter, or the figure of androgyny, there is a potentially ominous undercurrent that must be addressed. What once appeared as a dismissal of feminisms that founded themselves in a hope for equality between the sexes—perhaps best exemplified in Irigaray's engagement with Simone de Beauvoir[10]—has now morphed into problematic disdain.

Irigaray's understanding of the link between technology and the neuter is evident given the rhetoric she employs in her discussions of the neuter, which is particularly pernicious and dismissive. In both *I Love to You* and *Je, tu, nous*, discourses on performativity and identity are condemned as "delusional" and "decadent," caught up in some "fantasy" or "utopia" that has been painted by technocratic society. When Irigaray laments the impossibility of presenting "two subjectively sexed human beings," she notes that it is this failure that has "doomed man to technical being" (Irigaray 1993 [1987], 122). Elsewhere, she claims that "the enclaves of the neuter, which seek to be ethical, outside the war of the sexes, are, for as long as the tragedy of difference of the sexes and its fecundity remains unsolved, linked historically to the ascendancy and rule of technocracy" (Irigaray 1993 [1987], 117). The figure of the neuter hence becomes an instrument of technocratic reason on Irigaray's account, complicit in a misogynist cultural order where masculine cultural codes masquerade as neutral.

To question feminist strategies that are founded in the drive for equality is one thing, but to conflate a discourse on the propriety of social-political objectives with a different discourse on performativity and sexual identification is quite another. There is a great deal at stake in this vacillation between Irigaray's hesitation regarding egalitarian feminist strategies and her forthright dismissal of androgyny and the neuter. While there is doubtless reason to heed Irigaray's warning that one should be wary of embracing a "world that claims to be neuter but is man's alone," the manner in which her reticence in this regard easily slips into a vitriolic dismissal of contemporary discourses on gender identification and androgyny is worrisome (Irigaray 1993 [1987], 122).

For instance, Irigaray claims that an appeal to androgyny amounts to an attempt to suppress sexual morphology beneath the cloak of "more or less delusional mental forms" and that it "represents a utopia of decadents plunged in their own world of fantasy and speculation" (Irigaray 1993 [1987], 123). She further claims that such an appeal could only be the function of a "very small" portion of the community that remains seduced by a concept of identity that is radically bound to fashion, commerce, and technocratic society. She claims that she finds philosophies of gender that employ notions of androgyny, performativity, and imitation to be "delusional" and "weird" in this regard (Irigaray 1993 [1987], 123/137). It is difficult if not impossible to interpret these comments as anything other than a forthright dismissal of gender discourse that takes notions of performativity and gender identification to be as central and relevant as any notion of sexual morphology. And it is here that Irigaray's investment in a certain conception of nature, and of natural bodies, comes to the fore, as it justifies, somewhat deceptively, this very dismissal.

At its most hyperbolic, and arguably its most ominous, Irigaray's investment in nature is accomplished as an appeal to a discourse that is, at best, dismissive and, at worst, hostile towards certain gender narratives, among them transsexuality and transgenderism. She writes:

Some of our prosperous and naïve contemporaries, women and men, would like to wipe out this difference by resorting to monosexuality, to the unisex, and to what is called identification: even if I am bodily a man or a woman, I can identify with, and so be, the other sex. This new opium of the people annihilates the other in the illusion of a reduction to identity, equality, and sameness, especially between man and woman, the ultimate anchorage of real alterity. (Irigaray 1996 [1992], 61–62)

To privilege the natural and even morphological differences between men and women in a way that justifies the pejorative and even vitriolic treatment of the contemporary discourse on gender identification is to come dangerously close to exemplifying the dismissive and phobic manner in which some have navigated the philosophical discourses on transgenderism and transsexuality. Of particular interest is the manner in which Irigaray repeatedly associates gender identity with commerce, fashion, and decadence. Such comments have the cumulative affect of relegating the discourse on identity and performativity to the status of an indulgent fiction. The problematic consequence of Irigaray's dismissal of this discourse is that it amounts to a dismissal of the very framework that has been credited with urging the recognition of those gender identities that resist normative assumptions surrounding the "natural" relationship among sex, gender, sexual practice, and desire. Transgender narratives, for instance, reinstall the validity of the break between the bodily experience of one's sex and the external performance of gender. Indeed, the rift between sex and gender is implicit in the logic of transgenderism and transsexuality, as the figure of one's gendered imaginary is not always commensurate with the contours of one's material body. Given Irigaray's reluctance to valorize narratives such as this, and moreover given her rather pernicious dismissal of them, the heterosexist and heteronormative tenor of Irigaray's project becomes worrisome.

What needs to be guarded against in this endeavor is the attempt to normalize or naturalize experience on phenomenological grounds, by making claims that while transsexuals and transgendered individuals may *look* like men or women, they could never *feel* so. Irigaray hardly seems reticent in this regard. In the context of her indictment of the discourse of gender identification, Irigaray's aversion to the claim that "even if I am bodily a man or a woman, I can

identify with, and so be, the other sex" is demonstrative of her preoccupation with the biological and morphological difference that, for her,
constitutes the "ultimate anchorage of real alterity" (Irigaray 1996 [1992],
62). One must wonder, however, if such a privileging might ever be
accomplished without condoning the denigration and vilification of
those sexual identities that are not so readily located on the Irigarayan
landscape. In short, if Irigaray's own remembrance of sexual difference
can only be accomplished at the expense of certain gendered narratives—androgyny, transsexuality, and transgenderism for instance—then
her readers are obliged to be critical of the framework of sexual difference when it is used as a naturalist paradigm, a paradigm that unfairly
valorizes certain gendered identities at the expense of others.

These comments made by the later Irigaray reveal that she has
moved beyond the subversive parody of the natural that she performed in her earlier work and has become significantly invested in
a category she once insisted lay well beyond discourse's grasp, and was
thus always and only rendered as a projection of the masculine, as its
other. One might argue that this is simply a rhetorical or stylistic shift
away from mimicry to the more concrete discourses, but such a movement is not benign.

In her later work, what had once appeared as the subversive
appropriation of a forgotten voice has morphed into a voice that is no
longer trying to subvert a masculine discourse, but rather issue prescriptions. That once unnamable 'nature' is becoming more concrete,
it seems, and when parody dissolves into prescription, the subversive
force of Irigaray's mimicry is abandoned. More worrisome still is that
Irigaray's prescriptions are issued at the expense of other discourses on
gender and, in particular, at the expense of those discourses that have
tirelessly sought the recognition of marginalized sexual identities.

Indeed, given Irigaray's criticism of Heidegger, her own reluctance to acknowledge the naturalism that justifies her treatment of
sexual difference is noteworthy, if not surprising. Could it be that
Irigaray herself has forgotten, in her haste to diagnose the evils of
technocratic society, that there is a gendered landscape wherein allegedly 'natural' bodies and technological figures morph to the point
where it is impossible to say where nature ends and technology begins? It would appear that the later Irigaray's reticence concerning the
hegemony of technocratic culture lends itself to the embrace of a
naturalism wherein certain gender identities are ridiculed and themselves subject to erasure.

NOTES

1. In the interview "Words to Nourish the Breath of Life," in *Why Different? A Culture of Two Subjects*, ed. Luce Irigaray and Sylvère Lotringer (New York: Semiotexte, 2000).

2. See, for instance, Donna Haraway's discussion of the ways in which nature is constructed, not discovered, in her *Simians, Cyborgs, and Women: The Reinvention of Nature* (New York: Routledge, 1991), or Helen Longino's contention that the assertion of a value-free natural science is "nonsense" in *Science as Social Knowledge* (Princeton: Princeton University Press, 1990).

3. See Tina Chanter, *The Ethics of Eros* (New York: Routledge, 1995), 131.

4. Just as Heidegger accuses Western metaphysics of the forgetting of ontological difference, Irigaray reformulates this difference as sexual difference; in the forgetting of this difference, Being has come to be.

5. Martin Heidegger, "The Question Concerning Technology," in *Basic Writings*, ed. David Farrell Krel (San Francisco: HarperCollins, 1993).

6. Every mode of revealing or unconcealment is necessarily a danger for Heidegger, insofar as these modes block our even more primal understanding of the essence of what is being unconcealed, and the unconcealment itself (BW, 331). Thus, we are in many ways endangered by the technological mode of revealing in which we are enveloped. This endangerment has two moments. When we become the orderer of the standing reserve that is nature—when nature no longer concerns us as an object—we come "to the brink of a precipitous fall"—that is, we arrive at a place where humanity itself may be conceived as a standing reserve (BW, 332). In response to this threat, we assert our reign over the earth, thereby generating the illusion that everything we encounter is to some extent our own construct. This illusion, in turn, implicates us in a pattern of thinking that seems to dictate the possibility that we only ever encounter ourselves in the world (BW, 332).

7. Thus technology as the way in which the actual reveals itself as standing reserve is not revealed in a realm beyond all human doing, but neither does it happen exclusively in or through man (BW, 329). This process by which humans are made to render nature as standing reserve is, for Heidegger, *Gestell*, or enframing.

8. For Levinas, the Other was "forever unknowable." Although this Other did interrupt the boundaries of the self, he or she was preserved in exteriority and not assimilated by the logic of the subject.

9. Here Irigaray echoes the argument in "Commodities Amongst Themselves," where she claims that while ho(m)mo-sexuality may be the organizing principle of the sociocultural order, homosexual relations among men openly interpret this law for what it is and thus threaten to shift the horizon of that very law; hence, they must remain abject, if not invisible.

Male homosexual relations also threaten the sociocultural order to the extent that they subvert the necessity of product exchange, or the traffic in women (*This Sex*, 193).

     10. See Luce Irigaray, "A Personal Note: Equal or Different?" in *Je, tu, nous*, tr. Alison Martin (New York: Routledge, 1993).

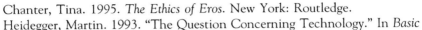

WORKS CITED

Chanter, Tina. 1995. *The Ethics of Eros*. New York: Routledge.

Heidegger, Martin. 1993. "The Question Concerning Technology." In *Basic Writings*. Edited by David Farrell Krell. San Francisco: HarperCollins.

Irigaray, Luce. 1985 [1977]. *This Sex Which Is Not One*. Translated by Catherine Porter. Ithaca, N.Y.: Cornell University Press.

———. 1993 [1987]. *Sexes and Genealogies*. Translated by Gillian C. Gill. New York: Columbia University Press.

. 1999 [1983]. *The Forgetting of Air in Martin Heidegger*. Translated by Mary Beth Mader. Austin: University of Texas Press.

———, ed. 2000. *Why Different? A Culture of Two Subjects* (with Sylvère Lotringer). Translated by Camille Collins, Peter Carravetta, Ben Meyers, Heidi Bostic, and Stephen Pluháček. New York: Semiotext(e).

RECONSIDERING IRIGARAY'S AESTHETICS

Elaine P. Miller

INTRODUCTION

In 1994, a debate ran through the pages of the British *Women's Art Magazine* (now M.A.K.E. magazine). First "A Natal Lacuna," Luce Irigaray's only discussion of a contemporary woman visual artist, Unica Zürn (1917–1970), was translated and published with an introduction by Margaret Whitford.[1] Two issues later, Whitford published a critique of and commentary on Irigaray's article and other writings on art, coming to the conclusion that Irigaray's writings on art are uncharacteristically conservative in that they focus almost exclusively on figurative and complete representations of women.[2] Finally, Hilary Robinson, one of the only Irigaray scholars to have commented extensively on Irigaray's aesthetics, added her voice to the debate.[3] Robinson's conclusion is that "Irigaray's main interest for the feminist artist is not in what she has to say about other visual artists. . . . Instead, Irigaray's main usefulness is at the point where practice and theory are intimately linked; where the experience of reading becomes an experience of theory in practice; where the visual as process and praxis is acknowledged and integrated into this experience" (Robinson 1994, 20). I wish, in this essay, to develop this claim of Robinson's through an extensive look at the historical basis for Irigaray's aesthetic theory. At the same time, however, I argue that although Irigaray's discussion of specific artists and artworks does go against the contours of her aesthetic theory, her conviction that idealized—that is, beautiful in the traditional sense—representations of women must predominate in feminist art is simply a first step, a *precondition* for the flourishing of

a feminist aesthetic in all its diversity. As Whitford shows, Irigaray
envisions such ideal presentations of women in art, such as that of the
Madonna or mythical female goddesses, as contributing to the development of a feminine imaginary and eventually a transformed symbolic order that would symbolize the couple and not simply male
identity. In particular, I argue that, for Irigaray, the question of aesthetics cannot be severed from the consideration of nature in general
and sexual difference in particular, and that the focus on women and
women's art reflects Irigaray's critique of the way in which nature has
been represented in the history of philosophy. Furthermore, Irigaray's
writings on art can provide a paradigm for her readers of the shift in
her writings from a primarily critical and deconstructive, albeit poetic
stance, to the attempt to show what it might mean to construct positive, ideal representations of women's identity as a transitional phase
in developing a less one-sided symbolic order. If this split might be
thought along the lines of early/late Irigaray, this distinction has value
for us only analytically. Ultimately, I hope to indirectly show that
drawing such a sharp divide between these ways of considering Irigaray's
work in order to criticize her for making an essential "turn" is simplis-
tic and unhelpful.

    I argue that a parallel can be drawn between Luce Irigaray's
appropriation of nature for freedom (ethics of sexual difference) and
Theodor Adorno's aesthetics of the beauty of nature. Both Irigaray's
delineation of nature, which is very close to that of Friedrich Schelling,
and Adorno's articulation of the beauty of nature, are explicit responses to the philosophy of G. W. F. Hegel. Adorno claims in his
Aesthetic Theory that Kant's *Critique of Judgment* was the last philosophical work to take the beauty of nature seriously, and points out
that Hegel denied that, properly speaking, nature can be called beautiful at all (Adorno 1997 [1970], 61; see also Hegel). Even Schelling,
who gave nature a far more important role in his system than Hegel
did, according it a kind of freedom, focused his aesthetics on works of
art (Adorno 1997 [1970], 61). For Adorno, the beauty of nature and
its counterpart in nonrepresentational (modern) art must retain an
important place in aesthetics by virtue of its resistance to the pervasive qualities of use-value and self-preservation generally associated
with nature under the rubric of capitalism, on the one hand, and the
legacy of social contract theory in liberal democracy, on the other.
Art "slough[s] off . . . the aims of self-preservation," Adorno writes,
and in doing so "keep[s] nature's promise" (Adorno 1997 [1970], 61).

Irigaray, despite her references to "keep[ing] faith with [natural] life" and "maintain[ing] the becoming of living things as they are" (Irigaray 1993 [1987], 140), conceptualizes nature in general and sexual difference in particular, I will argue, in ways that preclude biological essentialism and complicate the psychoanalytic framework that provides her point of departure. Irigaray's use of "nature" reflects both the legacy of German Idealism, as it draws on Kant and Goethe's philosophy of nature, under the presupposition that nature and spirit are not conceptually isolatable categories, and Marxist assumptions about the relationship between social and economic conditions and the development of bodily sense.

Adorno argued that access to nature is always mediated by history, and he conceptualized nature as a socially constituted alterity. This very construction as other leads to the articulation of the beauty of nature, explicitly in Adorno, and, I will argue, implicitly in Irigaray, as a resistance to the realm of calculation and use value, and a reminder that not everything fits the definitions and categories of scientific reasoning. Irigaray's use of what I am calling (as she does not), following Adorno, the aesthetics of nature, becomes an important resource for her critique of the history of the way in which nature has been conceptualized within philosophy. In order to construct this argument, I will begin with a consideration of Hegel's discussion of the beauty of nature in his *Lectures on Fine Art* (*Aesthetics*), followed by a reading of Adorno's discussion of the beauty of nature in *Aesthetic Theory*. I will then, using Benjamin to illuminate the structure of allegory, show how Irigaray uses nature allegorically in a manner similar to Adorno to critique the history of metaphysics and in particular to articulate sexual difference (nature) as a way of resisting the domination of instrumental reasoning and the tyranny of the logical sublation (*Aufhebung*) that equates form with content. This critique provides a bridge between Irigaray's earlier, more textual readings of canonical philosophical texts, in particular her readings of Marx and Hegel in *This Sex Which Is Not One* and *Speculum of the Other Woman*, and her later, more political and practical philosophy in *I Love to You, Je, tu, nous*, and *Sexes and Genealogies*. Because Irigaray always describes beauty in terms of sexual difference, the colors of nature, and the flesh, it is fair to attribute an aesthetics of the beauty of nature to her. Because of her rooting of aesthetics in sexual difference, which fundamentally destabilizes beauty and precludes the possibility of an exact coincidence between form and content, I argue that her conception of

the beauty of nature can perform the function of subverting traditional aesthetics that Adorno gave it even more effectively than his
own. In overlooking the gendered nature of both traditional representational art and modern art, Adorno overlooked one of the potentially most powerful forces inherent in "the beauty of nature."

HEGEL, NATURE, AND AESTHETICS

Hegel famously argues that nature can be said to be beautiful only
implicitly, in that the Idea is present in nature in merely an immediate sense, as "individual and adequate actuality" (Hegel 1975 [1835],
123). Because of this "purely sensuous immediacy," nature, insofar as
it is beautiful, is produced "neither *for* nor *out of itself*," but merely for
another (123). Thus, Hegel concludes, nature cannot be called beautiful properly speaking.

Hegel, like Kant, thinks that beauty is present only in form. But
when we call a natural entity beautiful, he argues, we are thinking not
of its form, but of its "inner unity" or "soul" (126). This is to say that
natural entities *qua* appearance are characterized by "capricious movement" and "irregular features," by "indeterminacy and abstraction"
(129), and by contingency rather than necessity. It is only by considering the organism in thought that we recognize in it a "unity of
configuration and its forms" (127). If we apprehend the "soul" of the
organism, in accordance with its concept, through thought rather
than external appearance, then we may call the organism beautiful.
But, says Hegel, if we do so, then there is a disjunction between the
perception of the so-called beautiful thing and the intellectual conception of it. This ought not be the case in the perception of beauty
(128). By extension, since the intellectual apprehension of soul would
not be possible with regard to natural beings other than organisms, we
realize that, for Hegel, a sunset or a landscape could not be called
beautiful properly speaking at all.

At the same time, Hegel acknowledges the common practice of
calling things in nature beautiful or ugly. And, he adds, we talk about
the beauty of nature even when we have before our minds no organic
or even living creation. He nods to the Kantian and Romantic conception of sublimity by acknowledging further the connection to the
noumenal, or the human soul, because it arouses emotional moods
that uplift us (131). Nevertheless, even animal life (the highest form
of natural life, according to Hegel's *Philosophy of Nature*) is thoroughly

limited to determinate qualities and is never present to itself as an ideal unity. The lack of self-awareness in the animal forever cuts it off from the realm of the ideal. We can only surmise a soul in the animal by looking at its form, never know it. This, Hegel says, is the primary deficiency in the beauty of nature (132). Only the self-conscious ego is the ideal, both in itself and for itself—it knows itself as the unity that it is and thereby "gives itself a reality which is no mere external, sensuous and bodily reality, but itself one of an ideal kind" (132).

The beauty of nature has the ideal "still lying ahead of it" (133). According to Hegel, nature exhibits no regularity or symmetry, but mere repetition. The forms of things in nature also do not conform to the exactitude of mathematical laws, although conformity to law determines the forms of the higher living organisms (140). Finally, although the colors of nature harmonize in an "essential totality," even harmony is not "free ideal subjectivity and soul" (141). Although it is the highest stage of abstract form, the harmony of colors in nature does not manifest spirituality in the same way that harmony in music forms the basis for a spiritual expression.

Even in its perfect appearance, then, natural beauty always lacks (142). For Hegel, the Idea, which in the sphere of aesthetics must be considered as a conceptual unity expressed in a determinate form that perfectly coincides with it, requires ideal subjectivity, which, as we have seen, is linked to self-consciousness. The immediate existence of nature is a finitude that does not correspond with its inner essence and thus can never be inherently infinite and free (151). Its beauty is purely interior to the reflection of the intellect, never visibly entering external reality as "the full expression of itself" in "*one* expression and *one* shape" (152). These deficiencies point to the ideal of beauty as being possible only in art, which Hegel spends most of his *Aesthetics* considering. Both Adorno and Irigaray will oppose this privilege and emphasize the beauty of nature against Hegel's critique; the beauty of nature, however, will align itself for each with a specific kind of art.

ADORNO'S THEORY OF THE BEAUTY OF NATURE

Contemporary discourses in aesthetics often argue or take it as given that beauty ceased to play a central role with the advent of modern art. Adorno himself might be read to make such a claim.[4] Adorno's use of the concept of "natural beauty," however distinct it ultimately is from any traditional concept of beauty in art, nevertheless retains the term "beauty" as central to transformative art. Adorno's discussion of natural beauty in his *Aesthetic Theory* is largely a response to Hegel's critique, but also refers to Kant's third *Critique*. Adorno notes the complete transformation of the central importance of the beauty of nature in Kant to the almost complete eclipse of nature by the beauty of art in aesthetic theory subsequent to Schelling.

Adorno begins by criticizing the elevation of human beings beyond the animal realm in idealism. He refers to the attempted redemption, by theorists like Karl Krauss, of phenomena repressed by idealism, in particular animals, landscapes, and women, subjects deemed inferior by virtue of not expressing freedom. Adorno points out that by limiting beauty to the autonomy of the (male) subject, idealistic aesthetic theory, with Schiller and Hegel at the vanguard, spelled out unfreedom for its other (Adorno 1997 [1970], 62). In using the word "repressed" Adorno intimates that the Hegelian theory that natural beauty can be negated and maintained on a higher plane within art merely masks an oppressive colonization of natural beauty by aesthetic theory (61). In the experience of nature within such aesthetic theory, "dignity reveals itself as subjective usurpation that degrades what is not subordinate to the subject" (62).

Even though natural beauty disappeared from aesthetic theory through Hegel's influence, Adorno shows how the concept of natural beauty continued to provide significant impetus for art itself. He gives the example of Proust, but also gestures toward the Romantic movement as he describes the historical amalgamation of the appreciation of natural beauty with the suffering of the lone subject, the one who does not fit in the context of Hegelian collective freedom. For Adorno, natural beauty ultimately functions as a way for authentic artworks to "step outside of themselves . . . as if in need of a breath of fresh air" (63).

This is not to say that the concept of natural beauty is ahistorical or untransformed by material shifts, however. Adorno describes natural beauty as "at its core historical" (65) and constantly returns to the notion that natural beauty and the beauty of art are intertwined. It is false to oppose the two. He notes that times in which nature overpowers human achievement are times in which nature has no beauty for human beings, just as the agricultural worker who has nature as her object of action has little impetus to appreciate its beauty. Times when nature regularly posed a threat are times with a predilection for symmetrical arrangements of nature, whereas a romantic delight in the irregularity of nature reflects the progress of civilization. Even when the subject's fear of nature becomes anachronistic, this fear gives way to an anxiety in the face of the unfreedom that comes with societal constraints; "In the experience of natural beauty," Adorno writes, "consciousness of freedom and anxiety fuse" (65). Art, for its part, seeks to redeem the promise of "sloughing off the aims of self-preservation" that the beauty of nature manifests (65). Art fulfils nature's goals in allowing it to appear as fully itself in a way that it could not when it was conceptualized purely through its antithesis to society (66).

Adorno's argument avoids at all cost a simple return to claims about the beauty of a sunset or a mountain range, or their represen-tation in art (indeed, the fact that kitsch art can infect the beauty of a sunset further strengthens the thesis of the interdependence of beauty in nature and in art). Adorno writes that artworks that represent nature merely repeat the gesture of industry in relegating nature to raw materials (66). Natural beauty as a concept itself arose in the early bourgeois period out of the historical progress of art, and the purportedly pure representation of nature in art occludes this histori-cal emergence. Natural beauty is nothing innocent; it makes an ap-peal to an escape from domination (its strength), yet it deceives because the freedom that it represents is really the unfreedom of fate, of mythical ambiguity, of divination by natural signs. Only what escapes nature as fate, Adorno writes, can aid in its restitution; art, organized by the subject, can speak "according to the model of a nonconceptual, nonrigidified significative language" that is perhaps closest to what the medievals called the "Book of Nature" (67), that is, it speaks through "ciphers" that have to be interpreted. Through art, human beings can become aware of what the tyranny of rationality and the autonomous subject have erased from view, but which cannot be brought to presence in any other way, namely, what Adorno calls the promise of nature.

Nature cannot be represented purely, Adorno writes, because to do so would be to refuse to recognize the historicity of the concept of the beauty of nature. The Old Testament prohibition on images has an aesthetic as well as a theological significance; one should not make images of that which by definition cannot be represented (67). Du-plication in art of the beauty of nature robs nature of its being-in-itself; art can be true to nature only where it presents the expression of its negativity (68).[5] What is beautiful in nature is what appears to be more than what is literally there (70–71). The aporia of natural beauty, which is the aporia of aesthetics as a whole, is that, Adorno writes, its object is determined negatively, as indeterminable (72). This position directly counters the Hegelian definition of beauty as the perfect coincidence of conceptual unity and formal expression.

Adorno contrasts his view to Hegel's; for Hegel, the weakness of natural beauty, as we have seen, is that it exists only for another, for us, to be precise. For Adorno, by contrast, natural beauty allows for the anamnesis of precisely what does not exist for another, what "presents itself as independent from the subject, as absolutely something [which is] not made" (74–75). Both Hegel and Adorno refer to this quality as indeterminacy, yet they interpret this indeterminacy in contrary ways. Hegel cannot acknowledge the "speech of what is not significative" (75). Nature is redeemed only through the consciousness that initially is set up over and against it. For Adorno, nature represents the promise of something higher than cognition or consciousness.

This "something higher" is also precisely what successful artworks express. "With human means, art wants to realize the language of what is not human" (78), and in doing so artworks converge with nature. However, this convergence with nature precludes the attempt to represent the natural in art, the tendency to imitate anything real. Rather, art, traditionally thought of as a quintessentially subjective, intentional activity, seeks, through the unconscious mediation of the artist, to divest itself of intentions, to move into a realm that surpasses human calculation and rationality. Adorno calls this "making the mute eloquent," where the "mute" would be nature free of human intervention, and the eloquence would not be the willed signification of instrumental reason. This constitutes what Adorno calls a desperate effort to bring about what cannot by definition be willed (78).

As Heinz Paetzold points out, Adorno's theory of natural beauty aims to parallel experiences of explicitly modern art.[6] Both transcend paradigms of representation, and both go beyond the principle of exchange and commodity production (Paetzold 1997, 219; Adorno 1997 [1970], 68). Despite the contemporary commodification or relegation of nature to a space for preservation (a national park, or as part of the tourist industry, for example) and despite the fact that access to that nature as a solace is a social privilege, natural beauty remains an *allegory* of a sphere beyond social mediatedness (Adorno 1997 [1970], 69). In emphasizing the allegorical character of the experience of natural beauty, Adorno seeks to avoid the possibility of the cult of natural beauty becoming an ideology (Adorno 1997 [1970], 68); in calling the beauty of nature an *allegory* of a sphere beyond social mediatedness rather than such a sphere itself, Adorno rejects the possibility of unmediated access to pure nature, another possibility of such an ideology. Like contemporary art, nature frustrates the attempt to capture meaning in a totalizing manner. Adorno refers to this quality as "the trace of the nonidentical in things under the spell of universal identity" (Adorno 1997 [1970], 73).

Adorno's naming of the beauty of nature as an allegory of a sphere beyond social mediatedness surely reverberates with the meaning accorded to allegory in Walter Benjamin's extensive discussion of it in *The Origin of German Tragic Drama* and other texts. Benjamin's discussion of allegory poses itself against romanticism's "tyranny" over more than one hundred years of aesthetics through its mistaken articulation of the symbol and attribution of a symbolic nature to beauty in general (Benjamin 1977 [1928], 160). In describing the "romantic" symbol as the "indivisible unity of content and form," Benjamin clearly points to the Hegelian ideal of beauty.[7] To this "comforting" popular tendency to equate the history of art with the progressive attempt to unify spiritual content and external form, Benjamin counterposes the baroque "speculative counterpart" of the allegory, which was not theoretically developed at the time. To name only one, albeit a "decisive" characteristic of allegory, its temporal dimension, according to Benjamin, is an extension in death, a "petrified, primordial landscape" that contrasts with the momentary, instantaneous "transfigured face of nature . . . fleetingly revealed in the light of redemption" in the symbol (Benjamin 1977 [1928], 166). What this means is that allegory displays the ruination of nature in the light of its salvation, rather than its ephemeral symbolic preservation in the illusion of beauty, preserving the truth of nature even in its destruction of faithful representation of it.

Two things are interesting to note in Adorno's appropriation of Benjamin's discussion of allegory. First, while Benjamin addresses allegory within the context of the seventeenth century German *Trauerspiel*, as a historically specific phenomenon, Adorno makes no such explicit historical correlation. The baroque period in which *Trauerspiel* flourished as an artistic form manifested a preoccupation with finitude and transience and the fleeting nature of truth, historically brought about by the Thirty Years War, the upheavals of Counter-Reformation political intrigue, and the separation of this-worldly

existence from the possibility of salvation brought about by the de-
cline of influence of a monolithic church (see Wolin 1994, 71f.). The
Trauer ("mourning") of the seventeenth century *Trauerspiel* is in its
essence the contrary of the redemptive Hegelian *Aufhebung* or
its correspondence in Benjamin's conception of the symbol, which in
its essentially momentary nature aspires to an immediate unity with
that which it intends. In the pre-romantic theory of the symbol beauty
is linked with instantaneity and immediate completion; by contrast,
allegory, as Benjamin describes it, possesses a necessary historical and
dialectical unfolding in time. Whereas the time of the symbol is redemptive, the allegory expresses "everything about history that, from
the very beginning, has been untimely, sorrowful, unsuccessful" (Benjamin 1977 [1928], 166).

Benjamin's historically specific location of allegory has a counterpart in his own time. Richard Wolin claims that the allegorical
method "immediately calls to mind the proliferation of like-tempered
artistic movements that came into existence at this historical juncture
as a self-conscious reaction to the mechanization of social life that
had proceeded unchecked since the time of the industrial revolution"
(Wolin 1994, 75), and Eric Santer points out the rebirth of Benjamin's
discussion of the allegorical mode of representation in postmodern
critical theory (Santner 1990, 11–12). Wolin mentions Kandinsky
and the *Blaue Reiter* Almanac, Andre Breton's "Manifesto of Surreal-
ism," the automatic writing techniques adopted by surrealist artists,
the novels of Proust and Joyce (Wolin 1994, 75). This "rejection of
realism" is easily aligned with Adorno's approbation of the rejection
of representation in modern art.

The allegorist, according to Benjamin, possesses a power never
accorded to the interpreter of symbols. Since the allegory never exists
in a self-sufficient relation to the idea it represents, but always remains in need of completion, allegory always has a necessary conceptual or linguistic counterpart, provided by the interpreter or critic.
Benjamin asserts that the allegory must "hold its own against the
tendency to absorption," and as such it must "constantly unfold in
new and surprising ways," unlike the symbol, which remains "persis-
tently the same" (Benjamin 1977 [1928], 183). Thus the "redemption" of the allegory is never accomplished once and for all; it seeks,
but never fully succeeds, in revitalizing the dead, fragmentary landscape to which nature has been reduced once beauty no longer has
the power to sustain the illusion of totality.

The second aspect of Adorno's use of allegory that is worth noting in its contrast to Benjamin's description of it is his equation of the beauty of nature with allegory. For Benjamin, allegory contrasts with symbol precisely in its rejection of beauty in its symbolic and momentary coincidence with the idea that it presents. It remains to be seen, then, it what sense the beauty of nature can perform allegorically, since, according to Benjamin, the allegorist saw nature not "in bud and bloom, but in the over-ripeness and decay of her creations . . . [as] eternal transience. . . ." (Benjamin 1977 [1928], 179). As Benjamin puts it in his essay on Goethe's *Elective Affinities*, it is the task of the philosophical critic, as opposed to the mere commentator, to burn away the external shell of beautiful appearance in order to penetrate to the truth content, or to allow the "expressionless" (*Ausdruckslose*) to appear (Benjamin 1996 [1924–25], 298). Perhaps we might productively read Irigaray as just such a philosophical critic.

IRIGARAY AND NATURE AS ALLEGORY

It is Adorno's depiction of the beauty of nature as allegory that parallels Irigaray's discussion of sexual difference as the primary delineating force in nature. Despite Irigaray's insistence that sexual difference is a "natural reality," but also contrary to claims that this kind of language represents only a strategic essentialism on her part, I believe that this realism is to be understood in the sense of the philosophy of nature of Goethe and German Idealism, in the sense of allegory in Romanticism that Benjamin discusses, which seeks for parallels between nature and human thought and understanding in which the real is spiritual and the spiritual is real, to put a twist on Hegel's phrase, and in the Marxist tradition which provides a link between the two.

Irigaray's description of the "constitution" of an authentic form of sexual difference in *I Love to You* is representative of this intertwining, which Irigaray believes can be altered and transformed in more or less enabling ways. She writes of "becom[ing] aware of being a woman or a man, and wanting to become one." This effort would be a "retroactive intentionality" that avoids both "simple projection" and "natural immediacy," that results in neither an "artificial construct" nor a "reducing [of] the natural to procreation" (Irigaray 1996 [1992], 39). The language makes it clear that Irigaray is studiously avoiding a reduction of nature to the simple opposite of culture or construct. Nature is "a universal that exists prior to me," but it is something that I must "accomplish . . . in relation to my particular destiny" (39).

She goes on to write: "The intention is to assure [the] cultivation [of my natural identity], so that I may become who I am. Equally, it is to spiritualize my nature in order to create with the other" (Irigaray 1996 [1992], 39). She contrasts this "ingathering (*recueillement*) of spirit's into the self," which she also calls a "return to nature" (38), with both patriarchy itself as an imposition and the simple critique of patriarchy that might prove nihilistic if not accompanied by the creation of new values. The aim is to liberate the "reality of sex and gender from subjection to a metaphysics or religion that leaves them to an uncultured and instinctual fate" (39). Instinct itself, nature represented as raw, the identification of woman with her ability to give birth and her hormonal fluctuations, are all the projections of a specific metaphysics, so that any return to nature will also involve a reconsideration of spiritual becoming. I will read Irigaray's philosophy of nature first with reference to its roots in German Idealism and second in line with the Marxist critique of a reductive understanding of work and property that limits bodily experience and sensible understanding, together with the imagining of how this limitation could be transformed into an enabling sense of the natural.

Irigaray's schematic philosophy of nature follows that of Goethe and the German Idealists in its identification of a rhythmic polarity as the predominant force that suffuses all of natural life. Irigaray emphasizes this natural, non-dialectical polarity as the way in which sexual difference must be thought:

> [Natural powers] are . . . regulated by alternations that do not truly contradict each other. Spring is not autumn nor summer winter, night is not day. This is not the opposition that we know from logic in which the one is opposed to or contradicts the other, where the one is superior to the other and *must put the inferior down*. There is a rhythm of growth in which both poles are necessary . . . (Irigaray 1993 [1987], 108)

Goethe called polarity (*Polarität*) and enhancement or intensification (*Steigerung*) the "two great driving forces of nature." Polarity, according to Goethe, is a property of nature insofar as it is thought of as "natural," and intensification is a property of nature thought of as spiritual, an identification we also find in Irigaray. Goethe calls polarity "a state of constant attraction and repulsion" and intensification "a state of ever-striving ascent." These two forces affect mind and body equally: "Since matter can never exist and act without spirit, nor spirit without matter, matter is also capable of undergoing intensification and spirit cannot be denied its attraction and repulsion" (Goethe 1988, 6). Goethe used the concept of polarity to explain the metamorphosis of plants in terms of expansion and contraction—also important terms for Irigaray in her description of nature (see, for example, Irigaray 2000 [1994], 111)—as well as to explain his theory of color. In accord with Lessing, Herder, Baader, and Schelling, among others, Goethe described the phenomena of magnetism and metamorphosis as "originary" in the sense that neither phenomenon belongs strictly to either the realm of matter or that of spirit, and neither fluctuation can be called purely qualitative or purely quantitative. Baader called the "polarity of conjoining and liberating" the "key" to all nature (Hoffmeister 1932, 28–29). For all of these thinkers, polarity signified far more than a simple material phenomenon. Polarity was considered to be spiritual, both in the sense that it was significant for understanding human freedom and thinking, but also in that it was a universal explanatory principle for all natural phenomena. In addition, whatever most transforms itself manifests the highest spirituality. The process of natural development is thus not simply a dialectical overcoming of opposition, but an enhancement that retains the tension of difference. Both Schelling and Hegel also use the notions of polarity and intensification; Schelling describes intensification in terms of potencies, and Hegel creates out of this conception of potencies and intensification the different levels of actuality of the *Begriff*. It seems likely that Irigaray takes her description of nature from Hegel's *Philosophy of Nature*, which in turn relies heavily at times on Goethe's natural science.[8]

Irigaray argues that sexual difference, as the fundamental polarity in nature, is an immediate delineating force that must be preserved and addressed in all theorizing about nature or spirit (human activities). "Nature" thus functions similarly in Irigaray's writings to the way in which Adorno describes it, as a cipher for that which resists the overarching contemporary economy of instrumental reason and calculative exchange value, or, as Irigaray might rather put it, of the male symbolic order. Another way of putting this claim is that Irigaray opposes the Hegelian retroactive appropriation of nature by spirit in the sense of spirit's positing nature as its opposite and thus "creating" it, then using it to overcome itself in (sexually neutral) spirit. This critique aligns itself with Adorno's critique of the representation of nature in art, as that which "analogous to industry . . . relegates nature to raw material" (Adorno 1997 [1970], 66). For both thinkers, the beauty of nature represents a resistance to the colonizing power of a specific mode of thinking, that thinking that reduces alterity to something to be reworked and consumed. Contrary to Hegel, then, the *only* art that is beautiful is the art that keeps this promise of the beauty of nature, that distorts the lens that purports to reflect reality back faithfully but in doing so reduces the other to the same.

As such, Irigaray's ethics of sexual difference has implications that have yet to be drawn out for a specifically feminist aesthetics. Irigaray's critique of market culture and her linkage of it with patriarchy is well known (see, for example, "Women on the Market," in Irigaray 1985 [1977], 170–91). According to Irigaray, our culture is based not just upon exchange and instrumental value, but specifically upon the exchange of women. As commodities, women are "a mirror of value of and for man" (Irigaray 1985 [1977], 177). The economy of exchange is "man's business" (ibid.), and for men, "commodities . . . share in the cult of the father, and never stop striving to resemble, to copy the one who is his representative" (ibid., 178). This resemblance is achieved through the capacity of the commodity, any commodity, to represent paternal authority. The linkage of paternal authority, representation, and commodification raises the question of how to escape the logic of exchange and instrumentality. This is where, potentially, Irigaray might articulate not just an *ethics* but also an *aesthetics* of sexual difference.

In order to draw out an aesthetics from a critique of commodification, consumer culture, gendered individualism, and instrumental reason, we might turn to Marx for instruction. Although Marx's most nuanced analysis of the commodity comes, as is well known, in chapter 1 of *Capital*, I would like to turn instead to his discussion of private property and communism, understood as both a humanism and a *naturalism*, in the 1844 *Economic and Philosophic Manuscripts*. This essay is, for good reason, sometimes included in aesthetics' anthologies, for it develops an account of the relationship between private property and the development of the senses that has important implications for aesthetics, and indeed it influenced a whole line of Marxist aestheticians from Lùkacs to Adorno.

In an essay on the various stages of private property and communism, Marx appropriates and elaborates the Hegelian notion of property as the most primordial form of the human self-development into freedom from *The Philosophy of Right*. Here, Hegel writes that "I possess my body, like other things, only so long as I will to possess them. . . . In so far as the body is an immediate existent, it is not in conformity with spirit. If it is to be the willing organ and soul-endowed instrument of spirit, it must first be taken into possession by spirit" (Hegel 1952 [1821], 43). Marx develops the notion of the necessity of the body being possessed by spirit, beyond the individualism of abstract right, where Hegel locates it, into the social and economic sphere. Our reductive, estranged notion of private property, Marx writes, "has made us stupid and one-sided so that [we think] the object is only ours when we *have* it, when it exists for us as capital or when we directly possess, eat, drink, inhabit, use it" (Marx 1988 [1930], 214). By contrast, property, including the possession of one's body, must be understood as "the appropriation of human reality" or social reality. Through a series of moves, Marx argues for an ontological link between property, humanity, social being, and nature:

> The human essence of nature exists only for social man; for only here does nature exist for him as a bond with other people, as the vital element of human reality, as the basis of human existence. . . . Society is therefore the perfected unity in essence of man with nature, the true resurrection of nature, the realized naturalism of man and the realized humanism of nature." (Marx 1988 [1930], 213)

This conception of nature refers most immediately to the body, and explicitly to the senses, which, through the transformed understanding of property,[9] can develop in a way that will foster true aesthetic awareness. When the one-sided sense of property as mere consumption and possession is superseded through the establishment of true communism, as opposed to crude communism, the senses and attributes of the human body will also be emancipated (Marx 1988 [1930], 214). Marx writes that "only through the objectively unfolded wealth of human nature can the wealth of subjective human sensitivity—a musical ear, an eye for the beauty of form—be either cultivated or created" (Marx 1988 [1930], 215). Thereby "subjectivism and objectivism, spiritualism and materialism, activity and passivity lose their antithetical character, and hence their existence as such antitheses, only in society (ibid.).

If "the senses of social man are different from those of non-social man" (Marx 1988 [1930], 215), then the body itself, nature as a concept, cannot be understood in isolation from its incorporation in society. To talk of a mere body makes no sense in Marxist terms. Understanding nature, be it the body or any other natural thing, as "raw material," is a product of commodity culture, an estrangement. Similarly, for Irigaray, "becoming who I am" is a cultivation of the "natural" identity that I am given, but can only be identified retroactively, as a result of my having taken a hold of it and made it my own. As Marx writes, "History is a real part of natural history and of nature's becoming human" (Marx 1988 [1930], 216). For Irigaray, of course, it makes a great deal of difference whether one's "taking a hold" of one's own identity and "making it one's own" occurs via the mediation of representations of one's own sexuate identity, or whether one is doomed to appropriate alien, dominating representations that pervert one's becoming-for-self, as women in a male economy have been.

In the essay on Unica Zürn, Irigaray refers to this disjunction between what one is (nature) and what one might become as "this space between herself and herself" (Irigaray 1994, 12). Margaret Whitford explicates the psychoanalytic underpinnings of this distinction (which I argue is equally a Hegelian and Marxist conception of becoming-for-self or a hybrid of the two traditions) in her commentary on this essay. In "A Natal Lacuna" Irigaray calls beauty the truth of art, in that art holds the promise of becoming the *means* for the creation of a new and transformed symbolic order, one that "would symbolize the couple and not simply male identity" (Whitford 1994, 16). Irigaray defines beauty, Whitford explains, as a moment of "happiness" or projective drawing-together of what was previously fragmented, namely the female imaginary. Beauty, in women's art, functions or *could* function as the projection or possibility of an ideal self that is specifically feminine, what Whitford calls "the ideality of a woman's identity-for-herself" that "depends upon the divine woman," the "ideal self which transcends the particularity of individual women" (Whitford 1994, 15). What Irigaray objects to in Zürn's art is that it projects precisely the contrary of an ideal self. "Everything that Unica Zürn writes/draws expresses a relationship to the void . . . the weight of the body, of bodies, is sought and found only in dislocation, fragmentation . . ." (Irigaray 1994, 11).

This fragmentation is a reference to the Lacanian vision of the imaginary in "bits and pieces." As Whitford explains, Irigaray interprets Freudian drive theory in a Lacanian manner, such that drives, including the death drive, are not pre-formed instincts, but derive their organization from the structure imposed on them by the symbolic order (Whitford 1994, 16). The death drive is the source of both destruction, and, when sublimated, of creativity. Irigaray argues, according to Whitford, that what is missing from the symbolic order are the ideal representations of women that would allow them to sublimate their own death drive and create their own art rather than simply functioning as a means for the sublimation of the death drive of men (Whitford 1994, 16). Irigaray reads Zürn's art through the artist's difficult relationship with a male artist, Hans Bellmer. Zürn's art manifests the impossibility of truth in women's art when it relates itself only to the projective fantasies of male being-for-self. For Irigaray, art that expresses anguish and ugliness has "failed in its quest" (Irigaray 1994, 12). Zürn herself, according to Irigaray, "fails to be born" (Irigaray 1994, 13) in the sense of the birth of the spiritual self.

This gap between ideal self and real self might also be thought in terms of Hegel's master/slave dialectic and its appropriation by Marx. If the master is thought as the projection of desire, the embodiment of what the slave wants to become, then the truth of independent self-consciousness only comes about when the slave realizes, through his labor, that it is his relationship with the thing (work, art) into which he puts his labor, that accomplishes his being-for-self (Hegel 1977 [1807], 117). The master in this case *might* be an alien (male) consciousness, but might also become the positive projection of the possibility of specifically feminine fantasy, or of a new, positive representation in the feminine imaginary, and ultimately a revised symbolic order.

For Irigaray, as Whitford notes with some surprise, this positive projection with reference to women's art seems to privilege figurative and complete representations of women. A woman's identity in the male symbolic order is already fragmented. Critical and desconstructive art, then, offers women only a male-constructed identity. Thus, although representations of fragmentation may have a place in psychoanalysis, in women's art, beauty must preclude such dismemberment. Whitford quotes Irigaray to the effect that the artist has an ethical responsibility to present to women an ideal self, "discovering and displaying her identity" (Irigaray 1994; Whitford 1994, 16). But is

Irigaray's idea of a feminine aesthetics really limited to figurative or representational art? How is this representation to be understood?

In 1984, Irigaray calls for "a new age of thought, art, poetry, and language: the creation of a new *poetics*" (Irigaray 1993 [1984], 5), a poetics of sexual difference. Not until three years later does she flesh out what this new poetics might look like, not just in the realm of literature, but with respect to the visual arts. In a short essay entitled "How Can We Create Our Beauty?" Irigaray expresses first the same dissatisfaction with the presence of anguish in much of women's art, and then a desire to help women exteriorize the beauty of which they are capable in works of art (Irigaray 1993 [1990], 107). Yet, when it comes to expanding on what this beauty might mean, Irigaray makes an interesting allusion to what Lyotard calls the contemporary sublime, the privileging, not of form or figure, but precisely of materiality over form, appropriating this rhetoric for feminism in its subversion of traditional power structures and linking it to the natural:

> In breaking out of our formal prisons, our shackles, we may discover what flesh we have left. I think color is what's left of life beyond forms, beyond truth or beliefs, beyond accepted joys and sorrows. Color also expresses our sexuate nature, that irreducible dimension of our incarnation. When all meaning is taken away from us, there remains color, colors, in particular those corresponding to our sex. Not the dullness of the neuter, the non-living or problematically living (stones, for example) but the colors that are ours owing to the fact that we are women. Colors are also present in nature—particularly plant life—and there they express life, its becoming and its development, according to days, seasons, years. In the world around us, they also express what is sexuate in life. (Irigaray 1993 [1990], 109–10)

The linkage of color with nature, and in particular with the plant, is an implicit reference to and transformation of Hegel's philosophy of nature and his philosophy of right, in which he first describes the plant in the language of passivity and impotence and then explicitly links these qualities with women and their inability to take an active role in the fundamental move toward freedom of appropriating their bodies through spirit.[10]

In a slightly earlier lecture, "Flesh Colors," Irigaray sheds light on what she might mean by colors expressing sexuate nature. In this essay, Irigaray advocates the practice of painting as a means to compensate for the "perceptual modification" or "imbalance" that psychoanalysis brings about. According to Irigaray, the sole focus on hearing within analysis risks draining a patient of image and color, "sinking down and seeing everything go *gray*" (Irigaray 1993 [1987], 153–54). In addition, when patients are lying down, their balance, which is normally attuned to both visual surroundings and a variety of aural cues, may become skewed through the very lack of need to pay attention to it. For these reasons, Irigaray proposes painting as a means of rectifying the "temporary perceptual equilibrium" that may give rise to delirium, paranoia, transference, and other weaknesses that threaten the very success of the analysis (Irigaray 1993 [1987], 155).

What is interesting about Irigaray's theory of painting presented in this essay is its relationship to the rhythms of life identified in her philosophy of nature and alluded to in the reference to plant life. The rhythm of nature, Irigaray writes, is silent or melodic, while other rhythms, those that bring about the pathologies that give rise to the necessity of analysis in the first place, are noisy and "risk destroying or effacing the color properties of matter, of perception, of the dream, of the painting" (Irigaray 1993 [1987], 156). She describes painting in the vocabulary of temporality, citing Paul Klee's idea that the point of painting is to make time simultaneous (Irigaray 1993 [1987], 155). Music and rhythm were central interests for Klee (anything but a representational artist), who had to decide between music and painting as careers and who chose painting only because he believed that music had already exhausted all its possibilities by the early-twentieth century. Klee singled out rhythm as the way in which music and art could be brought into proximity with each other. Klee writes that polyphony in music, like that found in Mozart's *Don Giovanni* expresses the simultaneity of yesterday, tomorrow, and today, and that painting, too, must eliminate time (Klee, *Diaries*: see Hajo Duechting, *Paul Klee: Painting Music*. Munich: Prestel Verlag, 2002, 14.) It is hard to imagine that Irigaray's own appropriation of Klee does not have as part of its background Heidegger's analysis of the three ecstases of existential temporality in *Being and Time* (Heidegger 1962 [1929], 377f).

Painting can succeed in making past, present, and future simultaneous, and thereby aid psychoanalysis, which risks being uniphonic,

in releasing crystallized past events and affects into the present of the
subject, freeing up energy through "poetry" or *poiesis*.[11] Here, Irigaray
relates art explicitly to sexual difference and gives us a clearer idea of
what she might mean by a new poetics or aesthetics of sexual difference. The voice (timbre, intensity, pitch) and colors, which Irigaray
calls "two components of human identity," differ according to sex. But
because polarities in color and voice are not binary, colors and timbre
do not obey the rules established by the seemingly universal cultural
logic of sexual difference (Irigaray 1993 [1987], 157).

Irigaray also relates color and voice to the materiality of the
human body, the sensuous fleshiness of nature that gets literally covered up or made over into something non-natural in an idealist account of art like Hegel's. Deliberately setting her theory of art apart
from a mere reflection on the linguistic arts, Irigaray writes that the
emphasis in our culture on writing as a medium for meaning has split
the subject from his or her body. By representing sexual difference in
terms of color, one can avoid the tendency toward dichotomization
evident in philosophy. Psychoanalysis, too, tries to encapsulate everything, including sensoriness, affectivity, parental relations, individual
and collective history, dreams, fantasies, into narrative. Visual art, for
Irigaray, thus fills in the lacunae of meaning left by the inadequacy of
the word. Irigaray writes enigmatically that "Time can . . . be made
simultaneous by couples in tension, colored couples, sound couples,
sexualized couples" (Irigaray 1993 [1987], 159). What I think this
means is that meaning, in the painting, should *never* coincide exactly
with its form. This theory of art resists Hegelian sublation in exactly
the way Irigaray's ethics of sexual difference does. It also accords a
greater role to the interpreter by virtue of its lack of immediate transparency (color that moves beyond the inadequacy of the word).

This asymmetry that Irigaray locates in a productive or progressive aesthetics complements her revision of Hegelian recognition. In
"You Who Will Never Be Mine," Irigaray writes that:

> As for the "absolute spirit," the recognition of sexed identity
> as a dimension of a spiritual culture renders the unity of this
> totalization impossible. In fact, each gender must define and
> retain mediations appropriate to it, and we must determine
> mediations enabling communication and exchange between
> the genders. But there will be no final synthesis. There will be
> no definitive "negation of negation." Man being irreducible

to woman and woman to man, there no longer exists any *absolute* spirit nor *one* finality of being. The relation between man and woman, men and women, takes place on the grounds of a groundless ground. It is without definitive resolution or assumption, always becoming in the outward and return jour- neying between one and the other, the ones and the others, with no end or final reckoning. (Irigaray 1996 [1992], 107)

Thus, *initially* ideal representations of women taken in the most literal sense may be necessary to put the transformed feminine imaginary into play in order to work toward a revised symbolic order of the couple. But this kind of art is not the final statement, the finality of aesthetic being.

Let us recall Benjamin's theory of allegory and consider whether this structure might translate into the visual arts. Allegory, as opposed to (the Romantic) symbol, as Benjamin articulates it, cannot be cap- tured in a moment. It lacks the immediate recuperative significance of the symbol in that its meaning never fully coincides or never forms an indivisible unity with its form. Nevertheless, Benjamin does de- scribe allegory as having a "saving power," but one that interrupts the possibility of redemption within time. Rather, Benjamin, too, is drawn to Klee's painting, painting that aims to disrupt time, and that does not attempt to "make whole what has been smashed."[12] In the alle- gory, the bodily, or nature, can never get completely taken up into meaning; its significance never allows the materiality that mediates it, however fragmentarily, to disappear.

Jean-François Lyotard would argue that this asymmetry of form and content really belongs to a theory of the sublime. According to Lyotard, the idea of a natural fit between matter and form is implied in Kant's analysis of the sublime, and modern painting had no op- tion but to turn to matter as its focus after the advent of the sublime into the artistic imagination (Lyotard 1991 [1988], 139–40). Mate- riality signifies, above all, the color and timbre on which Irigaray focuses. Sublimity and allegory would seem to align in the same way as beauty and symbolism do in Kant. However, Lyotard locates modern art as a symptom of the logic of capitalism rather than in resistance to it. The forces of skepticism, destruction, and imperma- nence that capitalism brings into play "encourages among artists a mistrust of established rules and a willingness to experiment with means of expression, with styles, with ever-new materials" (Lyotard

1991 [1988], 105). Thus, capitalism has something of the sublime in it, according to Lyotard.[13]

We might see something analogous to this observation in Hegel's aesthetics. Although Hegel divides the history of art into three stages, only the first of which is called symbolic art, by Benjamin's articulation, for Hegel all art is symbolic.[14] What Hegel calls symbolic art is unsuccessfully symbolic art. Here, in the art of ancient Egypt and India, the linkage of a symbol with its meaning is either external and purely arbitrary (Hegel 1975 [1835], 304) or unmediated and crude (a god present in the form of an animal, for example) (ibid., 324). Classical art, by contrast, achieves a complete reciprocal interpenetration of meaning and expression. Romantic art, which for Benjamin represents the apotheosis of the symbol in its linkage with beauty, for Hegel, is the realization by spirit that its truth does not consist in its immersion in corporeality. Beauty thus becomes something subordinate to the "absolute inner life" (Hegel 1975 [1835], 518). Interestingly, then, romantic art, in Hegel's sense, which tends toward the de-emphasis on outward form, might correspond to the tendency toward first minimalism and then conceptualism in modern art. In Irigaray it might correspond to a reduction to pure color or pure tone.

For these reasons, I contend that Benjamin's articulation of the allegory corresponds better to Adorno and Irigaray's conception of the critical function of the "beauty" of nature in aesthetics in art than either the symbolic (which would characterize figurative art) or the sublime, precisely because of the symbol's tendency toward either stasis or the hyper-irony of some German Romanticism, and toward the attempt to absolutely unify content and form, and because of the possible collusion of the sublime with the logic of profitability and calculation. This beauty of nature and the fulfilment of its promise in non-representational art, would, if successful, resist commodification and remain "true to nature," not in the sense of portraying the beauty of nature directly, but in remaining in the play of a non-dialectical difference with it, a play that would take as its model the polar interplay, not to be overcome, of the difference between the sexes.[15]

Hilary Robinson notes that Whitford's equation of symbolic representation and figuration in Irigaray's account of art is premature. Irigaray's suggestive concept of mucous, for one, seems to work against a simple notion of figuration. Robinson also points out that Irigaray's call for a "presentation of a woman's sexual organs . . . as the place where the universe was generated" is tempered by the words "without reducing it in any way to anatomy and physiology" (Robinson 1994, 13). I would agree that, for Irigaray, "nature" never refers to what we might in our most common-sensical moments presume. The beauty of nature is a beauty that must preclude its exact representation in art, for such a representation risks becoming complicit with the very order that it seeks to subvert. This does not mean that the kind of art that would be most consistent with Irigaray's philosophy would be, on the contrary, deconstructive and critical. It is precisely such a reductive oppositional evaluation, manifest also in critical contrasts of Irigaray's earlier and later works, that we are seeking to avoid.

NOTES

1. Luce Irigaray, "A Natal Lacuna," *Women's Art Magazine* 58 (1994): 11–13.

2. Margaret Whitford, "Woman With Attitude," *Women's Art Magazine* 60 (1994): 15–17.

3. Hilary Robinson, "Irigaray's Imaginings," *Women's Art Magazine* 61 (1994): 20.

4. See, for example, Jean-François Lyotard's *The Inhuman* and Arthur Danto's *The Abuse of Beauty*, to take examples from both continental and analytic philosophy. Adorno discusses the demise of beauty due to its formalization, as well as the inclusion of the category of the ugly in modern art, but his argument is ultimately against the fixation of the concept of beauty, which results in its incorporation into the very commodity culture that is its role to resist (see Adorno 1997 [1970], 45–53).

5. This point is also Kant's in the third *Critique*. For Kant, "free beauty" is superior to adherent beauty, under which representative art would be classified, because free beauty "does not presuppose a concept of what the object is [meant] to be" (Kant 1987, 76). Kant gives the examples of designs *à la greque* and the abstraction of foliage on borders or on wallpaper that are so stylized as to no longer point to the concept of what they represent. He also calls the Judaic and Islamic prohibition on images "sublime" (ibid., 135).

6. Again, this point is arguably anticipated by Kant in the *Critique of Judgment*.

7. Benjamin is specifically targeting the Romantic theorists of beauty, rather than Hegel or the Idealists, for reasons with which Hegel himself would concur. Although Hegel calls beauty the perfect coincidence of material form and ideal content, as is well known, he also diagnoses the death or end of art precisely as the incapacity of form to truly capture ideal content, so that first religion and then philosophy must take over the task of absolute spirit (Hegel 1975, 11, 539). Thus, Hegel's critique of the Romantics might align itself with

Benjamin in arguing against the impossibility of the merging of the beautiful with the divine in an unbroken whole (Benjamin 1977, 160). Nevertheless, Benjamin's critique of the symbol also points to the Hegelian articulation of beauty as the perfect and instantaneous coincidence of meaning and form, and to Hegel's privileging of symbolism over allegory. Hegel tends to treat allegory in the dismissive way that Benjamin describes as "a conventional relationship between an illustrative image and its abstract meaning" (Benjamin 1977, 162). It must also be noted that, for Hegel, symbolic art, which he locates in the ancient East as the first stage in the evolution of absolute spirit within art, remains a "continuing struggle for the compatibility of meaning and shape" in an attempt to "escape from this defective unification" (Hegel 1975, 317), not a merging, however ephemeral, of the two.

8. For a more complete account of Irigaray's philosophy of nature and its connection to her political theory, see Alison Stone's article "The Sex of Nature: A Reinterpretation of Irigaray's Metaphysics and Political Thought," in *Hypatia* 18:3 (Summer 2003): 60f.

9. Marx's notion of property revises the common, crude, or one-sided understanding of property as *having*, not Hegel's conception of property. Hegel, too, distinguishes between mere possession and property (Hegel 1975, 42). For Hegel, "the fact that I make something my own as a result of my natural need, impulse, or caprice, is the particular interest satisfied by possession. But I as free will am . . . an actual will, and this is the aspect which constitutes the category of *property*, the true and right factor in possession" (ibid.). Hegel considers mental aptitudes, artistic skill, talents, and so on to be things that can be considered my property in the sense of *propre*, ownness. In addition, Hegel understands that property implies a social reality. However, at this stage of the philosophy of right (abstract right), consciousness is not yet aware of this reality.

10. See Hegel (1970), 45–101, and Hegel (1952), 263–64. For more on Irigaray's appropriation and subversion of Hegelian plant figures as tropes for femininity, see my *The Vegetative Soul: From Philosophy of Nature to Subjectivity in the Feminine* (Albany: State University of New York Press, 2002), 187–200.

11. The mention of *poiesis* and building here seems to be an implicit reference to Heidegger (see "Building Dwelling Thinking"), although it is outside the scope of this paper to follow this thread.

12. See Benjamin's account of Klee's "Angelus Novus" in *Illuminations* (1968 [1955]), 257–58.

13. This view is contested by Adorno's earlier analysis of modern art as sublime. For Adorno, modern art's sublimity, unhinged from Kant's recourse to the supersensible, lies not in its obtrusive materiality but in the freedom of nature from the domination of subjectivity. The reduction of spirit to its natural dimension annihilates the individual not in its cognitive constitution (to be rescued through a recourse to noumenal humanity), but

in its pathetic self-aggrandizement, placing the sublime in a healthy way very close to the ridiculous, a category that Adorno finds crucial to modern art, in particular in the writings of Kafka and Beckett (see Adorno 1993, 196f and 118f).

14. Hegel accepts that this might be said of all art, but insists that in his account he will be emphasizing the distinction between art that presents symbols proper and art that has advanced to the point of a less explicit form of representation, namely, the classical and the Romantic. My point is that, nevertheless, classical and Romantic art as Hegel describes them remain symbolic in the sense that Benjamin articulates the symbol, that is, they aim toward an indivisible unity of form and content. For Benjamin, the apotheosis of symbolic art is Romantic.

15. This part of my argument was in large point developed out of a very productive dialogue with Ewa Plonowska Ziarek, who gave a paper entitled "The Soul of the Commodity and the Body of the Sphinx: Toward a Different Model of Social Mediation of Bodies" as part of the Linda Singer Memorial Lecture Series at Miami University in the spring of 2003 (it may well be published somewhere by the time of this book's publication). Ziarek argues, taking Irigaray's call for a "new poetics" as a point of departure, that a feminist critique of aesthetics might elaborate a new model of mediation which preserves the body as the site of a two-way passage between flesh and spirit, nature and culture, the unconscious and the conscious. In doing so, she rereads Hegel's discussion of symbolic art through the lens of Adorno's aesthetic theory, in particular Adorno's discussion of enigma. The two papers, which were being written simultaneously without any knowledge of the other, address very similar questions. However, whereas Ziarek invokes a reconsideration of symbolic art, I believe that the allegory is the form for art that captures what it is that Adorno and Irigaray are trying to achieve in their discussion of natural beauty. I am indebted to Ziarek for her nuanced and thought-provoking essay.

WORKS CITED

Adorno, Theodor W. 1997 [1970]. *Aesthetic Theory*. Translated by Robert Hullot-Kentor. Edited by Gretel Adorno and Rolf Tiedemann. Minneapolis: University of Minnesota Press.

Benjamin, Walter. 1968 [1955]. *Illuminations*. Translated by Harry Zohn. Edited by Hannah Arendt. New York: Schocken Books.

———. 1977 [1928]. *The Origin of German Tragic Drama*. Translated by John Osborne. London: NLB.

———. 1996. *Walter Benjamin: Selected Writings, Volume One: 1913–1926*. Edited by Marcus Bullock and Michael W. Jennings. Cambridge, Mass.: Harvard University Press.

Danto, Arthur. 2003. *The Abuse of Beauty: Aesthetics and the Concept of Art.*
    Chicago: Open Court.
Düchting, Hajo. 2002. *Paul Klee: Painting Music.* Translated by Penelope
    Crowe. Munich: Prestel Verlag.
Goethe, Johann Wolfgang von. 1988. *Scientific Studies.* Edited and translated
    by Douglas Miller. New York: Suhrkamp Publishers.
Hegel, G. W. F. 1952 [1821]. *The Philosophy of Right.* Translated by T. M.
    Knox. Oxford: Oxford University Press.
————. 1970. *Hegel's Philosophy of Nature,* 3 volumes. Translated by Michael
    John Petry. New York: Humanities Press.
————. 1975 [1835]. *Hegel's Aesthetics. Lectures on Fine Art.* Translated by
    T. M. Knox. Oxford: Clarendon Press.
————. 1977 [1807]. *Hegel's Phenomenology of Spirit.* Translated by A. V.
    Miller. Oxford: Oxford University Press.
Heidegger, Martin. 1962 [1929]. *Being and Time.* Translated by John Macquarrie
    and Edward Robinson. New York: Harper & Row.
Hoffmeister, Johannes. 1932. *Goethe und der Deutsche Idealismus.* Leipzig:
    Verlag von Felix Meiner.
Irigaray, Luce. 1985 [1977]. *This Sex Which Is Not One.* Translated by Catherine
    Porter. Ithaca, N.Y.: Cornell University Press.
————. 1993 [1984]. *An Ethics of Sexual Difference.* Translated by Carolyn
    Burke and Gillian C. Gill. Ithaca, N.Y.: Cornell University Press.
————. 1993 [1990]. *Je, tu, nous: Toward a Culture of Difference.* Translated
    by Alison Martin. London and New York: Routledge.
————. 1993 [1987]. *Sexes and Genealogies.* Translated by Gillian C. Gill.
    New York: Columbia University Press.
————. 1994. "A Natal Lacuna," *Women's Art Magazine* 58, 11–13.
————. 1996 [1992]. *I Love to You: Sketch of a Possible Felicity in History.*
    Translated by Alison Martin. London and New York: Routledge.
————. 2000 [1994]. *Democracy Begins Between Two.* Translated by Kirsteen
    Anderson. London: Athlone Press.
Kant, Immanuel. 1987 [1793]. *Critique of Judgment.* Translated by Werner S.
    Pluhar. Indianapolis: Hackett Publishing Company.
Klee, Paul. 1968. *The Diaries of Paul Klee, 1898–1918.* Edited by Felix Klee.
    Berkeley and Los Angeles: University of California Press.
Lyotard, Jean-François. 1991 [1988]. *The Inhuman.* Translated by Geoffrey
    Bennington and Rachel Bowlby. Stanford, Calif.: Stanford University
    Press.
Marx, Karl. 1988 [1930]. *Economic and Philosophic Manuscripts of 1844.* Trans-
    lated by Martin Milligan. Amherst, N.Y.: Prometheus Books.
Miller, Elaine. 2002. *The Vegetative Soul: From Philosophy of Nature to Subjec-
    tivity in the Feminine.* Albany: State University of New York Press.
Paetzold, Heinz. 1997. "Adorno's Notion of Natural Beauty: A Reconsidera-
    tion." In *The Semblance of Subjectivity: Essays in Adorno's Aesthetic*

Theory. Edited by Tom Huhn and Lambert Zuidervaart. Cambridge, Mass.: MIT Press.

Robinson, Hilary. 1994. "Irigaray's Imaginings," *Women's Art Magazine* 61, 20.

Stone, Alison. 2003. "The Sex of Nature: A Reinterpretation of Irigaray's Metaphysics and Political Thought," *Hypatia* 18:3, 60f.

Whitford, Margaret. 1994. "Woman With Attitude," *Women's Art Magazine* 60, 15–17.

Wolin, Richard. 1994. *Walter Benjamin: An Aesthetic of Redemption*. Berkeley and Los Angeles: University of California Press.

VISION, RECOGNITION,

AND A PASSION FOR THE ELEMENTS

Kelly Oliver

Throughout her work, Irigaray has been concerned about our connection to materiality or the elements that make all experience possible. She has criticized Western culture for forgetting the elements to which we owe our lives. She has forcefully argued that this forgetting revolves around the erasure of sexual difference at the heart of Western culture, an erasure that gives rise to one sex—the masculine—defining the role of the other—the feminine—as existing for him and not in herself. The materiality of our existence is continually forgotten, appropriated, usurped, and enslaved because of its association with the feminine/maternal and vice versa, which, within patriarchal culture, exists for man and not in itself. Irigaray's insistence on the elemental throughout her work sustains and transforms her critical relation to the notions of vision and recognition in Western philosophy. If we examine her remarks on vision from her early works—*Speculum; This Sex Which Is Not One; An Ethics of Sexual Difference*—through her latest works—*I Love to You* and *To Be Two*—, we will see that although vision is still central to her thinking and she continues to focus on the materiality of vision, while in her earlier work she criticizes the priority of vision in western thinking, in her later work she suggests a reconception of vision as a loving look that can inform an ethics and politics of vision.

In her first book, *Speculum of the Other Woman* (Irigaray 1985 [1974]), Irigaray rails against the masculinist privileging of vision in

Freud and Plato. She argues that, for Freud, "*nothing to be seen is equivalent to having no thing. No being* and *no truth.* The contract, the collusion, between *one* sex/organ and the victory won by visual dominance therefore leaves woman with her sexual void, with an 'actual castration' carried out in actual fact" (Irigaray 1985 [1974], 48). She levies a similar criticism on Plato's allegory of the cave when she argues that he has forgotten the cave/womb as generatrix and substitutes an "unbegotten begetter" born out of the specular economy that unites the soul, the eye, and the eye of the soul, what she calls a "speculogamy" and a "specular suto-gamy" because it reproduces its self same (Irigaray 1985 [1974], 294). In her next book, *This Sex Which Is Not One,* Irigaray continues to challenge the priority of vision over touch, which she associates with the priority of masculine over feminine: "Within this logic, the predominance of the visual, of the discrimination of form and individualization of form, is particularly foreign to female eroticism. Woman takes pleasure more from touching than from looking, and her entry into a dominant scopic economy signifies, again, her consignment to passivity . . ." (Irigaray 1985 [1977], 25–26).

If her early works *Speculum* and *This Sex Which Is Not One* substitute touch for vision because touch engages the fluidity of the body while vision fixes and objectifies bodies with its gaze, her work from the 1980s renegotiates the relation between vision and touch. In *The Ethics of Sexual Difference* (Irigaray 1993 [1984]), she acknowledges her debt to Merleau-Ponty and Levinas by critically analyzing the connection between vision, touch, and sexual difference in their philosophies. Even though she criticizes Merleau-Ponty for reducing touch, to vision and she objects that vision needs touch but touch doesn't need vision and therefore the senses aren't reversible (Irigaray 1993 [1984], 162), she is indebted to him for her notion of a tactile look and the connection between vision and touch.[1] And even though she criticizes Levinas for making woman a mere object of the caress, she is indebted to him for her notion of the look as a caress.

In *The Visible and the Invisible,* Merleau-Ponty describes palpitations of the eyes as analogous to tactile palpitations in a vision-touch system (Merleau-Ponty 1968). "Vision is a palpitation with the look" (Merleau-Ponty 1968, 134) and the world is visible because it is tactile. Vision is dependent upon tactility and the necessary connection, even reversibility, between the body and the visible world. For Merleau-Ponty the corporeality of the visible world is the connective tissue that nourishes and sustains the possibility of seeing. He describes vision in terms of thickness, corpuscles, tissues, grains, waves, channels, circuits, currents, embryos, and pregnancy, the very corporeality out of which sensation, thought, and language are born. As part of the vision-touch system, vision is proximal in that it is possible because our flesh touches the flesh of the world. It is possible because the world also has flesh. Vision touches the world and people in it not in order to fix it or them in the gaze. Rather, for Merleau-Ponty, vision is movement, more like a caress than a grip, more like a motion picture than a photograph (Merleau-Ponty 1964, 162). And space is thick with the flesh of the world.

At once taking and turning from Merleau-Ponty, Levinas makes a distinction between touch as palpation and touch as caress. To get beyond the subject-object hierarchy, he suggests that we also have to get beyond the notion of touch as palpation. Touch is not intentional and rather than return me to myself, it takes me out of myself toward the other (Levinas 1993, 119). As a caress, touch has no object. A caress *is* relationship and not its aim or medium. Levinas says that "what is caressed is not touched" (Levinas 1987, 89). The caress cannot possess the other or the relationship. "In starting with *touching*," he says, "interpreted not as palpation but as caress, and *language*, interpreted not as the traffic of information but as contact, we have tried to describe proximity as irreducible to consciousness and thematization. . . . Incapable of remaining in a theme and of appearing, this invisibility that becomes contact does not result from the nonsignifyingness of what is approached but rather from a way of signifying wholly other than that of exhibition from a *beyond* the visible" (Levinas 1996, 80; cf. 1991, 100). Even Merleau-Ponty's palpation is too subject-centered for Levinas. The caress, on the other hand, does not take place between subjects and objects. And all sensibility, even vision, begins with caress: "sensibility must be interpreted as touch first of all . . . The visible caresses the eye. One sees and one hears like one touches" (Levinas 1993, 118). Working through Merleau-Ponty and Levinas, Irigaray begins to reconceive of vision rather than merely challenge its priority. Indeed, in her later works— *I Love to You* (Irigaray 1996 [1992]), *To Be Two* (Irigaray 2001 [1994])— vision, the gaze and the eye become essential elements in her theory of intersubjectivity; there she develops what I will call a loving look or the look of love.[2] Irigaray's introduction of love into the look suggests that what in her earlier work appears as a concern with the

materiality of the senses and priority given to vision over touch becomes in her later work the ground for a reconceived ethics and
politics of vision.

Irigaray's move from challenging the priority of vision in her
early work to reformulating the notion of vision is enabled by her
emphasis on the materiality of vision, most notably in her book on
Heidegger, *The Forgetting of Air* (Irigaray 1999 [1983]). It is her concern for the materiality of vision that most centrally links her earlier
and later work around the themes of vision, gaze, and look. At around
the same time that she is reformulating the relationship between vision and touch, and moving from rejecting vision as masculinist to
reconceiving of vision as sensation, she becomes more intensely focused on the materiality and density of air, and the elements generally, which make vision and all sensation possible. In addition to her
focus on air in *Elemental Passions* (Irigaray 1992 [1981]) and especially
in *The Forgetting of Air*, in *Marine Lover* (Irigaray 1991 [1980]), she
argues that Nietzsche forgets water.[3]

My intention, however, is not to develop a chronological account of Irigaray's philosophy of vision or materiality, but rather to use
her insistence on materiality not only to explain her move away from
criticizing vision per se towards a new theory of vision, but also to
explore and develop this new vision and its implications for thinking
about subjectivity and ethics. Although her criticisms of the priority
of vision in her early work are associated with her attention to the
elements, and although she mentions the elements, especially air, in
passages associated with vision, she does not present an analysis of
how her focus on the elemental necessarily gives rise to a new conception of vision. Using Irigaray's attention to the elemental as a
starting place, I am interested in developing a new theory of vision
that can ground Irigaray's more recent thoughts on intersubjectivity,
particularly her carnal theory of vision and recognition.[4]

Irigaray's insistence on the importance of the role of material
elements in vision, perception, thought, and philosophy in general
suggests a new direction for theories of recognition and intersubjective
relations. Throughout her work, she is concerned to recall and remember the material elements—water, earth, fire, and air—out of
which we are born and through which we live, together. In *Marine
Lover of Friedrich Nietzsche* (Irigaray 1991 [1980]), she reminds us of
the importance of water, fluids, especially those out of which we were
born. In *Forgetting of Air in Martin Heidegger* (Irigaray 1999 [1983]),

she suggests that air has a special place among the elements: "Is not air the whole of our habitation as mortals? Is there a dwelling more vast, more spacious, or even more generally peaceful that that of air? Can man live elsewhere than in air? Neither in earth, nor in fire, nor in water is any habitation possible for him" (Irigaray 1999 [1983], 8). Can we expand Irigaray's theories of air and light to develop a new conception of vision that can give birth to a new conception of relationships beyond subject-object/other hierarchies?

Although Irigaray is indebted to Emmanuel Levinas and Maurice Merleau-Ponty in her attempts to reformulate the role of vision in relation to subjectivity, she takes us beyond their theories. For our purposes here, suffice it to say that, unlike Levinas, rather than favoring touch over vision because traditional theories of vision presuppose subjects dominating their objects, Irigaray also tries to reconceive of vision; and, unlike Merleau-Ponty, Irigaray refuses to fuse vision and touch, and instead insists that they cannot be reduced one to the other.[5] In her book *Textures of Light* (Vasseleu 1998), Cathryn Vasseleu argues that Irigaray goes further than either Merleau-Ponty or Levinas towards developing an alternative theory of vision by developing an alternative vision of light as textured. Rather than reduce vision to touch, which is one of her (debatable) criticisms of Merleau-Ponty, Irigaray emphasizes the touch of light on the eye. For Irigaray, it is not, then, that vision and touch are not separate senses, but rather that vision is dependent upon the sense of touch.

Vasseleu argues that conceiving of light's texture challenges the traditional separation of the senses that serves the separation of sensible and intelligible. The separation between sensible and intelligible, between body and mind or soul, has been constructed around the notion of the mind's eye and an immaterial seeing cut off from the body and sensation, a more accurate seeing. The split between the mind's eye and the body's eye is interlaced with the split between objective theoretical knowledge and subjective personal feeling. Objective theoretical knowledge requires a notion of vision as a distancing sense that separates the mind's eye from the body and gives it a privileged perspective devoid of contaminating sentiment. Information gathered through touch and more proximal senses is thought to provide only subjective feeling and cannot be grounds for knowledge (Vasseleu 1998, 12).[6]

If, on Irigaray's theory, however, vision involves touching light, then we are touched by, and touching, everything around us even as we see the distance between ourselves and the world or other people in the world. The texture or fabric of vision is even more tightly woven than Merleau-Ponty's reversible flesh (cf. Merleau-Ponty, 1968). It is not just that the fabric of vision is reversible between subject and object, invisible and visible, ideal and material; rather, the texture of vision is the result of an interweaving of elements both distinct and intimately connected in their sensuous contact. The texture of light is what is between us and other people in the world. We are both connected and made distinct by the texture of light that wraps us in the luxury and excesses of the world.

In addition to what Vasseleu calls the texture of light, Irigaray's insistence on material elements, especially air, provokes us to rethink vision in terms of its dependence upon the density of air, upon the elements. Irigaray concludes her *Elemental Passions* with an ode to the density of air: "I opened my eyes and saw the cloud. And saw that nothing was perceptible unless I was held at a distance from it by an almost palpable density. And that I saw it and did not see it. *Seeing it all the better for remembering the density of air remaining in between.* But this resistance of air being revealed, I felt something akin to the possibility of a different discovery of myself" (Irigaray 1992 [1981], 105; emphasis added). Space is not empty because it is filled with the density of air. And the density of air connects and separates everything on earth. Remembering air and the density of air reminds me that I am both connected to and different from those around me. Remembering what cannot be seen, the density of air, allows me to better see the difference and communion between myself and others. Seeing what is different from me and what is between me and difference opens the possibility of a different discovery of myself, a discovery that is not the hostile Hegelian struggle for recognition and is not based on the paranoia of the Sartrian accusing look or the Lacanian evil eye.[7]

Irigaray's most sustained reflections on air and the density of air are in *Forgetting of Air in Martin Heidegger* (Irigaray 1999 [1983]). There she takes Heidegger to task for forgetting the air that makes possible any clearing, being, or Being of being. Leaving behind the context of her criticisms of Heidegger, which is interesting in itself, I am interested in her descriptions of air and how they can help reconceive of vision. Throughout *Forgetting of Air*, Irigaray suggests that the philosopher has forgotten air and thereby forgotten that he is nourished and supported by air. By forgetting air, the philosopher imagines

that he is thrown into an empty abyss where he confronts only nothingness (Irigaray 1999 [1983], 98, 137, 147, 157, 162, 166, 169). The
abyss, she reminds us, is not empty; it is full of air. And air is not
nothing. The philosopher's supposition that we are alienated from the
earth or others by an abyss is the product of what Irigaray calls the
"forgetting of air" (Irigaray 1999 [1983]). She says that "the elementality
of *physis*—air, water, earth, fire—is always already reduced to nothingness in and by his own element: his language" (Irigaray 1999 [1983],
74). Irigaray asks what happens when the philosopher focuses on the
things within air and forgets air itself: "And what becomes of air when
the being appears within it? It is reduced to nothingness" (Irigaray
1999 [1983], 162). By forgetting the elements, the philosopher forgets
that space is not empty. By forgetting that space is not empty, the
space between us and others or our own image seems unbridgeable,
empty, alienating. But what if space is full and not empty?

Even light is dependent upon air. The texture of light cannot
touch without the air that opens onto that touch. Vision, speech, and
life itself require air. In response to Heidegger, Irigaray says "it is not
light that creates the clearing, but light comes about only in virtue of
the transparent levity of air. Light presupposes air. No sun without air
to welcome and transmit its rays. No speech without air to convey it.
Day and night, voice and silence, appear and disappear in air. The
extent of space, the horizons of time, and all that becomes present
and absent within them are to be found gathered together in air as in
some fundamental thing. The originary intuition of which recedes
indefinitely. Free beyond all vision. Dwelling out of sight. . . . And
thought attains the heart of this assembly only by assimilating itself
to this serene spatiality—air" (Irigaray 1999 [1983], 166-67). The
serene spatiality that is air cannot be seen and yet there is no seeing
without it. It fills space with the plentitude of life.

For Irigaray, air occupies a unique place among the elements in
that it is place. She says that "[n]o other element can for him take the
place of place. No other element carries with it—or lets itself be
passed through by—light and shadow, voice or silence. . . . No other
element is in this way space prior to all localization and a substratum
both immobile and mobile, permanent and flowing, where multiple
temporal divisions remain forever possible. Doubtless, no other element is as originarily constitutive of the whole of the world, without
this generativity ever coming to completion in a primordial time, in
a singular primacy, in an autarchy, in an autonomy, in a unique or

exclusive property" (Irigaray 1999 [1983], 8). Air generates life but without hierarchy, genealogy, domination, or ownership. More than this, Irigaray marvels at the way that air gives without demanding anything in return: "But this element, irreducibly constitutive of the whole, compels neither the faculty of perception nor that of knowledge to recognize it. Always there, it allows itself to be forgotten" (Irigaray 1999 [1983], 8). The recognition of this giving without demand for recognition is what opens the possibility of a different discovery of myself in relation to what gives me life and nourishes me. Irigaray's discussion of gifts and indebtedness to the elements and mediums of perception adds an ethical dimension to vision. She suggests that because we see and live in and by air and light, we have an ethical obligation to the earth and sky. Our indebtedness is not the debt of some economic exchange that must be paid off in full or in kind; rather, our indebtedness can only be acknowledged through wonder, marvel, love, and care (Irigaray 1999 [1983], 28; cf. 1980, 1984, 1992, 1994).

Irigaray proposes that remembering air and the gift of life that it gives provides us with another way of looking. The look is no longer the philosopher's gaze that rips opens and penetrates the other or fixes us in its piercing intensity. Reminiscent of Merleau-Ponty, she says that the look is the look of the flesh living in and off the air (Irigaray 1999 [1983], 116). The flesh does not respond to the demanding gaze of the philosopher but to the loving look of another body. Irigaray's poetry suggests this alternative: "The flesh sources indefinitely, never moving away from the setting that gives rise to it. The flesh opens, petal after petal, in an efflorescence that does not come about for the look, without for all that avoiding the look. These blooms are not seen. Unless by another sort of look? A look that allows itself to be touched by the birth of forms that are not exposed in the bright light of day? Yet, nonetheless, are there. Invisible substrate for the constitution of the visible. These gifts give themselves in the direction of an outside that does not cross the threshold of appearance. They suffuse the look without being noticed by sight. Irrigation by a sense-intuition that flows back and forth from the flesh to the look, from the look to the flesh, with neither the ek-stasis that attends a contemplation that has been resolved, nor a confinement in lack of light. Irradiances that imperceptibly illuminate" (Irigaray 1999 [1983], 116).

The unseen source of sight is a sensuous caress that touches and is touched by another sort of look, a tactile look that does not pry or gaze, but caresses in the flow of irrigation and irradiances. This look that sees without seeing, this look that touches the unseen substrate of the visible, seems to be an immersion in the ebb and flow of the moving elements that give birth to and nourish sensation and therefore thought, vision, and visions. A loving look becomes the inauguration of "subjectivity" without subjects or objects. Irigaray suggests that the loving look involves all of the senses and refuses the separation between visible and invisible (Irigaray 2001 [1994], 42). A body in love cannot be fixed as an object (Irigaray 2001 [1994], 42). The look of love sees the invisible in the visible; both spiritual and carnal, the look of love is of "neither subject nor object" (Irigaray 2001 [1994], 42). Irigaray describes the look of love as that which brings us together through our difference by virtue of both embodiment and transcendence: "Perhaps loving each other requires that we look at the invisible, to abandon the sight of it to the breath of the heart, of the soul, that we preserve it in its carnality, without staring upon it fixedly as a target" (Irigaray 2001 [1994], 42).

Perhaps it is in *To Be Two* that Irigaray's attention to air is most explicitly connected to a vision of the invisible as a vision of ethical intersubjectivity. Irigaray begins the book with an ode to Earth and concludes it with an ode to Air. Air is what separates us and thereby makes relationships between us possible. It is the between that brings us together as distinct individuals: "Air, . . . you who flow between one and the other but without destroying either's boundaries proper, you who respect the skin and nourish it, and who procure the medium for every contact . . . you without whom we cannot touch each other . . . whose distance allows us to approach each other. . . ." (Irigaray 2001 [1994], 116, cf. 2, 6, 10, 11). Irigaray calls air "a living being, a bridge, a relationship" (Irigaray 2001 [1994], 5). In *To Be Two* it is this third being, the air or element itself, that makes a relationship between two possible without one assimilating or annihilating the other.

Here the gaze is always mediated by this third element, by air; and this mediation insures that the gaze cannot capture or objectify the other. This gaze sees beyond the visible to the invisible elements between two and within the other. This is not to say that this is an omnipotent gaze; to the contrary, this gaze recognizes and acknowledges that it cannot see. In this sense, love is blind . . . not because the lover overlooks the faults of her beloved and doesn't see him clearly, but because "only love consents to a night in which I will never know you. Between those who love each other, there is a veil"

(Irigaray 2001 [1994], 9). Yet "the eyes are a bridge between us" and this veil, this crucial mediation that enables love and desire, is available through the visible and its very limitations: "Looking at the other, respecting the invisible in him, opens a black or blinding void in the universe. Beginning from this limit, inappropriable to my gaze, the world is recreated" (Irigaray 2001 [1994], 47, 9). It is recreated as love. The loving gaze that sees beyond the visible is not a harsh or accusing stare. Rather, affective psychic energy circulates through loving looks. Loving looks nourish and sustain the psyche, the soul, as well as the body.

Irigaray's formulation of what I am calling the loving look as an alternative to the objectifying look, and her reformulation of recognition beyond domination through love, suggest that the ethical and political power of love can be used to overcome oppression. If objectification is essential to domination and oppression, and love can bring us together outside of the hierarchy of subject/object/other, then relations beyond domination are possible. "The caress does not seek to dominate a hostile freedom" (Irigaray 1993 [1984], 188). In the caresses of love, there is no subject or object/other. The caress is the between, both carnal and divine, both sensible and transcendental. As such, the caress, and the look as caress, do not fix an object for a subject, but open a realm in which the two remain two but cannot be separated. Irigaray insists that "the other of sexual difference is each time contiguous and transcendent to me, and subjective and objective; he is matter and spirit, body and intention, inclinations and liberty" (Irigaray 2001 [1994], 165). Love and difference take place in between. Love does not exist without difference. And difference is not recognized beyond recognition without love.

Rather than trying to think outside of a Hegelian notion of recognition by abandoning recognition altogether, Irigaray reconceives of recognition as a connection between two different sexes. In I Love to You (Irigaray 1996 [1992]), she describes an alternative non-hierarchical recognition that does not and cannot dominate the other. She argues that to recognize another person requires that neither party is the One against the Other nor the Whole against its part (Irigaray 1996 [1992], 103). We cannot recognize that of which we are a part, whether it is the Whole or the One. Therefore, recognition requires two who are not greater or lesser than each other, not master and slave. Yet, these two are also not equivalent; their differences cannot be sublimated in a Hegelian dialectic. They cannot be substituted for each other or reduced one to the other: "I recognize you goes hand in hand with: you are irreducible to me, just as I am to you. We may not be substituted for one another" (Irigaray 1996 [1992], 103). Recognition requires that we are two different beings, inaccessible to each other, and yet able to communicate because of what is between us.

Communication does not demand subordination or assimilation. It does not require a master-slave relationship. But, "in order to avoid master(s)/slave(s) relations," says Irigaray, "we have to practice a different sort of recognition from the one marked by hierarchy, and thus also by genealogy" (Irigaray 1996 [1992], 105). Difference that is irreducible cannot be categorized or prioritized according to hierarchy or genealogy because it cannot be reduced to one system. Irigaray argues that when difference is recognized as irreducible "the power of the one over the other will be no more. Difference that is irreducible never ceases to curb the capitalization of any such power, of mere authority over" (Irigaray 1996 [1992], 105). For difference to be recognized as irreducible, it must be recognized as beyond recognition.

Irigaray suggests that we are different and that we can communicate because of what, following Hegel, she calls the "labor of the negative" between us. Most simply, the labor of the negative is the labor of limitation. Each individual has its limits that define it in relation to others. While these limits cannot be penetrated, they enable rather than disable communication: "I recognize you is the one condition for the existence of I, you and we . . . This *we* is the work of the negative, that which cannot be substituted between us, the transcendence between us. It is constituted by subjects irreducible one to the other, each one to the others, and thus capable of communicating out of freedom and necessity" (Irigaray 1996 [1992], 104).

We is the result of a recognition of our limitations that bring us together. Gender is one of our primary limitations in the sense that we cannot know the other gender (Irigaray 1996 [1992], 106). Irigaray goes so far as to say that the limitation of gender might serve as a third term in the psychoanalytic sense, which implies that the paternal function or law of the father is not necessarily the only third term that brings with it the possibility of social relations (Irigaray 1996 [1992], 106). It is through our limitations, or the labor of the negative between us, that we come together. It is through a recognition of our limits that we become social beings capable of relationships. For Irigaray, limit and limitations do not have *negative* connotations because the negative itself is reworked as a positive labor, a giving birth. She says that "Recognizing you gives me measure. Because you are, you impose limits upon me. I am whole, perhaps, but not the whole. And if I receive myself from you, I receive myself as me" (Irigaray 2001 [1994], 15). If recognition conceived as a recognition of sameness makes any relationship between two (or more) and therefore any ethics or politics impossible, recognizing our differences and the limits or boundaries that separate us makes an ethics and politics of love possible.

Irigaray says that it is the "negative that enables me to go towards you" (Irigaray 1996 [1992], 104). It is the negative in the sense of the phrases "I cannot know you," "I cannot be you," "I will never master you," that allows for relationships beyond domination, beyond recognition. As soon as I am sure that I know you, that I know what you will do next, I have stopped having a relationship with you and instead have a relationship with myself, with my own projection onto you. When I think that I know you, our relationship is over.

Unlike more traditional theories of recognition, the notion of recognition that Irigaray proposes is not connected to vision or seeing someone.[8] In fact, for her, recognition is acknowledgment of that which cannot be seen in vision, the invisible or beyond recognition. This recognition is not a recognition of sameness but precisely a recognition of difference. It is not a recognition of my mastery or a recognition that gives me mastery but, on the contrary, a recognition that recalls my limits and the boundaries of myself. For Irigaray, recognition is not based on seeing the otherness of the other and overcoming that otherness through assimilation or sublimation of the otherness within myself. Rather, recognition begins and ends with seeing the otherness of the other. This "seeing" requires fluidity between the visible and the invisible. What I recognize when I recognize the other is, in an important sense, beyond recognition.

It is precisely what we do not see that attracts us to each other: "I recognize you supposes that I cannot see right through you. You will never be entirely visible to me, but thanks to that, I respect you as different from me. What I do not see of you draws me toward you . . . I go towards you as towards that which I shall not see but which attracts me" (Irigaray 1996 [1992], 104). Recognition is a form of love that requires witnessing to that which is beyond recognition, witnessing to what cannot be seen. For Irigaray, love is witnessing to that which is *between* us, the invisible bond created through the labor of the negative, which is not nothing. In order to emphasize the between in love, Irigaray insists on saying *I love to you* rather than *I love you.* The *to* adds the dimension of movement and the in between *I* and *you* missing from the formulation that sounds as if my love can assimilate you (Irigaray 1996 [1992], 109–13).

Irigaray proposes love outside of domination as a nonhierarchical love between two. She emphasizes the between, which both connects and separates the lovers. This negative limit, which is not a negation, sets up the boundaries necessary to imagine a nontotalizing love across difference. She imagines a love that does not fix a beloved as an object, a love that does not reduce one to the other, love as a dynamic movement towards another: *I love to you.* She suggests that by reconceiving love, we can transform ethical, social, and political relations. Indeed, in order to transform ethical, social, and political relations, it is necessary to reconceive of love.

The love imagined by Irigaray is beyond recognition. Her discourse of love would challenge many, if not most, of our contemporary cultural representations of love. The notion of love itself—the experience of love and its representations, which cannot be separated—must be open to social and political transformation. Love too must be reinterpreted and elaborated, especially in terms of its performative dimension. What is love beyond domination? Love beyond domination is necessarily a critical love that recognizes its own limitations. On Irigaray's analysis, it is only through coming to terms with our own limitations that we can love an other without domination or assimilation. We can love an other as other only through vigilant self-limitation. This vigilant self-critical process of interpretation of our own limitations is not a sacrifice of ourselves to the other; rather, if anything, it is an acknowledgment of our indebtedness to others and otherness. This love within limits is clearly not traditional romantic love through which one or both lover and beloved are assimilated. Irigaray imagines moving beyond the subject-object dualism without simply assimilating difference to the same. Rather, she imagines love by virtue of difference, love that has become ethical and political.

NOTES

1. Irigaray's criticism of Merleau-Ponty may not be fair in that he does not claim that touch can be assimilated into vision or that one sense can be reduced to another. Rather, he argues that the senses are interrelated and always work together to produce sensation and perception (cf. Grosz

1993). For Merleau-Ponty, vision is tactile in that it is analogous to touch and dependent on it. On my reading, Irigaray's thesis that vision is founded on touch seems to echo rather than contradict Merleau-Ponty. For another interesting comparison between senses, see Irigaray's discussion of the connection between sight and sound in "Flesh Colors" in *Sexes and Genealogies* (1987). There, Irigaray argues that sight and sound operate in different registers and yet she endorses bringing them together to talk about the color of sound and the sounds of colors.

2. *To Be Two* was written in Italian and originally published in Italy in 1994. The English translation is from this Italian original. Irigaray has also written *To Be Two* in French, published as *Être deux* (1997).

3. For a discussion of Marine Lover, see my *Womanizing Nietzsche: Philosophy's Relation to the "Feminine"* (1995).

4. For an attempt to develop this new theory of vision out of an Irigarian sense of the elements, see my *Witnessing: Beyond Recognition* (2001).

5. I develop this claim in *Witnessing: Beyond Recognition* (2001).

6. Martin Jay's analysis of the nobility and then denigration of vision in philosophy substantiates this analysis (1994).

7. In *Witnessing*, I analyze Sartre and Lacan's notion of the gaze in relation to Irigaray's (Oliver 2001).

8. For a discussion of the connection between theories of recognition and a particular theory of vision, see my *Witnessing* (2001).

WORKS CITED

Grosz, Elizabeth. 1993. *Merleau-Ponty and Irigaray in the Flesh. Thesis 11*, no. 36:44, 37–59.

Irigaray, Luce. 1985 [1974]. *Speculum of the Other Woman*. Translated by Gillian Gill. Ithaca, N.Y.: Cornell University Press.

———. 1985 [1977]. *This Sex Which Is Not One*. Translated by Catherine Porter. Ithaca, N.Y.: Cornell University Press.

———. 1991 [1980]. *Marine Lover of Friedrich Nietzsche*. Translated by Gillian Gill. New York: Columbia University Press.

———. 1992 [1982]. *Elemental Passions*. Translated by Joanne Collie and Judith Still. New York: Routledge.

———. 1993 [1984]. *An Ethics of Sexual Difference*. Translated by Carolyn Burke and Gillian Gill. Ithaca, N.Y.: Cornell University Press.

———. 1993 [1987]. *Sexes and Genealogies*. Translated by Gillian Gill. New York: Columbia University Press.

———. 1996 [1992]. *I Love to You*. Translated by Alison Martin. New York: Routledge.

———. 1997. *Être deux*. Paris: Grasset.

———. 1999 [1983]. *Forgetting of Air in Martin Heidegger*. Translated by Mary Beth Mader. Austin: University of Texas Press.

————. 2001 [1994]. *To Be Two*. Translated by Monique Rhodes and Marco Cocito-Monoc. New York: Routledge.

Jay, Martin. 1994. *Downcast Eyes: The Denigration of Vision in Twentieth-Century French Thought*. Berkeley and Los Angeles: University of California Press.

Levinas, Emmanuel. 1969. *Totality and Infinity*. Translated by Alphonso Lingis. Pittsburgh: Duquesne University Press.

————. 1987. *Time and the Other*. Translated by Richard Cohen. Pittsburgh: Duquesne University Press.

————. 1989. *The Levinas Reader*. Edited by Seán Hand. Cambridge, Mass.: Blackwell Publishers.

————. 1991. *Otherwise Than Being*. Translated by Alphonso Lingis. Boston: Nijoff.

————. 1993. *Collected Philosophical Papers*. Translated by Alphonso Lingis. Boston: Kluwer Academic Publishers.

————. 1996. *Emmanuel Levinas: Basic Philosophical Writings*. Edited by Adrian Peperzak, Simon Critchley, and Robert Bernasconi. Bloomington, Ind.: Indiana University Press.

Merleau-Ponty, Maurice. 1962. *Phenomenology of Perception*. Translated by Colin Smith. London: Routledge.

————. 1964. *The Primacy of Perception*. Edited by James Edie. Evanston, Ill.: Northwestern University Press.

————. 1968. *The Visible and the Invisible*. Translated by Alphonso Lingis. Evanston, Ill.: Northwestern University Press.

Oliver, Kelly. 1995. *Womanizing Nietzsche: Philosophy's Relation to "the Feminine."* New York: Routledge.

————. 2001. *Witnessing: Beyond Recognition*. Minneapolis, Minn.: University of Minnesota Press.

Vasseleu, Cathryn. 1998. *Textures of Light: Vision and Touch in Irigaray, Levinas and Merleau-Ponty*. London: Routledge.

BETWEEN EAST AND WEST AND THE POLITICS OF 'CULTURAL INGÉNUITÉ': IRIGARAY ON CULTURAL DIFFERENCE

Penelope Deutscher

With the 1999 publication of *Entre Occident et Orient* (*Between East and West*) (2002 [1999]) Irigaray introduces her politics of cultural difference. To some extent the work reiterates Irigaray's depiction of sexual difference as universal. It claims that sex binarism runs through all races, cultures and traditions. However, *Between East and West* argues that we should recognize and cultivate relations of sexual difference because they will contribute to a plural and multicultural community. Multiculturalism becomes for the philosopher of sexual difference the overall focus in relation to which sexual difference takes on a more instrumental status. *Between East and West* speculates that a culture of sexual difference would facilitate improved relations between those of different cultures, races and traditions. Following Irigaray's previous fleeting comments in this regard, she now develops the argument more fully.

Many critics have questioned the cultural and race-blindness of Irigaray's work. Gail Weiss affirms that, "To the extent that Irigaray is suggesting that each of us should be a horizon of significance for the other, it is clear that this claim does not and should not apply only to relationships between the sexes." Weiss proposes that, in addition to same-sex relations Irigaray's claim should be extended to "individuals of different races" (Weiss 1999, 82). It might seem that the publication of *Between East and West* represents just this possibility.

In the work, Irigaray speaks for a politics of cultural *ingénuité* (1999, 14; 2002, 5). As she uses the term, it has the connotations of being both ingenuous and the ingenious. It is the aptitude for growth, invention and construction in addition to the stance of *naïveté*, a foetus-like openness to the new, 'to be born to my life' (Irigaray, 2002 [1999], 5). Irigaray recommends that we actively cultivate the conditions for living with the possible differences of other cultures, taking such active cultivation to be a social good. She argues that we currently lack these conditions, lacking a politics that values difference. We tend to suboordinate our respect for the other to a benchmark of sameness represented by Western whiteness (Irigaray 2002 [1999], 145). Irigaray is particularly suspicious of public professions of enthusiasm for multiculturalism. We believe in equality, and, she argues, we also believe that we are all a little bit masculine and feminine, and a little bit multicultural. We may even think we are post-gender, or post-race. But models of equality or neutrality are dubious,

> To make the Black equal to the White, the woman equal to the man, is still to submit them, under cover of paternalist generosity, to models put in place by Western man, who resists living together with the different. He even accepts becoming a little Black or a little female rather than going through a revolution of thinking that is today unavoidable. (Irigaray 2002 [1999], 127)

To see all humans—men and women—as a little bit feminine or masculine, or all humans—black and white—as a little bit colonized, a little bit colonizer, is in her view, problematic. Such models imply that we are all fundamentally similar, and strips out the real difficulty of living with difference. She argues that these are fundamentally integrationist models in which difference is submerged to sameness. In addition, even when it may seem otherwise, the ethos of similarity levels potential differences to a white Western and masculine reference point. Irigaray proposes that we cultivate a new and positive philosophical basis for living with difference and diversity given that we still lack 'a culture of between-sexes [*inter-sexes*], between-races [*inter-races*], of between-traditions [*inter-traditions*]' (Irigaray 2002 [1999], 139).

The problem with the account of the between [*inter*], is that it seems to erect as a monolith the notion of culture. Culture seems to be rendered homogenous, and difference seems to be deemed that which lies 'between' cultures. We can only speculate about whom Irigaray may have in mind with her negative depictions of the politics which claims that we are all a little bit black, white, male, female, colonizer, colonized. The intent of such depictions may be to interrupt the suggestion that we belong to a monolithic and fully realized gender, culture, or sexuality. But Irigaray's response is that the love of a metaphorics of fragmentation does in the end collapse into a return of the love of sameness. These fragmented bodies are, she thinks, considered fundamentally akin in their fragmentation.

Another objection Irigaray aims at multiculturalism concerns the tension between the apparently espoused value of difference, and the prevalent ideology of integration. In this sense also, multiculturalism tends to favor the assimilation of difference (Irigaray 2002 [1999], 134). This is seen in both conceptual and political manifestations. One example she provides of the latter is the European Community, which while sometimes associated with an ideology of inclusive multiculturalism, has also been connected to a wholesale depiction of immigration in terms of crisis—a crisis dominated by the language of possible (or impossible) integration of foreigners (Irigaray 2002 [1999], 135). Having criticized many manifestations of multicultural ideology, Irigaray offers an alternative deployment of the multicultural as an emblem of the basic social unit.

Earlier in her work, the couple formed by a man and a woman had represented the emblem of a positive difference on which community could be founded,[1] to replace the raceless sexless individual (Irigaray, 1996 [1992]). In *Between East and West*, the couple formed by a white woman and a black man, the one Catholic and the other Muslim (Irigaray 2002 [1999], 144), is so presented. Irigaray does not argue of this emblematic couple that their cultural and race differences are unimportant; instead, 'difference has nourished desire' (Irigaray 2002 [1999], 136).[2] Imagined thus, this emblematic couple becomes the 'site of civic education' (Irigaray 2002 [1999], 135). Irigaray had previously provided alternatives to the model of community founded in implicit contracts formed by individuals supported by usually invisible family units. She had proposed an imaginary couple as the conceptual basis for community in which positive difference nourishes the attraction of each to the other, rather than the supposition that either is either the complement, the opposite, or can be assimilated to the other. Irigaray now hopes to replace her earlier model of culture as founded on the sexually different couple (implicitly, it had seemed,

assumed to be of the same race) with a model of society as founded
in the existence of citizens whose public and private relations—their
private, familial and public bond—require the constant negotiation of
their own different races and cultures. Many couples consist of individuals whose desire for each other bears little tie to their cultural
background, or are not especially attracted to each other's differences.
Nonetheless, Irigaray takes as a reference point the ideal of a civic
community founded in the supposition that it is constituted of couples
positively negotiating the difference of culture and race:

> From this point of view, [racially and culturally] mixed fami-
> lies represent a key place for the construction of our future
> societies . . . The demands of cultural mixedness [mixité] dis-
> turb our mental habits, our common laws, our legislative cri-
> teria. They compel us to transformations of desire, of thinking,
> to hitherto unheard of civic forms of meeting and cohesion.
> (Irigaray 2002 [1999], 144–45, translation modified)

Between East and West allows readers to ask what resources
Irigaray's work offers for the theorization of differently raced individuals whose racial difference could allow each to serve as a horizon of
significance for the other. One can assess whether this horizon of
significance (in which cultural difference would become the basis for
restructured community and civic life) is imagined according to the
same model offered in Irigaray's theorization of sexual difference. Interestingly, it seems that it is not.

For example, in her discussion of multiculturalism, Irigaray
chooses not to reiterate the politics of performativity and identities-
to-come developed in her theorization of sexual difference. She says
of sexual difference, 'I am thinking of a relation between the sexes in
which a woman and man each have a different subjectivity, based
notably on both a relational identity of their own and a relation to
language of their own [*propre*]' (Irigaray 2002 [1999], 136–37). There
is no equivalent account of differently raced and encultured individuals having different subjectivities and specific relationships to language and identity-[always]-to-come.

Consider the way in which Irigaray emphasizes differences between Asian and Western cultures and religions. *Between East and
West* criticizes western approaches to ecology, nature, the elements,
the senses and embodiment, by contrast to an approach attributed to

'India.' Compare this with her previous discussion of differences between men and women (whose race was not specified, but where the context seemed to be European) in their relation to appropriation, narcissism, mediation, self-abnegation, guilt, hysteria, objectification, consumption, the third party, etc. According to Irigaray, such differences between men and women do not reflect a culture of sexual difference. Instead, they reflect the absence of sexual difference. This point allows us to reflect on the status of sexual difference in her work. Irigarayan sexual difference is not reducible to real differences between men and women. This is partly because the Irigarayan concept is forward-looking, anticipating alternative identity structures for the sexes. It is also because Irigaray criticizes existing identity structure for the sexes, in which women are conceived as the opposite, the complement or the same to a masculine reference point. Irigarayan sexual difference is a hypothetical non-hierarchical field of difference between the sexes. Men and women would situate themselves in the context of an open-ended field of all those belonging to their sexuate *genre*. This sexual contextualization would mediate self-other relations. Present differences between men and women reflect impoverished sexual relations, and the absence, not the existence, of a culture of sexual difference.

To give one example, Irigaray has claimed that masculine discourse is typically self-reflexive.[3] The speaker muses to himself, or to a general other akin to himself. The speaker does not assume that a different other is going to speak back to, or with, him. Typically masculine discourse positions both the 'I' and the 'you' as,

> . . . two unequal parts of the world that are capable neither of exchange nor of alliance . . . This leads to social crises, to individual illnesses, to schematic and fossilized identities for both sexes, as well as to a general sclerosis of discourse, a hardening of language. (Irigaray 1993 [1984], 135)

Irigaray does believe that discourse is sexed, as when she states that,

> . . . anyone who denies that discourse is sexed is advised to carry out a statistical investigation of taped materials and analyze the results. If he still claims to discern no difference, then his or own interpretation would have to be analyzed to see how it reproduces one of the patterns of the taped material,

even, or perhaps especially, in the denials. (Irigaray 1993
[1984], 136)

Though Irigaray takes the sexedness of language to be empiri-
cally irrefutable, the sexedness of discourse is not evidence of the
reality of sexual difference. To the contrary, it is evidence of the
absence of sexual difference in the Irigarayan sense. It demonstrates
that there is no adequate exchange or communication between sexed
subjects. In fact, according to Irigaray, men and women have never
yet adequately communicated (Irigaray 1993 [1984], 140). Her linguistic samples may demonstrate the sexedness of discourse, but they
do not demonstrate adequate sexual difference in our culture. They
demonstrate the contrary. This point contributes to an understanding
of what sexual difference (and difference more generally) are for
Irigaray. She means an ideal, hypothetical, adequate difference, not
the currently impoverished relations between men and women. Is this
the case for other kinds of difference as they are discussed in her
work? What about Irigaray's discussion of cultural difference?

Irigaray offers a highly idealized depiction of the different relationship to embodiment, the mind/body distinction, the emotions,
nature, and sexual difference to be found in Eastern cultures and
religions. The idealization of Eastern cultures interconnects with
Irigaray's denunciation of the West, 'Unfortunately, most patriarchal
philosophical and religious traditions act in this way, they have substituted words for life without carrying out the necessary links between the two' (Irigaray 2002 [1999], 51). Opposing East to West, her
valuation of Eastern cultures can read as an appropriation that bol-
sters her own depreciation of the West[4] and its depreciation of women.
The nuanced dilemma formulated by Gayatri Spivak[5]—according to
whom we must argue both that the subaltern woman can speak and
cannot speak, that one must hear her and one does not hear her—
would be welcome in Irigaray's work. Irigaray is too sure of her ability
to listen to and represent a culture depicted as other. She does not
acknowledge the inevitable differend at the heart of those depictions.

Irigaray's tendency to idealize the East is reminiscent of the idealization of femininity that indicates an impoverished culture of sexual
difference. Her discussion of Asian cultures and religions could be
interpreted (through an extension of her own methodology) as a symptom of the absence, not the presence, of an adequate culture of culture difference.

In short, there is a striking discrepancy between the conception of difference which grounds Irigaray's approaches to race and to sexual difference. She considers that we do not currently live in a culture of sexual difference. The conditions for sexual difference must be created. This gives the impetus to the Irigarayan bill of sexuate rights, for example. Contrast Irigaray's approach to cultural difference, seen by her as a problem of creating the conditions for living with others. In *Between East and West*, her defense of a multicultural integration that does not assimilate difference (Irigaray 2002 [1999], 134) assumes as a viable referent (rather than an open reference to that which is to come) the differences between cultures. In other words, the fact that Irigaray lauds the different conceptions of embodiment, rationality, nature, the elements, the senses, and sexuality in the East over those of the West, indicates more than a highly naïve and idealizing sense of India. It indicates that a modification of her politics of difference has occured, at least in this context.

For, of course, the differences between the East and West as Irigaray depicts them should not be the differences in the name of which she wants multicultural integration. They should be evidence of the impoverishment of cultural difference. Such depictions should indicate to Irigaray the need to anticipate alternative formations of cultural difference. The approach consistent with Irigarayan difference would ask how cultural difference can *not* be represented today. For example, we might usefully ask how cultural difference is not represented in her own writing? How does its non-depiction in her writing connect with the patterns in its non-depiction through the histories of philosophical and cultural treatments of race? What possibilities for understanding other races and other cultures are excluded from her writing? What possibilities for race and cultural difference are actively foreclosed by her own formulations? Though these questions are critical of Irigaray, they also speak to the importance of her approach to difference. Directed at her own writing, Irigarayan questions about difference are still good questions to ask. Despite the author, Irigaray's own blindspots eloquently make a case for critical Irigarayan interpretation of depictions of difference, even where such depictions are her own.

The question Irigaray takes up in her recent politics is how to live with the (culturally different) other. Is cultural difference just a matter of learning new means of living with difference? As Irigaray asked of sexual difference, what about fostering the conditions for new formations of difference? What if Western culture has been founded on the exclusion of the possibility of such formations? The conditions for the invention of new formations of difference might be as important as a politics of recognition of and living with difference. Such a point would be more consistent with Irigaray's own approach to sexual difference.

Recall that Irigaray's formulations on sexual difference are based on an 'aporia' of recognition. Widely interpreted as a poetic and performative remetaphorization of the feminine, Irigaray speaks in the name of a feminine identity she considers to be excluded from culture. She emphasizes how women have *not* been represented. She searches for repetition in such exclusions. Focussing on such repetition, she hypothesizes about concepts of the feminine that are antithetical to our cultural history. Her positive references to feminine identity lead to the accusations of essentialism. However Irigaray emphasizes that the hypothetical feminine in whose (contentless) name she speaks has been excluded from culture, and lacks identity. In this sense, sexual difference is not a misrecognized subjective reality. It is an excluded possibility. Inventing possibilities for femininity for which there has to date been no scope, she emphasizes that the project belongs to the politics of invention rather than recognition. When she sometimes uses the language of recognition, she mimics or performs a feminine speaking voice deemed culturally intolerable.

Irigaray's turn to issues of multiculturalism and cultural difference could engage with the writings on race which make up part of the French literary tradition, in addition to those of the cultures on whom she reflects. Without this or some other alteration in her approach, she ends up reiterating the stance she has long decried in relation to sex, where women, Asia and Africa are the object, not the subject or interlocutor, in Western discussion.

Following on from Toril Moi's reflections on the possible relationship between feminism of difference and the earlier politics of *négritude* (Moi 1994, 291n), one can reflect on how Frantz Fanon amongst many others have explored some of Irigaray's later concerns.[6] For Fanon, for example, the problems of cultural difference in the wake of colonialism involved more than the development of new models for living with cultural differences. Fanon argued that the very identity formations of colonized peoples were impoverished. One needed to foster the conditions for the flourishing of new modes of identity. How could the colonized form a new identity in which they did not merely follow Europe? "We must find something different. We today can do everything, so long as we do not imitate Europe, so long as we are not obsessed with the desire to catch up with Europe" (Fanon 1963, 253). Irigaray and Fanon share their concern about the detrimental effects for those who assert their equality with a pre-given standpoint belonging to a colonizing group. They agree about the dilemmas of equality politics. They agree in their resistance to an affirmation by the disenfranchised of ancient or traditional identity. They agree that identity politics must avoid stereotypes of African or female proximity to nature, "No, there is no question of a return to Nature" (Fanon, 1963, 254). Instead, Fanon argues, we should see "the human condition, plans for mankind and collaboration between men" as "new problems which demand new inventions" (Fanon 1963, 253).

Though his depictions of women were sometimes problematic, Fanon also offered comments about the role of women in the politics of colonization that resonate with an Irigarayan politics. In "L'Algérie dévoilée" (Fanon 1968) he notes the attempt by French colonialists to undermine Algerian society by promoting the view that the veil represented the subjugation of Algerian women to Algerian men. Not attempting to fully account for the status of the veil in Algerian society, Fanon instead offered an analysis of the cynical deployment of such arguments to the purposes of colonial rule. He pointed out the way that it seemed to destabilize the French colonizer's appropriative perspective on Algerian woman, frustrating the European investment in the visibility of the feminine. Algerian women represented to the European eye the threat of an object who sees without being seen. From her earliest work, Irigaray has discussed the regularity with which women have been depicted as objects of a male gaze which they also frustrate and elude.

In addition to their emphasis on the destabilizing effects of women who elude the certainty and control of those who objectify them, some other points of theoretical connection shared by Fanon and Irigaray include their concern for the highly conflicted psychic state of those who adopt the ideal of likeness to white men, in addition to their interest in a forward-looking identity politics which affirmed prospective identity formations

An engagement with the work of Fanon, Senghor and others preoccupied with conceptual problems and imperatives surrounding Afrocentrity might have allowed Irigaray to reflect further on the theoretical approaches appropriate to sexually and racially colonizing histories. Such an engagement might encourage her to ask why the particular formulation of her identity politics is applied so differently to sex and to race in her work. What aspects of her philosophy of difference are appropriate to the postcolonial context? Her philosophy of difference emphasizes (sexuate) identities which have been 'impossible' in Western history. Would it not be appropriate to emphasize impossibility in her reflection on cultural difference also? It seems Irigaray's politics of cultural difference has become more akin to a politics of 'recognition' then her work on sexual difference has ever been.[7] An Irigarayan politics asks how to live well with existing formations of cultural difference. Above all, it does not ask what formations of cultural difference are excluded by our own discourse. Yet theorists of race and postcolonialism, both contemporary and historical, have long considered such questions critical. In relation to sexual difference, Irigaray asks what hypothetical differences can *not* be represented in a given context. What conceptual possibilities for the existence of difference are excluded from it? How can our analysis of the pattern of such exclusions form the basis for imagining hypothetical, alternative identity formations? Irigaray need not restrict the relevance of such questions to the interpretation of sex.

Irigaray's politics of sexual difference is not a politics that supposes men and women to be different. Instead, it asks for the recognition of their potential difference in law, culture and language. Gesturing towards the possibility of that difference (as excluded and impossible), Irigaray emphasizes that ours is not a culture of sexual difference. Irigaray's material on linguistics (amongst many other aspects of her work) makes this clear. By contrast, it can be argued that Irigaray's politics of multiculturalism supposes multicultural difference to be a pre-existing difference, which Irigaray thinks both nourishes culture, and to which our cultural and legal institutions should be more responsive. One element that seems to weaken her work on multiculturalism is the absence of her treatment of postcolonialism. Again, consider the role of this omission as compared to her approach to sexual difference. In the latter, Irigaray argues that women have, in a sense, been colonized. They have no 'original' difference that has been stolen, appropriated or eradicated by male colonizers. Nonetheless, the very possibility that there should be a culture of sexual difference has been, in her view, annexed from the outset. The argument that there should be sexual difference dovetails with the argument that there is not, and has never been sexual difference. Both arms of this argument need to be intertwined.

It might be argued that Irigaray's apparent argument that there is multiculturalism, and that it offers the potential of nourishing and reforming human identity, really operates as the simultaneous argument that there is no multiculturalism. In this case, readers would suppose that cultural difference occupies the same structural status as sexual difference in her work. I think this interpretation is excluded because the crucial second arm of Irigaray's argument is missing. The potentially Irigarayan argument that there could be a positive multiculturalism would need to be complemented with the argument that there has never yet been multiculturalism in this sense. This would require the same finesse that Irigaray brought to her analyses of sexual difference, close interpretations of the texts of Western philosophy, anthropology and psychoanalysis, in which Irigaray analyzed the repeated depictions of the colonized and marginalized cultural other as—(for example) concurrently devalued and noble savage—in the very same writers she has already closely analyzed. One can well imagine an intricate Irigarayan demonstration that there has never been cultural difference in the full and positive sense we could only imagine (in which non-white cultures were seen by European whites neither as same as, the opposite of, or the absence of civilization, nor the complement to Western civilization). Her engagement in such a project would give a different meaning to her recent statements praising the enriching possibilities of cultural difference. Similar statements about the positive potential for a refigured sexual difference do indeed operate quite differently, because of the concurrent and intricate project undertaken by Irigaray to demonstrate that there never has been this sexual difference. Because of this work, we understand that any positive resonance given to sexual difference lies on the side of reinvention—sometimes through poetic re-imagination, sometimes through speculating on legal and other kinds of reform, and sometimes through mimicry or other forms of displacing occupation of traditional representations of the feminine.

No theorist preoccupied with the status of Afrocentricity has not wrestled with the relationship (complementary or conflicting?) between the project of, a) depicting an annexed, colonized culture; b) revaluing tradition in the face of a colonizing tradition; and/or c) emphasizing the values of reinvention of culture rather than 'simple' traditionalism. Possibilities for (positive) cultural difference have been constantly eroded. In their erosion, there has been a constant, simultaneous, 'pointing' or 'calling' to excluded possibilities for reinventions of cultural difference. In this sense, one can imagine Irigaray's formulation of a politics of cultural difference that did follow, to some extent, the shape of her politics of sexual difference, but both arms (deconstruction intertwined with reinvention) should be in place—and they are not.

For this reason, Irigaray's use of the term *ingénuité* (given its connotations of *naïveté*) to depict the individual rebirthing of the subject which might accompany a refiguring of the status of cultural difference (Irigaray 2002 [1999], 5), seems particularly indicative of the problems embodied in the project. Consider the parallel with the positive refiguring of the concept of women's virginity which also occurs in her politics of sexual difference (Irigaray 1994 [1989], 60). Cultural *ingénuité* might be considered the equivalent, in the domain of cultural difference, of virginity in the context of her discussions of sexual difference. But Irigaray's project to remetaphorize the conventional connotations of virginity occurs in the context of a close reading of the historical and patriarchal connotations of virginity elsewhere in her work. For this reason, the remetaphorization of virginity is not, we could say, naïve. Irigaray's revaluation of *naiveté* (*ingénuité*) in the context of cultural difference works differently. Since it does not occur in the context of a close reading of the Eurocentric philosophical depictions of cultural difference going back to Plato, we have no sense of what a revalued concept of *ingénuité* displaces. In the absence of an interpretation of that history, the project seems literally naïve, rather than a positive and inventive refiguring of *naïveté* as a cultural value. Irigaray's new work on cultural difference suggests a new response to the considerable debate, first addressed by Margaret Whitford (1991), about whether Irigaray's controversial later work is best understood in the context of her earlier work. The Irigarayan project on cultural difference can be fruitfully re-imagined or refigured by readers insofar as it could alternatively follow a structure closer to her approach to sexual difference.

NOTES

1. This led to considerable concern about the heterosexism of this metaphorics. Jagose (1994) is one of the many critics to have taken up this problem, and it is also given further consideration in Deutscher (2002 [1999]).

2. However, Irigaray does not suppose that love of difference always nourishes the relationship between those of different cultures and religions, any more than it systematically nourishes the relationship between those of different sexes.

3. Note that masculine discourse is deemed a type, without Irigaray claiming that it is found in the speech patterns of all males. Irigaray holds a doctorate in linguistics, in addition to doctorates in psychoanalysis and philosophy, and the claims are made based on empirical linguistic studies undertaken with research teams. On this, see in particular the anthology *Sexes et genres à travers les langues* (Irigaray 1990) and Gail Schwab's discussion of this material in Schwab 1998.

4. For this reason, an important shift occurs where Irigaray finally turns to discuss limitations, as she understands these, in her vision of Eastern cultures (Irigaray 2002 [1999], 49ff.), after several depictions of the East in writings preceding *Between East and West*, and comes to question, in one chapter of the latter work, the status of women in some aspects of Indian culture and religion. Her criticisms, while perhaps equally problematic, at least indicate that Irigaray is to some extent prepared to let go of her idealising view of the East.

5. For this argument see in particular Spivak (1988).

6. Fanon is also a figure one would want to see included in Irigaray's responses to French existential phenomenology in *To Be Two* (2001), for example.

7. This point is developed further in Deutscher (2002).

WORKS CITED

Deutscher, Penelope. 2002. *A Politics of Impossible Difference: The Later Work of Luce Irigaray*. Ithaca, N.Y.: Cornell University Press.

Fanon, Frantz. 1963. *The Damned*. Translated by Constance Farrington Paris: Présence Africaine.

———. 1968. 'L'Algérie dévoilée,' pp. 16–47 in *Sociologie d'une révolution/L'an V de la révolution algérienne*. Paris: Maspero.

———. 1970. *Black Skin, White Masks*. Translated by Charles lan Markmann. London: Paladin.

Irigaray, Luce (ed.). 1990. *Sexes et genres à travers les langues: Elements de communication sexuée*. Paris: Grasset.

———. 1993. *An Ethics of Sexual Difference*. Translated by Carolyn Burke and Gillian C. Gill. Ithaca, N.Y.: Cornell University Press.

———. 1994. *Thinking the Difference: For a Peaceful Revolution*. Translated by Karin Montin. London: Athlone Press.

———. 1996. *I Love to You*. Translated by Alison Martin. New York: Routledge.

———. 1999. *Entre Orient et Occident*. Paris: Grasset.

———. 2001. *To Be Two*. Translated by Monique M. Rhodes and Marco F. Cocito-Monoc. New York: Routledge.

———. 2002. *Between East and West: From Singularity to Community*. Translated by Stephen Pluhácek. New York: Columbia University Press.

Jagose, Annamarie. 1994. *Lesbian Utopics*. New York: Routledge.

Moi, Toril. 1994. *Simone de Beauvoir: The Making of an Intellectual Woman*. Oxford, London and Harvard, MA: Blackwell.

Schwab, Gail M. 1998. 'The French Connection: Luce Irigaray and International Research on Language and Gender,' pp. 13–24 in *Untying the Tongue*. Edited by L. Longmire & L. Merrill. Westport, CT: Greenwood.

Spivak, Gayatri Chakravorty. 1988. 'Can the Subaltern Speak?,' pp. 271–313 in *Marxism and the Interpretation of Culture*. Edited by C. Nelson and L. Grossberg. Urbana: University of Illinois Press.

Weiss, Gail. 1999. *Body Images: Embodiment as Intercorporeality*. New York and London, Routledge.

Whitford, Margaret. 1991. 'Introduction,' in *The Irigaray Reader*. Edited by Margaret Whitford. Oxford: Basil Blackwell.

IRIGARAY'S COUPLES

Debra Bergoffen

OPENING

Irigaray seems to be out of step with the current feminist agenda. The European Union ignored her proposals for sexed rights (Irigaray 2001 [1994], 80–91). Her insistence on sexual difference is at odds with contemporary feminist theories which identify the two-sex distinction as arbitrary (for example, Judith Butler, *Gender Trouble: Feminism and the Subversion of Identity* and Monique Wittig, *The Straight Mind and Other Essays*). Her privileging of the sexual difference does not accept the premise, central to third wave feminism, that critiques of sexism must also attend to matters of sexuality, race, class, ethnicity, and nationality (for example, Diana Fuss, *Essentially Speaking: Feminism, Nature and Difference* and Elizabeth V. Spelman, *Inessential Woman: Problems of Exclusion in Feminist Thought*).

Irigaray is aware of her disputed position—that she is criticized for advocating an essentialism characteristic of an earlier (and repudiated) feminist thinking, and repudiated for invigorating reactive patriarchal forces in her validation of the heterosexual couple. She responds,

> The whole of human kind is composed of women and men and of nothing else. The problem of race is, in fact a second-ary problem—except from a geographical point of view? . . . and the same goes for other cultural diversities—religious, eco-nomic and political ones. Sexual difference probably repre-sents the most universal question we can address. Our era is

151

faced with the task of dealing with this issue, because across
the whole world . . . there are only men and women. (Irigaray
1996 [1992], 47)

This response is not likely to convince her critics. It gives no
sense of what she means by sexual difference and seems to invite
rather than address the charge of essentialism. And yet it gets to the
heart of Irigaray's thought. It signals the ways in which Irigaray teth-
ers material and cultural forces and exposes the ways in which her
thinking carries both promissory and reactionary valences. This dangerous ambiguity is part of the power of Irigaray's thinking. I am
interested in probing it. I think that it comes from Irigaray's refusal to
accept the nature-culture divide; that it is embedded in the way she
grounds her understanding of the sexual difference in the materialities
of our desire; in the way she looks to these materialities for ethical
directives; and in the way she calls on these ethical directives to
structure our political commitments. I also think that we can best
delineate the ways in which the sexual difference works its way through
(is worked through) Irigaray's thought by understanding the essential
relationship between the sexual difference and coupled life. With
these thoughts in mind I propose the following thesis: For Irigaray, the
question of the sexual difference is the question of the couple.
    I think the place to begin sorting these issue out is Freud's *Three
Essays on Sexuality*. I choose this beginning not only because Irigaray
begins from the psychoanalytic site, but because Freud's *Essays* alert us
to the difference between the way the analyst conceives of the sexual
difference and the ways in which it is represented in everyday life. I
also begin here because the *Essays* alert us to the crucial point at
which Irigaray breaks with two key psychoanalytic premises. The first
of these premises is that sexual desires ought not be judged by moral
standards but by medical ones. Freud saw this as critical to breaking
the knot of guilt and repression. Irigaray finds that ignoring the intimate relationship between sexed desire and ethical and political life
may have been the first blind spot of psychoanalysis. The second
premise concerns the inevitability of the Oedipus complex. Though
Freud's *Essays* begin by severing biological sex from psychological
sexuality, they conclude by affirming a happy harmony between the
biological requirements of the species and the psychological mandates
of the Oedipus complex. Irigaray finds no evidence of this Oedipal
benevolence. She finds the effects of the Oedipus complex disastrous

for our species life. The Oedipus complex perverts the heterosexual relationship, forecloses the possibility of ethical relationships, and is the source of the unjust politics of patriarchy.

Irigaray works through her differences with the founder of psychoanalysis (and his followers) and develops her alternative understanding of the sexual difference through her discussions of couples. The couple, (the placental couple, the mother-daughter couple, the heterosexual couple), whether or not it is the site of what patriarchy calls sexual difference, is the site, according to Irigaray, where desire and difference are either nourished or repressed. As the scene of desire and the site of the possibility of difference, the couple is the ground of ethical and political life. Whether or not the ethical intentionality and political promise of the sexual difference is realized depends on the ways in which we image, represent, and live our coupled existence.

THE SEXED LAW OF DESIRE

As Irigaray sees it, desire is driven by the law of return. Our desire, she tells us, is born as a longing to return to the place where we began (Irigaray 1985 [1974], 68). It is structured by the ways in which we map out routes of return and is assuaged by the assurance that such routes can be found. Given that we are all of woman born, the maternal body stands as the origin of the human. Given that we are not all born women, however, we cannot all return to this body in the same way. Thus the source of the sexual difference. We learn who we are by discovering how our lived bodies are related to and differentiated from the source of our desire. This is what analysts call resolving the Oedipus complex. For the patriarchal analysts, Freud and Lacan, resolving the Oedipus complex requires the entry of the third, the father. The bond between the maternal body and its issue must be cut by the paternal figure. For Freud and Lacan, remaining coupled with the mother is the equivalent of a death warrant. For Irigaray, marking the mother's body as taboo is a recipe for violence and destruction. Resolving the Oedipus complex is not a matter of abandoning the mother's body, but of learning its lesson of relational autonomy so that the desire to return to it is neither coded as a matter of rights, property, and possession, nor repressed as scandalous.

Resolving the Oedipus complex is also a matter of understanding that each embodiment of the human must map out sexually distinct routes of return. Currently only one map exists. The patriarchal map of Oedipus. The Oedipus complex, Irigaray tells us, scripts the male fantasy of return. This fantasy reduces woman to the mother (the origin of his being and ground of his desire) and then transforms her into the wife (the one through which he will/can return to the origin/ground). It establishes the penis as the phallus and images the phallus as the only possible solution to the problem of origin. It will bring him back to the lost mother (through the wife-mother). Because the penis is the only recognized solution to the question of the origin, woman, the one who has no penis/solution, is simultaneously frozen in the place of the origin (woman = mother) and designated as the means for the ends of men's desire (woman = wife). Serving as the image of the desired origin and the possibility of his return, woman guarantees man's desire. So long as she is denied her desire, she can be counted on to anchor and secure his. This does not mean that he is not anxious. This does not even mean that he really believes that the equation woman = mother = wife reflects something other than his desire. The unconscious has its ways of speaking. Here it surfaces in the strategies of the obsessive.

> Peter Peter pumpkin eater.
> Had a wife and could not keep her.
> Put her in a pumpkin shell.
> And there he kept her very well.

It is tempting to follow the line of this story to Irigaray's conclusion, women do not exist, and to close the book; but things are more complicated. For if it is the case that woman is the castrated, wounded, melancholic sex whose desire is foreclosed, it is also the case that man, identified by Irigaray as the only sex that does exist, is a mere ghost of the subject he claims to be (Irigaray 1985 [1974], 60–61). In exposing the fact that women, having no access to their desire, do not exist, Irigaray also exposes the fact that men, who do exist insofar as they assert their desire, do not experience themselves as the source of their desire. Their affirmation of male autonomy is a myth. Having denied women's existence in order to secure their own, men discover that they are haunted by the absent presence of the woman who anchors their desire. If she does not exist, he is lost. If she does exist, her desire may take her away. "Peter, Peter pumpkin eater . . ."

It is, I think, important to note that Irigaray is not critical of the desire to return to the origin (Irigaray 1985 [1974], 66–73). Whatever may or may not be historical about current structures of subjectivity and sexual difference, this much is not: there is a sexual difference and this difference is a matter of our desire for and relationship to the maternal body. The maternal body and its issue is the original couple. Our current inability (refusal?) to imagine and symbolize the sexual-ethical difference of this couple is repeated in the absence of a sexual-ethical relation everywhere else. We might think of this generationally. Lacking an ethical inter-generational ground, ethical intragenerational relationships cannot be created.

Speculum ends on two notes. One concludes the argument against the Oedipal imaginary-symbolic. The other points to the possibility of another imaginary-symbolic that opens routes for female desire and an imaginary-symbolic proper to it. This possibility resides in women's dreams, in the hysteric's body, and in the repressed memory of blood: "Red blood. Woman, virgin and mother represents the blood reserves. This natural source of profit—acknowledged as such in "prehistory" when the value of blood was recognized and exalted above all else—is denied, censored in favor of other goods and powers when patriarchy is established. . . . Blood rights are . . . completely neglected . . . But blood is not easily repressed . . ."(Irigaray 1985 [1974], 125). Speculum ends by detailing the return of the repressed blood in patriarchal violence. Irigaray's later works return us to this blood differently: first to the maternal body and its coupled placental economy, then to the mother-daughter couple, and finally to a rescripted heterosexual couple whose validation of the sexual difference anchors the politics of the democracy to come.

If the road is not straight forward, it nevertheless seems psycho-analytically correct. It is a way of working through the myths of woman rather than evading them. If the myth of woman distorts women's desire insofar as it reduces women to the maternal body, it also points to the materiality of the birthing body as harboring a different truth about women. This truth speaks of her sexual difference without reference to the discourses of the father or Oedipal lack. Likewise, if current Oedipal myths construe the mother-daughter relationship through the lexis of hate, they also point to the emotional depths of this relationship. If we remember that the hatred of father and son also speaks of a deeper love and that one of the functions of the Oedipus complex is to teach the son to use his love to sublimate the hate, we may find resources in current configurations of mother-daughter antagonisms for sublimations that speak of the singularity of women's love for each other.

The strategy of working through the myths of woman as mother (the patriarchal reproductive vessel) and daughter (the one who hates her mother and envies her father and brothers) may be seen as both supplemental and corrective. It teaches us how to understand what *Speculum* means when it speaks of the ways in which patriarchy systematically erases the gap between men's and women's desire. It also shows us that the discourse of the gap is vulnerable to appropriation by patriarchal discourses of difference unless it is supplemented by and understood through the discourse of the between. Moving into the territory of the between, the between of the placental and mother-daughter couples, we avoid thinking of the sexual difference in reductionist biological terms or essentialist psychoanalytic ones. Rather than reading the sexual difference as the site from which difference first speaks, as its own ground, we learn to see it as a species of difference grounded elsewhere.

THE ALMOST-ETHICAL PLACENTAL ECONOMY

The Oedipus complex speaks of the desire to know and to return to the origin of our desire, the mother, as impossible. Invoking the incest taboo, it bars us from the maternal body, imbuing it with devouring, annihilating powers. The mother's body, according to Oedipus, is a lure to the end of our desire—death.

In "On the Maternal Order" in *Je, tu, nous*, Hélène Rouch, an expert in the in utero mother-child couple, knows nothing of this devouring, threatening maternal body. The maternal body she knows is structured through the placenta "a tissue formed by the embryo which while being closely imbricated with uterine mucosa remains separate from it" (Irigaray 1993 [1990], 38). The child, even before it becomes a child, is never the plaything of the mother. It is, in utero, an other. It forms the placenta, the tissue that effects its individuation. Rouch continues, "However, although the placenta is a formation of the embryo it behaves like an agent that is practically independent of it. It plays a mediating role . . . it's the mediating space between mother and fetus . . . there's never a fusion of maternal and embryonic tissues . . . it . . . establishes a relationship between mother and fetus" (Irigaray 1993 [1990], 38–39). Concluding her descriptions of this placental economy by describing the placenta as relatively autonomous, she finds descriptions of the fetus-maternal body relationship that appeal to images of fusion and aggression "quite poor and . . . extremely culturally determined" (Irigaray 1993 [1990], 39).

Thinking through these meanings of the maternal body requires that we rethink the meaning of autonomy. We can no longer identify it with independence and separation. We need to think of it as both relative and relational. Placental mechanisms support the autonomy of fetus and mother by regulating an exchange between them such that the otherness of the fetus is distinguished from the otherness of the foreign object that threatens the mother's body. These mechanisms do not define the fetus's autonomy against the autonomy of the maternal body. The placental mechanisms do not allow the fetus to establish its difference by attacking the maternal body's defense mechanisms. Neither do they demand that the maternal body, in deactivating its defense mechanisms vis à vis the fetus, forfeit its ability to deflect infection. Within the maternal body, recognition of otherness is not coded as a Hegelian contest of wills where only one or the other survives or where the survival of both is conditioned on one forfeiting its identity to the other. The maternal body teaches a different lesson: autonomy figured as an absolute is a pawn of the death drive. A fetus identifying itself as absolutely other would set itself up for attack by an auto immune system designed to identify the foreign as threatening. If, however, the fetus were saved from this fate by the effect of a placenta which compelled the maternal body to accept the fetus as an absolute other, the maternal body's defenses would have to be defused. To ensure the survival of the fetus, the maternal body would have to become an auto immune deficient body; becoming a maternal body would become the equivalent of contracting AIDS. Happily for the survival of the species, the placental economy does not work this way. Its mechanisms are ignorant of the Dialectic. They deploy what Irigaray will later call the labor of love (Irigaray 1996 [1992], 29).

The placental economy thinks autonomy according to a deconstructive logic of difference and a feminist ethics of generosity. One's being as the differential of the autonomous can only come into being through an inscription in the other. Thus, though the placenta is described as a tissue formed by the embryo, Rouch tells us that in order for it to be produced, "There has to be a recognition of the other, of the non-self by the mother and therefore an initial reaction from her. . . . It's as if the mother always knew that the embryo (and thus the placenta) was other and that she lets the placenta know this, which then produces the factors enabling the maternal organism to accept it as other" (Irigaray 1993 [1990], 41). So the otherness of the embryo is first given to it by the maternal body. Its generosity provides the ground for the placental tissue's production. In order for the fetus to come into being and survive, however, it must produce the placental factors that allow the maternal organism to accept it as other. The logic of active or passive, master or slave, autonomous or dependent, one or the other, cannot describe this process by which the maternal body and the fetus negotiate their relationship. Patriarchy, following the logic of Oedipus, calls this ambiguous relationship impossible. Yet it exists.

Biology gives us two models of autonomy and otherness: one maternal, the other medical. The medical model might be described as a paradigm of independent autonomy. In this model of disease, infection, and antibodies, the other is identified as a threat to the body's integrity. Acting to preserve itself as independently autonomous, the body treats that which is foreign to it as an enemy which must either be destroyed or expelled. Thus, its health is maintained. If we follow Irigaray's assessment of the relationship between nature and culture, that there is no break between the two but a process by which one is taken up by the other, then we might suggest that the sexed culture of Oedipus, the culture of the independently autonomous subject and the binary logic of the either/or, is a cultural appropriation of the medical mechanisms of the body.

In directing us toward the cultural possibilities of the placental economy, Irigaray is not arguing that this body leads us to the truth of our desire. Her point is ethical and political, not epistemological. It is that by choosing the maternal rather than the medical paradigm of autonomy and otherness we can replace our current exploitative modes of sociality with ethical ones. Irigaray, responding to Rouch's descriptions of the placental economy's mechanisms of relative and relational autonomy, calls the fetal relation "almost ethical." Almost ethical, a resource for ethics. Calling the placental economy almost ethical is, I think, Irigaray's way of alerting us to the fact that the utopian moments of her thought are not thoughts of a not yet that come from nowhere. They are materially grounded in the distinctive features of the maternal body. As such they are no more impossible than current patriarchal structures grounded in the realities of the body's medical materialities.

MOTHERS AND DAUGHTERS

The almost-ethical placental relationship is not expelled in the afterbirth. It speaks in the young daughter's words to her mother. As almost ethical, the reciprocities of the placental economy know nothing of the sexual difference. They pay no attention to the dialectic of the individual and the universal. As taken up in the young daughter's sexed discourse, however, these reciprocities become ethical. They take root in the sexual difference and affirm the principle of individuation.

By investigating the ways in which women and men use language, Irigaray discovers sexually distinct patterns of discourse. Men, she finds, privilege relations to the object. Women privilege relations between subjects. This sexual difference is already evident in young children. Only little girls create a situation with their mothers where there are always two people speaking to each other. The little girl, Irigaray tells us, shows her mother a loving ethical intention. She creates a just and communicative microsociety between her mother and herself (Irigaray 1996 [1992], 130). The mother, however, does not show the same intersubjective respect for her daughter: "A dominant male culture has intervened between mother and daughter and broken off a loving and symbolic exchange" (Irigaray 1996 [1992], 131). Rejecting the young daughter's opening to/of the difference of the between that makes their twoness possible, the mother encloses the daughter in the order of the same. She insists that the daughter listen and obey. Only one voice prevails. Though it was the mother's body that birthed the almost-ethical relationship of the placental economy, it is her young daughter who transforms the almost-ethical materiality of the mother's body into a realized ethical intentionality. The little girl remembers what the mother has been taught to forget.

Reading Irigaray, I discover that it is not the incest taboo that secures patriarchal culture, but the taboo that deflects the daughter from her ethical intentionalities. By outlawing mother-daughter love, patriarchy secures the status quo. Prohibited from loving each other in their singularity, mothers and daughters see each other only as instantiations of the universal. The singularity of the female is erased in the patriarchal duties of the mother and wife. Women (the sexed singular) are disappeared into woman (the patriarchal universal). In Irigaray's words: "The girl's only reason for being is to become a wife and mother. In this respect her mother represents this abstract role for her as she does for her mother . . . With this erasure within the universal, or this sacrifice to the spirit of the relationship between mother and daughter, there occurs the most extreme loss of human singularity" (Irigaray 1996 [1992], 26).

I hear the refrain of Beauvoir's, "One is not born a woman but becomes one." I ask Irigaray's question: How does the one who is born a daughter become alienated from her ethical intentionality? How does she become a mother? The answers lie in her own mother's alienation and in men's desire. The one will rob her of a cultural mediation for relating to other women and teach her to abdicate her singularity. The other will seduce her desire for ethical relationships. The mother will deliver the daughter to the fathers and brothers. They will promise her love. The promise is a ploy. He wants an open road home. If she will embody the idea of his origin and promise to love, honor, and obey his desire, he will play at her game of relationships. Believing that he will respond to her ethical call, she will become a women by sacrificing her singularity to her universal duty as wife and mother. (This account is accurate for those parts of the world where the ideology of romantic love prevails; where it does not, no male seductions are necessary. It is simply a matter of power.)

Is there an antidote to the mother-daughter taboo? Must we quarantine the daughter from the threat of her mother and the men? This seems to be where the argument leads. It is not, however, the conclusion of Irigaray's line of thought. For her, challenging the taboo does not entail orphaning the daughter and abandoning the men. For her, the prohibition that bars women from their relational singularity will be reinforced, not undermined, if daughters, in defense of their singularity, turn away from their mothers, or if women, insisting on their desire, refuse to grant men theirs. Though patriarchy forbids women's relationships in order to affirm men's absolute autonomy, the true target of the mother-daughter taboo is the relationship that enacts the relational autonomy of the placental economy. Men's domination of women is symptomatic of this more fundamental problem. What must be eradicated is the relationship that validates the one by negating the other.

Advocating that mothers and daughters (re)discover their individuated gendered identity through their relationship to each other, Irigaray directs women to take up the task of becoming themselves so that they can take on the task of creating a between-two relationship with men. In her words: "female genealogies had to be disinterred from oblivion, not . . . to eliminate the father . . . but to return to the reality of the two . . . [to affirm that] genealogical authority belongs to man and to woman" (Irigaray 2001 [1994], 131, see also Irigaray 1996 [1992], 27). As the mother-daughter relationship articulates the almost-ethical relationship of the placental economy, the woman-man relationship fulfills the political promise of the mother-daughter bond;

for, as Irigaray presents it, the ethical intentionality of the difference of the between is brought to its highest articulation where the gap that sustains the between of the two is anchored by a two whose difference so intensifies the space between them that their relationship must be anchored in a promise to abandon all hope of reaching, understanding, or possessing the other. As the relationship that confronts the patriarchal relationship of possession head on, Irigaray envisions her revisioned heterosexual couple as poised to fissure the ground of patriarchal politics.

WOMEN AND MEN

The between-men sociality of patriarchy is said to be grounded in the incest taboo. Reading the accounts of the origins of this taboo in *Totem and Taboo, The Future of an Illusion,* and *Civilization and Its Discontents* alerts us to two things: 1. The incest taboo, an agreement among men, only recognizes women as the universal and passive principle of femininity; 2. The men who accept this taboo recognize the universal of the sexual difference only as a means of affirming their own independent autonomous identity. As autonomous, the men recognize and relate to each other as equals, that is, as the same. Recognizing the woman as the one who is different, they refuse to relate to her. She is no party to their contracts. The link between the incest taboo and patriarchy's misogyny is grounded here.

There is a telling gap in this account. How can we account for the thing that makes the incest taboo possible—women's passivity? Irigaray directs us to the mother-daughter taboo. As the condition of the possibility of the incest taboo, insofar as it renders the women passive and allows for their exchange among men, it is also the point at which patriarchy is most vulnerable. If we note that prior to the patriarchy of the brothers the patriarchy of the father ruled, and if we see that this patriarchy, grounded in the passivity of sons and daughters, was undone when the sons found their voice, then we can see how/that the end of the mother-daughter taboo, by giving women their voice, could/would end the reign of the incest taboo and dismantle modern patriarchy.

The very thought of lifting the incest taboo seems terrifying. It conjures up images of abused children, ravaged women, violence, and chaos. The indoctrinations of patriarchy are powerful. That children and women are not protected by this taboo is readily available in the statistics. Children are the victims of their families. Women are readily raped. Domestic violence plagues women's and children's lives. The incest taboo grounds the violences of patriarchy by establishing men as the protectors of passive women and vulnerable children and by ensuring that the protectors have little interest in policing each other. We need only read the daily paper to see that the basic promise of the incest taboo, peaceful fraternal coexistence, has yet to be fulfilled. The end of the incest taboo may be the end of civilization as we know it— that may not be such a bad thing (see Irigaray 1996 [1992], 135–36).

Understanding the connections between the mother-daughter taboo, the incest taboo, autonomous man, and misogyny, we are prepared to understand why Irigaray identifies the question of the sexual difference as the question of our age; for now we see that the question of the sexual difference concerns the difference between legitimating a paradigm of sociality that welcomes the singularity of the difference and enforcing a paradigm of sociality that recognizes individuals only insofar as they instantiate the universal of their patriarchal sexed identities. Read as the culminating stage of a developmental process that began in utero, the affirmation of the sexual difference is not a declaration of an essential difference between women and men, but an invitation to an alternative sociality. We see this most clearly if we trace the meaning of the sexual difference to the couple; for the ethical intentionalities of the couple, not just the heterosexual couple, are the sexual difference.

As I read her, I find Irigaray using the phrase "the sexual difference" much like the way Freud used the term "sex." In both cases the terms refer us to commonsense definitions but are deployed to counter their sedimented everyday meanings. In both cases the tensions between the commonsense and the newly crafted meanings create ambiguities that render the thought overdetermined and undecidable. I think that this overdetermination is part of the structure of both Freud's and Irigaray's thought. I do not wish to erase it. I do, however, think that we best understand it if we see that, as Freud's term, sex must be translated as sensual pleasure such that his thought challenges our genital understanding of sexuality without delegitimizing it. Irigaray's phrase sexual difference must be translated as the between that makes the two possible such that it leads us to think of this difference in heterosexual terms while showing us that these terms are too restrictive. Whether the two of the between exists as a placental negotiation where the sex of the fetus is a matter of indifference;

as a mother-daughter dialogue where the two embody the same sexed identity; or as a heterosexual intimacy where what we commonly identify as the sexual difference is present; so long as the principle of the between is in play the sexual difference is at work. Whether the sexed identity of those engaged in the dialogue of the between is irrelevant, the same, or distinct, however, changes how the sexual difference works. The difference between the placental and mother-daughter couple resides in the distinction between an almost-ethical intentionality and a realized one. The difference between these couples and the heterosexual couple lies in the emergence of the sexual difference as a political force.

Approaching the question of politics through the lense of the sexual difference and the couple, Irigaray structures her political thinking along social contract lines. For her, as for the social contract theorists, the rightness of our political commitments depends on accurately addressing several fundamental questions: What is the relationship between the natural and social worlds? Who may rightly be called a citizen? How does one become one? What are the rights of the one so called? Agreeing that we are not born citizens but become them, Irigaray and the social contract theorists then part company. The issue between them (which is at issue in Irigaray's critique of the liberal democratic tradition) concerns our civil identity. Is it one or two? Is it the effect of a moral rebirth which alienates us from nature (Rousseau), or the consequence of cultivating our natural embodied identities? Does one become a citizen through an act of unsexed consent, or through an affirmation of the mutually sexed limits of our subjectivity?

Irigaray's argument with social contract politics may be traced to this matter of the limit. Social contract patriarchy identifies the citizen as male and then identifies the male with the universal. Though it speaks of the limits placed on citizens vis à vis each other and the state, in fact its delineation of the subject invites those designated as subjects to see themselves as absolute. This becomes clear in the ways in which the liberal state severs the public and private realms and in the ways sovereign states relate to each other. In severing the public and private realms, the state sanctions the absolute authority of husband over wife and children. In their imperialist behavior, democratic states rely on their power to assert their authority over people who have not consented to their rule. These apparent anomalies of the social contract tradition are, from Irigaray's perspective, not anomalies at all. They speak the truth of democratic patriarchal politics:

Only those who are the same will be respected in their persons and rights. Politics, for Irigaray, however, is about respecting the difference. It is about taking up the natural difference of the lived sexed body and cultivating the meanings of this difference to create sexed civic identities. Where the polity of the universal subject of the same can blind itself to the injustice it inflicts on those it designates as other, the polity of the sexed subject cannot exile the other from the rules of justice.

What was identified in the placental economy as the hope of the ethical relationship and analyzed in the mother-daughter couple as the promise of individuated identity is now considered from the perspective of the we of the community and the limits of subjectivity. Moving from the almost ethical to the ethical, and from the ethical to the political, the question now becomes: What sort of identity will/can ground a social order where the boundaries of the self are protected and the difference(s) of the other(s) is respected? Irigaray's answer: An identity grounded in the sexual difference and lived in the man-woman couple—grounded in the sexual difference because it is this difference that establishes the limit(s) of our subjectivity, lived the heterosexual couple because it is here, in this first we, that I intimately encounter an other whose difference, in its absoluteness, lays claim to my love. The rules of justice speak of respect for the other. The ground of justice lies in our ability to love the other.

Packed into this affirmation of the sexual difference and the man-woman couple is a critique of current family arrangements and the current assessment of the family as the ground of the political order; a critique of identity politics and of a politics focused on the rights of the exotic other; a critique of our formulation of the question of the relationship between nature and culture; and a critique of the political traditions of human rights. Briefly put, in arguing for a politics of sexual difference, Irigaray argues that it is not the family but the couple that grounds the social order; that it is easy to defend the rights of the distant and exotic other; that arguments for the social construction of the sexed subject are as misguided as arguments claiming that we are the products of our biological inheritance; and that universal human rights are as much a figment of the male imaginary as is the idea of an autonomous subject. In all of this the number two prevails: the two of the couple, not the many of the family; the two of the intimate one and the other, not the many of the one and the distant others; the two of nature and culture, not the either/or of the one or the other; the two of sexed subjects, not the one of the neutral subject.

Irigaray is insistently specific: the transition from natural to civic identity occurs in the intimacies of the man-woman couple or it does not occur at all. The affections of friendship, the love of parents and children, same-sex love, cross-cultural respect, interracial affiliations, and so on—all of these socialites of difference are possible only if and after the erotic desires of a man and a woman are enacted in accordance with the requirements of the between of the difference. We must, Irigaray insists, live the difference through the flesh of our desire for the sexed other and become so habituated to living the difference in our everyday lives that it becomes a part of our way of being in the world. The capacity to become a civil person, a person responsible for him or herself and for the community is realized only if, through the love of the sexually distinct other, we come to understand that being responsible for the community means protecting the relationship between us that makes communal life possible and that being responsible for ourselves means securing our bodies and ourselves from the authority of church, state, father, and husband (Irigaray 2001 [1994], 133). Love of the sexually distinct other does not guarantee this understanding. It is, however, the condition of its possibility; for it is through this love that we can learn to love and live the limit of the subjectivity that marks us as human, not as an abstract affirmation of an ethical ideal, but as embedded in the concrete familiar gestures of everyday life. Further, experiencing the limits of my finitude through my desire for an other whom I can embrace but not possess disentangles the meaning of finitude from the specter of death.

From the perspective of the preservation of the species, the heterosexual couple is the most natural relationship. There is nothing distinctly human about the two by two collected by Noah to preserve the earth's life forms. It is this apparent and real naturalness that makes the matter of the heterosexual couple so difficult and so crucial in Irigaray's thought. The social contract tradition addresses the matter of the naturalness of the heterosexual couple by distinguishing the husband-wife relationship from the citizen-citizen relationship. The citizen relationship is characterized by equality. The family relationship is characterized by subordination. Rejecting this degradation of their humanity, feminists have demanded their equal rights as citizens and have argued against severing husband-wife relationships from the rules of civic equality. Irigaray finds both positions flawed. She appeals to the phenomenological understanding of the lived body to reject both the social contract politics of difference that delegitimates the woman's lived embodied experience and the feminist politics of equality that legitimates women's experience by divesting it from its embodied realities. The naturally different male and female bodies are the source of different natural rhythms. They are the ground of different ways of engaging the world (Irigaray 2001 [1994], 112). These differences are not amenable to the syntheses of the dialectic. In Irigaray's words: ". . . neither man nor woman can manifest nor experience its [humanity's] totality. Each gender possesses or represents only one part of it. This reality is both very simple and quite foreign to our way of thinking. It is evident that male and female corporeal morphology are not the same and it therefore follows that their way of experiencing the sensible and of constructing the spiritual is not the same" (Irigaray 1996 [1992], 37–38).

The challenge critically framed in the heterosexual couple is: "To pass from the state of nature to civil life without abandoning the relationship to nature" (Irigaray 2001 [1994], 47). What cannot be abandoned is the sexual difference. This is the relationship to nature. We cannot, however, assume too much about the relationship between our natural and civic identities. Criticizing the European Union Women's Commission for not addressing the matter of sexed rights, Irigaray writes: ". . . how are the female members of parliament on the Commission to be defined as women? Is it purely a question of a biological identity? This is not enough to ensure representation for either sex, especially if the dimension of sexed civil identity is denied. To be born a woman should not be sufficient grounds for claiming to represent the rights of women. . . . It is dangerous to govern in the name of the state of nature!" (Irigaray 2001 [1994], 83).

Arguing against the neutral subject, Irigaray appeals to the sexual difference grounded in nature. Arguing against women who do not share her ideas of sexed rights, Irigaray appeals to the difference between being born a woman and affirming one's civil identity as a woman. What Irigaray means by natural is not entirely clear. She is most helpful in directing us to what she means when she speaks of the power of the negative of the sexual difference to cultivate our sensibilities of the limit (Irigaray 2001 [1994], 13). Here she seems to identify the natural with the forces of the life drives such that a culture that draws on its relationship to nature is "A culture of life . . . the body . . . natural sensibility . . . [and] of ourselves as living beings" (Irigaray 2001 [1994], 57).

The clearest discussion of how Irigaray envisions the give and take between the natural and civic domains comes in the essay "Toward a Citizenship of the European Union." There she describes the civil code as "a code for us and the between us" (Irigaray 2001 [1994], 64). This code sets the conditions for "a civil relationship between a man and a woman" that safeguards and protects "human identity . . . and coexistence in the community" (Irigaray 2001 [1994], 65). This code defines civil identity ". . . at the intersection of individual, natural identity and of community, relational identity, a transition which each person, male and female would have to make on their own behalf and consent to the other, male or female" (Irigaray 2001 [1994], 65).

AND YET . . .

There is no doubt that the argument is cogent. It is also consistent with recent scientific findings, which find the nature-nurture dispute misguided and support an interactive view that refuses to reduce us to our DNA code and rejects the idea that nurture trumps nature. Further, the concept of sexed rights is at the forefront of the feminist human rights agenda. Feminist organizations are arguing that the right of a woman to control her reproductive choices is a fundamental human right. They have hailed the recent conviction of Bosnian Serb soldiers, not only because their conviction for the crimes of rape and sexual slavery represent a departure from the attitude that these crimes should be "forgiven" as the "natural" consequence of war, but also because this conviction held that rape and sexual slavery are crimes against humanity, the most serious category of crime under international law. Irigaray might object to the language of human rights, but she would surely see that feminists are using the tools of human rights discourse to establish that there are such things as sexed rights, rights that only apply to women, and that state governments and the international community are obliged to recognize and protect these rights. We can see that these global women's rights claims rely on a central tenet of Irigaray's thought: whatever their cultural, racial, or economic differences, women, because of their embodied difference, require certain sexed protections. The observation of the Center for Reproductive Rights that "even in countries with democratic governments, a woman's right to control her reproductive life is rarely linked to her fundamental human rights or to her basic rights as a citizen."[1] The words of Nancy Northup, the Center's president, may not be based on a reading of Irigaray. They indicate, however, that their thinking and politics appeal to Irigaray's ideas of sexual difference, and they demonstrate the radical political ramifications of these ideas: "The Center for Reproductive Rights exists to hasten the arrival of a time when a woman's right to control her reproductive life is secured as a fundamental human right, which cannot be denied in the name of religion, culture or politics."[2] Determining how and where to draw the line between sexed protections grounded in our bodies and sexed protections grounded in and serving patriarchal ideologies, however, is not entirely clear. Should women be given preferential treatment in custody cases? Should pregnant women be barred from certain types of work? Did Judge James Lawrence King speak for Irigaray when, in denying a gay male couple's petition to adopt a young boy, he agreed with the Florida state lawyers who argued that children should be raised in heterosexual homes because of the "contribution of male and female influences to childhood growth and development"?[3]

Beyond the concrete difficulties of sorting out the implications of advocating the sexual difference as the basis of sexed rights, there are stubborn theoretical problems. Allowing that only the male-female couple can ground a just civic culture, rather than finding that this couple is one among several routes to a culture where our relationships are not mediated by money or property, does not necessarily follow from Irigaray's line of argument. This conclusion may be drawn from her arguments concerning the intensification of the between-two when the subjects anchoring the between embody lived irreducible differences, but, by Irigaray's own account, these are not the only relationships that challenge patriarchal mediations. She convincingly argues that the mother-daughter relationship is tabooed by patriarchy precisely because it is a relationship that refuses the patriarchal dialectic of mediation by power and mastery. She argues that releasing this relationship from its prohibitions would create a between-women genealogy that would render the one of the patriarchal genealogy impotent. Why abandon this conviction? Why, against the argument that the between-woman relationship might also be the ground of a challenge to the patriarchal order, suggest that fostering such relationships would only create an inversion of the patriarchal structure, that it would ground a matriarchy of the one? Why suggest that a relationship that refuses to compromise the difference of the between would betray itself? In only allowing the heterosexual couple to play the revolutionary role, Irigaray seems to forget the maternal body's almost-ethical placental relationship. This relationship is the ground of our ethical intentionalities and political demands. It teaches us that the between of the relational autonomy that guarantees the individuated life of the mother and the fetus is not dependent on the sexual difference but on the generosity of the exchange between two.

But must this be an exchange between two? Is the couple as cosmically grounded as Irigaray suggests? The placental economy may support more than one fetus. Its almost-ethical mechanisms of the difference do not demand the difference of the two. The mother-daughter dyad may also be a triad or more. The male-female relationship may be enacted in plural rather than coupled ways. Do we want to call these plural intimacies unethical? Perhaps the most concrete way to get at this issue is to look at the politics of marriage.

Within the Western industrialized world, the matter of the ethics of the heterosexual couple is being played out in the politics of marriage. Globally, and in the United States in the mid-nineteenth century, the matter of the ethics of the heterosexual couple is/was played out in the politics of the couple. In the first case, the debate concerns the heterosexual structure of the couple. In the second it concerns the ethical status of the couple *per se*. Approaching the marriage debates in the Western world through the lens of Irigaray's thought, it is important to note that none of the parties to this debate question the ethical status of the couple. Critics of the institution of heterosexual marriage find fault with the ways in which this institution either legally encodes the subordination of women to men (this now mostly a thing of the past), or socially endorses stereotypical sex roles (still a force today). Distinguishing between the legalities of heterosexist marriage and the lived realities of coupled man-woman intimacy, heterosexual feminists enact their endorsement of the couple and their critique of marriage by living their coupled lives "outside the law." Gays and lesbians articulate their endorsement of the couple by arguing that their coupled lives evade the inequalities and subordinations of the heterosexual couple. Thus, a distinction is made between the couple as an intimate ethical relationship and its current unethical institutionalized forms. Political theorists and historians, however, have noted that in turning away from the institution of marriage, the feminist and gay and lesbian communities are forfeiting an important political resource. They note that entering into legal recognized couple relationships was seen as the basis of legitimating the citizenship of former African-American slaves[4] and argue that gay

marriage ought to be at the top of the gay and lesbian political agenda
because without the ability to establish the legality of their coupled
relationships, gays and lesbians will remain marginal to the political
life of the nation.[5]

Within the modern Western world, only marginal utopian movements have challenged the ethics and politics of the couple. The
matter of affording gay and lesbian couples the legitimacy of marriage
is hotly contested. They are couples after all. When it comes to grant-
ing marriage rights to Mormon polygamists, however, there is no debate.
The answer is no. If it is taken for granted that heterosexual couples
are legitimate, if legalizing the status of gay and lesbian couples is a
matter of dispute, the question of acknowledging the right to arrange
one's intimate life polygamously or plurally is closed. No such social
approval or legal right exists in the Western industrialized world for
this presumed unjust marriage arrangement. Where it has been argued
that it is not the couple relationship that is exploitive but the legalities of patriarchy that make it so, similar arguments are not made for
polygamy. In the West, it is taken for granted that polygamy is inherently unjust. Is this a Western prejudice? Is it possible that if we
disengaged the polygamous relationship from its patriarchal context
we would discover the ethical and intimate possibilities of the polygamous bond? Would we discover that an ethics of sexual difference can
tolerate the difference of the one and the many? Might it be fostered
by this plural difference?

If these questions seem off the mark at best, and politically and
ethically dangerous at worst, they direct us to the dual valences of
Irigaray's thought. Today, when feminist thinking and politics must be
simultaneously local and global, we cannot presume that our Western
understandings of ethical intimacy preclude others. Our assumption
that the couple represents a higher form of sexual order than other
sexual arrangements may be as biased as the Enlightenment notion of
the white man's burden. If we wish to disenfranchise noncouple intimate relationships, if we wish to advocate an ethic of the couple, we
must, I think, provide clear justifications.

The argument against the one and the many is not as obvious
as it seems. If it is the case that the one man one woman intimate
arrangement is exploitative only under specific conditions, might this
also be true of the one man many woman or other plural configurations of erotic intimacy? That this cannot be dismissed out of hand is
suggested by the Mormon and Oneida community experiences in the

nineteenth century.[6] During the period of the Mormon experiment with polygamy, Mormon women were more active and influential in public and religious life than other women in the United States. They had the right to vote before other women did. They ran businesses. They published an influential women's newsletter. All of this during a securely patriarchal time and in the context of a firmly patriarchal religion. Suppose the patriarchal trappings were removed?

The complex marriage experiment of the Oneida community in the 1840s presents a more pointed challenge to our endorsement of the couple and to Irigaray's move to link the assumption of women's desire to the erotics of the two of the sexual difference couple. The Oneida community distinguished our need for erotic intimacy from our need for coupled intimacy. It separated the desire for sexual pleasure from the demands of procreation. Valuing the pleasures of the erotic but finding that bearing and birthing unwanted children drove women from these pleasures, and determining that rearing children was the source of women's inequality, the Oneida community mandated the practice of male continence or *coitus reservatus*. Here the requirements of procreation and male demand were subordinated to female desire. Men and women exchanged sexual partners frequently. Exclusive romantic attachments were described as "special loves" and characterized as antisocial behavior that threatened the well-being of the community.

As different as the Mormon and Oneida challenges to the ethics and politics of the couple are, however, their communities have this in common: they link their rejection of the intimate erotic couple relationship to a fundamentally antidemocratic vision of religious and communal life. In this they recall us to *The Republic*'s utopian politics. Plato too found the couple a threat to the life of an autocratic polity. So Irigaray is on to something? There is a connection between heterosexual coupled intimacies and democratic politics?

In the end there is an irreducible undecidability that attaches to the name Irigaray. The forces of utopian and dystopian powers find support in her thinking. In this, her writings repeat the tensions of Freud's *Three Essays*. Like the *Essays*, which open by directing us to the prejudices of common sense but which, by their end, seem to reinforce the very prejudices they were meant to refute, Irigaray's thinking alerts us to the ways in which patriarchy "naturalizes" its injustices by misreading the maternal body, tabooing the mother-daughter relationship, and perverting the erotics of the heterosexual couple. Her analyses and prescriptions for transformation, powerful as they are in destabilizing the structures of patriarchy, are themselves unsettling. To take up Irigaray's question of the sexual difference is to take up the challenge of following the forked roads of her thought. It returns us to the issues of repetition and sublimation. The question is this: Will accepting the question of the sexual difference as the question of our age take us on a road not yet traveled or return us to familiar territories by an alternate route?

NOTES

1. Center for Reproductive Rights, *Of Council* (winter 2003): 1.
2. Ibid.
3. Adam Liptak, "Gay Couple Challenges Florida Ban on Homosexual Adoptions," *New York Times*, 2 March 2002, A14.
4. See, for example, Nancy F. Cott, *Public Vows: A History of Marriage and the Nation* (Cambridge: Harvard University Press, 2000) and Amy Dru Stanley, *From Bondage to Contract: Wage Labor, Marriage and the Market in the Age of Emancipation* (New York: Cambridge University Press, 1998).
5. See, for example, Cheshire Calhoun, *Feminism, The Family and The Politics of the Closet: Lesbian and Gay Displacement* (New York: Oxford University Press, 2000).
6. For detailed accounts of these experiments, see Lawrence Foster, *Women, Family and Utopia: Communal Experiments of the Shakers, the Oneida Community and the Mormons* (Syracuse, N.Y.: Syracuse University Press, 1991).

WORKS CITED

Center for Reproductive Rights. *Of Council* (winter 2003).
Irigaray, Luce. 1985 [1974]. *Speculum of the Other Woman*. Translated by Gillian C. Gill. Ithaca, N.Y.: Cornell University Press.
———. 1993 [1990]. *Je, tu, nous: Toward a Culture of Difference*. Translated by Alison Martin. New York: Routledge.
———. 1996 [1992]. *I Love to You: Sketch for a Felicity Within History*. Translated by Alison Martin. New York: Routledge.
———. 2001 [1994]. *Democracy Begins Between Two*. Translated by Kirsteen Anderson. New York: Routledge.
Liptak, Adam. "Gay Couple Challenges Florida Ban on Homosexual Adoptions." *New York Times*, 2 March 2002, A14.

BETWEEN TWO: CIVIL IDENTITY AND THE SEXED SUBJECT OF DEMOCRACY

Emily Zakin

The question "what is . . . ?" is the question—the metaphysical question—to which the feminine does not allow itself to submit . . . There is no question of another *concept* of femininity. To claim that the feminine can be expressed in the form of a concept is to allow oneself to be caught up again in a system of "masculine" representations.

(Irigaray 1985 [1977], 122)

At the opening of *Democracy Begins Between Two*, a collection of lectures whose primary consideration is the meaning of civil identity in the formation of the European Union, Irigaray declares that, with regard to ensuring democratic values and especially equivalent opportunities for women, "it is a question of discovering what woman is and what she wants" (Irigaray 2001 [1994], 1). Irigaray here seems to be affirming the import of questions of identity and desire for establishing civil rights for women. Those of us familiar with Irigaray's earlier work on the constitution of feminine identity and its elision of feminine desire might at first be troubled by this approach to citizenship and rights. Hasn't Irigaray argued that we cannot say what a woman is or what she wants and that any attempt to do so is always already bound to an economy of violence? Is not the first question, of what woman is, inevitably one of metaphysical essence (as the above epigraph from "Questions" avers), and the second, of what she wants, allied with Freud's impossible quest to delimit a supposedly mysterious and dark desire and therefore implicated in the Freudian pursuit of feminine sexuality so aptly criticized in "Blind Spot of an Old Dream of Symmetry" (Irigaray 1985 [1974])? Why is Irigaray not only asking but also asserting the crucial value of these questions, both of which are repeatedly challenged in her earlier work? How do these questions of identity and desire mediate Irigaray's consideration of the predicament presented to women in the quest to attain a political, civil identity? In this essay, my aim will be to show how, in articulating a feminist politics of difference, Irigaray fortifies her earlier criticism of the masculine politics of desire that lie at the heart of civilization's social contract, while nonetheless elaborating a promising relation between democracy, sexed subjectivity, and civil identity.

In texts such as *Speculum of the Other Woman* and *This Sex Which Is Not One*, originally published in the 1970s, and *Ethics of Sexual Difference* and *Sexes and Genealogies*, originally published in the 1980s, Irigaray articulates the impasse of feminine subjectivity, showing the resistance that femininity and subjectivity present to one another. In arguing that metaphysically, psychically, and politically, the subject is masculine, Irigaray aligns the genealogy of the political subject with that of the sexual subject, insofar as both are premised on a symbolic structure that organizes the world according to patrilineal relations, homosocial bonds, patricidal fantasies of origin, and the sublation of particularity, embodiment, and nature, to universality, reason, and civil order. Within this symbolic universe, the right to be man is equated with a desire for mastery, a fetishizing ideal of independence, and a relation between the one and the many in which the closed atomism of the self adheres to a concept of law (autonomy) that cuts off political and psychical inheritances from the mother. It should thus be clear that Irigaray's work has always drawn connections between critiques of social organization (the politics of liberal democracy) and critiques of the formation of the subject (the birth of identity through the father's name), aligning the fraternal structure of liberal multiplicity (the 1+1+1 of monadic masculine citizens) with the unending metonymy of masculine desire (the 1+1+1 of substitutable women).[1] Irigaray's work testifies to the political and psychical bulwarks of the sexual contract and to its alignment of the body of woman with nature and blood, such that civil order provides itself a material substrate for civilization (the polis of men) to transcend. Yet, her earlier work also leaves us with a deadlock in many ways: if the human individual is always masculine, and if in fact it is the dream of perfect neutrality that enacts the separation of body and words, nature and culture, then the symbolic death[2] of the feminine seems enshrined within the very possibility of political order. How then can women embark on the passage from nature to culture without abdicating the specificity of feminine identity, embodiment, and genealogy? These concepts and questions re-emerge in, and provide a resource for, Irigaray's practical and theoretical attempts to refound democracy on the basis of sexual difference.

In more recent work, such as *Thinking the Difference*, *To Be Two*, *Democracy Begins Between Two*, and *Why Different?*, originally published, with the exception of the first in this list (1989), in the early 1990s, Irigaray begins to conceptualize a political right to difference as a way both to contest the masculine appropriation of subjectivity, which only grants women the right to be men (Irigaray 2000 [1998], 110), and to disrupt the scene of political inheritance, which only acknowledges a genealogy from father to son, by introducing what both that right and that scene exclude, the impossible[3] figure of a feminine citizen. If the right to be men entails assimilation and sacrifice of the feminine, the right to difference entails cultivation of the feminine and serves as an antidote to the masculine death grip on neutrality. Moreover, insofar as sexual difference takes form as 'two,' it resists the order of the one and the many (the ceaseless multiplication of ones in the liberal marketplace of desire), refusing to be submerged or sublated within this economy. The two instead represents the subject as divided and split, neither a self-enclosed atom nor a moment of particularity in a sea of multiplicity.[4] Irigaray thus grapples with both the logic of liberalism and the impasses of identity and desire through political creation of a subject who is neither mired in the masculine fantasies of women (nature, body, simultaneously mother and yet nongenerative) nor another man, but a different kind of subject, a woman who is returned from exile to her own subjectivity, the polis, and genealogical relations. The 'two' is thus simultaneously a promise and a threat, a promise of a new democratic form and a threat to the organizing conditions and practices of liberalism and patriarchal masculinity.

Before moving forward, it is probably useful to remind the reader that, in all her work, including the most recent, Irigaray promotes sexual difference[5] but rejects the idea of gender as either a sociohistorical determination or a merely natural phenomenon and writes instead of "different subjective configurations" (Irigaray 2001 [1994],

137) or "a different structuring of subjectivity" (Irigaray 2001 [1994], 151). She submits in regard to social constitution that the human being, whether woman or man, "is not a mere social effect, whatever its impact and historical importance. And, whosoever renounces the specificity of both the feminine subjectivity and identity, reducing them to simply social determinations, sacrifices even more women to patriarchy" (Irigaray 2000 [1998], 11). And with regard to nature she writes that women should "not accept being reduced to a pure body, a pure nature" (Irigaray 2000 [1998], 151). Refusing to abandon the psychoanalytic insight that subjectivity emerges in relation to parental others and that this relation is itself sexuate (Irigaray 2000 [1994], 31), Irigaray continues to maintain that the mother/child bond mediates the elaboration of sexed identity and that it marks the unconscious with the body that gives birth. Rather than presuming the givenness of nature or history, Irigaray is instead interested in reconceiving precisely how sexual difference might alter our understanding of the relation between the natural and the civil, making available new modes of political being through a "refounding of the relationships between man and woman" (Irigaray 2001 [1994], 25). For this to happen, however, "it is necessary to make sexual difference pass from the level of simple naturalness, of instinct, to that of a sexuated subjectivity" (Irigaray 2000 [1998], 165), a difficult task given that our current sociopolitical regime is premised on "a flaw in the relation between the state of nature and civil identity which makes civil coexistence impossible" (Irigaray 2001 [1994], 46). In other words, within the regime of liberalism, sexual difference is excluded from representation, in all senses of that word.[6] If sexual difference is not merely the historical residue of "an alienation of the feminine" (Irigaray 2001 [1994], 137), endlessly variable, abstract, and detached from nature, it is also not merely a natural immediacy, a brute reality outside the sphere of civilization with no political import.[7] Irigaray thus contests the idea that "starting from the cosmic or natural order is sufficient to build a social or political order" since here "one may risk falling again into the errors of the patriarchal world" whereas "a harmonious civil community, an accomplished democracy can only be founded upon relations between citizens" (Irigaray 2000 [1998], 149), that is, citizens who are women and men, who are not asexuate.[8] Irigaray is thus quite clear that a viable feminist politics requires a passage between nature and culture both as the condition for and the task of civil order.

It is within this context of the exclusion of sexual difference by an asexual democracy that Irigaray claims that the idea of human nature might be better replaced with the Greek sense of "coming to appear" (Irigaray 2000 [1998], 95) or with gender: "Maybe it would be better to talk about the human species as being divided into two genders, using a word that means 'genus,' 'generation' or 'family' among the Greeks" (Irigaray 2000 [1998], 95). In indicating that the word nature might be too "abstract and ambiguous" a term, Irigaray draws our attention to the link between it and the more "concrete" ideas of lineage and growth. We could say, in other words, that, insofar as human nature is always already attached to gender,[9] there is no *one* human nature and that therefore "human nature is two" (Irigaray 2000 [1998], 95), a two that can be traced genealogically and that therefore must be understood as fundamentally temporal.[10] If there can be no concept of human nature that might provide determinate content, we must instead apprehend the fundamentally divergent quality of nature's participation in the human and the vexed bond between the human and the natural.

When, therefore, Irigaray asks, "how are we to define the difference between woma(e)n and ma(e)n?" (Irigaray 2001 [1994], 150), she is not seeking a formula that might provide positive, substantive, unchanging realities or abstract concepts that could capture all particulars. To the contrary, she is quite explicit that the mistake is to quantify a calculable difference just as it is equally mistaken to abolish "the reality of the genders to resolve the domination of one by the other" (Irigaray 2001 [1994], 150). To resist both of these errors, essentialism and neutralization, Irigaray proposes the affirmation of a difference that mediates and limits, but does not imprison, the becoming of both identity and desire. We cannot expect to be emancipated from sex; there is no end of sex, as, for instance, might be fantasized in the liberal dream of an androgynous society.[11] It is instead sex that must be emancipated from liberalism.[12]

THE NAME AND THE NAVEL

The phallus becomes the organizer of the world through the man-father at the very place where the umbilical cord, that primal link to the mother, once gave birth to man and woman . . . Does the father replace the womb with the matrix of his language? But the exclusivity of his law refuses all representation to that first body, that first home, that first love. These are sacrificed and provide matter for an empire of language that so privileges the male sex as to confuse it with the human race.

(Irigaray 1993 [1987], 14)

In her essay "Body Against Body: In Relation to the Mother," Irigaray argues that "our society and culture operate on the basis of an original matricide" (Irigaray 1993 [1987], 11), and she suggests that the son's mother and the daughter's mother are asymmetrically placed or displaced within patriarchal political genealogies. Irigaray's approach to the impasse of feminine subjectivity thus begins with an analysis of the masculine appropriation of genealogy and its exclusion of maternal lines of inheritance and legitimacy. The father's genealogy provides our socio-political orientation, grounding individual identity in the inheritance of his name and property, and social identity and citizenship in the space of his absence. Allowing for only one origin, the father's language camouflages and petrifies the mother's body, denying its claim to generative power. Taking itself alone to legitimate the child's birth, the father's name suppresses the mother's body and blood. Both legitimation and generation are confiscated by the paternal principle.

Irigaray argues that sexual difference is not appropriately spiritualized or sublated in part because of this patriarchal substitution of the name for the navel: "when the father refuses to allow the mother her power of giving birth and seeks to be the sole creator . . . he superimposes upon our ancient world of flesh and blood a universe of language and symbols that has no roots in the flesh" (Irigaray 1993 [1987], 16). Since both have severed ties with nature, neither language nor law can subsequently speak with the body, a situation that leaves us with a chasm between word and body that is also the trace of their attachment: "just as the scar of the navel is forgotten, so, correspondingly, a hole appears in the texture of the language" (Irigaray 1993 [1987], 16). Irigaray claims of this bodily sacrifice, for the sake of an "exclusively male symbolic world" (Irigaray 1993 [1987], 17), that it desubjectivizes women and swallows their desire (Irigaray 1993 [1987], 18) while, at the same time, "the sacrifice of nature and the sexual body" (Irigaray 1994 [1989], 12) leaves men with no specific sexual identity of their own.[13] In differing ways, both sexes become asexuate. The "difficulty in relation to his mother and his corporeal, natural origin" permits men to "communicate only among themselves, the 'brothers' who share the same language, the same subjectivity" (Irigaray 2000 [1998], 130), while women have no symbolic access to their maternal heritage and hence to their own identity. For both children, the effect of this reduction to a single lineage is that maternity represents at best a merely natural origin, while paternity, the patronym that gives the child a name and legitimates him or her, represents a transcendental origin. It is in part with reference to this seclusion of the mother in the domain of the natural, "silent, out-lawed" (Irigaray 1993 [1987], 14), that Irigaray characterizes women's situation as one of exile.

The social contract, in establishing citizenship and democratic legitimacy through masculine lines of descent, represses the son's mater-nal birth and severs the feminine from civil identity. The subject is born of the father's death,[14] the father's name, establishing filiation as a strictly patrilineal affair. In this way, desire and politics collude to establish a masculine universal subject, delimiting a terrain of seeming neutrality in which the conflation between the universal and the mas-culine does not appear as such and founding the universal on an alli-ance between a neutered sexual identity and an all-encompassing political desire for unity. The effect is that "citizens as a gender are cut off from their roots in the body" (Irigaray 1993 [1987], 136). Without access to a double origin, to the mother as origin, and to the body as a resource for law, "the relation of citizens to birth, motherhood" remains unme-diated and severed from civil law so that *the social body splits off from the natural body*" (140). Here we can see clearly the dilemma of strand-ing sexual difference in the body, isolated as unmediated nature without access to language or law. While masculine subjects are denatured in-sofar as their birth is conceptualized through name and law and not as a bodily event, femininity is severed from the status of subject so that feminine subjects are not able to exist or to represent themselves as such at all.[15] It is this split between the natural and the social,[16] the severing of the mother from sexual, subjective, and political history, which fosters the illusion of a *"neuter universal"* and a neuter citizen. There is, hence, "no civil law in our era that makes human persons of men and women" (Irigaray 1996 [1992], 21), and thus "as sexed persons they remain in natural immediacy. This means that real persons still have no rights, since there are only men and women; there are no neuter individuals" (Irigaray 1996 [1992], 21). The absence of a medi-ated maternal relation is especially problematic for women since they have thereby surrendered both a necessary resource of identity and the capacity to formulate that identity in the public sphere as citizens. The effect of the patrilineal status of law is that "the law has a sex, justice has a sex, but by default" (Irigaray 1993 [1987], 193; 1994 [1989], 15). The lines of inheritance that establish the meaning of citizenship effec-tively produce and conceal a false universal.

In establishing a necessary relation of law to paternity, the posture of equality sustains only a masculine universal, while simultaneously governing the political sphere in the form of a fraternal structure. Irigaray recognizes two dimensions, vertical and horizontal, of masculine relationality, noting that "we live in a society of men-amongst-themselves that operates according to an exclusive respect for the ancestry of sons and fathers, and of competition between brothers" (Irigaray 1994 [1989], 7). The vertical aspect, tracing masculine lines of descent, and the horizontal aspect, binding men-amongst-themselves, together collude to exclude what they ostensibly include and incorporate what they ostensibly leave behind. Irigaray thus contends that only the "cultural restitution of the mother-daughter couple," that is, of lines of matrilineal descent, which, insofar as they are submerged within and by a culture between-men, have become the "lost crossroads of becoming woman" (Irigaray 1994 [1989], 99), could create the conditions necessary for a woman to "become who she is" (Irigaray 1996 [1992], 39).

Living within the political and subjective context established by masculine rationality and fantasy, woman has been encouraged "to become *man*. If she is to become woman, if she is to accomplish her female subjectivity" (Irigaray 1993 [1987], 64) and break free of the limit furnished by 'equal rights,' Irigaray postulates that she must access a genealogical and public relation of her own. A feminine subject (with her own agency and form of desire), cannot materialize without a creative imagination of both the vertical axis of inheritance and lineage, traced through feminine lines of descent, and the horizontal axis of public and universal relations among women, neither of which can be activated within a regime of masculine neutrality. For this reason, Irigaray believes it would be mistaken to "demand a right to subjectivity and to freedom for women without defining the objective rights of the female gender" (Irigaray 1996 [1992], 5), rights that are sexed and not neutral.

For women to be full citizens, to have access as women to the domain of the political, they must have recourse to their own becoming, which entails giving feminine identity a past and a future ('verticality' but also temporality) and feminine desire a public language in which to speak. This context explains why "for the daughter, discovering a relationship of words with her mother corresponds to discovering the path of her incarnation as a woman: the path of the relationship inside herself between body and words. So the woman is no longer the nature-body for which man will be the words . . . both woman and man are a different body and different words" (Irigaray 2000 [1998], 34). A relation to the mother's body and its loss, to "genealogical becoming" (Irigaray 1993 [1990], 94), might offer woman "an other of her own that she can become" (Irigaray 1993 [1987], 64), providing for a self-cultivation that is not divorced from the body and thereby contesting the fantasy of origin which begets fraternity and defines law/democracy as inheritance in and of the father's name.

Even within the context of her earlier work, it should thus not be surprising that in *Thinking the Difference*, Irigaray protests that "the written law is a law established for a society of men-amongst-themselves" (Irigaray 1994 [1989], 59). While her work has always focused attention on the failure of symbolic law to constitute sexed identity through Symbolic law, and on the question of how women are to become subjects, here she extends this concern to the realm of civil identity, in the domain of political power and law. The question of subjectivity takes on a practical (in addition to ontological) meaning: how can women become political subjects? Arguing that civil identity is an identity in which the rights of women are excluded from consideration by the 'Rights of Man,' with which they cannot be assimilated, Irigaray challenges the masculine hold on universality. "The *Universal Declaration of Human Rights* [La Declaration universelle des droits de l'homme, i.e., 'Declaration of the Rights of Man'] may be a moving document," Irigaray remarks, "but from the very first article, I, a woman, no longer feel 'human' [feel I am a 'man']. For I am not 'born free and equal in dignity and rights' [to other 'men']" (Irigaray 1994 [1989], viii–ix). Thus, "if we are not to be accomplices in the murder of the mother," we must transform the language of politics[17] by inventing "words that do not erase the body but speak the body," thereby establishing a different relation to origin and asserting "that there is a genealogy of women" (Irigaray 1993 [1987], 19).[18]

TOTALITARIAN DEMOCRACY

To become equal is to be unfaithful to the task of incarnating our happiness as living women and men.

(Irigaray 1996 [1992], 15)

Being we means being at least two, autonomous, different. This we still has no place, neither between the human genders or sexes, nor in the public realm where male citizens (women not yet being full citizens) form a social whole in the form of one plus one plus one

(Irigaray 1996 [1992], 48)

The equality of brothers has become the only legitimate basis for civil society and the definition of the individual. In confronting this fraternal order of politics, however, we confront a dilemma: as fraternity has become more developed, it is realized not through strict adherence to the sovereignty of men, but at that moment when its mechanisms have become so entrenched, and its form of universalization so extended, that even women are welcomed as citizen-allies, welcomed in 'brotherhood.' The problem, of course, is that with the arrival of this moment, women become fellow citizens on the basis of being or appearing to be (equal to) masculine (that is, neutral) subjects. The apparent political emancipation of women is at the same time the valorization, through de facto acquiescence, of the masculine ideal as the standard of citizenship. Given that women can neither wholly assimilate to the masculine generic nor evade its grasp altogether, a woman must inhabit an unhappy both/and: she both appropriates a language and an identity that does not arise from her (that, in fact, effaces her) and she also lives within a body taken to be pre-social and antithetical to culture. She is both masculine and silent. Moreover, with "the reduction of each and every subject to a single subjectivity: a human, universal, abstract, asexuate subject" (Irigaray 2000 [1994], 44), the imperialist ego appears, detached from the body and capable only of "appropriating the other" (Irigaray 2000 [1994], 43), in a world that is "a vast competitive market" (Irigaray 2001 [1994], 173). The politics of equality displaces women in both the public and the private realms, since femininity is absent from the former and severed from political agency in the latter. Equal opportunity to be a liberal self is hence also a demand for a further sacrifice on the part of women. Women are asked not only to sacrifice their 'pound of flesh' for the sake of becoming speaking subjects; they are also asked to sacrifice their sexed specificity for the sake of becoming citizens.[19] In addition to masquerading as women, women must masquerade as men, must in fact desire this masquerade: "We proclaim that we want to be free, equal brothers" (Irigaray 2000 [1994], 85).[20] Liberalism thereby enlists feminism in the service of patriarchy, asserting women's rights on the basis of fraternal individuality and therefore at the expense of femininity.[21] Alternative feminisms are rendered obsolete as the assertion of a specifically feminine identity becomes inevitably associated with an archaic traditionalism or mystifying nostalgia to the detriment of public legitimacy and sustenance. It is this effective regulation of the parameters of feminism that Irigaray resists; in pursuing the meaning and consequences of women's failure to garner their own civil identity and the attempt to settle instead for a pre-existing masculine model, she asks "will they not be supporting and promoting a male tradition and society to which they remain alien, and which, to some extent, annihilates them as persons?" (Irigaray 1994 [1989], 41) and thereby turns the charge of traditionalism against the accusers who are, in supporting egalitarianism, nourishing the basic structure of patriarchal politics.

As Jean-Joseph Goux argues on the basis of his reading of Irigaray, the quest for equal rights is a ruse of patriarchal masculinity (Goux, 182) in which "egalitarianism works toward the disappearance of women, in the totalitarian order of the masculine-neutral" (Goux, 185): the "ultramodern" fantasy of neutralization extends and sediments the sovereignty of the masculine in the form of a radical substitutability and infinite exchange wherein all can be measured by the same virile standard. The logic of modernity thus sustains masculine hegemony in the form of a "generalized equivalence" (Goux, 180) of persons even while purporting that the latter undoes the former. The neutral thereby succeeds in consolidating the masculine, not destabilizing, evading, or overcoming it. In decrying a form of democracy that has devolved into the totalitarian fantasy of interchangeable subjects, Goux also supports Irigaray's contention that the modern ego is "imperialist" (Irigaray 2001 [1994], 10), incapable of brooking excess or externality and fundamentally antidemocratic in its desire to possess rather than connect and to establish unity rather than enjoy alterity.

As Goux writes, "the inexorable logic" of sexual neutrality is that "it is women who are destined to disappear, not men . . . in the end only women lose their distinctive characteristics and their difference"[22] (Goux, 177). If modern egalitarianism is driven by its assault on traditional values, and particularly by its assault on a form of social domination legitimated by "the immutable decrees of nature, or through the dignity of an eternal essence" (Goux, 178), then, Goux claims, the "intransigent affirmation of equality" will always be haunted by the "specter" of that which it contests, not least because both share a devalorization of the natural and thus operate on a common ground. The threat to women is thus less essentialism than erasure of sexuation, women's "metamorphosis into the masculine-neutral" (Goux, 178). On Goux's reading of Irigaray, therefore, egalitarian claims are intrinsically disposed to support rather than threaten masculine domination and in fact "are complicit with the deep logic of this domination"

(Goux, 180) as well as with "an ancient patriarchal ideology" that denies difference and devalues nature. Goux identifies this totalitarian logic with a Cartesian radicalization of rationalism and scientism (185) forcibly deployed against nature to create an "asexual universe of human ants" (Goux, 181). By contrast, Goux affirms Irigaray's commitment to an idea of sexed embodiment that is not degraded to "the primitive and shameful residue of humanity's animal origins, an ancient, prehistorical vestige" (Goux, 181), but is instead valued as "the drama of sexual alterity" and the fertile resource for a genuinely democratic politics.[23]

The logic of liberalism and the Modern victory of contract over status[24] thus means that we must distinguish masculine sovereignty from the domination of women by men. Goux reminds us that the former can persist beyond the eradication of the latter and that so long as the "structural and abstract reign of the masculine-neutral" provides a "horizon" of value, femininity will continue to be suppressed in "an indefinite play of substitution and interchangeability" (Goux, 188). Goux agrees with Irigaray that to resist this dispossession (of human nature), we must refuse to abandon sexuate identity.

If egalitarianism has reached its limit in "the deadly impasse of the neutral sex" (Goux, 189), deadly because it cuts us off from life, transforming life into exchange in the conquest of reason over embodiment, then sexual difference offers a different kind of limit, "the most radical limit opposed to the totalizing will of the subject" (Irigaray 2001 [1994], 6). The opposition between "living persons, man and woman" and "abstract, artificial individuals" (Irigaray 2001 [1994], 155) that characterizes the logic of liberal democracy Irigaray calls "death" (Irigaray 2001 [1994], 117), writing that "although life, obviously, is always sexed, death on the contrary no longer makes this distinction" (Irigaray 2001 [1994], 34). Only a necropolis denies the temporality that inheres in sexual difference, preferring the stagnant guarantee, the closed order, of the neuter to the risks and promises of becoming that inhabit carnal subjects. To deny mortality through an evasion of sexual difference that displaces it onto a denigrated nature is actually to take the side of death and disembodiment wherein "life and singularity are erased in an abstract universal" (Irigaray 2000 [1994], 64).

If, instead, sexual difference becomes a civil difference with a "political value" (Irigaray 2000 [1998], 109), the sensible as the site of temporality will be honored while the between-two as the site of transcendence[25] will be preserved as a gap that cannot be closed and that, in resisting finality and totalization, fosters life. While the refusal of this form of cultivation fixes becoming into being, excludes temporality, and surrenders the body, the two of sexual difference mediates the passage from nature to culture, "the crossing between body and word" (Irigaray 2000 [1994], 12), neither leaving behind nor sublating the sensible, but inviting a never-ending process that marks the indebtedness of the latter to the former and their energetic connection.[26] For incarnate subjects, the sensible and the transcendental cannot be split apart, as though each might belong independently to a single gender, but are instead developed between us, not as possessions of a gender but as the movement of each gender's becoming. Irigaray's conclusion is unequivocal: "the civil law must be changed to give both sexes their own identity as citizens" (Irigaray 1994 [1989], xvi). While equality demands that the transcendental and the sensible be severed from one another, and that the one (the brother) be repeated over and over in the 'one plus one' without difference, sexed civil identity might respect sex (and the mother's mark, the navel) as the incarnate unity of sensible and transcendental.

So long as the concept of the citizen, of the individual as bearer of political right, is identified with neutrality, masculinity will emerge as the substanceless, shapeless form of subjectivity itself, submerging the difference of sex. The interchangeability of subjects in "a regime of generalized equivalence—incorporating everything, without residue" (Goux, 188), has led to a "dissolution of being into exchange value" (Goux, 188), abolishing alterity. Nonetheless, sexual difference haunts democracy as its living remainder, what gets lost in, but also sticks in the throat of, the formulation of totalitarian order. How, then, can we (politically) liberate the relation between the sexes and how, conversely, might sexual difference sustain and nourish a legitimate political relation? Against the closure of totality, Irigaray proposes that what sexual difference can accomplish, what a democratic politics should accomplish, is the preservation of that in-between space, which is collapsed by the Modern logic of egalitarianism and its concomitant pleasures of exchange. But this requires that women be citizens while neither acceding to an alienated femininity nor assimilating to a masculine identity; it requires, in other words, that women emerge as citizens in their own right and with their own rights. Here the choice between equality and difference is found to be a deceptive one as equality emerges as a "right to difference"[27] (Irigaray 1993 [1990],

11). For this reason, Irigaray's response to the limitations of limitless equality is that "each must have the opportunity to be a concrete, corporeal and sexuate subject, rather than an abstract, neutral, fabricated and fictitious one" (Irigaray 2000 [1994], 26). In reflecting on women's current situation with regard to law and civil identity, Irigaray thus proposes a sexed universality, a universality without neutrality: two universals in fact. If the universal has become occupied by the masculine (occupied in the sense of an invasion by hostile forces), then only a splitting of the universal can open up a feminine genealogy, while only another relation to origin can counter this occupation, forming a resistance that releases feminine subjects into a political identity of their own. While the masculine universal citizen functions in apparent neutrality, there has yet to be a feminine universal subject, one correlated with a distinctly feminine embodiment. Women must thus devise a way to "accede to a civil identity without denying their own nature" (Irigaray 2001 [1994], 140), thereby reconciling embodiment with civil status but without fixing or giving absolute value to an abstract concept of woman. By introducing and developing such a redefinition of rights, Irigaray claims to have found a way "to emerge from a critique of patriarchy that might well prove nihilistic if it is not accompanied by a definition of new values founded on natural reality and having universal validity" (Irigaray 1996 [1992], 39).

BEING TWO

I do not believe that to question the universal subject starting from the multiple is sufficient, because the multiple can always be equivalent to a multiple or a sub-multiple of *one*.

(Irigaray 2000 [1998], 145)

In order to question the universal subject, it is necessary to approach another logic . . . The universal therefore is no longer *one* nor unique, it is *two*.

(Irigaray 2000 [1998], 146–47)

As we have seen, the totalitarian structure of liberal egalitarianism is perhaps best understood as "an undifferentiated state of universality" that erases or sacrifices sexuate, but also specifically feminine identity, in establishing "a neutral asexual community" (Irigaray 2001 [1994],

37). Within this order, "we are no longer two, but subjugated, both of us, to an abstract order which divides us into one+one+ . . . parts of a community" (Irigaray 2000 [1994], 31–32). Such ones must be whole, self-enclosed, solitary, self-generating, neither split nor related to otherness (including the otherness within). The atomistic subject is the other side of totalitarian politics, the support for the "undifferentiated magma . . . of a male kind of power (Irigaray 1996 [1992], 48).

While the many is simply an "ensemble of ones"[28] (Irigaray 2000 [1994], 33), the two opens an entirely different relation, a relation that is not additive but mediating, not the "juxtaposition of one+one subjects" but rather "a relationship *between*" (Irigaray 2000 [1994], 35). It is in connection to this "between" that Irigaray writes that "the universal is within you and develops out of you as a flower grows from the earth" (Irigaray 2001 [1994], 29). The universal emerges between-two, at their "cross-roads" and in their "encounter" (Irigaray 2001 [1994], 29). Since the between-two is also within, it precludes monadic identity in favor of self-division. In this regard, Irigaray posits sexual difference as a limit to wholeness, writing that "being a man or a woman already means not being the whole of the subject or of the community or of spirit, as well as not being entirely one's self" (Irigaray 1996 [1992], 106). Sexual difference presents itself as the antithesis to the principle of totalization, subverting the unity, the self-identity, and the definite boundaries of both the self and the community.

The one is an illusion of patriarchy and complicit with the imperialist forces of containment that can recognize no outside, no exteriority, and which are thus fully totalizing. Irigaray's response to this closed order is not multiplicity since, she asserts, the many is merely a plurality of ones or a one that has been fragmented. The logic of the one and the logic of the many are inseparable, both promising the infinite malleability that is the hallmark of liberal individualism. The logic of the two, however, resists this bond and respects both the obdurate aspect of human nature[29] and its fundamental capacity for change, growth, and development. In the very division that is its mark, we are, Irigaray reminds us, "children of the flesh, but also of the word;" the two has the capacity to energetically mediate them while respecting that the unity of the self is limited by incarnation (Irigaray 2000 [1994], 59). Historically, the sensible transcendental has been split, with natural birth assigned to maternity and cultural birth to paternity, equating the woman-mother with body and the man-father with language and law. As a result, human

subjectivity has been masculinized, while human flesh is both femi-
nized and animalized. Language is disincarnated (Irigaray 2000 [1994],
107) and rendered foreign to our bodies (Irigaray 2000 [1994], 106).
Since sexual difference entails that subjectivity is always already incarnate, "woven of bodies and words" (Irigaray 2000 [1994], 28), it
also makes possible "new bridges between nature and culture, between
instincts or drives and civility, between the individual body and the
collective body" (Irigaray 2000 [1998], 78). In traversing this perilous
chasm, such an incarnate universal "overcomes the deadly split between body and spirit" (Whitford, 393), the death entailed by totalitarian, asexuate, and egalitarian democracy. The between-two thus
provides a new basis for democracy and an alternative to both liberal
individualism and the disguised atomism/egoism of multiplicity.[30]

Moreover, if the two is extricated or "disinterred" from the one
(Irigaray 2001 [1994], 131), then the feminine might become subject,
might be freed "from the world of man," thereby acknowledging "this
scandal for philosophy: the subject is neither one nor singular, but is
two" (Irigaray 2001 [1994],130). A feminine subject would be an *other*
subject and also an *other* sex (not a second sex). Irigaray's point is that
only 'twoness' unlike 'secondness' can represent or partake of difference. Since the two addresses itself both to the other's alterity and the
subject's own divided nature, a democracy founded on sexual difference could, unlike the fraternal liberal democratic order (operating
on the logic of the one and sustained by its own impasse), represent
and cultivate all its citizens and reconnect nature with culture across
the barrier of illusory wholeness. And the two also, unlike the disem-
bodied 1+1+1, begins with 'thinking from the body,'[31] and thereby
enables a passage from natural to civil identity without erasure of sex
in the illusion of neutrality. As such, the two provides a radically new
basis for political order, a basis in living beings. Since there is no such
thing as a generic human, such an abstraction cannot provide a legitimate basis for democratic politics. There is no neutral human. But,
Irigaray proposes, there is a sexed universal. If politics requires a subject, and the subject is always sexually differentiated (if there are two
forms of subjectivity), then the universal must be sexuate as well. In
proposing a new logic of the universal, Irigaray refuses the regime of
the one and the many in a paradoxical doubling or division of the
universal that not only subverts its pretensions to neutrality, but thereby
also resists both atomism and particularism while opening feminine
access to civil identity.

The idea of the universal seems inseparable from a concept of the (modern) subject, necessary to its very political (and sexual) structure. To be a subject (in either sense) has required the sacrifice of substance, that is, it has required the universal as the abstraction in which substance might be abandoned and the principle under which particularity might be subsumed. "The universal," Irigaray writes, "has been thought as *one*, thought on the basis of *one*. But this *one* does not exist" (Irigaray 1996 [1992], 35). Irigaray instead maintains that nature contains its own limit, its own finitude, a limit that we can designate as that of sexual difference: " 'I am sexed' implies, 'I am not everything' " (Irigaray 1996 [1992], 51). I am sexed implies an acceptance of lack, loss, and division. It is through sexual difference that the body becomes subject and attains its fundamental relation to alterity. With this acceptance, that which poses as the (one, or only) universal, which purports to "represent human kind" (Irigaray 1996 [1992], 39), must be seen as an exclusion of the body and an exhortative invitation to disavow human nature.

In order to reconceive the universal as two, the human must first accept its foundation in the natural (rather than in the opposition between reason and nature). Since human nature is two (is split, contains difference), no one gender can represent the totality of human being, and such totality itself becomes suspect. As "he dreams of being the whole" (Irigaray 1996 [1992], 40), the brother of fraternal order also radically severs nature from culture, maternal origin from paternal origin, commiting himself to a kind of faith in the sacrificial logic of subjectivity in which the social contract, the origin of the political, is only possible through the murders that allow him to inherit in the father's name and that guarantee him the seemingly infinite permutations of unlimited self-development. The universal of liberal democracy, though severed from nature and committed to culture, is nonetheless saturated with masculinity (and even with the masculine body on which its imaginary unity is modeled). But we can think the limit of sexual difference in a different way, as a creative limit (creative of the universal), one which is generative, between two. In saying "I belong to a gender, which means to a sexed universal and to a relation between two universals" (Irigaray 1996 [1992], 106), sexual difference becomes not only the mark of mortality on the body, but also the promise of finitude. It is this idea of a between-two that is at the heart of Irigaray's development of an ethics of sexual difference in the recognition of a sexual relation between two universals. The relation between these two universals is not to be resolved or sublated into a neutrality that is its telos. The maintenance of sexual difference requires instead that the two remain two, capable of being in relation because they represent a difference and not a mere opposition or mirroring of the same. With a sexed universal, feminine and masculine would emerge as immanent universals, rooted in singularity but not determined by any already existing content.

A divided or doubled universal (simultaneously founded in and founding a feminine genealogy) would thus foster "the right to sexual identity" (Irigaray 1994 [1989], 81), and hence also provide for a specific set of women's rights while catalyzing "a redefinition of the rights and responsibilities of male citizens" (Irigaray 1994 [1989], 62) no longer strictly bound to the delusion of neutrality and equality. With the sexual dimension "recognized as part of civil identity" (Irigaray 1994 [1989], 81), a universality that respects the singularity of sex would reorient the human relation to nature. At first glance, Irigaray's claim that "the most appropriate content for the universal is sexual difference" might appear to be a contentious one. But this claim is intended to support a notion of originary difference at the heart of subjectivity. Sex "constitutes the irreducible differentiation that occurs *on the inside of the* 'the human race.' Gender stands for the unsubstitutable position of the *I* and the *you*" (Irigaray 1993 [1987], 170), for the ethical relation to an other. The individual contains the universal within, not the human universal but the universal of sexual difference, of man or woman (Irigaray 1996 [1992], 48). In departing from any determinate or abstract sense of universality, Irigaray redefines it as a mediating principle, both living and divided (Irigaray 1996 [1992], 50), effecting (defining, limiting, establishing) relations among individuals, as well as between individuals and the state. This living universal "is divided into two" (Irigaray 1996 [1992], 50) just as the subject is divided, since it is from the subject that it emerges. It can thereby do justice to sex, establishing rights to identity and dignity that would otherwise be dissolved in mythical unity.

Irigaray's wager is that women's access to political subjectivity can be brought about by raising sexual identity to the level of the universal, recognized by law, creating a civil identity that resists both the reduction of women's identity to the private function of motherhood and women's assimilation (through the concept of equality) to the public function of the masculine citizen. An abstract structure of rights is insufficient to this task because it fails to alter the legal conditions and grammatical structures necessary for actual accrual of rights to women; the singular conception of the individual can only represent while concealing, a sacrificial logic in which the universal emerges as a conceptual abstraction and the individual, segregated from feminine embodiment, emerges in a genealogy governed by the father's name.

In intervening in and transforming its possibilities, Irigaray alters the logic of the universal in such a way that it no longer bears the implication of fraternal neutrality. In proposing that we think the human as two, that there are two human universals, or that sexual difference is universal, Irigaray develops a relation between a feminine universal and the formation of a feminine subject mediated by maternal genealogy. Enshrining two universals in civil law is thus Irigaray's response to the paternal/fraternal lineage of Modern democracy, a way to mediate desire and identity, nature and law, and offer women a civil identity that does not deny their sexed embodiment. Women's liberation (or emancipation) could hence be understood not as a utopian release from alienation or sacrifice, but as "access to subjectivity" (Irigaray 1993 [1990], 71). By imagining this possibility, Irigaray responds directly to the impasse of a homosocial democratic order, both politically and psychically. She introduces sexual difference into the heart of rights and thereby transforms their meaning as well as that of civil identity.

The passage from nature to culture that takes form in the social contract exiles the difference of the body and excludes sexual difference from culture. A democracy of sexual indifference founded on a history of the one (and the many) but not of two is one that is irreconcilably barred from living beings. To counter this sacrifice and its repudiation of the natural, Irigaray claims we need a new form of incarnation and a new logic of division (rather than the logic of multiplicity). A divided universal is neither one nor its dispersal or dissolution in a sea of particularities. It is, instead, a paradox, tension, and dehiscence at the heart of subjectivity, ethics, and politics, and, as such, it disrupts the fantasy of harmony, unity, and perfect fraternal equality and marks instead a democratic possibility of a "law of persons appropriate to their natural reality,"[32] that is, to their sexed identity" (Irigaray 1996 [1992], 51). Such a law brings into the public sphere speaking bodies, bodies with words (and not just bodies with needs, natural bodies). Here "bodies are invited to participate in the becoming of thought, ethics, and History. It's no longer about overcoming the body, more specifically the sexed body" (Irigaray 2000 [1998], 124). Moreover, as a law of the divided universal, it preserves what is indigestible to it without assimilating it, a "gap" in our encounter with the other that cannot be overcome. Because "difference is present everywhere, in us and between us" (Irigaray 2001 [1994], 13), taking sexual difference as the principle of universality and democracy can disorder the totalitarian kernel that is otherwise the truth of liberal democracy.

CONCLUSION

'Women's liberation' requires an exacting cultural effort, and not just strategies for social emancipation. Deconstructing the patriarchal tradition is certainly indispensable, but is hardly enough. It is necessary to define new values directly or indirectly suitable to feminine subjectivity and feminine identity . . . We need to go back a few steps in order to analyze the grip on the feminine subject by one or many tradition(s) created by a sole subject, de facto masculine.

(Irigaray 2000 [1998], 10)

We have seen that the development of sexual difference in Irigaray's more recent work has taken on an increasingly political significance, allying itself with a notion of democracy that might depart from its fraternal lineage and thus provide women with a civil identity. Irigaray claims of the norms of citizenship being developed in the institution of the European Union: that "women's identity is outlined negatively, through what it lacks . . . The request is above all to be recognized as a 'citizen' [gram. masc.) on an equal footing. But there is no statement nor question concerning who woman is and what her needs are" (Irigaray 2001 [1994], 83). The inquiry into woman's identity and desire is crucial to a democratic politics because only an approach that responds to the danger of 'neutral' citizenship and its destruction of sex can refound democracy on a different kind of passage between nature and culture. Questions about identity and desire are hence questions about how we develop "civil self-representation" (Irigaray 2001 [1994], 101) mediated by appropriate rights (Irigaray 2001 [1994], 100) and not about a mandate aligned with determinate nature (Irigaray 2001 [1994], 101). Since "becoming a woman means acquiring a civil dimension which is appropriate to 'feminine identity' " (Irigaray 2001 [1994], 36), Irigaray's insight is that we must both revive feminine lines of descent and reconfigure the universal if we hope to engage "the battle for the passage from the state of nature to civil identity" (Irigaray 2001 [1994], 105). A law that is addressed to sexed bodies might return temporality and public space to politics. Irigaray's idea of the between-two makes possible not only a political becoming-woman (i.e., it serves as a response to the question with which Irigaray's work has always been concerned: how do we become woman?), but also, as sexed universal, mediates and calls forth new forms of democracy. Sexed rights, written laws that allow women to redefine themselves and become self-determining, allow women to escape the deadly choices of sexual indifference: subject (masculine) or mother (essentially and only the pale reflection and resource of the subject). Inviting a civil identity and dignity that doesn't sacrifice the body, that establishes a passage between nature and culture, these embodied rights are rights for the living (unlike neutral rights which are rights for the dead, for those who have left their bodies).

The point of Irigaray's work on identity and desire is thus to depict women as feminine subjects (and not as eternal essences or masculine subjects as the liberal state implicitly conceives them). Rather than interpreting Irigaray's call to sexed embodiment as a renewal of metaphysical essentialism or as a regression to social empiricism, we should instead appreciate how the language of bodies provides a necessary resource for the cultivation of sexual difference and a permanent reminder that sexual difference is a limit that mediates rather than grounds our relations to identity and desire, transforming their very logic and making possible civil recognition of the singularity of citizens in precisely their non-unity and self-differentiation. By offering "an elaboration of *sexualized subjective identity*" (Irigaray 1993 [1987], 153), Irigaray thus inaugurates a transformative project, a new passage from nature to civil life that solicits a radical reconstitution of the subject as well as of politics. In suggesting that we think about "the establishment of another era of civilization, or of culture, in which the exchange of objects, and most particularly of women, would no longer form the basis for the constitution of a cultural order" (45), her politics is directed against the order of generalized equivalence, breaking with the Modern and liberal quest for closure in favor of the generative promise of sexuation which is itself a futural/temporal promise and not a determinate concept.

We can now see how the fate of the sexed subject, the subject of desire, is implicated in the formation and identity of the civil subject and in the idea of sexuate rights for women. If human nature is fundamentally two, then the masculine "relationship between the one and the many, between the I-masculine subject and others: people, society, understood as *them* and not as *you*" (Irigaray 2001 [1994], 171) is inadequate, and so also are the ideas of the citizen and the universal with which it is mired By contrast, as a relation "between two," rather than one of lack in either self or other, a politics of sexual difference binds us to bodily finitude, corporeal limits, and sexed possibilities. The "between-two" is thus Irigaray's response to the structural and political appropriation of democracy by masculinity (fraternity), a rewriting of subjectivity as self-division and becoming, and a refounding of democracy on living, sexuate human life. Feminine subjectivity is opened up to civil identity and becoming, not frozen as ontological being.

Irigaray is thus attempting, with the idea of sexuate rights, to introduce the feminine into politics, and the body into language, in a way that does not simply position the feminine as the outside, the limit, the subversion of the political. It would thus be mistaken to assume that the idea of a feminine universal must imply a reversion to content over form, status instead of rights, substance rather than subject, to a closed concept of the feminine. By demanding rights as women and not as persons, Irigaray is not basing political claims on an essential or substantive identity, but on the formation of universality itself. In this way, she aims precisely to give form to a feminine subject. Since politics has been the politics of a universal taken to be fraternal, Irigaray's feminism can also be seen to be a wholly other democratic politics whose correlate is the sexed subject, and which therefore doesn't preclude there being an outside, since it isn't an enclosed totality.[33]

In rethinking the conceptual bases of democracy, Irigaray is thus not appealing to concepts that have already been destabilized or dismantled in her earlier work, but is instead drawing out the overtly political implications of this work, demanding the necessary transformations that might enable the formation of a democracy no longer allied with or premised on the hom(m)osexual citizen, the solitary, self-enclosed, atomistic, wholly autonomous masculine subject. Starting from the monadic subject, whole within himself, a totality to himself, we can only conceive of democracy as also a totality, as self-enclosed, without remainder or excess, without unwieldy troublesome elements, a democracy that excludes or incorporates its other but does not acknowledge any debt. But a democracy premised on a divided subject, a subject who is divided within, who is her/himself not a totality (but a becoming), that is, a sexed subject, will be a democracy capable of respecting the differences that might otherwise threaten it without attempting either to exclude or assimilate them, a democracy open to difference of all kinds and to its own lack of closure.[34] Sexual difference thus presents us with a capacity for thinking through the body that is politically transformative, a capacity that must be tethered to a divided universal to be realized in democratic politics.

NOTES

1. In this formulation of multiplicity we can also see the alliance of liberal democracy with capitalism (the 1+1+1 of unmoored commodities amid an economy of "infinite dispersal" [Irigaray 2001 (1994), 164]) insofar as both represent a politics of the one and the many.

2. This idea of Symbolic death refers to the rupture with nature and the body demanded by entry into language. This very rupture is itself, moreover, predicated on a prior sacrifice of the maternal body whose loss is required to establish the infantile body in the first place and for which language is meant to compensate. The body is hence doubly surrendered.

3. Both Penelope Deutscher and Ewa Ziarek in recent books develop the language of impossibility to characterize Irigaray's approach to sexual difference. See Deutscher 2002 and Ziarek 2001. As Deutscher points out, "Irigaray speaks in the name of a female civic identity that is impossible . . . The formulation does not suggest that women need to rediscover their identity. Rather, there needs to be a cultural reinvention or reconception of sexual difference" (34). And elsewhere Deutscher writes that Irigaray is wrongly read as positing sex as a substantive entity; difference is, for her, not at all a list of predicates or a set of predefined, obligatory roles: "Irigaray does not justify her sexuate rights by reference to a blunt fact of sexual difference which the law should recognize, she avoids projecting sexual difference as external, transcendent, or original" (Deutscher 2000, 97). And, for Ziarek, sexual difference is a site of permanent "disappropriation" (Ziarek 2001, 152) in which "the impossible of sexual difference is fundamentally linked to the *possibility* of becoming" (Ziarek 2001, 154). Gender is not, for Irigaray, a substance but an insubstantial gap, fissure, or excess; this is the 'nature' of gender and for this reason sexual difference is the rupture of impossibility within democracy that cannot be represented.

4. "Irigaray regards multiplicity as complicit with the logic of the one. In her view the multiple is the one in its self-willed dispersal into unrelated atomistic singularities, many others of the same" (Cheah and Grosz 1998, 6).

5. Sexual difference is opposed to a culture of sexual indifference in which the only avenues available to women are those of conventional femininity (the mirror of patriarchal desire) or its repudiation in the public sphere (in the guise of neutral citizenship). In this view, the language of sexual difference available to us is just words, concealing the lack of a concept. As suggested above, Irigaray is not interested in finally determining the appropriate concept but in opening up a space in which contested meanings might invite new forms of feminine becoming.

6. This lack of representation is intimately connected to the culture of sexual indifference that Irigaray defies. Cultivating a culture of sexual difference might, rather than representing women, instead present women with new avenues for growth and development. In this sense, political representation would not entail representational content but a mode of being addressed by the law. A law that is addressed to bodies, a language of address between body and law, would itself transform the meaning of being a woman-citizen. Deutscher makes a similar point (Deutscher 2000), arguing that civil rights for women are not about representing feminine sexual difference, but transforming the meaning of femininity, making way for the impossible, though it will never be realized. As Deutscher writes, "structural, symbolic, and institutionalized mediation are necessary to the generation of new sexuate identities" (Deutscher 2000, 95). We need civil rights to "found, rather than reflect, sexuate identity" (Deutscher 2000, 94). Women and men are thus not represented by the two, because the two doesn't reflect or recognize gender but generates sexual difference. The two is not representative but transformative.

7. In thinking about how to establish a passage from sexual to civil identity rather than severing each from the other, claims about whether sexual difference is natural or historical are not so much opposed as mutually reinforcing, since in both discourses nature and history are cut off from one another, usually with the effect of separately assigning one gender to each (masculine history, feminine nature), thereby also separating body and word between the sexes.

8. This should also make clear that Irigaray is referring to the sexed and not the sexual couple; it is not the domesticated, private (married) couple who desire one another sexually, but the public couple of man-citizen and woman-citizen who speak to and listen to one another in civil society that concerns Irigaray. The two is not the sexual two of erotic intimacy, but the sexed two of public life and discourse, the two of embodied difference. Irigaray is attentive to the missing couple, the couple who does not appear and is not represented. This couple might also be the genealogical couple of mothers and daughters—in both cases the focus is on the missing relationship, the one that doesn't exist (even if there is apparently a plenitude of such, since these are relations to a same and not an other, the appearance is just that) and which, in its absence, precludes woman's relationship with both herself and other women.

9. At the same time, we cannot think of sex as an immediate sensuous reality (nature) which might undergo various human alterations (culture); rather, its appearance crosses and determines this very divide at the same time as it enacts the social bond. Sexual difference performs a kind of border function, representing the overflow of culture into nature and vice versa.

10. This temporality is marked by the rhythms of human life: mortality, carnality, and sensibility, just those aspects that are, ironically, deemed immaterial by civil law as it now stands.

11 The critique of androgyny is the premise of Jean-Joseph Goux's essay "Luce Irigaray Versus the Utopia of the Neutral Sex" (1994) which will be discussed further below. As Irigaray puts it, "the exploitation and the alienation of women are located in the difference between the sexes and the genders, and have to be resolved in that difference, without trying to abolish it, which would amount to yet another reduction to the singular subject" (Irigaray 2001 [1994], 126).

12. This is not simply a reassertion of what Foucault has analyzed as the repressive hypothesis but instead a claim about what the juridical realm classifies as outside its borders. First, Foucault's analysis is directed toward discourses of sexuality, not those of sexual difference. Second, it might be possible to argue (though it is outside the scope of this paper) that the very (ostensible) exclusion of the body from law is precisely what enables power (biopower) to rebound onto the body in virulent form.

13. Of course, men still have a genealogy, a signifier of desire, and a public law via the relation to the father.

14. As Freud shows in *Totem and Taboo*, patricide is the mythological structure of the social contract and democratic order, central to its story of origins. See Zakin 2002.

15. Those representations that do exist are sedimented concepts (the eternal feminine) that order and maintain the absence or disappearance of sexual difference.

16. The theory of the social contract is about this very split/passage. Social contract theory generally tells the story of how both the chaotic wilds of nature and the savagery of human nature are left behind in the passage to civil order. In establishing a border between the natural and the social, the social contract guards against the threatening pre-social, an uncivil space purportedly manifested and ascertained in women's bodies.

17. With regard to the politics of language, we might ask not only about the use of 'he' as the neutral pronoun, but also about the use of the subjective 'I.' The problem of the masculinization of the subject is compounded in French, where 'le Je' (literally 'the I,' but in psychoanalysis used to denote 'the subject' in distinction to 'the ego' which is rendered 'le moi') takes the masculine article. The language here is neither trivial nor accidental, but indicates something fundamental to the nature of 'the subject' as

such. Much of the second half of the book *I Love to You* is taken up directly
with questions of language and with the way in which both grammar and the
semantic privileging of pronouns prevents a relation of sexual difference
from forming. For instance, Irigaray contends that "we need to go through
this valorizing of the two pronouns *he* and *she* in order to uphold the intentionality of the *I* that operates in the relation between *I* and *you*; otherwise
it becomes pathological" (Irigaray 1996 [1992], 67). In this context also, as
well as throughout the book, the question of love assumes a kind of priority.
Irigaray's thesis hence raises questions not only about the language of politics
(the Rights of M*an*) but also about the politics of language.

   18. Just as sexuate rights do not represent the body, neither does the
universal which must be figured "not as the underlying principle explaining
identity but as a 'missing fullness' in each identity" (Ziarek, 174), a universal
that cannot be inhabited. A sexed universal means one that is immanent
within, but not reducible to, the body, nature: "apart from the minimal
natural determination that sex is two, sexual identity is paradoxically without content because it is also formed by the spiritual work that occurs through
one's *respect for* the other sex . . . one's natural sex needs to be actualized and
spiritualized through the development of sexual identity" (Cheah and Grosz
1998, 13). Sexual difference is the work of living/becoming, a significance
that comes in time not that determines a destiny. It can therefore never be
about a common womanhood or shared essence or immutable nature, con-
firming one in a pre-given identity. As universal it is not about sameness or
essence, nor that which substists behind difference as more primary. As an
embodied rather than abstract universal, sex undermines the opposition
between sensible and transcendental and the tyranny of predication, keeping
me moving beyond myself.

   19. It is for this reason that, insofar as it demands political emancipation for women, liberal feminism is evidence of the compatibility of modernity and patriarchy, rather than the departure of the one from the other.
And, in fact, the form of feminism which appears at the historical moment
of modernity is that which claims equal rights on the basis of some fundamental sameness to, or identity with, men, a sameness or an identity usually
associated with being a rational animal. We might thus question whether
such a feminism is really a threat to patriarchal structure, given that it aims
to capture women in a sign of the universal which remains masculine. The
effect of liberal feminism has been to conceptualize and produce women
subjects on the model of masculine subjects. Yet it leaves undisturbed the
masculinization of politics: men bring masculinity to politics in a way that
women cannot bring femininity to it, precisely because of the association of
masculinity with the universal. So long as masculine sexuality is on the side
of the universal, the public/private divide works effectively to recapitulate
the split between being human and being woman. The neutrality of the state
with regard to sex thus turns out in fact to have as its basis masculinity, in

two related senses: first, because the concept of the subject is the concept of the masculine subject, with the effect that women are subjects only insofar as they are, or appear to be, like men; and second, because public neutrality is the perfect ruse of patriarchal masculinity. We can thus name as a 'fraternal feminism' the view that, in expressing "the demand to be equal presupposes a point of comparison" in which the standard is masculine: "To whom or to what do women want to be equalized? To men?" In response, Irigaray asks, "Why not equal to themselves?" (Irigaray 1993 [1990], 12).

20. Already we can see that the language of desire does not return us in a simple way to a mysterious dark continent or an immediate social empiricism (let's just ask them what they want) since Irigaray takes as her starting point, as precisely the datum to be interrogated, that what (some) women "want" is equality. Irigaray invites us to reconceive the meaning of freedom and desire, such that freedom is understood not as the antithesis of nature but rather as its cultivation. If the modern, masculine definition of freedom is one that is understood as mastery over nature (especially the nature of one's own body) and distance from its precepts (Irigaray 2000 [1994], 88), Irigaray develops a concept of freedom that is not foreign to the body (Irigaray 2000 [1994], 90) but encourages a relationship to it. Rather than "giving oneself subjectivity despite a natural birth" (Irigaray 2000 [1994], 88), she proposes a freedom that comes from, and is founded on, cultivation of the body. And, just as freedom is mediated by the body and its desires, so too is desire mediated by freedom, with the implication that what women want is not immediate but detoured and delayed. If freedom to become a subject cannot be purchased at the price of sex neutrality and disembodiment, or with the denial of bodily difference, then neither can desire be purchased at the price of dignity and identity.

21. As Ziarek puts it, "liberal citizenship . . . excludes sexual difference from political identity" (Ziarek 2001, 173).

22. Or, as Whitford puts it, "if the universal is not sexuate then women are effaced" (Whitford 1994, 392).

23. Sexual difference is "the site for the formulation, cultivation, and dissemination of values that respect the generative difference of living nature" (Cheah and Grosz 1998, 8). Again, nature is here understood as the site of freedom, not its opposite or limit. Our bodies encounter difference in other bodies in different contexts and with different responses, and these bodily encounters with difference are also bodily possibilities.

24. Pateman develops the implications of this Modern victory in her book *The Sexual Contract* (Pateman 1988).

25. Sex constitutes a difference or division within the subject, a limit or form of finitude and alterity that renders any possibility of unitary wholeness fantastic or phantasmatic. The idea of a subject divided by sex, unlike that of "heterogenous multiplicities," retains a connection to organic, earthly life, while still disrupting identity. As such, sex is a 'sensible transcendental.'

The transcendental is to be found within the body and between bodies, between incarnate subjects (i.e., it is not a vertical transcendence). Transcendence is hence conceptualized as a space between (immanent within) that must be respected in order to found a democratic politics (a space of division): "transcendence exists in the difference of body and culture that continues to nourish our energy" (Irigaray 1996 [1992], 104), creating a "transformation that limits the empire of my ego" (Irigaray 1996 [1992], 105). This is why we need to "learn to lay it [transcendence] between us. Each one of us is inaccessible to the other, transcendent to him/her. The most irreducible space is between woman and man and it's only out of the impossibility of their reciprocal substitution—hence in the respect for each other's transcendence—that the social and cultural order can be thought anew and founded again" (Irigaray 2000 [1998], 58). Gender is here understood as "an opening to the other gender, both genealogically and horizontally" (Irigaray 1996 [1992], 107) and therefore as a site of transformation to and for the other.

26. In disturbing the mythological passage from nature to culture, Irigaray's tactic is one of displacement, displacing the idea of origin, reminding us of exiled debt, and not allowing us to be comfortable in our place, the *oikos*, the public/private split, the appropriation (incorporation, digestion) of women. Irigaray is pointing toward something indigestible, something that cannot be, has not been, captured or contained by the fraternal imaginary, something that threatens (creatively) to rupture enclosed space with time (see Ziarek 2001,159).

27. Or in which equal rights are pursued in terms of difference (Irigaray 2001 [1994], 90).

28. In other words, "the binary opposition between the abstract concept of liberal citizenship and its opposite, the reification of proliferating differences as unmediated particulars" (Ziarek, 173) are actually mutually reinforcing.

29. The cultivation of sexual difference is a cultivation of limits premised on understanding limits as generative (and always generative because always with a remainder): Irigaray calls for "a cultivated, civilized *we/us*, owing to a respect for the *not*" (Irigaray 2000 [1998], 92). Becoming is here figured not as radical transcendence but as the "not" of limits, the impasse of identity.

30. As in supposedly anti-liberal multiculturalism.

31. Adrienne Rich develops the idea of "thinking through the body" as a challenge to the body politic, which represents only the masculine body while denying that it represents any body (Rich 1976). Like Irigaray's 'sensible transcendental,' such thought is not about capturing or containing difference within the borders of the feminine body (it is not merely reactive to the figuring of the body politic as masculine), but about disseminating difference and alterity throughout the body politic. To come into the polis as sexually differentiated is not to enter politics with identities and desires intact but with both bodies and words.

32. As should already be clear, Irigaray's notion of 'natural reality' is not reducible to scientific, anatomical, or empirical conceptions or to a biological facticity of sex. Irigaray is committed to the "the liberation of women from subjection to a natural function" (Irigaray 2001 [1994], 3). As with the 'sensible transcendental' natural reality is situated (like Freud's drive) on the frontier between the psychic and the somatic, the interior collaboration of body and psyche, the taking form of identity that must occur for a subject to emerge. The sensible transcendental refuses the opposition between sensible and intelligible, rooting the possibility of the subject in a natural, bodily reality; as a bridge between nature and freedom, it is rooted in the sensuous particular but also informed by language and law, making possible a subject whose universality lies not in an abstraction from the body, but in the form of the body itself. As a demand made on the body by language, and on language by the body, sexual difference is thus, again, not a determinate concept under which particular identities can be subsumed, but a sensible form of identity, the condition of possibility for identity as such. To say that sexual difference is a universal difference is also to say that it is a difference of/within the universal: the universal of sexual difference mediates identity and desire, makes possible their becoming, imbuing the body with significance, possibility, and its own excess. Sexual difference is a transcendence immanent within our bodies and relations to others, a protean site of development and motility (but not infinitely so, not without limits).

33. While it is outside the scope of this paper to develop this argument further, it is worth suggesting that this form of antitotalitarianism might also resonate with antinationalist politics and with the formulation of the nation-state as a container of identity. In contrasting civic neutrality with sexed citizenship, the relation between the citizen and the nation-state, and among citizens and nation-states, can also be rethought. Irigaray's interest in introducing difference, a split in being, at the founding level of politics (in, for instance, the writing of a constitution) prevents the universal from being total since the universal can never be all and is always entangled with the animal and natural, (as both intransigent and changeable, temporal, and dynamic). Irigaray writes that "respect for difference between the genders is a possible way towards coexistence between all the other forms of difference" (Irigaray 2001 [1994], 90) and "respecting the man-woman difference would protect a democratic Union founded in diversity." Rather than abandoning others symbolically in the state of nature without passage to culture (as the globalizing forces of liberal democracy do), the between-two opens a dynamic space for movement, providing a necessary support so that the multiple doesn't revert to the one. Sexed rights organize a defining framework for the respect of difference. Democracy, it could be argued, needs a divided universal, not a multiple one, because this latter is too easily accommodated and recuperated by atomistic liberalism or repeats and consolidates it. While the disguised liberal atomism of the many might be just another form of

totality, the 'two' pressures the state for its citizen-others. The sexed two is thus not a primordial moment prior to or subtending differentiation, but a possibility of the sexed body attained through singularity itself: "a cultural becoming that doesn't claim to overcome singularity in the universal but rather save this singularity through a relationship of the two" (Irigaray 2000 [1998], 124). In this way, the "disjunctive temporality of sexual difference" might lend itself to "the emergence of new modes of life" (Ziarek 2001, 158). In further thinking through the necessity of disjunction and dissensus for democratic politics, I argue in *Fantasies of Origin: The Birth of the Polis and the Limits of Democracy* (in progress) that what I call radical republicanism would accept and even foster a split between subjectivity and citizenship, thereby breaking with the logic of identity and difference while promising a new form of cosmopolitan universalism. Radical republican politics would be a force that, in rupturing the human with the political, resists social harmony and thereby promises political movement and reconstitution. This argument is, however, grounded more on a reading of Kristeva than Irigaray and so cannot be developed in this discussion.

34. This still leaves us with a crucial question: Can the two present itself to politics? Or only present itself as the impasse to politics? If sexual difference is the difference that prevents the closure of totality, that is permanently at odds with the resolution of democracy, does it redefine or re-found the democratic project? Or does it break with it? Perhaps it is less an impasse than a permanent 'interval,' a space between, a space of love, mediation, and alterity. The in-between or between-two of the sexual relation is homologous to the in-between of the political relation—neither encounter is about appropriation or teleology. As Ziarek argues, sexual difference is the permanent aporia of democracy and therefore its very definition (as that which is forever open, futural, agonistic).

WORKS CITED

Burke, Carolyn, Naomi Schor, and Margaret Whitford, eds. 1994. *Engaging with Irigaray*. New York: Columbia University Press.

Cheah, Pheng, and Elizabeth A. Grosz. 1998. "Of Being Two." *diacritics* 28:1.

Deutscher, Penelope. 2000. "Luce Irigaray's Sexuate Rights and the Politics of Performativity." In *Transformations: Thinking Through Feminism*. Edited by Kilby Ahmad et al. New York and London: Routledge.

———. 2002. *A Politics of Impossible Difference*. Ithaca, N.Y.: Cornell University Press.

Freud, Sigmund. 1914 [1968]. *Totem and Taboo*. In *The Standard Edition of the Complete Psychological Works of Sigmund Freud*. Vol. XIII. Edited and translated by James Strachey. London: The Hogarth Press.

Goux, Jean-Joseph. 1994. In *Engaging With Irigaray: Feminist Philosophy and Modern European Thought*. Edited by Burke and Margaret Whitford. New York: Columbia University Press.

Irigaray Luce. 2001 [1994]. *Democracy Begins Between Two*. Translated by Kirsteen Anderson. New York and London: Routledge.

———. 2000 [1998]. *Why Different? A Culture of Two Subjects, Interviews with Luce Irigaray*. Translated by Camille Collins. New York: Semiotext(e).

———. 2000 [1994]. *To Be Two*. Translated by Monique M. Rhodes and Marco F. Cicito-Monoc. New York and London: Routledge.

———. 1996 [1992]. *I Love to You: Sketch of a Possible Felicity in History*. Translated by Alison Martin. New York and London: Routledge.

———. 1994 [1989]. *Thinking the Difference*. Translated by Karin Montin. New York and London: Routledge.

———. 1993 [1990]. *Je, tu, nous: Toward a Culture of Difference*. Translated by Alison Martin. New York and London: Routledge.

———. 1993 [1987]. *Sexes and Genealogies*. Translated by Gillian C. Gill. New York: Columbia University Press.

———. 1993 [1984]. *An Ethics of Sexual Difference*. Translated by Carolyn Burke and Gillian C. Gill. Ithaca, N.Y.: Cornell University Press.

———. 1985 [1977]. *This Sex Which Is Not One*. Translated by Catherine Porter. Ithaca, N.Y.: Cornell University Press.

———. 1985 [1974] *Speculum of the Other Woman*. Translated by Gillian C. Gill. Ithaca, N.Y.: Cornell University Press.

Pateman, Carole. 1988. *The Sexual Contract*. Stanford, Calif.: Stanford University Press.

Rich, Adrienne. 1976. *Of Woman Born*. New York: Norton.

Whitford, Margaret. 1994. "Irigaray, Utopia, and the Death Drive." In *Engaging With Irigaray: Feminist Philosophy and Modern European Thought*. Edited by Carolyn Burke and Margaret Whitford. New York: Columbia University Press.

Zakin, Emily. 2002. "Beyond the Sexual Contract: Traversing the Fantasy of Fraternal Alliance." In *Between the Psyche and the Social*. Edited by Oliver and Edwin. Rowman & Littlefield, 2002.

Ziarek, Ewa. 2001. *An Ethics of Dissensus*. Stanford, Calif.: Stanford University Press.

IRIGARAY AND THE CULTURE

OF NARCISSISM

Margaret Whitford

In this paper, I want to situate the work of Irigaray in a new context. The framework one adopts determines to a large extent what one sees and what one discards. Seeing Irigaray primarily as a dissident Lacanian who was responding to the gaps in Lacan's theory where 'woman' or 'women' ought to have been made for a rather restricted account. I want to propose that we look at Irigaray in the light of psychoanalytic theories of narcissism, in general, and the work of Melanie Klein and the post-Kleinians in particular. I think what this will enable us to do is to see more connections between Irigaray's critique of Western civilization and other related critiques. Irigaray's utopianism and her rather radical theory of sexual difference make it easy to dismiss her work as extreme and to see her as a rather isolated figure. The argument that Western culture is monosexual and that it is marked by the absence of an imaginary or symbolic register corresponding to women has aroused quite a lot of controversy. However, I think that to concentrate too exclusively on the unlikeliness of the advent of her 'new era' of sexual difference or on the impossibility of a female symbolic (a critique which is often, though not exclusively, made from a Lacanian point of view) can be a distraction. When one reads Irigaray in the light of contemporary psychoanalytic theory, she seems rather less extreme and strange, since the fantasies she is ascribing to western culture are a commonplace in clinical accounts.

In the present paper, I will suggest two things: firstly, that Irigaray is delineating a cultural pathology of narcissism which could be usefully contextualized with reference to post-Freudian theories of narcissism; secondly, that her account could be understood in terms of the Kleinian concept of projective identification and its post-Kleinian development. I have in mind particularly her 1993a [1984] work *An Ethics of Sexual Difference* and the essays collected in *Sexes and Genealogies*, but most of her work of the '80s and '90s could be read in this context. I shall thus be shifting the emphasis away from an account which focuses exclusively on the Oedipus complex, castration, and the role of the phallus (that is, the Lacanian context) to an account which includes reference to other models of the psyche. In this way—although I won't be spelling out the links here—her work can be linked more readily to that of other cultural theorists who draw on psychoanalytic theory for their models.

My title comes from Christopher Lasch's well-known book *The Culture of Narcissism*. Irigaray and Christopher Lasch seem poles apart, and indeed, in many ways, they are. However, I think it makes sense to see Irigaray's work as an account of 'the culture of narcissism,' although what she means by this is something rather different from Lasch's analysis of the ills of the contemporary United States. In particular she argues that Western culture only recognizes one sex and that the narcissism in question is male narcissism.

THEORIES OF NARCISSISM

Freud's legacy here is perhaps more pertinent than the theory of Freud himself. I will therefore situate Irigaray within a distinctively European tradition of psychoanalysis, which stretches from Freud's early colleagues (Sándor Ferenczi and Karl Abraham) to their modern and contemporary heirs (Béla Grunberger, André Green, Melanie Klein).

There are several quite distinct theories of narcissism. The ones used by Lasch are those of Kohut (1971) and Kernberg (1985, originally published 1975), both developed in the U.S. I think it is rather more likely that Irigaray is making use of Béla Grunberger's theory, put forward in *Narcissism: Psychoanalytic Essays*, a collection of articles published in France in 1971, but written over the period 1957–1967 and published earlier in journals and periodicals. (See also Grunberger 1989.)

Using the work of his fellow Hungarian, Ferenczi (see, for example, Ferenczi 1999), Grunberger sets out to develop a theory of narcissism as a psychic agency, distinct from the topology of ego, superego, and id elaborated by Freud, but which nonetheless integrates the new theory with classical theory.

As far as I know, there is no other attempt to explore Irigaray's psychoanalytic context—apart from the Lacan connection—although as a psychoanalytic trainee in France, she would obviously have read widely in the available psychoanalytic literature. My argument is that Irigaray has been concerned from the outset with the problem of cultural narcissism. Although this is clearer in her later work, all her work, in my view, has been informed by the post-Freudian psychoanalytic account of narcissism.

Freud's theory of narcissism was left in quite a sketchy form. When he wrote his essay "On Narcissism" (1914), he had not yet developed the theory of identification, which appears a few months later in "Mourning and Melancholia" (1915). So he was trying to conceptualize narcissism within an economic framework—libido theory—which was not adequate for the conceptualization of an internal world (Segal and Bell 1991). It was left to his successors to revise and amplify the theory. Freud hypothesized that the infant passed through a period of primary narcissism, a state preceding both the formation of the ego and object relations, in which the infant's libido was still attached to itself and not turned towards the others in its environment. The psyche was at that stage still a closed system. For quite a long time, the psychoanalytic world was divided on the question of primary narcissism, between those who accepted the hypothesis and those who rejected it. However, developments in child development theory (see Stern 1985) indicate that infants are object-seeking from the start, and narcissism is now more likely to be conceptualized as an object relation, but of a particular kind, one in which there is an active turning away from the object and a withdrawal to internalized objects. Child development theory tends to confirm what Melanie Klein claimed in 1952:

> The analysis of very young children has taught me that there is no instinctual urge, no anxiety situation, no mental process which does not involve objects, external or internal; in other words, object-relations are at the *centre* of emotional life. Furthermore, love and hatred, phantasies, anxieties, and defences are also operative from the beginning and are *ab initio* indivisibly linked with object-relations. (Klein 1988, 53)

Post-Freudian psychoanalysts have developed theories of narcissism along various lines suggested by their experience with those types of disorder—the psychoses and schizophrenia—which Freud did not attempt to analyze. Green (1983), for example, points out that Freud does not rework his theory of narcissism in the light of *Beyond the Pleasure Principle* and the theory of the life and death drives, and argues that narcissism needs to be theorized along two axes, which he calls the narcissism of life and the narcissism of death. Grunberger (1979) distinguishes between the ego (*moi* in French) and the self (*soi* in French), and argues that the sense of self—and injuries to it—requires its own conceptualization. In Grunberger's account, narcissism always has a dual orientation—it cannot exist in a pure state but only in conjunction with (or in an antagonistic relation to) other psychic agencies. Crucially, for Grunberger, narcissism is not libidinal. There is always a dialectical relation between instinctual (libidinal) and narcissistic components (Grunberger 1979, 6). In Grunberger's theory, narcissism is a striving towards the prenatal state, "a situation from which [man] was traumatically expelled and that he never ceases longing to recapture" (1979, 10). It should not be attributed to either id or ego libido, and its characteristics are not determined by the instincts alone.

There is some disagreement about whether to conceptualize narcissism in terms of the metapsychology of the life and death drives or instincts. Some continue to refer to the life and death drives (Rosenfeld, Green), while others (Grunberger) reject this late Freudian dualism or simply do not consider it at all (Kohut, Kernberg). Thus, Rosenfeld seems to accept it when he writes that "the death instinct *cannot be observed* in its original form, since it always becomes manifest as a destructive process against objects and the self" (Rosenfeld 1971, 169, my emphasis), while Grunberger dismisses the concepts of Eros and Thanatos as extra-scientific (Grunberger 1979, 9)—precisely because they cannot be observed—and argues that the Eros-Thanatos dialectic constitutes a closed system, rather than one which is open to subsequent research and investigation. There is a remarkable clinical consensus, however, despite the theoretical divergence. While there is considerable disagreement about the justification for hypothesizing a life-death drive dualism, there is general acceptance of the clinical phenomena and fantasies which call for an explanatory framework. Irigaray does not spell out her theoretical commitment; at some points she appears to accept the theory of the death drive; in her more recent work, she sounds more dubious. However, in my view, Irigaray's diagnosis of narcissism is a phenomenological one, and does not depend on any particular metapsychological formulation. What is more important for Irigaray is the unconscious phantasy informing the theory, the theory's 'imaginary.' This leads her to take a distance from psychoanalytic theory, even while she makes use of psychoanalytic theory's resources and techniques to discover the operation of the masculine imaginary in the various psychoanalytic theories. On this account, the theory of primary narcissism would itself be a masculine fantasy.[1]

In Grunberger's theory, we can find a description of almost all the elements which are specific to Irigaray's analysis of the Western masculine imaginary: the fantasies of merger and fusion and the nostalgia for the intrauterine state; the relation between narcissism and anality; the attempt to control the mother-container; the projection of the ideal on to the divine. Since narcissism is both inevitable and essential for Grunberger, (and Irigaray accepts this too), the question is then: when does it become pathological? Everyone, as an infant, has to face an early narcissistic wound—the discovery that one is not the center of the world—and some have greater inner or outer resources than others for dealing with that discovery. Irigaray's theory takes into account the sociocultural environment into which we are born. According to her cultural, rather than individual analysis, we have a scenario in which the man, via representations of the masculine imaginary, projects the wound on to the woman in order to deny need and dependence, protecting—more or less successfully—his own narcissism, but leaving women without the representational wherewithal to protect theirs. Irigaray's "culture of narcissism" is a description of an imbalance in which the sociocultural environment into which women are born has long been inimical to women's positive narcissism—or "narcissism of life" to use Green's phrase[2] (see Irigaray 1991 [1980], 105–17).

One way of describing narcissism is to say that it is the inability to give up the fantasy of omnipotence (see Benjamin, 1998). In Grunberger's theory, narcissism can be interpreted as the wish for an ideal sense of well-being in which, like the fetus, one knows nothing of need but, being ignorant of one's real dependence, feels autonomous and omnipotent, and in which one would feel loved because one *is*, rather than for any qualities, abilities, or deeds. One has only to be to be loved. This state would exclude, at least in fantasy, the recognition of dependence, of other people's existence, of needs, and particularly of the need to earn love or esteem. Grunberger writes that "not only is everything given to the foetus, but nothing is taken in return" (Grunberger 1979, 19). "The foetus does not have to exercise instinctual *control*" (Grunberger 1979, 19). He goes on to add that "all these characteristics also happen to be attributes of divinity, and one could say *that if God created man in his image, man has created God in his own prenatal image*" (Grunberger 1979, 21). The difficulties of development in childhood relate to the need to shift from this ideal, or idealized, position to one in which the child has to learn to relate to and negotiate the pressure of instincts, the need to conform to the demands of reality, and the difficulties and pleasures of negotiating the world with other people. "Narcissism utilizes the libido but is not one with it" (Grunberger 1979, 24). Where there are problems in the child's early life, and the narcissistic and instinctual trends are not balanced, problems arise for later development. There is, for Grunberger, a conflict between the requirements of the narcissistic state—which is basically asexual, based on the autonomy of the child in the prenatal state when it was unaware of mother or needs—and the requirements of the mother-child relationship, which is basically instinctual.[3] If the two cannot find a dialectic and the narcissism predominates, there will be difficulty in recognizing the real needs or even existence of other people. In his theory, therefore, Grunberger sets out to show the ways in which narcissism may be articulated with each instinctual stage.

Unlike Grunberger, Irigaray is not using a developmental theory, but focusing rather on the fantasies, since her analysis applies to Western culture in general. In *Luce Irigaray: Philosophy in the Feminine* (Whitford 1991a), I noted Irigaray's diagnosis of an anal ontology (Irigaray 1993a [1984], 101) which refuses to recognize sexual differ-ence,[4] but did not delineate the narcissistic diagnosis which seems equally important. There are several points however where it might have helped to refer to Grunberger's account. For example, his reflec-tion that "the equation of woman with castrated man seems to me to belong to the anal phase" (Grunberger 1979, 209) is precisely the aspect which Irigaray foregrounds. Grunberger's treatment of phallic omnipotence also seems relevant. Fantasies of omnipotence are asso-ciated with the memory or fantasy of the prenatal state. The phallus, for Grunberger, is a symbol of omnipotence (Grunberger 1979, 212). In Grunberger's view, the phallus stands in the unconscious for whole-ness and integrity and is a narcissistic indicator par excellence (i.e., not an instinctual one), regardless of sex. The question for Irigaray then becomes the question of woman's narcissism and whether there is a necessary connection with the phallus. From Irigaray's point of view, there would in fact be a difficulty in Grunberger's account, since he considers that instinctual drives must be narcissistically cathected, so that there is a "continual interaction of penile factors and phallic factors" (Grunberger 1979, 211). The question of women's instinctual drives and exactly what they are supposed to cathect in the absence of a penis is left rather unclear in this account, leaving the problem of women's narcissism, which Irigaray addresses in *An Ethics of Sexual Difference* and elsewhere. Grunberger writes further that: "We know that the child manages to preserve his narcissistic omnipotence by projecting it on to his deified parents and deifications in general" (Grunberger 1979, 212). This is how Irigaray describes the relationship with God in Western culture, and again she notes the way in which, in monotheistic religions, one of the deified parents seems to have disappeared, and wonders what effect this has for women's narcissistic needs.[5]

It is clear that Irigaray has such theories in mind when she describes Western thought as a pathology. She argues that the social body as well as the individual needs to give up "narcissistic self-sufficiency" (Irigaray 1993b [1987], 87). She diagnoses in various Western philosophers a nostalgia for the intrauterine state (Irigaray 1993a [1984], 11, 127) in which there were no needs since they were immediately met:

> If I wanted to apply some terms here which I do not like to use outside of their strictly clinical setting—where, moreover, I do not use them as such—I might say that Merleau-Ponty's seer remains in an incestuous prenatal situation with the whole. This mode of existence or of being is probably that of all men, at least in the West. (Irigaray 1993a [1984], 173)

Despite her disclaimer—or rather because of it—we can see that Irigaray is alluding to the theory of narcissism. What it means in practice is that "nothing new happens" (Irigaray 1993a [1984], 182), as she puts it succinctly: history is repetition; there is an "almost fatal repetition at the cultural level" (Irigaray 1993c [1990], 37). Narcissism here is the instinctive hostility to anything new or different or other than self (what for the infant was the impingement of reality on its fantasy of possession of, and permanent union with, the mother). The repetition compulsion—a manifestation of the death drive in late

Freudian theory ("nothing new happens")—does not allow anything to change. In clinical terms, the patient is unable to allow any change through contact with another mind. Since, according to psychoanalytic theory, one can only develop via contact with another mind, failure to make that contact, or inadequate and unsatisfactory contact, gives rise to destructive pathology. If the world of men fails to make contact with the world of women, there are problems for both.

Like the obsessional patient whom Irigaray describes in *Speaking Is Never Neutral* (Irigaray 2002 [1985]), everything takes place in the closed universe of the narcissist's own mind. Clinical vignettes from case histories describe this process quite explicitly. For example, Rosenfeld's patient cannot accept anything from the analyst, but must turn interpretations into his own possession: "He did not resent interpretations, but on the contrary took them up quickly and talked about them in his own way, feeling very self-satisfied with his knowledge since he did not feel that the analyst had made any contribution" (Rosenfeld 1982, 173). The omnipotence defends the patient against acknowledging his own envy and hostility—taking back his projections, in other words—and having to face them. Although narcissism is not necessarily overt psychosis, it is psychotic in its scotomization of the real existence of anyone else:

> In terms of the infantile situation, the narcissistic patient wants to believe that he has given life to himself and is able to feed and look after himself. (Rosenfeld 1971, 173)

> While ostensibly the narcissistic patient maintains that he has a superior and sometimes more creative breast in his possession, which gives him better analysis and food than the mother-analyst could ever produce, careful analysis reveals that this highly-valued possession of the patient represents his own faeces which have always been highly idealized, a fact carefully concealed by the patient. (Rosenfeld 1982, 175–76)

Again, the connection with anality is spelled out.

In Irigaray's terms, the narcissistic subject of Western thought cannot acknowledge the debt to the mother-woman and, by extension, the debt to nature or to the rest of the world. What this denial conceals is destructive envy. What he cannot possess, the narcissistic subject will denigrate, devalue, hold in contempt, and even destroy. The problem of narcissism is by no means an exclusively masculine one, since Irigaray is here talking about an entire culture in which the maternal imago is deficient or split. If the masculine self protects its narcissism through projection, the feminine self suffers from the effects of a narcissistic wound, that is, from destructive (oral) rage. In Irigaray's vision, there is no question of women being 'better' than men—they are simply less invested in a system which offers them fewer satisfactions corresponding to their own narcissistic needs: "The deceptive notion of obscurely being or potentially being men [. . .] condemns many women to self-exile and turns them into agents of social and individual destruction" (Irigaray 1993b [1987], 196). In the absence of an adequate representational support, it is difficult for them to avoid operating at an equally primitive level and directing their rage towards others, both women and men. Here is Irigaray on women's violence:

> The world [of women] seems very like that of certain primitive societies that have no official sacrifice, no recognized rites, no indigenous jurisprudence. Revenge is taken, outside of law or rights, in the form of private attacks, whether concerted or not. [. . .] Real murders occur as well as (if the two can be separated) cultural murders, murders of the spirit, the affections, the intelligence, that women perpetuate among themselves (Irigaray 1993b [1987], 85). Woman needs to develop words, images, and symbols to express her intersubjective relationship with her mother, and then with other women, if she is to enter into a non-destructive relation with men. (Irigaray 1993b [1987], 196)

There is a suggestion in Irigaray that the destructive reaction is only half the story. She proposes a different 'imaginary,' based on the fetus (a counternarrative to Grunberger, one might say), in which there is a mediator, the placenta, which enables coexistence. In the following extract from an interview between Irigaray and the biologist Hélène Rouch, Rouch is describing the mechanism:

> The embryo is half-foreign to the maternal organism. Indeed, half its antigens are paternal in origin. Because of this, the mother should activate her defense mechanisms to reject this other to her self. The placenta, which is also this other, prevents this mechanism from being activated. (Irigaray 1993c [1990], 40)

I won't be developing the theme of coexistence here, but I will remark only that one can see Irigaray searching for ways of conceptu-
alizing early fetal life that do not depend on the fantasy of primary
narcissism (which would be the masculine fantasy), but replace it
with a more female-centred conception in which self and otherness
are more open and negotiable. Again and again, particularly in *An
Ethics of Sexual Difference* and subsequent works, Irigaray insists that
the possibility of cultural growth and cultural change can only come
from openness to the other's difference: "This other, male or female,
should surprise us again and again, appear to us as *new, very different*
from what we knew or what we thought he or she should be" (Irigaray
1993a [1984], 74). In her work she has oscillated between an account
of the narcissistic hatred of otherness and its cultural effects, and a
quest for, or evocation of, non-narcissistic models. Sometimes she
recognizes the necessity for the work of mourning, in the process of
giving up the narcissistic defence: "a mourning for the self as an
autarchic entity" (Irigaray 1993a [1984], 75). But there are also more
utopian moments where the need for *work* is less clearly foregrounded
and she focuses on the hoped-for future rather than on the difficulty
of reaching it.

    I have discussed extensively elsewhere Irigaray's view that the
problem lies in the nonsymbolization of the relation (both men's and
women's) to the maternal (Whitford 1991a). What I want to continue focusing on here is the diagnosis of narcissism, and, at this
point, I think we need to move from the idea of omnipotence to that
of projective identification, which is one of the psychic mechanisms
by which omnipotence is secured in fantasy. The concept of projective identification is a specifically Kleinian concept and is not accepted by all analysts. Recent work however, indicates that it can be
put to use in an understanding of the types of social oppression in
which a whole group is targeted. For example, M. Fakhry Davids, an
analyst trained at the Institute of Psycho-Analysis in London, shows,
in an article on Frantz Fanon (Davids 1996), how this might work in
relation to race. He suggests that, in racism, as described by Fanon,
projective identification is the mental equivalent of colonial occupation (Davids 1996, 216). It was his paper that suggested to me that
Irigaray's account could also be understood in terms of projective
identification. So, at this point, I need to give some background to
explain the concept further.

PROJECTIVE IDENTIFICATION

A central theme of Irigaray's *An Ethics of Sexual Difference* is the diagnosis of splitting: the split between masculine and feminine, between body and thinking, between empirical and transcendental, between science and life. It is a split in the order of reason which "leaves the family with no future other than work for the state, procreation without joy, love without ethics" (Irigaray 1993a [1984], 119). And behind this split lie the envy, hatred, and destructiveness described by Klein and Bion.

Klein was analyzed by Ferenczi and Abraham. She was writing in Freud's lifetime and, like all psychoanalytic theorists at that time, was concerned to indicate her theoretical affiliation to Freud. But the main effect of her work was to displace the centrality of the Oedipus complex as the crystallizing 'event.' Klein claimed that she was questioning the timing of the Oedipus complex and situated its onset much earlier in psychic development than Freud had done. (Freud had hypothesized age three to five; Klein thought it began in the first twelve months.) The drama of childhood starts much earlier for Klein. In Klein's work it is less the pivot of the Oedipus complex that organizes her theoretical contributions than the concept of the two "positions"— the paranoid-schizoid position and the depressive position.

The paranoid-schizoid position is a way whereby the primitive psychic apparatus masters excitations, whether from internal or external sources. It is thought to precede the judgment of reality (internal-external) by dividing experiences into bad (projected outwards—this is not me) and good (introjected—this is me). The bad experience, however, returns since the 'me' is now surrounded by a bad environment. The role of the mother-caretaker in providing a good environment and containing the early projections is crucial. This basic splitting, argues Klein, is a position which is inherent in psychic life. It may be modified but is never definitively transcended. It is modified in the depressive position, in which the child realizes that the source of the bad experiences (or the absent breast) and the source of good experiences (the feeding breast) belong to one and the same person. The infant has to bring love and hate together and recognize that they are evoked by one person, not the two figures of angel and witch respectively. Similarly, the child has to recognize that some of the 'bad' experience is its own aggression, rage, and envy. In developmental terms, splitting is the more primitive position; it is thought to be a less arduous activity, psychically, than ambivalence—that is, the realization that the qualities one most loves and the qualities one most hates belong to the same source. It is easier to locate them in different places, to idealize the one and demonize the other, than to link the two together and endure their coexistence.

What happens when the rage, envy, and hatred become too great is that destructive fantasies overwhelm the good feelings. In her late work, Klein suggests that behind destructiveness lies primitive envy: "envy is an oral-sadistic and anal-sadistic expression of destructive impulses, operative from the beginning of life" (Klein 1988, 176). It is the unbearable feeling that someone else has something good which they are enjoying without me, and if I cannot have it too, then I am going to destroy and spoil what I cannot have. In terms of narcissism, envy disturbs the fantasy of omnipotence; if this is disturbed too early, before the child can cope, the result is that the child, and later the adult, is overwhelmed by envious feelings. They cannot enjoy what another person has to offer because the desire to spoil and destroy is too strong. Klein's theory links the paranoid-schizoid position with omnipotence: "splitting, denial and omnipotence play a role similar to that of repression at a later stage of ego-development" (Klein 1988, 7).

As I said earlier, projective identification is defined as one of the mechanisms in which omnipotence is secured in fantasy. It is easier to use projective identification—in which the unwanted feelings are projected permanently into someone else who is then felt to carry the feelings—than to suffer the pain of the depressive position. Projective identification is a concept which refers to the way in which feelings are either communicated or evacuated by a process which involves evoking them in someone else. For a preverbal baby, it may be the only way to communicate feelings. For an adult, it is often a way of getting rid of affective states that feel intolerable. These states can then be projected violently into others.

Projective identification is based on the splitting of the ego and the projection of parts of the self into other people (Klein 1988, 303). Splitting and projection are thought of as universal human characteristics (Klein 1988, 8–9). However, when they are used excessively, we find the triad of splitting, denial, and omnipotence, referred to just now, installed as an inflexible defensive structure. A number of consequences follow. Large areas of the self become unavailable, since they are located elsewhere, and this permanently split ego is weakened. The split becomes fixed—Benjamin describes it as congelation (Benjamin 1998, 197). Above all, to maintain its defensive position, the subject needs to control the person into whom the aspects of the self are projected; Benjamin talks of "the tendency of the subject to force the other to either be or want what it wants, to assimilate the other to itself or make it a threat. It is the extremism of reducing difference to sameness, the inability to recognise the other without dissolving her/his otherness" (Benjamin 1998, 86). In addition, the subject seeks—and creates—situations in which the split is self-evidently justified, so that the world seems to offer self-confirming examples of its necessity.[6]

It is difficult to do justice here to the concept of projective identification, whose scope has been elaborated and enlarged considerably since Klein first formulated it. However, one finds extensions or applications of the theory in most contemporary theorists of the Kleinian school, and my argument here can only gesture towards the hinterland of this immensely important and far-reaching concept. I would go so far as to argue that the theory of projective identification in its modern elaborations constitutes in itself a theory of narcissism. However, the main implication which concerns me here is the element of forceful control. Projective identification is used in defence of narcissistic omnipotence; it functions to affect the *mind* as well as the actions of others, and it is often powerfully effective. Projective identification is more than just projection (evacuation of unwanted parts of the self); it is far more extensive in its aims and effects (cf. the "colonial occupation" referred to earlier), which are evacuation, possession, and control.

Sandler (in Sandler (ed.) 1988, chapter 2) suggests that we can divide the evolution of the concept into three moments. The first moment is Klein's account of the internal world, in which projective identification refers to unconscious phantasies and in which an object is identified in *unconscious fantasy* with unwanted parts of the self. This does not necessarily affect the real object, since the projection is into internal objects, not external ones. The second moment is the post-Kleinian elaboration of counter-transference, in which the effect of unconscious fantasy on the analyst was taken seriously. Projective identification was then thought to be a process whereby the analysand communicates to the analyst the nature of the internal object-relationships by evoking feelings in the analyst. The counter-transference reaction of the analyst is then thought of as a source of information about the analysand's inner world. The third moment is Bion's development of projective identification and his concept of the mother/analyst as a container of the child's/analysand's unthinkable thoughts. In Bion's account, this is more than just something occurring in unconscious fantasy; it is the use of another person who needs to be literally affected by the projections in order to contain and process them. It is Bion and subsequent developments of the concept which I am principally referring to here.

There is, I believe, more than one source for Irigaray's concept of the maternal container (apart from philosophical sources, Winnicott is also probably in the background), but I think Bion's model of the mother-container is indispensable for understanding Irigaray. I would like to suggest that Irigaray is using a similar model for analyzing the masculine-feminine split in culture and all that this split brings in its train. It is a model in which male narcissism secures itself via projective identification on a cultural scale. This creates a problem for both parties, for those apparently benefiting from the evacuation of unwanted feelings and those designated as containers of them, since it creates a situation in which the container may readily be felt as persecuting if the feelings are either not contained or returned to the sender. The container can become "a substrate . . . peopled with monsters that have to be locked away" (Irigaray 1993a [1984], 103). Or:

> How can one not also feel [anxiety, phobia, disgust, a haunting fear of castration] on returning to what has always been denied, disavowed, sacrificed to build an exclusively masculine symbolic world? (Irigaray 1991 [1980], 41)

> The mother has become a devouring monster as an inverted effect of the blind consumption of the mother. (Irigaray 1991 [1980], 40)

Confronted with the wall of projections, Irigaray argues, it is difficult for women to make their distinct reality impinge, or even to retain any sense of being other than the projection.

> Historically, the female has been used in the construction of man's love of self. [. . .] a whole history separates her from the love of herself. (Irigaray 1993a [1984], 62, 65)

The love of self among women, in the feminine, is very hard
to establish. (Irigaray 1993a [1984], 101)

The women who are on the receiving end of the aggressive projections have often accepted the projections—seen themselves as lacking, or defective, relative to men, or have identified unconsciously
with the aggressor, seeking to be men themselves.

Again and again, we are placed in the sites of those projections. Again and again we become the captives of these fantasies, this ambivalence, this madness which is not ours.
(Irigaray 1991 [1980], 42)

Rebirth [of women] cannot take place unless it is freed from
man's archaic projection on to her. (Irigaray 1991 [1980], 42)

But freeing oneself from the projections is no easy matter. In a first
moment, the impulse will be hostile and aggressive—reactive, in other
words. The angry energy of the women's movement can be interpreted in this way. But, as Alison Jaggar pointed out in 1983, it is
important to problematize the emotional stances in feminist theory,
since they are not self-justifying. The optic on the world provided by
the position of "container of projections" ("oppressed victim" in 1970s
feminist language) may shed light on political and social arrangements, but it should be subject to critique: "A theory may require that
we revise even the descriptions of the world on which the theory
itself is based" (Jaggar 1983, 381).

In her work, Irigaray argues that the masculine-feminine split is
the most basic one. However, questions of priority may not be the most
important issue. It is easy to see the structural analogies between the use
of the fantasy of omnipotence, with its mechanism of projective identification, in a masculine-feminine context, and its use in any social
context where one group is used as a container for the unwanted aspects of another group. One might put Irigaray's analysis alongside
Memmi's classic account of colonialism (Memmi 1985), first published
in the fifties, to show the similarities. Shorn of its 'New Jerusalem'
aspects, Irigaray's theory holds much in common with related critiques
of Western culture from the point of view of one of the groups which
has found itself 'other' to the dominant ideology—whether this is conceptualized as eurocentric, phallocentric, ethnocentric, or whatever. To

suppose that her work concerns (white Western) women only would be to miss in a quite significant way the implications of her oeuvre, which—on my reading—is far from being a marginal analysis. On the contrary, it is structurally similar to some of the major currents of social and political critique of the postwar period.

NOTES

1. Michael Balint demonstrates that the theory of primary narcissism was only one of the theories entertained by Freud about the infant's earliest psychic state. He argues that Freud in fact held three mutually exclusive views of the individual's most primitive relation with his environment. (Balint 1968, chapter 7).

2. "I propose to distinguish a *positive* primary narcissism (attachable to Eros), tending towards unity and identity, from a negative primary narcissism (attachable to the destructive instincts" (Green 1986, 167).

3. In the light of recent child development theory, one would have to add a further dimension to the narcissistic-instinctual dialectic, that of the emergence of the child's sense of self in relation to the mother on a relational rather than an instinctual axis. See Stern 1985. This is Jessica Benjamin's project (see Benjamin 1995, 1998).

4. In the ontology of the West, according to Irigaray, there are only men and defective, castrated men (women). This corresponds to the undifferentiation of the anal phantasy (see Chasseguet-Smirgel 1985).

5. See Martin 2000 for a detailed account of Irigaray's work in relation to the divine.

6. Bion's essay "The Differentiation of the Psychotic from the Non-Psychotic Personalities" (Bion 1984) gives some indications of the persecutory and malevolent universe inhabited by someone who engages in excessive projective identification.

WORKS CITED

Balint, Michael. 1968. *The Basic Fault: Therapeutic Aspects of Regression.* London: Tavistock.

Benjamin, Jessica. 1990. *The Bonds of Love: Psychoanalysis, Feminism and the Problem of Domination.* London: Virago.

———. 1995. *Like Subjects, Love Object: Essays on Recognition and Sexual Difference.* New Haven and London: Yale University Press.

———. 1998. *Shadow of the Other: Intersubjectivity and Gender in Psychoanalysis.* New York and London: Routledge.

Bion, Wilfred R. 1977. *Seven Servants*. New York: Jason Aronson.

———. 1984 [1967]. *Second Thoughts*. London: Karnac Books.

Chasseguet-Smirgel, Janine. 1985. *Creativity and Perversion*. London: Free Association.

Davids, M. Fakhry. 1996. "Frantz Fanon: The Struggle for Inner Freedom." *Free Associations* 38 (6:2): 205–34.

Ferenczi, Sándor. 1999 [1913]. "Stages in the Development of the Sense of Reality." In *Sándor Ferenczi: Selected Writings*, edited by Julia Borossa, 67–81. London: Penguin.

Green, André. 1983. *Narcissisme de vie, narcissisme de mort*. Paris: Gallimard.

———. 1986. *On Private Madness*. London: Hogarth Press and the Institute of Psycho-Analysis.

Grunberger, Béla. 1979 [1971]. *Narcissis: Psychoanalytic Essays*. Madison Conn.: International Universities Press.

———. 1989 [1963–1988]. *New Essays on Narcissism*. Translated and edited by David Macey. London: Free Association.

Irigaray, Luce. 1991 [1981]. "The Bodily Encounter with the Mother." In *The Irigaray Reader*, edited by Margaret Whitford. Oxford: Blackwell.

———. 1993a [1984]. *An Ethics of Sexual Difference*. Translated by Carolyn Burke and Gillian C. Gill. London: Athlone Press.

———. 1993b [1987]. *Sexes and Genealogies*. Translated by Gillian C. Gill. New York: Columbia University Press.

———. 1993c [1990]. *Je, tu, nous: Toward a Culture of Difference*. Translated by Alison Martin. New York and London: Routledge.

Jaggar, Alison. 1983. *Feminist Politics and Human Nature*. Brighton: Harvester Press.

Kernberg, Otto. 1985 [1975]. *Borderline Conditions and Pathological Narcissism*. Northvale, N.J.: Jason Aronson.

Klein, Melanie. 1988 [1975]. *Envy and Gratitude and Other Works 1946–1963*. London: Virago.

Kohut, Heinz. 1971. *The Analysis of the Self: A Systematic Approach to the Psychoanalytic Treatment of Narcissistic Personality Disorder*. New York: International Universities Press.

Martin, Alison. 2000. *Luce Irigaray and the Question of the Divine*. Leeds: Maney Publishing for the Modern Humanities Research Association.

Memmi, Albert. 1985 [1957]. *Portrait du colonisé, précédé de Portrait du colonisateur*. Paris: Gallimard.

Morrison, Andrew P., ed. 1986. *Essential Papers on Narcissism*. New York and London: New York University Press.

Rosenfeld, Herbert. 1971. "A Clinical Approach to the Psychoanalytic Theory of the Life and Death Instincts: An Investigation into the Aggressive Aspects of Narcissism." *International Journal of Psycho-Analysis* 52: 169–77.

————. 1982 [1965]. *Psychotic States: A Psychoanalytical Approach*. London: Karnac Books.

Sandler, Joseph, ed. 1988. *Projection, Identification, Projective Identification*. London: Karnac Books.

————. 1991. *Freud's 'On Narcissism': An Introduction*. Edited by Ethel Specter Person and Peter Fonagy. New Haven, Conn.: Yale University Press.

Segal, Hanna and David Bell. 1991. "The Theory of Narcissism in the Work of Freud and Klein." In *Freud's 'On Narcissism': An Introduction*, edited by J. Sandler, E. S. Person, and P. Fonagy, 149–74. New Haven, Conn.: Yale University Press.

Stern, Daniel N. 1985. *The Interpersonal World of the Infant: A View from Psychoanalysis and Developmental Psychology*. New York: Basic Books.

Whitford, Margaret. 1991a. *Luce Irigaray: Philosophy in the Feminine*. New York and London: Routledge.

————, ed. 1991b. *The Irigaray Reader*. Oxford: Blackwell.

Wieland, Christina. 2000. *The Undead Mother: Psychoanalytic Explorations of Masculinity, Femininity and Matricide*. London: Rebus Press.

KNOWING THE OTHER:
ETHICS AND THE FUTURE
OF PSYCHOANALYSIS

Catherine Peebles

Early on in Luce Irigaray's work, in *This Sex Which Is Not One*, she summarized her attitude toward psychoanalysis by stating that it was not a matter of abandoning it as misogynist or hopelessly phallocentric, but of "implementing its still inoperative potential" (Irigaray 1985b [1977], 72). In the three decades since, have her writings offered articulations of such implementations? Do we have, in works from *An Ethics of Sexual Difference* to, say, *Being Two*, a vision of what *another* psychoanalytic thought would be, one that might begin from an Irigarayan understanding of sexual difference as necessary to, indeed constitutive of, any ethics? Can psychoanalysis listen productively to philosophical work on sexual difference? Has it? Is there, in short, a psychoanalysis yet to come (already happening?) for Irigaray's thought of sexual difference?

Although *Speculum of the Other Woman* (first published in 1974) is deeply engaged with the psychoanalytic project from Freud to Klein and Lacan, Irigaray's works after *This Sex* have been less overtly concerned with psychoanalysis per se. In her latest writings, she addresses it most often parenthetically or in short asides—usually noting that such and such a discussion would have significant ramifications for psychoanalytic thought. It is now quite common to hear that Irigaray's work is divisible into two distinct phases, that the earlier phase was open to and critically engaged with psychoanalytic thought, and that the latter phase largely ignores, fails to account for, or leaves behind psychoanalysis. Today, when we think of a practicing philosopher who engages psychoanalysis extensively and with ideas about its possible transformations, we are more likely to mention Jacques Derrida, whose work has consistently interrogated, drawn on, and challenged psycho-analytic knowledge, from *The Postcard: From Socrates to Freud and Beyond* (1987 [1980]) to, most recently, "Psychoanalysis Searches the States of Its Soul: The Impossible Beyond of a Sovereign Cruelty (Address to the States General of Psychoanalysis)" ([2002] 2000). Penelope Deutscher, in fact, has argued that now, Derrida's work is more productive for a feminist rethinking of ethics and psychoanalysis than is Irigaray's, especially because of what she calls the latter's as-sumption "that we know what the proper boundaries of the subject are" (Deutscher 1998, 182). In order to address the question of what, if anything, Irigaray's recent work offers to psychoanalytic thought, I would like to take up Deutscher's argument as a provocative starting place because she reflects upon and challenges the direction of Irigaray's thinking, and also because, although I differ from her in my conclu-sions, I think Deutscher is right to suppose that an engagement and comparison with Derrida will prove fruitful for our understanding of Irigaray's project today.[1] In order to come to this discussion of Irigaray with Derrida, then, I will first dwell at some length on the major points of Deutscher's argument.

In her essay, "Mourning the Other, Cultural Cannibalism, and the Politics of Friendship (Jacques Derrida and Luce Irigaray)," Deutscher contends that "Irigaray retains the belief that the other can be stably identified" (Deutscher 1998, 180)—in short, that the other is, in fact, knowable. This belief contrasts with Derrida's consistent emphasis on the failure of our knowledge of the other, on the extent to which even our appropriations and assimilations of the other, are necessarily incomplete. Deutscher frames her discussion with respect to the way each thinker addresses mourning and friendship. She be-gins her article with a reading of Michel de Montaigne's "On Friend-ship," in which she notes that Montaigne characterizes the ideal friendship (the one he shared with Etienne de la Boétie) as compris-ing a lack of any difference between the one and the other. In Montaigne's essay, Deutscher observes,

> [a] theme emerges about the structure of friendship. Montaigne articulates the identificatory mode in which the other is rec-

ognized in the mode of sameness to self. Montaigne also takes for granted that perfection in friendship is the fusion of two subjects as same, rather than resistance, mystery or difference between them. Yet, from the latter perspective, La Boétie is the friend whom Montaigne had assimilated too well, precisely because there is no account of a La Boétie who resists assimilation by Montaigne, the friend I do not know, or do not know how to mourn. There is no question of who La Boétie was. Montaigne is only too sure: his friend was a part of himself. La Boétie, as the perfect friend, is described as Montaigne's only true listener (de Certeau 79). By contrast, I might value in the friend what he or she could least comprehend about me, or I might value their refusal to be my perfect listener. Montaigne's love for his friend could be designated a cannibal love because of the telling sensation of mourning a half of oneself. If Montaigne has "not survived whole," had La Boétie been reduced to Montaigne's (same as) self? (Deutscher 1998, 161; Deutscher's reference)

Deutscher proceeds with a rich discussion of mourning, in which she describes Derrida's understanding of the inevitability of "cannibalizing" the other, or reducing the absent friend to the terrain of the self, *and* of the inevitable failure of such a reduction to ever be absolute. In *Mémoires: For Paul de Man*, for example, "Derrida describes the inevitability of cannibalism. But he also finds the means to articulate its failure and impossibility" (Deutscher 1998, 161). Although, in mourning, the friend exists no longer in the world, and has indeed been reduced to our interiorization of him or her, that interiorization or eating of the other always also meets an indefatigable resistance, one that we do not overcome. So, the question, for Derrida, becomes not how *not* to eat the other, but rather, given that we must eat the other, how to eat well (Deutscher 1998, 174).

Derrida's emphasis on the always ambiguous status of the other with respect to the self, Deutscher writes, has implications beyond the field of mourning and ought to be brought to bear on Irigaray's philosophy.

From this point on, we can ask what happens if this thematic [of the simultaneous inevitability and impossibility of cannibalizing the other] is introduced into the cannibal metaphor as it is deployed by Luce Irigaray in her work on the ethics of

sexual difference? Irigaray devises political programs that would
enable mediated relations between subjects in order to interrupt cultural cannibalism (the tendency to appropriate and
interiorize the other). Perhaps Irigaray overtheorizes the success of cannibalism, underemphasizing its necessary failure?
(Deutscher 1998, 169)

According to Deutscher, Irigaray underlined "very strongly" in her early
work the point that "[t]he other is always in excess of my reductions of
and identifications with him or her," but has since "de-emphasized" this
point, to the extent that the other is now vested in a stabilized and
knowable identity. Furthermore, she suggests that it is precisely this
issue that allows for a useful "comparison of interventions into psychoanalytic theory from Irigaray and Derrida" (Deutscher 1998, 170).

Before discussing such a comparison, I should explain why it is
that Deutscher believes Irigaray's thought has, as it were, fallen into
sameness. Deutscher's first and general point is that Irigaray's insistence on the need for cultural change is based on her assumption that
"cultural cannibalism" (the eating/appropriating of the other) does in
fact succeed. In other words, Irigaray's suggestions concerning the
need for cultural changes (linguistic, legal, religious, etc.) are proof
that her thinking is now "premised on her diagnosis of the success of
cultural cannibalism" (Deutscher 1998, 170), as opposed to Derrida's
more nuanced interpretation of how we consume the other. For example, "Derrida occupies psychoanalytic accounts of mourning in order
to destabilize the integrity of the subject who mourns the other and
the integrity of the other who is mourned," whereas Irigaray resists a
"reconsideration of the integrity of the self and other" that should be
"as important to feminism as a reconsideration of sexual difference"
(Deutscher 1998, 170). Thus, Deutscher's first challenge goes as follows: "how might Irigaray's anti-cannibal politics be affected by a
conceptualization of my appropriations [. . .] of, and identifications
with the other as always inevitable, *and* as always inevitably failing?
We will always be faithful to the other, and even our worst cannibalisms
must necessarily fail" (Deutscher 1998, 170).

Deutscher offers her second point by way of a comparison between Derrida's and Irigaray's accounts of narcissism, suggesting that
Irigaray is too quick to conclude that narcissism is simply "a successful
subordination of the other to the self" (Deutscher 1998, 174), whereas
Derrida stresses the ambiguity at the heart of narcissism. Still in the

context of mourning, Deutscher quotes Derrida from *Mémoires*, where
he argues that the relation to the absent other in mourning cannot be
reduced to a merely narcissistic fantasizing, and that, indeed, the structure of narcissism is itself already "too complex to allow the other,
dead or living, to be reduced to this same structure [of a subject
identical to itself]. Already installed in the narcissistic structure, the
other so marks the self of the relationship to self, so conditions it that
the being 'in us' of bereaved memory becomes the coming of the
other" (Derrida 1989, 22; qtd. in Deutscher, 173). By contrast,
Deutscher points to a recent Irigarayan denunciation of "narcissistic
self-other love relations precisely as a relationship to the other in
which s/he is subordinated to my nostalgia for unity" (Deutscher 1998,
174). In *Etre Deux*, Deutscher reminds us, Irigaray couches the destructive "nostalgia for the one" in terms of a narcissism that crowds
out the possibility of a relation between two. Such nostalgia, at times,
"corresponds to narcissistic self-love. It is often the equivalent of the
will to be or possess the whole. To remain two requires that one
renounce this fusional, regressive, autistic, narcissistic unity" (Irigaray
2000 [1997, 1994], 104, Deutscher's translation; quoted in Deutscher,
174). As opposed to Derrida's account of a paradoxical narcissism,
Irigaray offers "a simple reference to narcissism as unethical and as a
failure to recognize the two," whereas, Deutscher observes, "what is
needed is an emphasis on the instability of the 'identity' of narcissism,
an insistence that it is always at once exclusion and incorporation of
the other, infinitely complicated" (Deutscher 1998, 174). Irigaray's
failure to emphasize such instability, Deutscher argues, leaves her too
liable to be supposing a version of the self that is somehow uncon-
taminated by the other, a self that embodies a complete integrity with
respect to the other, an integrity that cannot be put into question for
fear of such questioning leading to a narcissistic "breakdown of boundaries" between self and other (Deutscher 1998, 175).

According to Deutscher, the resistance to any such breakdown
of boundaries stems from a recent change in Irigaray's conception of
sexual difference. "In her early discussion of mourning and melancholia, Irigaray's concept of feminine identity is represented as culturally
annihilated: 'I defend the impossible . . . But am I actually allowed to
do otherwise? Is not what is offered me already within a horizon that
annihilates my identity and my will?'" (Irigaray 1996 [1992], 9;
Deutscher, 177, Deutscher's ellipsis). Now, though, "the sexual difference that has been culturally annihilated is more concretely knowable

and speakable . . . much more precisely defined. Less obscure than was the definition of femininity in the early work, it is stabilized as a concept of sexuate identity" (Deutscher 1998, 177). Deutscher offers the following passage as an example: "the relation between genders is determined by man's needs with no consideration for women's identity . . . [O]ur tradition lacks the mediations enabling her to keep her identity as a woman. . . . It is from a desire for exchange that women's melancholy ensues" (Irigaray 1996 [1992], 135–36; Deutscher, 177, Deutscher's ellipses). In the interest of offering a new vision of sexuate identity that might enable the implementation of new political programs, which would in turn nurture such identity, Irigaray has forgotten her earlier[2] insistence on the resistance of the other to the same: she "seems to fail to remember the failure of appropriation" (Deutscher 1998, 177).

As a final and most striking instance of this forgetting, Deutscher cites Irigaray's description, in *I Love to You*, of her public encounter and exchange with the Italian politician Renzo Imbeni, and she compares this description with Montaigne's account of his perfect friendship with La Boétie. In the opening pages of *I Love to You*, Irigaray describes a 1989 meeting with Renzo Imbeni, mayor of Bologna, where she had been invited to participate with him in a debate about "New Rights in Europe" (Imbeni was being elected to the European Parliament). Irigaray portrays the event in very positive terms, expressing her pleasant surprise at finding that she could speak and be listened to, as a woman, in that public arena: "that night, a miracle took place. We talked; we talked to each other; he and I, his citizens and my insurgents. Between us, each and every woman and man, there were truths, questions, passions, fidelities, words. We stayed together exchanging our views for at least three hours" (Irigaray 1996 [1992], 7). Like Montaigne, Deutscher claims, Irigaray offers us a picture of a friend and listener whom she *knows*, whom she recognizes as a stable and identifiable other, of the other sex:

> There is no question of who Imbeni was. What Irigaray evokes is her very recognition of him, she is only too sure of who he was. The evocation of La Boétie as the perfect and true listener occurs in a politics of sameness in Montaigne's work. So it is telling that although Imbeni is evoked in the context of an Irigarayan politics of difference, he is again represented as the perfect and true listener. (Deutscher 1998, 178–79)

Furthermore, "Imbeni's personal qualities are depicted by Irigaray in ideal terms," as is her ability to speak of the qualities of the other; whereas, on the contrary, we would expect that "[i]f there has been an ethical encounter between herself and Imbeni, this should enable her recognition of 'another who will never be mine'" (Deutscher 1998, 179), another whom she cannot presume to know. This episode, Deutscher concludes, also offers support to the argument that Irigaray overprivileges heterosociality or heterosexuality as the realm of the ethical recognition of difference. Montaigne, in his depiction of the perfect friend as exactly like himself, may have privileged the homosocial in his assumption that we can only truly know what is similar, what is the same. For her part, "Irigaray supposes that we know the different, and that it specially occurs in the heterosocial friendship" (Deutscher 1998, 179).

For Deutscher, then, Irigaray's thought has strayed too far into the territory of stable identities, at the cost of the attention that must be paid to the ways in which the other always eludes one and in which identity always undermines itself, is never merely identical. This overemphasis on identity stems from and strengthens Irigaray's vision of *two* sexes, of a culture of sexual difference in which the hetero is too consistently figured as the privileged realm for ethics.

As I mentioned above in my introduction to Deutscher's argument, I do not come to the same conclusions as Deutscher, and I would like to begin with her last point in order to show why. For Deutscher, Irigaray's description of her meeting with Imbeni is emblematic and symptomatic of her recent forgetting of the nonintegrity and unknowability of selves and others. Instead of evoking Imbeni's resistance to her knowledge of him, what she underlines "is her very recognition of him, she is only too sure of who he was" (Deutscher 1998, 178). It seems, first, that Deutscher may be conflating recognition and knowledge here, whereas, for Irigaray, these are two very different notions. To recognize another, for Irigaray, is to recognize, among other things, that one does not and cannot completely know the other. As she explains in *I Love to You*, in the chapter on recognition,

> I recognize you, thus you are not the whole [. . .] and I am not the whole. [. . .] I cannot completely identify you, even less identify with you.
>
> I recognize you means that I cannot know you in thought or in flesh. The power of a negative prevails between us. I

recognize you goes hand in hand with: you are irreducible to me, just as I am to you. [. . .] You are transcendent to me, inaccessible in a way, not only as ontic being but also as ontological being [. . .]

Recognizing you means or implies respecting you as other, accepting that I draw myself to a halt before you as before something insurmountable, a mystery. (Irigaray 1996 [1992], 103–4)

Irigaray's concern here is to call attention to the incommensurate in what is commonly understood to signify identity, similarity, or a total knowing. So, the charge that Irigaray evokes "her very recognition of him" is irrelevant, since it in no way implies that she has some sort of absolute or complete knowledge with respect to Imbeni. On the contrary, as Irigaray herself explains in the same work, it implies an encounter in which his ultimate unknowability is acknowledged and respected. But does Irigaray otherwise imply that she knows only too well what and who Imbeni is? My reading of the passage yields the opposite conclusion. In fact, what Irigaray emphasizes is her lack of knowledge and the general uncertainty of her position vis à vis her interlocutor. For example, her description begins thus: "I *did not know* my interlocutor very well. He had publicly acknowledged me after I had spoken at his Party's 18th Congress. But, at the time, *I did not realize* the significance of that gesture" (Irigaray 1996 [1992], 6, emphases added). She goes on to repeat her lack of knowledge and to add that her distance from him was increased by the fact that she was not speaking her own language: "And so I found myself in a situation that *was new for me*, with someone *I did not know*, and I had to speak, listen and respond in another language" (Irigaray 1996 [1992], 6, emphases added). When she does indeed describe him positively, those descriptions come not from any arbitrary or secure knowledge she supposes herself to possess, but from her experience of him: "*By his reaction*, he thus *appeared to me* as a man worthy of trust," even though, indeed, "I was unable to follow all that he said," and his frankness and resolution, in fact, "took me by surprise" (Irigaray 1996 [1992], 8, emphases added). Now that the encounter has passed, "I cannot say whether it was a fecund experience for him," and "to be sure, a reality divides us" (Irigaray 1996 [1992], 9). But, if she cannot and does not claim to know the other, she can recognize him "by attesting to the qualities of the other, to what he communicates" (Irigaray 1996 [1992], 16). Irigaray is not, I would maintain, refusing to speak of "an Imbeni whose identity she can't be sure of" (Deutscher 1998, 179); rather, she is taking care to underline the necessary incompleteness of her descriptions and judgments of another.

Identity, indeed, is the term that Deutscher fears has become too stabilized and well-defined in Irigaray's recent work, but I would suggest that Irigaray's use of the term does not imply its secure definition. Irigaray does indeed speak of sexuate identity and of one's "identity as a woman," but to name something called "woman's identity" is not necessarily to stabilize it or define it. Deutscher contrasts such allegedly stabilizing statements with acknowledgments, in the early work, of the impossibility of pinning down something that might be called the feminine or femininity, acknowledgments of the annihilation of such a reality in a culture based on hom(m)osexuality. However, in her example, the contrasting (early and late) passages Deutscher cites are in fact from the same work, *I Love to You*, published in the 1990s. It is in this work that Irigaray says *both* that she is necessarily defending the impossible when she asserts that she wants "what is yet to be as the only possibility of a future" (Irigaray 1996 [1992], 10), *and* that "our tradition lacks the mediations enabling her [woman] to keep her identity as a woman" (Irigaray 1996 [1992], 13). These two statements, in the context of Irigaray's thought, are in no way mutually exclusive, and it should come therefore as no surprise that they are also not separated by years or decades in her oeuvre.

Perhaps Deutscher assumes that the phrase "to keep her identity as a woman" implies that there is a speakable, nameable identity in question here. But the context of this statement helps to show that just the opposite is the case: in this section of the book, Irigaray is discussing the inevitable impossibilities created by the structure of patriarchal family and civic relations. She continues her discussion as follows:

> [G]iven the prevalence of *one* genealogy, a patriarchal one, female filiation is erased, and while the wife (of a son) becomes mother (or a son), the father's virgin daughter, by virtue of her status as such, becomes a currency among men. Justice would mean woman's being virgin and mother for herself, these properties of her nature founding her spiritual becoming, her rights and duties. (Irigaray 1996 [1992], 136)

Justice, in other words, would require that the woman be able to maintain an identity proper to herself *as woman*, rather than as a function of man, and that, as a consequence, her nature would then be determined based on, and within, a culture that recognized her being as a value in itself, in its own terms. This is a point that goes back to *Speculum*. What this impossible future, and the identities it would afford, would look like, would be, is of course impossible to say, is as mysterious and transcendent to us as any other. It is, nevertheless, Irigaray asserts, necessary to think, imagine, and try to create such an impossibility "as the only possibility of a future."

As we noted above, Irigaray's underlining of woman's identity is not the only instance of what Deutscher suspects is a new certainty about the security, identity, and integrity of the self in Irigaray's work. The other example Deutscher cites deals with the treatment of narcissism, where Irigaray seems to claim that narcissism is simply and completely the subjection of the other to the self and the self's terms. The self, in other words, would be capable of excluding the other in a narcissistic self-love bent on being all, being complete, and thereby making impossible a relation between two. The matter of narcissism also touches on Deutscher's more general claim that Irigaray supposes we know "what the proper boundaries of the subject are" (Deutscher 1998, 182). Rather than offering "a simple reference to narcissism as unethical and as a failure to recognize the two," Deutscher writes, Irigaray might (but doesn't) suggest that "the success of narcissism fails and that the failure of narcissism succeeds" (Deutscher 1998, 174). In other words, Irigaray does not note the inevitable ambiguity attached to narcissism, which, for example, in incorporating the other within the self and the self's terms so as to do away with the otherness, has at the very least first to recognize that otherness and thus be changed by it in some way. When Deutscher worries that Irigaray supposes "too quickly that narcissism is a successful subordination of the other to the self" (Deutscher 1998, 174), she is concerned with the predominance that Irigaray's thinking of *the two* seems to bestow on the two as separate, identifiable, and discrete subjects. This concern, however, fails to take into account Irigaray's preoccupation, in this discussion from *Etre deux*, with the possibility of a change, in history, to the "infernal circle" of sexual difference, thought as merely two kinds of exteriority, which has led to woman trying to define herself by recourse to man, and man by recourse to the mother. The traditional attempt to escape this circle, she argues, has taken on various forms, all of which attempt to fix things by inventing a final, unassailable unity at the base of all things, including the sexes (and that unity, of course, has had the logical and historical effect of privileging as neutral values those that are in fact more proper to masculinity in the west's versions of it). "Logic imagined originary causality, philosophy the univocal character of the truth, our religious tradition the authority of a God-the-Father" (Irigaray [1997], 102, my translation). What such figures of external and unified authorities have in common, Irigaray suggests, is their failure to recognize that "what determines me, what is cause of me and for me belongs in part to the other, in particular the other of sexual difference. I receive my life as a woman, my interiority, also from the other-man; they are fecundated and come to growth starting from the encounter between me-woman and you-man, if we are each of us faithful to our gender" (Irigaray [1997], 103, my translation). The self is, in other words, constituted always in and as a relation to the other, and the task of her ethics of sexual difference, as she sees it, is to foster recognition of this interiority of the other as the very beginning of the self. Such a recognition leads to the realization that stories of single, unified origins (be they Plato's Forms, Christianity's God, or logic's primary Cause) occlude what are in fact multiple origins, origins which continue to multiply as the self finds itself in relation with others. She writes:

> There is then no longer a unique origin, nor for that matter an origin common to many: a *logos*, a civilization, a religious or civil authority. We do not belong only to one family, one people, one nation, one culture. There exist for me, for us and between us, singular and multiple origins, diverse genealogies. I was born in and of a family, in a determined epoch of History, in a specific place and in the context of a tradition. But I have encountered and criss-crossed other causalities with that. And so it is for each man and woman. Together, we represent many diversities, more or less compatible.
>
> Desire can bring us together, unite us. But, although it's as old as the world, this mediation for realizing a communitary life has not been cultivated. The nostalgia for the *one* has always supplanted the desire between *two*. (Irigaray [1997], 103–4, my translation)

Here is the context, then, in which Irigaray will take issue with a nostalgia that can present itself in several ways. It may appear as the desire for fusion with nature, with a god, or with the energy of others, for example; or it may "correspond to the narcisstic love of self"

(Irigaray [1997], 103–4, my translation). However it manifests itself, the problem with such a nostalgia is that it works against the cultivation of a desire between two, a desire that would be cognizant of the other's constitutive place in my origin, my self. While it is true that Irigaray does not offer, in this passage, a nuanced discussion of narcissism, it is also the case that here, narcissism is functioning on the level of one example among others, an example of broad cultural tendencies toward the fantasy of an original unity. A tendency toward narcissism, in other words, is for Irigaray here merely one symptom among many of a universal that is broadly conceived as originating in and heading toward the faulty ideal of the One. This is not, however, to say, that Irigaray is arguing that such a complete and fulfilled narcissism can actually obtain, only that the cultural tendency toward it has identifiable ethical effects. If we recall her most fundamental conceptual move—away from stabilized identities and towards what she calls being two—it becomes impossible to imagine that, for Irigaray, a kind of total narcissism (and the complete occlusion of the other it implies) succeeds entirely. But again, this is not to say that its tendency is not operative.

For Irigaray, leaving the ground of identity, and of the universal as one, is concomitant with a rethinking of what can constitute a ground, or what can constitute and ground a being. What she proposes is a new formulation of the universal, a universal based on the plurality of sexual difference. Her *being two*, taking its number from the two sexes, is the model she takes because of the specific sort of transcendence it implies, on both the inter and intrasubjective levels. To be two, and to be of two, means, for Irigaray, to acknowledge that the other is irreducible to the self and that even the self is never wholly identical to itself, belonging as it does to a universal gender, to a kind, which transcends its individuality and which the subject must remake, constituting her or his expression of the universal. In this sense, the universal of sexual difference can only be conceived as a process and as not yet having arrived—both in terms of a contemporary cultural poverty that does not allow for it and in terms of its own fluid nature. She writes, "The culture of this universal does not yet exist. The individual has been considered as a particular, without sufficient interpretation of that universal which is in the individual: woman or man" (Irigaray 1996 [1992], 48, translation modified).

In explaining that Derrida's understanding of narcissism is less restrictive than Irigaray's, Deutscher points to his emphasis on the impossibility of self-identity, since the other is always a part of what constitutes one. Thus, for example, Derrida will reject the Freudian distinction between a "normal" self and the self occupied, more or less pathologically, by an internalized other in mourning. She writes:

> Where he [Derrida] occupies psychoanalytic theory to theorize non self-identity at the heart of identity, he is led to the position that we are inevitably cannibal selves. The distinction between the abnormal (mourning) self and the normal self of integrity could not be sustained. The normal self does not possess integrity any more than the mourning self. The obvious lack of self-identity that is seen when the other is mourned in fact pertains in a more generalized way to every subject constituted with alterity at its heart. We are the constant interiorization/ incorporation of the other. (Deutscher 1998, 175)

And thus, Irigaray could add, we are transcendent to ourselves. For the logic here is entirely consistent with Irigaray's understanding of, to use her terms, subjectivity as always mediated, never immediate. Deutscher, however, suggests that Irigaray's concern about the effects of a narcissistic and unitary logic lead her to suppose that there can be a neat distinction between the self and the other. "Irigaray's concern is directed at the narcissistic breakdown at work when I suppose that I am already the other. But in response, we could also ask, who do I think 'I' am, if I think the other is 'over there'? What integrity for the self's identity do I hope to establish?" (Deutscher 1998, 175) Against an Irigarayan move that wants to ask *who* the other is, who or what the other represents in all the contemporary philosophical, religious, and political discourse about the other, Deutscher offers a Derridian response that "simultaneously put[s] into question the integrity of the *self*. The way he does so—by theorizing the self as always already the other—risks incurring Irigaray's accusations of narcissism and cultural appropriation. But despite her own concerns on this very point, the status of self and other may be too secure in her theory" (Deutscher 1998, 176). In fact, I don't think Derrida's emphasis on the mutual implication of self and other does go counter to Irigaray's question of the other; the terms, however, are different. For Irigaray, the important notions are incompletion and belonging to a gender.

If the other is to be respected in her or his alterity, this does not require, for Irigaray, maintaining boundaries that would guarantee a kind of individual integrity to each. On the contrary, what she argues for is an understanding (and living) of the self and the self's identity as always incomplete. This incompletion means both that it is possible for me to be open to the other and that it is impossible for me ever to fuse entirely with the other, even as I am constituted always in relation to the other. And in her attempt to forge an ethics based in sexual difference, Irigaray links this incompletion to the fact of belonging to a gender, a reality that limits my identity—not to any particular content, but rather to the necessity of my being constituted always *in relation to*, to you, to others, to another gender, to another in me, and so on. As she writes in *I Love to You*, "The being that I am is thus never the whole and it is always separate (from) insofar as it corresponds to a gender. Thus, it cannot be fusional, neither in infancy nor in love. What's more, this being is an opening to the other gender, genealogically and horizontally" (Irigaray 1996 [1992], 107, translation modified). While Deutscher acknowledges the legitimacy of what she calls Irigaray's suspicion that "the politics of difference sometimes does not render its conception of 'the other' sufficiently complex," she calls for a recognition, in Irigaray's work, that "an adequately complex account of what the other is requires an account of how we must already be the other" (Deutscher 1998, 176). This account, for Irigaray, is contained precisely in her notion of "belonging to a gender," which is both of me and more than me, both external to me and to be created by me.

What constitutes "cannibalism," then, for Irigaray, cannot be understood in quite the terms Deutscher employs when she refers to Derrida's recognition of the inevitability of cannibalizing the other. Insofar as my identity must always partake of the other, be "contaminated" by the other, and feed off of the other, then yes, Irigaray's work acknowledges the necessity of such a cannibalism, equally as strongly as Derrida's, and for similar reasons. But Irigaray herself uses the term "cultural cannibalism" to mean something quite distinct from this necessary appropriation of the other. In her use of it, in fact, we can say that cannibalism refers to the *failure* to take the other in as an other, to the failure to maintain an openness to the other that might allow him/her to participate in the constitution of the self. Here is the context in which she uses the term, in the title essay of *I Love to You*:

> The "to" is also a barrier against the alienation of the other's freedom in my subjectivity, my world, my language.

I love to you thus means: I do not take you for a direct object, nor for an indirect object by revolving around you. It is, rather, around myself that I have to revolve in order to maintain the *to you* thanks to the return to me. Not with my prey—you become mine—but with the intention of respecting my nature, my history, my intentionality, while also respecting yours. Hence, I do not return to me in the mode of: I wonder if I am loved. That would result from an introverted intentionality, going toward the other so as to return ruminating, sadly and endlessly, over solipsistic questions in a sort of cultural cannibalism. (Irigaray 1996 [1992], 110, translation modified)

Cultural cannibalism here describes "an introverted intentionality," one which fails to apprehend the other at all, except as a means to the end of building up the self as an introverted (and hence integral, self-contained?) whole. Irigaray's problem with such a cannibalism, then, is not that it eats the other, that it takes the other in, but precisely that it does not—that it does not allow in any way for an openness to the other as a site whereby I acknowledge my incompleteness, my belonging to a gender (also seen as incomplete and to be created), and the other's freedom with respect to me. In the context of mourning, we could then say that, insofar as such a cultural cannibalism were at work, it would be impossible for mourning to take place, because the self's relationship to itself has not been formed and constituted in relation to the other, but merely "fed" by a wholly (and whole) fantasized other, created entirely for the sake of maintaining the fantasy of the whole self. But if or when this type of cannibalism does not describe my relation to the other, if the self, in being a self, is attentive to, without alienating, the other's freedom *and* "my subjectivity, my world, my language," if the relation to the other acknowledges the incompleteness of both self and other as constitutive of the self, then, indeed, we can say from an Irigarayan perspective, and with Derrida, that the work of mourning, "the being 'in us' of bereaved memory, becomes the *coming* of the other" (Derrida 1989, 22, original emphasis), specifically, the other who is both in me and inaccessible to me.

What Irigaray and Derrida share, via their respective emphases on incompletion and alterity, is an emphasis on the yet to be, the impossible, as a site of possibility and of creation. The important difference, of course, is Irigaray's almost exclusive focus on sexual difference as an ontological category and as a privileged category when it comes to conceiving ethics. While it is true that her more recent works do not spend as much time as the earlier ones on what psycho-analytic thought might or ought to contribute to her ethics of sexual difference, it is nevertheless the case that in marking sexual difference off as *the* site for the creation of ethics, her work necessarily supposes the possibility of psychoanalysis, or a psychoanalysis to come, as a primary locus for ethical interrogations, because it is, by definition, and like no other field of knowledge, primarily concerned with elabo-rating the significance of sexual difference. Likewise, Derrida has sug-gested in his most recent writing on psychoanalysis that it is the field of knowledge most properly concerned with, for example, the ques-tion of radical evil, with questions upon which any ethics must base itself (Derrida 2002 [2000], 240). At the same time, Derrida takes what we might call an Irigarayan direction when he wonders whether we can think beyond psychoanalysis's present possibles, toward impos-sibilities still to come:

> My question will be [. . .]: is there, for thought, for psychoana-
> lytic thought to come, another beyond, if I can say that, a
> beyond that would stand beyond these *possibles* that are still
> *both* the pleasure and reality principles *and* the death or sov-
> ereign mastery drives, which seem to be at work wherever
> cruelty is on the horizon? In other words, altogether other
> words, can one think this apparently impossible, but other-
> wise impossible thing, namely, a beyond the death drive or
> the drive for sovereign mastery, thus the beyond of a cruelty,
> a beyond that would have nothing to do with either drives or
> principles? And thus nothing to do either with all the rest of
> the Freudian discourse that orders itself around them, with its
> economy, its topography, its metapsychology, and especially
> with what Freud [. . .] also calls its "mythology" of the drives?
> (Derrida 2002 [2000], 241)

In asking about the possibility of psychoanalysis going beyond certain of its tenets in order to be able, precisely, to think something that underlies those tenets, is he calling on the psychoanalysts he addresses in this lecture to leave the domain of psychoanalysis altogether, for philosophy (properly or improperly conceived)? And/or, is he asking psychoanalysis to burst its own proper dimensions in order to become

the improperly philosophical discourse it (also already) is? His questions here demand what he calls a "leap" into the ethical realm that
would require that psychoanalysis leave behind its legitimate and legitimating grounds. And in order to call for this leap, he makes a
claim about Freud's concept of indirection that will also bring to mind
Irigaray's thinking about the importance of indirection and mediation.
Furthermore, in suggesting the importance of indirection or mediation
for any ethics, both Derrida and Irigaray effectively urge a future psychoanalytic thinking that does the impossible and the necessary, that is,
a psychoanalytic thinking that is so only improperly. Derrida takes up
the importance of indirection specifically in attempting to read Freud
on the possibility of going beyond cruelty (in *Why War?*):

> Even though Freud does not say it, certainly not in this way,
> this concept of the *indirect* seems to me to take into account,
> in the mediation of the detour, a radical discontinuity, a het-
> erogeneity, a leap into the ethical (thus also into the juridical
> and political) that no psychoanalytic knowledge as such could
> propel or authorize. [. . .] Whether one is talking about the
> cruelty or the sovereignty drive, psychoanalytic knowledge as
> such has neither the means nor the right to condemn it. In
> this regard, it is and must remain, as knowledge, within the
> neutrality of the undecidable. Whence what I call the 'états
> d'âme,' that is, the hesitation, the confused mental state, or
> the soul-searching of psychoanalysis. To cross the line of de-
> cision, a leap that expels one outside psychoanalytic knowl-
> edge *as such* is necessary. (Derrida 2002 [2000], 273)

The relation of psychoanalysis to ethics is, then, necessarily indirect,
requiring that psychoanalytic knowledge leave itself in order, as it
were, to be taken into account by domains properly concerned with
judgments about good and evil (ethics, law, politics). Moreover, in
order for these domains to transform themselves, this indirection on
the part of psychoanalytic thought is necessary. As Derrida sees it, a
future transformed ethics will need the organizing force of "this taking
account of psychoanalytic reason without reducing the heterogeneity,
the leap into the undecidable, the beyond of the possible, which is
the object of psychoanalytic knowledge" (Derrida 2002 [2000], 273).
It is, he argues, precisely via such a discontinuous and indirect encounter (between ethics, law, and politics and psychoanalysis) that

both ethics and psychoanalysis may surpass themselves, becoming what they are not yet (Derrida 2002 [2000], 274).

In thinking toward a new ethics, an ethics of sexual difference, Irigaray is engaged in precisely such a task. It is no doubt for this reason that indirection has played such an important role in her own thought. This is most clearly proclaimed by the "to" in her phrase "I love to you," but it has been the case also from as early on in her work as *Speculum*, in which she presents an extended practice of indirection: thinking from Freud to Plato via the curved mirror of an ethical project that chooses, in a "leap," to situate itself in and from a sexual difference that is not (yet). Her project, in other words, suggests and inaugurates psychoanalysis's potential to participate in a redefinition of both the sexual and the ethical. And if it often seems that the terms in which she proposes such a redefinition are, from the perspective of psychoanalytic knowledge, off the mark, not to say impossible, this is precisely because they are oriented toward its "impossible beyond."

NOTES

1. The present essay represents the beginning stages of an attempt to formulate some of the implications of Irigaray's thought for psychoanalysis.
2. In fact, both of these quotations, representing an earlier and a later orientation, are taken from the same work: *I Love to You*. See below.

WORKS CITED

de Certeau, Michel. 1986. *Heterologies: Discourse on the Other*. Translated by Brian Massumi. Minneapolis, Minn.: University of Minnesota Press.
Derrida, Jacques. 1987 [1980]. *The Post Card: From Socrates to Freud and Beyond*. Translated by Alan Bass. Chicago: University of Chicago Press. (Translation of *La carte postale: de Socrate à Freud et au-delà*. Paris: Flammarion.)
———. 1989. *Mémoires: For Paul de Man*. Translated by Cecile Lindsay, Johathan Culler, Eduardo Cadava, and Peggy Kamuf. Edited by Avital Ronell and Eduardo Cadava. New York: Columbia University Press.
———. 2002 [2000]. "Psychoanalysis Searches the States of Its Soul: The Impossible Beyond of a Sovereign Cruelty (Address to the States General of Psychoanalysis)." In *Without Alibi*, edited, translated and introduction by Peggy Kamuf, 238–80. Berkeley, Calif.: Stanford University Press. (Translation of *Etats d'âme, de la psychanalyse: L'impossible au-delà d'une souveraine cruauté*. Paris: Galilée.)

————. 2002 [2000]. "The University without Condition." In *Without Alibi*, edited, translated, and introduction by Peggy Kamuf, 202–37. Berkeley, Calif.: Stanford University Press.

Deutscher, Penelope. 1998. "Mourning the Other, Cultural Cannibalism, and the Politics of Friendship (Jacques Derrida and Luce Irigaray)." *differences: A Journal of Feminist Cultural Studies* 10.3: 159–84.

Irigaray, Luce. 1985a [1974]. *Speculum of the Other Woman*. Translated by Gillian C. Gill. Ithaca, N.Y.: Cornell University Press.

————. 1985b [1977]. *This Sex Which Is Not One*. Translated by Catherine Porter. Ithaca, N.Y.: Cornell University Press.

————. 1991. *The Irigaray Reader*. Edited by Margaret Whitford. Oxford: Blackwell.

————. 1993a [1984]. *An Ethics of Sexual Difference*. Translated by Carolyn Burke and Gillian C. Gill. Ithaca, N.Y.: Cornell University Press.

————. 1993b [1987]. *Sexes and Genealogies*. Translated by Gillian C. Gill. New York: Columbia University Press.

————. 1996 [1992]. *I Love to You: Sketch of a Possible Felicity in History*. Translated by Alison Martin. New York: Routledge.

————. 1997. *Etre Deux*. Paris: Bernard Grasset.

————. 1999. *Entre orient et occident: de la singularité à la communauté*. Paris: Bernard Grasset.

ON LUCE IRIGARAY'S PHENOMENOLOGY

OF INTERSUBJECTIVITY:

BETWEEN THE FEMININE BODY

AND ITS OTHER

Sara Heinämaa

> He sees his body as a direct and normal connection with the world, which he believes he apprehends in its objectivity.
>
> (Beauvoir [1949] 1993, 15/15)*

Luce Irigaray's work is often interpreted as an argument about Western philosophy as a whole. Irigaray is claimed to maintain that woman—or the feminine—is the "other" of the Western theoretical tradition. On this reading, Irigaray's works aim at demonstrating that our philosophies and theories are based on an exclusive operation which rejects or suppresses everything that is feminine.

Thus understood, the feminist problem with philosophy would not just be that women are excluded as subjects—as speakers, writers, and topics—from the institutions of philosophy, but more severely that the philosophical activity itself, independently of its subjects, somehow defines itself in opposition to the feminine. Women would not just suffer from the practical difficulty of finding access to philosophical forums, but more severely from the principal problem that no appearance or event of the feminine is possible within the philosophical praxis.

Irigaray's critique would not just concern the factual or actual state of philosophy but its possibilities.

Two alternatives would be left open for women: either women can try to work to disrupt and unsettle the founding principles of Western theory and philosophy—the principles of reason, truth, and objectivity—or they must abandon the whole philosophical project.[1]

The problem with this extremist line of interpretation is that it makes Irigaray's work seem self-refuting. For, on the other hand, Irigaray presents in her own publications philosophical claims about the nature of the feminine and suggests that she is speaking in a feminine voice. Several commentators have been perplexed by this tension. Thus, for example Shoshana Felman, an early critic, asks:

> [. . .] if "the woman" is precisely the Other of any conceivable Western theoretical locus of speech, how can the woman as such be speaking in this book [in *Speculum*]? Who is speaking here, and who is asserting the otherness of woman? (Felman 1975, 3)

And, further:

> If, as Luce Irigaray suggests, the woman's silence, or the repression of her capacity to speak, are constitutive of philosophy and of theoretical discourse as such, from what theoretical locus is Luce Irigaray herself speaking in order to develop her own theoretical discourse about the woman's exclusion? (Felman 1975, 3)[2]

Another problem of the extremist reading is that it fits Irigaray's early works but conflicts with her later writings. In *Ce sexe qui n'en est pas un* (1977), for example, Irigaray seems to propose an all-encompassing "critique of philosophy." She writes:

> (. . .) it is indeed the philosophical discourse that we have to question, and *disturb* [*deranger*], (. . .) For each philosopher—beginning with those who determine an era in the history of philosophy—we have to identify the operation which cuts with the material contiguity and puts together the system, the operation of the specular economy. (Irigaray 1977, 72–73/74–75, cf. 153–55/158–60)[3]

But already in 1984, in *Éthique de la différence sexuelle*, Irigaray takes a very different attitude towards classical philosophical works. Instead of disturbing or disrupting the texts of Plato or Descartes, she follows closely their distinctions and develops further their concepts of love and wonder.[4] The constructive work continues in the later publications.

This suggests that there would be a change or a turn in Irigaray's thinking. The problem, however, is that she explicitly rejects such readings. For her, they are part of the misunderstandings and confusions concerning her work (Irigaray 1992, 50/59, Irigaray with Hirsch and Olson 1995, 106).

In this chapter, I present an alternative to the extremist reading of Irigaray's critique of philosophy. I argue that Irigaray's claims are more specific than such readings suggest. She does not maintain that the very principles of philosophical thought exclude woman or the feminine. Her critique is more focused.[5] It concerns the ways in which our modern predecessors and contemporaries have reflected on *living bodies and bodily persons*, and it hinges on the very idea of unprejudiced philosophical thinking.

These problematic reflections on bodies and persons tangle with different practical and ethical topics, such as political life, work, production and reproduction, friendship, and love, but Irigaray argues that, ultimately, they also distort our ontological and epistemological concepts, the concepts of objectivity and knowledge in particular. She states:

> [. . .] what still remains hidden is the limit of a culture based upon a single subject. And how it impedes intersubjectivity—particularly between the two kinds [*genres*]—defining, for example, objectivity and all the forms of representation from the point of view of a single subject. (Irigaray 1994, 103, 1997 161/90, cf. 1994, 43–44, 1997, 63–65/33–36)

FROM INTERSUBJECTIVITY TO OBJECTIVITY

In *J'aime à toi*, Irigaray explicitly rejects the notion that there is a theoretical turn in her thinking. She makes clear that the thematic and conceptual differences between *Speculum* and *Éthique* are superficial and that there is a deeper continuity in her thought. The permanent goal has been to think through, and to work for, the constitution of "the feminine identity" [*l'identité féminine*] or "the feminine generic" [*le générique féminin*] (Irigaray 1992, 103/60, 1994, 83, 1997, 129/72).

The question is not just about the feminine identity as an empirical fact or reality, but more crucially about the feminine generic as the condition of possibility for objectivity and ideality (Irigaray 1992, 103–10/60–64, 1994, 120–21, 1997, 188–89/106). What does this mean?

My suggestion is that to understand what is at issue in Irigaray's discussion of the feminine generic, we need to get clear about the connection between *intersubjectivity* and *objectivity* as described and analyzed in the phenomenological tradition of modern thought. This discussion forms the background for Irigaray's reflections. And to get to the root of the problem we have to go deeper into the tradition than to Irigaray's close predecessors. Even though her critical remarks are directed against Heidegger's, Merleau-Ponty's, Sartre's, and Levinas's notions of intersubjectivity,[6] they are more fundamental and carry more far-reaching consequences.

The constitutive connection between objectivity and intersubjectivity was first explicated by Edmund Husserl, the founder of the phenomenological movement. In the fifth of his Cartesian meditations (*Méditations cartésiennes* 1931, *Cartesianische Meditationen* 1950), Husserl focused his inquiry on the meaning of objectivity. The phenomenological analysis that he put forward was designed to show how the ideas of objective reality and objective truth are constituted on the basis of the relation between self and other.[7]

The fifth Meditation thematizes the other first in the sense of *another self* or *alter ego*, that is, another conscious, experiencing subject. Husserl then extends his inquiry to cover the sense of *anything alien to me*, irreducible to me. Ultimately, his analysis is about the sense of objective nature and objective world: How is objective being constituted in experience such that it transcends all the possible contents of my experience?[8]

The sense of objectivity proves to depend on our experiences of other experiencing subjects. So, the fifth Meditation asks: How do we experience other subjects, in what way are they given to us, and on what conditions?

The principal sense of another subject in Husserl's analysis is *another ego similar to me but irreducible* (1950, §49 137/107). The other is constituted as similar to me but at the same time as irrecoverably and endlessly transcending my experiences. He is similar to me in that he too is conscious[9] of the world and experiences the world in his own way. But, at the same time, he is irretrievably separate from me and different from me because my experiences do not, and cannot, encompass his experiences (Husserl 1950, §48 135–36/105–6, §51–52 143–44/113–14).

The other also has experiences of me which are alien to me; I appear to him as part of the world. Thus, his appearance reveals to me a new aspect of my own being (Husserl 1950, §43 123/91, 1952, §18f 81/86). We both experience the world and each other as part of the world, but the ways and relations in which we encounter the world are different. This is crucial: neither he nor his living body are mere phenomena for me; rather, the other establishes an independent unity of phenomena in its own right.

Thus, in Husserl's analysis of sense, objectivity is constituted on the basis of intersubjectivity and otherness.[10] The transcendence of the world that I experience is based on the experiential fact that the other, his conscious life, is definitely beyond my reach. I cannot grasp his experiences as I can grasp entities of the world. Eventually this means that the perception of another *perceiving* body is the experience in which my solitary environment opens up and receives the sense of the world.

Irigaray's ethical reflections are based on this fundamental analysis of sense. In *J'aime à toi*, she writes:

> I recognize you means that I cannot know you by thought or by flesh. The power of a negative prevails between us. I recognize you is on a par with: you are irreducible to me, just as I am to you. We may not be substituted for one another [. . .] (Irigaray 1992, 161/103, cf. Irigaray 1994, 50, 1997, 76/40)

In *Éthique*, she directs the Husserlian arsenal against Merleau-Ponty's notion of intertwining. Her claim is that the subject thematized by Merleau-Ponty in *Le visible et l'invisible* (1964) remains on the level of solitary life. It never really enters the world, for it lacks the other necessary for the step:

> This subject, as it were, never comes to the world. He never emerges from an osmosis which would allow him to say to the other, "Who are thou?" But also, "Who am I?" [. . .] The phenomenology of the flesh that Merleau-Ponty presents is

without question(s). It is without spacing or interval for the
freedom of questioning between two. Without an other or
the Other who would guard the open world. (Irigaray 1984,
170/183)

But Irigaray's main argument is not just directed against Merleau-
Ponty's later philosophy. Her critique is more general and applies
equally to Husserl's followers as to his critics. She argues that phenomenological and postphenomenological thinkers neglect the fundamental difference between two sexual types, and that their
descriptions, explications, and analyses of otherness and intersubjectivity[11] suffer from the identification of human with male (1974,
165/133, 1984, 17/5–6). This also means that, ultimately, their understanding of objectivity is seriously defective.

Irigaray's attempt to constitute the feminine identity or the generic feminine must be seen in this light. Her work is an uncompro-
mising attempt to problematize the sexual neutrality of subjects as
they are thematized in the existentialist-phenomenological tradition
of philosophy. This is not done in the equalitarian aim of keeping our
theories of human subjects and subjectivity as plural or liberal as
possible (Irigaray 1992, 105/61, cf. 1977, 148/152, 160/166).[12] Rather,
the main task is to study subjects in their sexual differentiation and
to understand this difference as the foundation of sense that provides
for the constitution of intersubjectivity and objectivity, living beings
and the world.[13]

Irigaray connects these topics explicitly in her later works of '80s
and '90s. At the same time, she emphasizes that neutrality is not just
a problem in ethics, it also impairs our philosophical understanding of
perception, knowledge, and being (Irigaray 1984, 13/5–6, 117–20/
121–24, 1994, 29ff., 120, 1997, 41ff./22ff., 188–89/106). The fundamental flaw is in a restricted, superficial understanding of the bodily
difference between the two sexes. Male theorists have failed to think
through their own bodily condition:

In all his creations, all his works, man always seems to neglect
thinking of himself as incarnated, as one who has received his
body as this first home or native place (this *Gestell*, as
Heidegger would say . . .) which determines the possibility of
his coming into the world and the potential opening of a
horizon of thought. [. . .] (Irigaray 1984 123/128, cf. 98/98)

To see how a mere bodily difference can be crucial to our understanding of objectivity, we need to go deeper into Husserl's discussion of intersubjectivity and to compare it to Irigaray's remarks on the specificity of the feminine body.

ANOTHER BODY—SIMILAR TO MINE

In Husserl's analysis, the experience of an other is founded on two kinds of affective perceptions: the perception of one's own living animated body and the perception of another body similar to mine in its shapes, postures, and movements. Thus, the self-other relation is established between two bodies, and not between pure consciousness and its object.

However, the two bodies are not on equal grounding. The experience of one's own body as a living sensing whole is an independent, primary formation (Husserl 1950, §44 127–28/96–97). The other body is experienced as living only on the condition that it resembles this self sensing and moving in space.

The analogy between the two separate bodies does not have to be total or comprehensive. But I have to perceive the two bodies as "similar" for a connection to arise between them in my experience. According to Husserl, such "pairing" [Paarung] of the bodies makes possible a transfer of sense between them: the other body receives the sense "living" from mine. As the result, it presents itself as another living being having its own sensations, perceptions, and directions (Husserl 1950, §50–51 139–42/111–13).

So, in Husserl's analysis, the sense "living" or "sensing" has its origin in my experience of my own living body.[14] All other bodies acquire the sense "living" from my body (Husserl 1952, §18f 81–82/ 83–86, 1954, §62 221/217–18).

Several commentators, in the first place Emmanuel Levinas ([1947] 1994, [1961] 1988), have complained that Husserl's approach reduces the other to a mere phenomenon or meaning. Also, Irigaray warns against such reductions (1994, 18, 1997, 23/9). However, Husserl's analysis does not imply that the other body is merely a phenomenon for me. On the contrary, the explicit aim is to account for the experiential fact that the other is given to me as an independent and autonomous bodily subject irreducible to any of my experiences.[15]

Husserl's thesis of the primacy of my own living body does not concern the other's being, but concerns my possibility of relating to

his being. It contains the claim that I can experience material things
as living bodies *only because* I experience my own body in this specific way. Conversely, if I did not experience this particular body as
animated—if I did not experience this skin as sensing, these hands
as touching, and these eyes as seeing—then I could not, through any
manoeuvre, understand or approach an other body as a sensing living being.[16]

The critical questions Irigaray launches against the Husserlian
framework focus on the idea of similarity between the two bodies. She
argues that we should not neglect the obvious difference involved in
all perception of living beings:

> The natural, aside from the diversity of its incarnations or
> ways of appearing, is at least *two*: masculine and feminine.
> This division is not secondary nor unique to human kind. It
> cuts across all realms of the living which, without it, would
> not exist. (Irigaray 1992, 69/37)

Irigaray argues that, in the framework outlined by Husserl, and
reshaped by Heidegger, Levinas, and Merleau-Ponty, perception of the
other is discussed as if the human and animal bodies that we can see,
hear, and touch would not have any sex or were without sexual characteristics. Her main argument is that phenomenologists have neglected
an obvious perceptual fact, the fact that human bodies, and living
bodies more generally, come in two different kinds or genres. We do not
see "bodily persons," as Husserl suggests, neither do we find ourselves as
being simply there "with others," as Heidegger contents. These descriptions already abstract from the concrete bodies encountered in perception (Irigaray 1994, 55, 104–5, 1997, 77/44, 164/91).

What we meet and encounter, in our experience, are living bodies,
animal and human, and we experience these bodies as being composed and as moving in two different ways:

> It is evident that the corporeal morphology of the feminine
> and the masculine are not the same and it therefore follows
> that their way of experiencing the sensible and of construct-
> ing the spiritual is not the same. (Irigaray 1992, 69/38, see
> also 105/61–62)

In the phenomenological and post-phenomenological discussions,
the other is certainly often named "female" or "feminine": Levinas

describes a female beloved and the feminine body; Sartre studies the experience of desiring a woman; Merleau-Ponty identifies a feminine way of moving; and Derrida entertains the idea of being woman. But, Irigaray claims, this name "woman," this generic name or common noun, has remained unthought. Sexual difference is presupposed in numerous philosophical discussions on desires, passions, and emotions, but the difference has not been thematized or thought through. This is the task that Irigaray sets to feminist thinkers: to investigate the sexual difference and its founding role in our experience of ourselves and the world (Irigaray 1984, 13/5).

The critical side of her argument is that our notions of inter-subjectivity are restricted by our inability to think beyond one kind of bodily subject, or even to recognize this subject as of one kind. What we call intersubjective is actually just relations between bodies of one kind and their diverse versions, inversions, opposites, complements, and residuals (Irigaray 1974, 167–68/134–36, 1977, 72/74, 154/159, 1992, 107/63). We speak about "individuals" but fail to see that we interpret them all through one paradigm, one model, that disregards bodily—morphological and sensory[17]—differences (Irigaray 1992, 85/48).

Irigaray's constructive suggestion is that by thinking through the sexual difference in its bodily concreteness, we can arrive at the recognition of two different kinds of corporeal subjects (1984, 13–15/5–8, 148/157, 1994, 45–46, 1997, 67/36). And this recognition serves as a basis for a true understanding of intersubjectivity, between "at least two." She writes:

> The other as other, the other who guarantees irreducible alterity belongs to a genre which is not mine. (Irigaray 1994, 105, 1997, 165/92)

To summarize, following the phenomenologists, Irigaray sees the constitution of intersubjectivity as crucial to objectivity and truth. Thus, her position is transcendentalist and anti-naturalistic. However, she challenges the Husserlian heritage by problematizing the unity of the category of the other.[18] What phenomenologists have described, varied, and analyzed, is not an experience of a concrete other, but an abstraction based on the male sex. The result of their investigations is not, as promised, a philosophical understanding of intersubjectivity, but a prejudiced and interested notion. We still lack an adequate description of the difference between the self and its other, and this perverts our understanding of the foundations of objectivity.

THE OTHER IN ME

Beginning from *Speculum*, Irigaray continuously reminds us that the bodies that we meet in perception and emotion are feminine and masculine. She argues that the feminine body has a specific morphology as well as a specific way of moving and relating to itself and to its objects. Its scope of self-affection, tactile sensation, proprioception, and kinesthesia are specific, different from that of the masculine body (e.g., Irigaray 1977, 24–27/24–27, [1977] 1990, 82, 1984, 48–56/43–52, 1992, 105/61).

The most challenging case that Irigaray presents against phenomenological discussions on intersubjectivity is the experience of a woman carrying an unborn child in her womb. The argument is that the phenomenological analyses prove prejudged when we try to extend them to cover women's experiences of their own bodies. If we take into consideration the fact that a woman is able to apprehend another living being in her own body, and to house or host this other, then we have to question the presupposition that self and other are necessarily separated by a spatial *distance*. The subject that feels a sensing and moving other inside her own living body is different from the subject that sees the other at a distance over there.[19] The relations between self and other are crucially different in these two cases.

To understand the radical nature of Irigaray's reflection, we need to return again to the details of Husserl's analysis of intersubjectivity.

Husserl points out that the transfer of sense that makes possible the experience of the other does not happen directly between the other body and my own living body. It happens between the other body and my own body *imaginatively* taking the place of the other. More precisely, the necessary transfer of sense presupposes an act of imagination in which I picture my own body in the place of the other. Husserl explains:

> I do not apperceive him as having [. . .] the spatial modes of appearance that are mine from here; rather, as we find in closer examination, I apperceive him as having spatial modes of appearance *like those I should have if I should go over there and be where he is.* (Husserl 1950, §53 120/117, my italics)

Husserl's analysis shows that my experience of my own living body is invested with the specific sense of "being here." My body is the zero-point of orientation for all my perceptions and movements (Husserl 1952, §32 127/135, §41a 158/165–66, cf. Merleau-Ponty [1945] 1993, 106/90, 163/140). All other things, including the other's body, are given to me as being there at a distance from my primordial here. This "here" is always with me, so that when I change position and location, I do not leave it behind, but, on the contrary, carry it with me and thus give a new organization to spatial things. The transfer of sense, necessary for the experience of the other, happens between the other's body over there and my own body as it would be if it were there *in his place* (Husserl 1950, §54 148–49/117–19).

Irigaray's argument is that woman's experience of the child moving in her own body constitutes an anomaly in this descriptive and analytic framework. Thus, her critique is not the principled suspicion that Levinas presents against Husserl's analysis;[20] she is not arguing for the general impossibility of replacing any other. More precisely, her reflection points to the difficulty of imagining oneself taking the place of someone who *lives in me*. This difficulty raises questions about the sense of *owness* and one's *own body* presupposed in the phenomenological analyses of intersubjectivity.

The experience of a pregnant woman diverts from the paradigmatic case in three respects. First, the other's body that the woman experiences is *not* somewhere *there at a distance*, but here present with her in every movement and position of her own body. There is no variable distance between the two, but a permanent closeness or proximity (Irigaray 1992, 161/103).[21] For the woman to imagine herself in the *place* of this particular other means that she would have to, at the same time, imagine a third living body in her own place. For if she leaves her position, even if imaginatively, in order to take the place of the child, then she undoes that inner place and environment which she is about to enter (Irigaray 1984, 155–56/165–66). To compensate for this, the woman would have to imagine another body in her own place. So, the substitution or pairing would not happen simply between her own body and another body "in here," but between her own body and another body living inside a third one.

Second, the woman *cannot see* the movements and positions of the other inside her, she can only feel them. This means that the spatiality of her *own* moving body proves to be more complex than in the paradigmatic cases studied in the tradition.

In the Husserlian framework, my own living body is disclosed as a specific material thing in that *I can see only part of it*. Other parts are absent from my visual field, and this absence is constitutive of my own body (Husserl 1952, §41b 159/167, cf. Merleau-Ponty [1945] 1993, 106/92, Irigaray 1984, 159–60/169–70).

A somewhat similar specificity seems to characterize the experience of a unborn child living in one's own body. This other can become visible, and eventually he[22] will, but my experience of him, as living and sensing, does not require that he is visible or becomes visible (Irigaray 1984, 163–64/174–75, 174–75/187). It is enough that I feel him moving in me in a similar—autonomous and spontanious—way, which characterizes my own movements (cf. Husserl 1950, §52 144/114). The living body of the child is constituted in my experience merely *on the basis* of touch sensations and kinesthesia, as is my own body (cf. Husserl 1952, §37 147–49/155–56).[23]

This specific mode of proximity does not cancel the separateness between the child's body and the maternal body. The child's sensations are beyond the mother's reach in a way similar to the sensations of those visible others that move in space at a distance. She cannot feel what the child feels, or hear what he hears, in the way he does (Irigaray 1984, 157–58/168), and she cannot govern his movements as she can govern her own.[24]

As a result of this "intertwining," her own body is given to her not just as the zero-point of visual perception, but also as an invisible "inner space" structured by tactile sensations ([1977] 1990, 82–83, 1984, 156/166). Accordingly, her body is not a visible object for this specific other who lives in her, but rather functions as a living milieu for his movements and sensations (Irigaray 1984, 149–50/159, cf. 1994, 39, 1997, 57/30).

Irigaray describes the intertwining of these two bodies and their different relations to the visible:

> [. . .] the one who is still in this night does not see and remains without a visible (as far as our knowledge is exact). And the other who sees cannot see him. The other does not see him, he is not visible for the other, who nevertheless sees the world, but without him. (Irigaray 1984, 144/152)[25]

Third, this mode of experience lacks that particular form of reciprocity that is characteristics of the paradigmatic examples of phenomenology: two visible subjects gazing at each other at a distance. The symmetry of such perceptions was already described by

Husserl in *Cartesianische Meditationen* (e.g., Husserl 1950, §56 158/130); and later his followers repeated the account in their own terminology, as did Sartre, for example, by writing:

> [. . .] if the other-as-object is defined in contact with the world, as the object which sees what I see, then my fundamental contact with the other-as-subject must be able to be referred back to my permanent possibility of *being seen* by the other. (Sartre [1943] 1988, 296/345)[26]

Against this, Irigaray argues that women relate to their unborn children in a different way. Reciprocity—this particular mode of symmetrical reciprocity—is not (yet) established (1984, 161–63/172–74). For even if we could perhaps say that the child's body is, or lives, in the perceptual field of the woman, we should not assume that the woman's body is given to the child in a similar or analogous way as a tactile object. Rather, the maternal body constitutes for the child the background of all possible tactile sensations (cf. Merleau-Ponty [1945] 1993, 399).

To summarize, Irigaray's descriptions of the mother-child relationship emphasize three aspects that raise questions about the adequacy of the standard analysis. In this case, the self-other relation is not symmetric; it is not governed by visual but by tactile (and auditory) perceptions, and this complicates the discussion about one's own body and its spatiality.[27]

One could, of course, insist that these differences show exactly that the child living in the mother's body is not an other self but merely a plantlike formation.[28] However, the phenomenological description of the self-other relation is not intended for providing criteria of belonging to the objective category "others." Instead, the phenomenologist is committed to the task of taking lived experiences [*Erlebnis*] in their own terms and of studying the intentional relations and ontic meanings involved in them. Thus, if the woman's articulated experience is that there is "someone in her," then the phenomenologist—or she as the phenomenologist—needs to inquiry into the conditions of this experience and not restrict herself to the more familiar experience of "someone over there."

Irigaray's descriptions might also be countered by arguing that the experience of having someone living in one's own body is dependent, in its meanings, on the experience of seeing others at a distance.

In his Cartesian meditations, Husserl gives a short discussion of "abnormal others" with "abnormal appearance systems." As examples, he
refers to deaf and blind humans and to nonhuman animality (Husserl
1950 §55 154/125–26). His argument is that "the constitution of
abnormality is possible only on the basis of an intrinsically antecedent
normality" (Husserl 1950 §55 154/125). However, he does not suggest
that this remark closes the case, but, on the contrary, emphasizes that
"this points to new tasks, which belong to a higher level of phenomenological analysis of the constitutional origin of the objective world"
(Husserl 1950 §55 154/125). In any case, a new question comes up:
In what sense can pregnant women be characterized as "abnormal
others" or "abnormal egos," and from whose viewpoint?

At the core of Irigaray's discussions is the claim that, experien-
tially, the feminine body has a specific sensory and morphological
organization, different from that of the male body (Irigaray 1984, 157/
148, 166/156). My own body is not constituted for me as a solid
closed volume, but rather as a fold which is capable of opening to
form an inner space that can house an other sensing being. This
opening is experienced in erotic encounters but more vigorously in
pregnancy. Thus, the others that are crucial for the constitution of
intersubjective space and objectivity are not always there at a distance but can also be here within me.

What consequences does this possibility have for the phenomenological analysis of intersubjectivity or for our understanding of
objectivity? The answer is that we do not yet know, for our choice of
examples and models has thus far been guided by the still dominant
assumption that sexual difference is inconsequential for philosophical
reflections.

Irigaray's suggestion is that if we manage to study the self-other
relation in the specific case of mother-child—if we manage to fight
the habit of bypassing this specific case as an insignificant exception
or an emotive projection—then our reflections on intersubjectivity
will be enriched to form a basis for a reconsideration of objectivity.

This requires that we study without prejudice the specificity of
the feminine body and the experiential differences between feminine
bodies and masculine bodies, not in order to construe theories of
women or female subjects, but in order to realize objectivity.

I am grateful to Martina Reuter, Antti Kauppinen, and Virpi Lehtinen
for helpful suggestions and critical insight.

NOTES

*In my documentation, my primary reference is to the original sources in French, Italian, and German. The original year of publication is given in square brackets. I also give the reference to the English translation, separating it by a slash. For example, in my epigraph, (Beauvoir [1949] 1993, 15/15) refers to Simone de Beauvoir's *Le deuxième sex*, which was first published in 1949 and from which I have used the 1993 printing. The English pagination is given after the slash, all bibliographic information about translation being given in the bibliography.

1. Such readings were common in early commentaries; see, for example, Burke 1981, Whitford 1988, Butler 1990a, 13–14.

2. Cf. Burke 1981, 302, Moi 1985, 139, Butler 1990b, 326–27.

3. Cf. this statement to the thesis of *Speculum* (1974): "Toute théorie du 'sujet' aura toujours été appropriée au 'masculin.' A s'y assujettir, la femme renonce à son insu à la spécificité de son rapport à l'imaginaire" (Irigaray 1974, 165), and to the explanation given in an "interview" in *Ce sexe*: "[. . .] l'articulation de la réalité de mon sexe est impossible dans le discours et pour une raison de structure, eidétique. Mon sexe est soustrait, en tout cas comme propriété d'une sujet, au fonctionnement de la prédication qui assure le cohérence discursive" (Irigaray 1977, 145).

4. On Irigaray's interpretation of Descartes's notion of wonder, see Heinämaa 1999; on her reading of Plato's *Symposium*, see Heinämaa 2001.

5. Compare to what Heidegger says about his *destructive* reading of the philosophical tradition in *Sein und Zeit*: "The destruction does not relate itself negatively [*negiered*] towards the past; its criticism hits the 'today' and the prevalent way of treating the history of ontology, whether doxographic, intellectual history, or history of problems" ([1927] 1993, §6 22–23/44). Also, compare Irigaray's framing of the problem of sexual difference (1984, 13) to the idea of the "unthought" in Heidegger (e.g., 1957, 123–24/71) and in Merleau-Ponty ([1960] 1998, 202/160). On Merleau-Ponty's understanding of the "intentional history" of thought, see Heinämaa 2000, 83–85, Reuter 2003.

6. On this side of Irigaray's critique, see Chanter 1995, 127–24, Deutscher 2002, 142–63.

7. Husserl starts formulating this argument in the 20s. In the second book of *Ideen*, written between 1914 and 1928, he already argues that objective being is constitutively based on intersubjectivity (Husserl 1952 §18 e–f 77–84/83–89).

8. Husserl explains his topic right at the beginning of the fifth Meditation: "The Objective world is constantly there before me as already finished, a datum of my living continuous Objective experience [. . .] It is a matter of examining this experience itself and uncovering intentionally the manner in which it bestows sense, the manner in which it can occur as

experience [. . .] (Husserl 1950, §48 108–9/106). And then in paragraph §49 he is able to state: "[. . .] *the intrinsically first other* [. . .] *is the other Ego*. And the other Ego makes constitutionally possible a new infinite domain of what is 'other': an objective nature and a whole objective world, to which all other Egos and I myself belong" (Husserl 1950, §49 137/107, cf. Husserl 1959, 495).

9. Compare to Levinas's reflections on the meaning of femininity in *Le temps et l'autre* ([1947] 1994 81/88), and to Beauvoir's critical response in *Le deuxième sexe* ([1949] 1993, 15–16/15–16, esp. n.1). On this debate, see also Chanter 2001, 1–11, Heinämaa 2003, 88–91, 125–27.

10. For the fundamental role of intersubjectivity in Husserl's phenomenology, see Dan Zahavi's *Husserl und die transzendentale Intersubjektivität* (1996). Cf. also Hart 1992, Steinbock 1995, Donohoe 2003.

11. Dan Zahavi (2001) gives an illuminative overview of the different aspects and levels of intersubjectivity discussed within the phenomenological movement.

12. Irigaray's radical, "gynocentric" feminism of difference is often contrasted to Simone de Beauvoir's "equalitarian" approach (e.g., Grosz 1989, 15–19, Hekman 1990, 73ff., Gatens 1991, 113–20, Schor 1994, 62–66, Chanter 1995, 47–79). I have argued elsewhere (2003) that the contrast is superficial and that there is a deeper continuity between these two approaches, cf. La Caze 1994, 101–3.

13. This does not imply that the feminine generic is a closed totality. Irigaray explicitly argues against attempts to subsume the feminine under a substantial term or concept. Rather, the unity of the feminine should be described by the modal concepts of style (Irigaray 1984, 76/79). As such, the feminine constitutes an open evolving whole and not a closed unity (Irigaray 1977, 122/122, 151–52/155–56, 1984, 111/115). Thus, there can be no "theory" of the feminine, if by theory we mean a system of theses formulated in exact concepts (Irigaray 1977, 122/123). For an explication of the concept of style as used by phenomenologists in describing embodiment and sexuality, see Heinämaa 2003, 37–44, 66–70, 78–83.

14. Husserl gives his analysis of our experience of our own bodies in the second book of *Ideen*. This is elaborated further by Merleau-Ponty in the first part of his *Phénoménologie*. For an introduction to the topic, see Heinämaa 2003, 26–44.

15. For a forceful argument against Levinas's reading, see Derrida 1967a, cf. also Marion [1983] 2002. For an illuminative critical overview of Levinas's rejection of Husserl's analysis, see Overgaard 2003.

16. Cf. Marion [2001] 2002, 87–91, Heinämaa 2003, 31–37.

17. More precisely, differences in the proprioceptic, kinesthetic, and tactual systems of the lived body [*Leib*].

18. However, in this enterprise too, Irigaray's roots are deep in the existentialist-phenomenological tradition. For earlier remarks on the "prob-

lem of the sexes," see Stein ([1928–1932] 2002), Husserl ([1936–1937] 1954, §55 192/187–88), Beauvoir ([1949] 1993, 11–30/13–28), Fink (1988, 274).

19. Birth has a different role in Irigaray's critique of Heidegger than in the critiques that Hannah Arendt (1958) and Levinas (1947) directed against Heidegger. Even though Irigaray too emphasizes natality as a universal condition of humankind, her main argument is that sexual difference is fundamental to our experience of embodiment and alterity. On the Arendtian line, see Schües 1997, 2000, cf. also Alter 1993, Oksala 2003. Compare Irigaray's arguments also to Beauvoir's critique of Heidegger in Pyrrhus et Cinéas (1944).

20. See, e.g., Levinas 1989.

21. For empirical investigations into experiences of pregnancy and early child-parent interaction, see Stern 1985, Piontelli 1992. For a philosophical discussion on experiential results investigations into prenatal and infantile self-awareness, see Zahavi 2004. For Husserl's remarks on these issues, see Husserl 1973, 510–14, 582–83, 604, cf. Smith 2003, 243–47.

22. No assumptions about the sex or gender of the child is made here; the personal pronouns "he" and "his" are used in a neutral sense.

23. Cf. Marion [2001] 2002, 89.

24. So the mother and the child form together a special pair "we," and not a nondifferentiated totality.

25. But notice that Husserl points out already in the second book of Ideen that the self-other relation, in its genetically primary mode, is not visual but auditory-tactile: "It seems, from my observation, that in the child the self-produced voice, and then, analogously, the heard voice, serves as the first bridge for the objectification of the Ego or for the formation of the 'alter,' i. e., before the child already has or can have a sensory analogy between his visual body and that of the 'other' " (Husserl 1952, 96, n.1). Irigaray's argument emphasizes the fact that already before auditory self-objectivication, tactile sensations and kinesthesia are at work constituting one's own living body.

26. Cf. Merleau-Ponty: "Through phenomenological reflection, I discover vision, not as a 'thinking about seeing' to use Descartes' expression, but as a gaze at grips with the visible world, and that is why for me can be another gaze; that expressive instrument called a face can carry an existence, as my own existence is carried by my own body [. . .]" ([1945] 1993, 404/351). For an illuminative explication of Irigaray's critique of Sartre, see Deutscher 2002, 153–63. For Merleau-Ponty's understanding of the self-other relation and his notion of alterity in self, see his Phénoménologie (398–419/346–65), but also his "L'expérience d'autrui" ([1951] 1988), "Les relations avec autrui chez l'enfant" (1951), and Le Visible 1964, 113/81, n.14.

27. Compare Irigaray's descriptions to those of Julia Kristeva in "Motherhood according to Giovanni Bellini" ([1975] 1980, 236) and "Stabat mater" ([1977] 1986, 177–78).

28. Christina Schües, for example, claims that the child living in the mother's womb still lacks certain forms of intentionality necessary for human subjectivity (Schües 1997, 244, cf. 2000, 112). Irigaray's argument does not, however, depend on the claim that the child manifests all possibile forms or levels of intentionality; it is enough that the child moves and behaves in ways that manifest primitive motor and perceptual intentionality.

Recent empirical studies indicate that perception is not a capacity acquired after birth, but develops already prenatally. There is strong empirical evidence that suggests that unborn children perceive auditory objects, such as rhythmic and intonational structures, and are able to recognize these after birth. For such studies, see DeCasper and Fifer 1980, DeCasper, Lecanuet, Busnel, Deferre-Garnier, and Maugeais 1986, DeCasper and Spence 1994, Moon, Cooper, and Fufer 1993.

WORKS CITED

Arendt, Hannah. 1958. *The Human Condition*. Chicago: Chicago University Press.

Beauvoir, Simone de. 1944. *Pyrrhus et Cinéas*. Paris: Gallimard.

———. 1993 [1949]. *Le deuxième sexe I: Les faits et les mythes*. Paris: Gallimard. In English *The Second Sex*. Translated and edited by H. M. Parshley. Harmondsworth: Penguin, 1987.

———. 1991 [1949]. *Le deuxième sexe II: L'expérience vécue*. Paris: Gallimard. In English *The Second Sex*. Translated and edited by H. M. Parshley. Harmondsworth: Penguin, 1987.

Burke, Carolyn. 1981. "Irigaray Through the Looking Glass," *Feminist Studies* 7:2: 255–88.

Butler, Judith. 1990a. *Gender Trouble: Feminism and the Subversion of Identity*. New York and London: Routledge.

———. 1990b. "Gender Trouble, Feminist Theory, and Psychoanalytic Discourse." In *Feminism/Postmodernism*, edited by Linda Nicholson. New York and London: Routledge.

Chanter, Tina. 1995. *The Ethics of Eros: Irigaray's Rewriting of the Philosophers*. London and New York: Routledge.

———. 2001. "Introduction." In *Feminist Interpretations of Emmanuel Levinas*, edited by Tina Chanter. University Park, Penn.: Pennsylvania State University.

DeCasper, Anthony, and William Fifer. 1980. "Of Human Bonding: Newborns Prefer Their Mother's Voices." *Science* 208: 1174–76.

DeCasper, Anthony, J.-P. Lecanuet, M.-C. Busnel, C. Deferre-Garnier, and R. Maugeais. 1986. "Prenatal Maternal Speech Influences Newborn's Perception of Speech Sounds." *Infant Behavior and Development* 9: 133–50.

DeCasper, Anthony, and M. J. Spence. 1994. "Fetal Reactions to Recurrent Maternal Speech." *Infant Behavior and Development* 17: 159–64.

Derrida, Jacques. 1967a. "Violence et métaphysique." In *L'écriture et la différence*. Paris: Seuil. In English "Violence and Metaphysics." In *Writing and Difference*. Translated by Alan Bass. London: Routledge & Kegan Paul, 1985.

———. 1967b. *La voix et le phénomène*. Paris: Presses Universitaires de France. In English *Speech and Phenomena*. Translated by David B. Allison. Evanston, Ill.: Northwestern University Press.

Deutscher, Penelope. 2002. *A Politics of Impossible Difference: The Later Work of Luce Irigaray*. Ithaca and London: Cornell University Press.

Donohoe, Janet. 2003. "Genetic Phenomenology and the Husserlian Account of Ethics." *Philosophy Today* 47:25: 160–75.

Felman, Shoshana. 1975. "Women and Madness: The Critical Phallacy." *diacritics* 5:4: 2–10.

Fink, Eugen. 1988. *VI. Cartesianische Meditation: Teil 2: Ergänzungsband*, Husserliana, Dokumente, Band II/2. Edited by Guy van Kerckhoven. Dordrecht, Boston, and London: Kluwer.

Gatens, Moira. 1991. *Feminism and Philosophy: Perspectives on Difference and Equality*. Cambridge: Cambridge University Press.

Grosz, Elisabeth. 1989. *Sexual Subversions: Three French Feminists*. Sidney: Allen & Unwin.

Hart, James G. 1992. *The Person and the Common Life: Studies in a Husserlian Social Ethics*. Dordrecht: Kluwer.

Heidegger, Martin. 1993 [1927]. *Sein und Zeit*. Tübingen: Max Niemeyer Verlag. In English *Being and Time*. Translated by John Macquarrie and Edward Robinson. Oxford and Cambridge: Blackwell, 1980.

———. 1957. *Der Satz vom Grund*. Pfüllingen: Verlag Günter Neske. In English *The Principle of Reason*. Translated by Reginald Lilly. Bloomington, Ind.: Indiana University Press, 1971.

Heinämaa, Sara. 1999. "Wonder and (Sexual) Difference: Cartesian Radicalism in Phenomenological Thinking." In *Norms and Modes of Thinking in Descartes*, edited by Tuomo Aho and Mikko Yrjönsuuri. Acta Philosophica Fennica, 64.

———. 2000. *Ihmetys ja rakkaus: esseitä ruumiin ja sukupuolen fenomenologiasta*. Helsinki: Nemo.

———. 2001. "Filosofi—praktik och dialog." *Filosofisk tidskrift* 22:2: 32–39.

———. 2003. *Towards a Phenomenology of Sexual Difference: Husserl, Merleau-Ponty, Beauvoir*. Lanham, Boulder, New York, and London: Rowman & Littlefield.

———. 2004. "The Soul-Body Union and Sexual Difference: From Descartes to Merleau-Ponty and Beauvoir." In *Feminist Reflections on the History of Philosophy*, edited by Charlotte Witt and Lilli Alanen. Dordrecht, Boston, and London: Kluwer, 2004.

Hekman, Susan J. 1990. *Gender and Knowledge: Elements of a Postmodern Feminism*. Cambridge: Polity Press.

Husserl, Edmund. 1950. *Cartesianische Meditationen und pariser Vorträge*, Husserliana, Band I. Edited by Stephan Strasser. Haag: Martinus Nijhoff. In English *Cartesian Meditations*. Translated by Dorion Cairns. Dordrecht and Boston: Martinus Nijhoff, 1960.

―――. 1952. *Ideen zu einer reinen Phänomenologie und phänomenologischen Philosophie, Zweites Buch: Phänomenologische Untersuchungen zur Konstitution*, Husserliana, Band IV. Edited by Marly Bimel. Haag: Martinus Nijhoff. In English *Ideas Pertaining to a Pure Phenomenology and to a Phenomenological Philosophy, Second Book: Studies in the Phenomenological Constitution*. Translated by Richard Rojcewicz and André Schuwer. Dordrecht, Boston and London: Kluwer, 1993.

―――. 1954. *Die Krisis der europäischen Wissenschaften und die transzendentale Phänomenologie: Eine Einleitung in die phänomenologische Philosophie*, Husserliana, Band VI. Edited by Walter Biemel. Haag: Martinus Nijhoff. In English *The Crisis of the European Sciences and Transcendental Phenomenology: An Introduction to Phenomenological Philosophy*. Translated by David Carr. Evanston, Ill.: Northwestern University Press, 1988.

―――. 1959. *Erste Philosophie (1923/24), Zweiter Teil*, Husserliana, Band VIII. Edited by R. Boehm. Haag: Martinus Nijhoff.

―――. 1973. *Zur Phänomenologie der Intersubjektivität, Texte aus dem Nachlass, Dritter Teil 1929–1935*, Husserliana, Band XV. Edited by Iso Kern. Haag: Martinus Nijhoff.

Irigaray, Luce. 1974. *Speculum, de l'autre femme*. Paris: Minuit. In English *Speculum of the Other Woman*. Translated by Gillian C. Gill. Ithaca, N.Y.: Cornell University Press, 1986.

―――. 1977. *Ce sexe qui n'en est pas un*. Paris: Minuit. In English *This Sex Which is Not One*. Translated by Catherine Porter with Carolyn Burke. Ithaca, N.Y.: Cornell University Press, 1985.

―――. 1990 [1976]. "Women's exile," interview. Translated by Couze Venn. In *The Feminist Critique of Language*, edited by Deborah Cameron. London: Routledge.

―――. 1983. *Amante marine, de Friedrich Nietzsche*. Paris: Minuit.

―――. 1984. *Éthique la différence sexuelle*. Paris: Minuit. In English *An Ethics of Sexual Difference*. Translated by Carolyn Burke and Gillian C. Gill. Ithaca, N.Y.: Cornell University Press, 1993.

―――. 1990 [1986]. "Egales ou différentes." In *Je, tu, nous: Pour une culture de la différence*. Paris: Grasset. In English "Equal or different?" In *The Irigaray Reader*, edited by Margaret Whitford. Oxford: Basil Blackwell, 1991.

―――. 1992. *J'aime à toi: Esquisse d'une félicité dans l'histoire*. Paris: Grasset. In English *I Love to You: Sketch for a Felicity Within History*. Translated by Alison Martin, New York and London: Routledge, 1996.

―――. 1994. *Essere due*. Torino: Bollati Boringhieri.

————. 1997. *Être deux*. Paris: Grasset. In English *To Be Two*. Translated by Monique M. Rhodes and Marco F. Cocito-Monoc. London and New Brunswick: Athlone Press, 2000.

Irigaray, Luce, with Elizabeth Hirsch and Gary A. Olson. 1994. "Je—Luce Irigaray: A Meeting with Luce Irigaray." *Hypatia* 10:2: 93–114.

Kristeva, Julia. 1980 [1975]. "Motherhood According to Giovanni Bellini." In *Desire in Language*, translated by Thomas Gora, Alice Jardine, and Leon S. Roudiez, edited by Leon S. Roudiez, 237–70. New York: Columbia University Press.

————.1986 [1977]. "Stabat mater." Translated by Léon S. Roudiez. In *The Kristeva Reader*, edited by Toril Moi, 161–86. Oxford UK & Cambridge USA: Blackwell.

Levinas, Emmanuel. 1994 [1947]. *Le temps et l'autre*. Paris: Quadrige/PUF. In English *Time and Other*. Translated by R. A. Cohen. Pittsburgh, Penn.: Duquesne University Press, 1987.

————. 1988 [1961]. *Totalité et infini: Essai sur l'extériorité*. Paris: Kluwer. In English *Totality and Infinity: An Essay on Exteriority*, translated by Alphonso Lingis. Pittsburgh, Penn.: Duquesne University Press, 1969.

————. 1989. "Philosophie et trancendance." In *Encyclopédie philosophique universelle*. Paris: PUF.

La Caze, Marguerite. 1994. "Simone de Beauvoir and Female Bodies." *Australian Feminist Studies* 20: 92–105.

Marion, Jean-Luc. 2002 [1983]. "The Intentionality of Love, in Homage to Emmanuel Levinas." In *Prolegomena to Charity*, translated by Stephen E. Lewis. New York: Fordham University Press. Original *Prolégomènes à la charité*.

————. 2002 [2001]. "Flesh or the Givenness of the Self." In *In Excess: Studies of Saturated Phenomena*, translated by Robyn Horner and Vincent Berrand. New York: Fordham University Press. Original *De surcroît: Études sur les phénomènes saturés*.

Merleau-Ponty, Maurice. 1993 [1945]. *Phénoménologie de la perception*. Paris: Gallimard. In English *Phenomenology of Perception*. Translated by Collin Smith. New York: Routledge & Kegan Paul, 1995.

————. 1951. "Les relations avec autrui chez l'enfant." Paris: C.D.U.

————. 1988 [1951]. "L'expérience d'autrui." In *Merleau-Ponty à la Sorbonne: Résumé de cours 1949–1951*. Paris: Cynara.

————. 1998 [1960]. *Signes*. Paris: Gallimard. In English *Signs*. Translated by Richard C. McCleary. Evanston, Ill.: Northwestern University Press, [1964] 1987.

————. 1964. *Le visible et l'invisible*. Edited by Claude Lefort. Paris: Gallimard. In English *The Visible and the Invisible*. Translated by Alphonso Linguis. Evanston, Ill.: Northwestern University Press, 1975.

Moon, C., R. P. Cooper, and W. P. Fufer. 1993. "Two-Day-olds Prefer Their Native Language." *Infant Behavior and Development* 16: 495–500.

Oksala, Johanna. 2003. "The Birth of Man." In *Metaphysics, Facticity, Interpretation: Phenomenology in the Nordic Countries*, edited by Dan Zahavi, Sara Heinämaa, and Hans Ruin. Dordrecht, Boston and London: Kluwer.

Overgaard, Søren. 2003. "On Levinas' Critique of Husserl." In *Metaphysics, Facticity, Interpretation: Phenomenology in the Nordic Countrie*, edited by Dan Zahavi, Sara Heinämaa, and Hans Ruin. Dordrecht, Boston and London: Kluwer.

Piontelli, Alessandra. 1992. *From Fetus to Child: An Observational and Psychoanalytic Study*. London: Routledge.

Reuter, Martina. 2003. "Tensions and Continuity: Merleau-Ponty on the History of Philosophy." Paper presented at the First Annual Meeting of the *Nordic Society for Phenomenology/Nordisk Selskab for Fænomenologi*, Helsinki, April 25–27, 2003.

Sartre, Jean-Paul. 1998 [1943]. *L'être et le néant: Essai d'ontologie phénoménologique*. Paris: Gallimard. In English *Being and Nothingness: A Phenomenological Essay on Ontology*. Translated by Hazel E. Barnes. New York: Washington Square Press, 1956.

Schor, Naomi. 1994. "The Essentialism Which Is Not One: Coming to Grips with Irigaray." In *Engaging with Irigaray: Feminist Philosophy and Modern European Thought*, edited by Carolyn Burke, Naomi Schor, and Margaret Whitford. New York: Columbia University Press.

Schües, Christina. 1997. "The Birth of Difference." *Human Studies* 20: 243–52.

———. 2000. "Empirical and Transcendental Subjectivity: An Enigmatic Relation?" In *The Empirical and the Transcendental: A Fusion of Horizons*, edited by B. Gupta. Lanham: Rowman & Littlefield.

Smith, A. D. 2003. *Husserl and the Cartesian Meditations*. London and New York: Routledge.

Stein, Edith. [1928–1932] 2002. *Die Frau: Fragestellungen und Reflexionen*. Edited by Maria Amante Neyer OCD. Freiburg, Basel, and Wien: Herder.

Steinbock, Anthony J. 1995. *Home and Beyond: Generative Phenomenology after Husserl*. Evanston, Ill.: Northwestern University Press.

Stern, Daniel. 1985. *The Interpersonal World of the Infant: A View from Psychoanalysis and Developmental Psychology*. New York: Basic Books.

Whitford, Margaret. 1988. "Irigaray's Critique of Rationality." In *Feminist Perspectives in Philosophy*, edited by Morwenna Griffiths and Margaret Whitford. London: MacMillan.

Zahavi, Dan. 1996. *Husserl und die transzendentale Intersubjektivität: Eine Antwort auf die sprachpragmatische Kritik*. Dordrect, Boston and London: Kluwer.

————. 2001. "Beyond Empathy: Phenomenological Approaches to Inter-subjectivity." *Journal of Consciousness Studies* 8/5–7: 151–67.

————. 2004. "The Embodied Self-Awareness of the Infant: A Challenge to the Theory of Mind?" In *The Structure and Development of Self-Awareness: Interdisciplinary Perspectives*, edited by Dan Zahavi, Thor Grünbaum, and Josef Parnas. Amsterdam and Philadelphia: John Benhamins.

IRIGARAY IN DIALOGUE WITH HEIDEGGER

Maria C. Cimitile

Luce Irigaray has had an ongoing conversation with Martin Heidegger. Is it a relation of lovers? Of paternity? Maternity? Of patricide? One thing for certain is that the dialogue gives us access to the influences on Irigaray's thought and the subtleties that emerge out of them. Through her speaking with Heidegger, we encounter Irigaray the phenomenologist, the psychoanalyst, the existentialist, and the neo pre-Socratic thinker, all of whom are interspersed, inform, and sometimes conflict with one another in Irigaray's writings. The most interesting aspect of this conversation is Irigaray's ability to be thoroughly Heideggerian in her method, while at the same time disclosing Heidegger's thought to remain within a metaphysics, the metaphysics of sexual difference. Though Heidegger's project is exactly to overcome metaphysics, the metaphysics of presence, Irigaray puts him through the rigors of his own process of thought, a test which he ultimately fails.

Although Heidegger did not ask the question of sexual difference, he did ask the question of being. Irigaray takes up the question of being to bear on sexual difference, using the same phenomenological probings that Heidegger uses, to examine the being of woman. Her earlier work sets out for us the necessity of a feminine symbolic to free woman from the definitions and limitations imposed by the phallic economy, and is the first step toward grounding a politics of a relationality of difference. In other words, Irigaray allows us to grasp what Heidegger would have said had he applied his questions and concerns to sexual difference. That fact that he did not is due in part to the phallocentric assumptions hidden in Heidegger's thought. Uncovering these while maintaining her closeness to Heidegger enables Irigaray to find a new relationality. In some ways, Irigaray takes up the same question that Beauvoir raises in the initial question of *The Second Sex*, "What is a woman?" In Irigaray's early work, in her phenomenology and psychoanalysis, she shows both how woman has been conceived in terms of man, and what sensible transcendentals of feminine materiality we might find as a resource beyond woman's reflective economy within phallocentricism. In her later work, she can now turn to imagining a new community whereby woman and man are different and respectful of the difference and the political realities concomitant to it. There is no question in my mind that as readers of Irigaray we would be remiss in isolating any part of her trajectory as a thinker apart from the overall politic that guides her thinking, and that her project is always in dialogue with Heidegger's thought. This is not to say that Irigaray does not engage in dialogue with others, a claim easily refuted. It is to say, however, that I believe Heidegger to be Irigaray's most important and formidable interlocutor, a claim I hope to give evidence for here.

From her early to her late writings, Irigaray's agenda is always political, and her writing is liberatory in intent. The earlier critical works reveal patriarchy at work in the very structures that allow for the reification of hegemony in the everyday realities of women's lives. Her overtly political writings from this same time period must be read in tandem with this critical process. Irigaray has always been clear with regard to the importance of nonstatic thinking, a stance inherited from Heidegger, and makes obvious what Heidegger leaves implicit, the essential political component of nonstatic thinking. As feminist scholars, we should take Irigaray at her word and recognize the movement that strategically empowers her thought across the time of her writing. She offers a path of steps from one idea to another, steps of thinking rather than a Hegelian resumption. Irigaray continues to merge and layer multiple theoretical perspectives. She can be seen to employ a historical materialism through the lens of sexual difference, but without the ideological attachment to rationality and linear progress—difference as both produced by patriarchal culture, but as positively aligned with the materiality of bodies; hers is a phenomenological method that incorporates materiality and difference, thereby forestalling abstraction into idealism.

In taking fundamentally different perspectives to create an innovative understanding both of how philosophy has been and might be enacted, Irigaray calls for a new logic, one that is necessary for a politics to emerge apart from the phallocentric economy that dominates Western thought. We find this new logic embedded throughout Irigaray's work; it occurs very strongly in her recent thinking on relationality and its challenge to the traditional subject/object dichotomy, which Heidegger himself undertook to reveal the metaphysics of presence. My assertion here is that it is *because of* the dialogue with Heidegger that Irigaray can enact her political strategy, as it is Heidegger that taught Irigaray the power of nonstatic thinking. Irigaray's analyses are of course a demonstration of this. But also, it resides in the movement of Irigaray's thinking, across engagements within the canon, in the enactment of her methods and strategies. It is, as Heidegger would say, in the thinking itself.

What follows is a tracing of the dialogue between Irigaray and Heidegger. By initially examining Irigaray's appropriation of Heidegger in her early deconstructive projects, then her direct contestation with him in *The Forgetting of Air in Martin Heidegger* (Irigaray 1999 [1983]), we can find that her latest engagement with Heidegger in *The Way of Love* (Irigaray 2002) exemplifies the relationality of her recent thought. She says, "In this dimension of ourselves [where we live together with the other in communion] where Being still quivers, identity is never definitively constituted, nor defined beforehand. It is elaborated in relation-with, each one giving to the other and receiving from the other what is necessary for becoming" (Irigaray 2002, 93). At once, Irigaray offers a critique of Heidegger in her invocation of "relation-with," which harkens to Heidegger's inadequate treatment of being-with, and implicitly reveals her transformative dialogue with him. In her analysis in *The Forgetting of Air*, Irigaray applies the deconstructive tools she learned from Heidegger to his own thinking such that we find that there is a hidden element in Heidegger's thought that acts as the condition for the possibility of langange, namely, air. The lyrical and pointed encounter with Heidegger shows that the materiality of air, symbolic of woman, remains covered over and invisible in the same way that Heidegger, before her, demonstrated the covering over of presencing. The interesting move in Irigaray's thinking is when we find that, in *The Way of Love*, she again takes up the symbolic of air and its attachment to language; but here air is not the underside of the phallocentric system of language, as it was in *The Forgetting of Air*, but is transformed into the symbolic of the third that is both created by and makes relationality between two possible. Through Irigaray's treatment of the symbolic of air from 1983 to 2002 in conversation with Heidegger, we become witness to the changes and development in her thought as exemplifying dialogue between two. Irigaray has received from and given to Heidegger, and though he cannot receive in death (both literally and metaphorically speaking), we can imagine his thought after Irigaray, thanks to her engagement with him. Out of the dialogue, there is a becoming, a coming into the new. To be clear, my claim is not obvious when one reads *The Way of Love*; it is perhaps even controversial. Nearly every moment of the text offers a critique of Heidegger, as any Heidegger or Irigaray scholar will recognize. However, this is only part of the story between the two. We must read Irigaray's corpus as a conjoined project in order to understand the complexities of her thinking and from whence they emerge. While it is easy to read Irigaray's latest work on Heidegger with an atomistic perspective, and thus as a dismissal or overcoming of Heidegger's thought, to do so does not provide the means for a full understanding of what Irigaray offers us in her latest work, the importance of which lies not only in the text, but in the movement of thinking that has brought this text to us. With her Heideggerian legacy, Irigaray brings Heidegger to us, in difference.

FIRST SPEAKING, WITH HEIDEGGER

From her earliest works, Irigaray challenges discourse by using Heidegger's phenomenological tactic of revealing the hidden condition for the possibility of, in this case, discourse. As for Heidegger, language is a central component of Irigaray's thinking. She understands the power within it to structure thought and relations between men and women. In an interview from 1975 entitled "The Power of Discourse and the Subordination of the Feminine," (Irigaray 1985 [1977], 68–85), Irigaray advances an account of her overall project put forth in *Speculum of the Other Woman*, which was published the previous year in 1974. In the interview she claims that it is philosophical discourse that must be "challenge[d]" and "disrupted" (Irigaray 1985 [1977], 74), as it is the foundation for all other discourses. When Irigaray discusses discourse here, she is not merely referring to speech. Rather, she intends the meaning of "discourse" to indicate the way in which we understand the world through the particular apparatus of the philosophical system. In this vein, she comments that philosophical discourse has "a *position of mastery*, and of potential reappropriation of the various productions of history" (Irigaray 1985 [1977], 74).

She uses the term "mastery" to indicate that the system of discourse orders, and thereby controls, our knowledge. In this, Irigaray adopts a basic hermeneutic position, one forcefully argued by Heidegger, that there is no bare knowledge apart from interpretation. Language does not act merely as a conduit of meaning but itself creates meaning. Our knowledge is biased by philosophical discourse and the inherent positions and attitudes within it. Philosophical discourse, in its desire to offer a theoretical standpoint that yields understandability, takes what is different and forces it under the same rubric; it reduces difference to sameness (Irigaray 1985 [1977], 74).

Exemplifying this insight, what Irigaray deems the economy of the same, we find the traditional dualisms that characterize metaphysics in general, and Enlightenment thought in particular. Within the conceptual schema of the philosophical discourse of liberal theory, the differences in male and female are subsequent to the similarity in sharing the essence of humanity. Contrary to its intent, this sameness is not a neutral position; rather, it is a male position under the guise of neutrality. It posits the ideals of universality, egalitarianism, and individualism as applying to all persons. However, these ideals, at the time of their inception, applied only to men. What is put forth as neutral is actually male. However, discourse acts to cover over this truth of sameness, here in the Enlightenment political system of thought, but also in general. Masculinist discourse has structured our thought without opening the way to sexual difference, appropriating the feminine into the system of masculinist thought and rendering woman silent with regard to her 'ownness' as an active subject. This hidden phallocentricism occurs because everything, including woman, is defined in terms of the male symbolic. For every historically great philosopher, we find a model of woman being defined in terms of the male order, as *Speculum* demonstrates. In this, Irigaray follows in the path of Simone de Beauvoir, despite the very different outcomes of their individual analyses. Beauvoir, in the introduction to *The Second Sex*, famously offers:

> In actuality the relation of the two sexes is not quite like that of two electrical poles, for man represents both the positive and the neutral, as is indicated by the common use of *man* to designate human beings in general; whereas woman represents only the negative, defined by limiting criteria, without reciprocity . . . Thus humanity is male and man defines woman

not in herself but as relative to him; she is not regarded as an
autonomous being . . . She is defined and differentiated with
reference to man and not he with reference to her; she is the
incidental, the inessential as opposed to the essential. He is
the Subject, he is the Absolute—she is the Other. (Beauvoir
1980, xxi–xxii)

Like Beauvoir in the above passage, Irigaray shows right from the
start of her early work that the place of woman in this discourse is to
be other, namely other than male. However, there is another but not
unrelated task for woman within this discourse, which consists in providing the condition for the possibility of that discourse. While woman
has been marginalized, she is needed and plundered for the feminine
element that implicitly defines the male. To reveal this hidden element
within the tradition, Irigaray "interrogates *the conditions under which
systematicity itself is possible*" (Irigaray 1985 [1977], 74). Her claim here
is that woman, as matter, symbolizes that which allows the masculine
discourse to cohere in a systematic manner or methodology. As long as
this role remains concealed by the system of discourse, discourse functions properly. That is also to say then that woman is not proper to this
discourse: "[woman's functions] ensure its coherence so long as they
remain uninterpreted" (Irigaray 1985 [1977], 75). Providing the matter,
and having been expected to uphold and facilitate the masculine element, establishes woman as the *place* of reflection. What allows for this
reflection, namely, woman herself, has been denigrated and her place as
reflective element has been covered over. Woman is expected to
silently provide the copy at the expense of her own subjectivity.
    This brief overview clearly shows Irigaray's earliest work as an
engagement with Heidegger's phenomenological method. We might
recall Heidegger's own examination of metaphysics and the dualism
thereof in his many critiques, which open up the dynamic between
dualistic categories, Being and beings, absence and presence, identity
and difference, Truth and falsehood. Heidegger's point is to show the
relationality between two, the dynamic of presencing which allows for
the categories to emerge as if whole unto themselves. Heidegger's
lesson is to reveal the hidden element that undergirds what is present
before us—his ontological inquiry into the metaphysics of presence.
Irigaray adopts his analysis of the metaphysics of presence, but in its
form of masculinst discourse. Irigaray's assertion of woman as movement and nonidentity analogously reflects the function of presencing

as Heidegger explains it—the movement of being rather than being itself. While Heidegger names the covering over of this process errancy, we find on Irigaray's analysis that woman herself is covered over in becoming Other. Irigaray's conversation, however, does not end in her education from Heidegger. There is a reversal of this mentoring relationship. Heidegger asserts the movement and emergence of being out of the relation of truth and untruth, but he does not critically apply the question of sexual difference to his own discursive project of investigating being and truth.[1] It is Irigaray's feminist perspective that takes up the phenomenological workings of Heidegger and reveals the unseen that makes appearance possible, exercising it upon the question of sexual difference, and effectively undermining the whole of the philosophical project, including Heidegger's.

DECONSTRUCTING BEING AND THINKING[2]

Irigaray's dialogue with Heidegger takes a critical turn whereby she applies the search for the unseen in Heidegger's own discourse in yet another of her earlier works, *The Forgetting of Air in Martin Heidegger*. Irigaray's critical voice both draws on Heidegger's analysis of language and draws out the implications of this analysis. Using the mimetic strategy that marks her early work, that is, adopting or miming the prescriptions and symbolics of an analysis in order to reveal the assumptions and presuppositions that underpin that theory, Irigaray demonstrates the abjection of women in Heidegger's philosophy of language. It is a yawning gap that self-alienates Heidegger the philosopher, who prefers the abstraction of theory to the material elements that act as the transcendental condition for thought itself. An investigation into Being, for Heidegger, relies on the uncovering of presence and absence and that which subtends that relation. However, and through the interrogation of Parmenides, which Heidegger draws upon frequently in his writings, Irigaray notes that the absent that truly subtends this relation is the unthought, the Nothing, which Irigaray shows to correlate with the place of woman. As Heidegger does not take sexual difference into account, he neglects the unseen, transparency, air, that which lies in the Nothing. Here we find Irigaray to be both pupil and teacher of Heidegger, almost disappointed by his lack of insight given the importance and strength of his analysis of presence and technological culture. Her careful and nuanced critique of Heidegger is phenomenological in method, political in outcome.

Irigaray begins her conversation with Heidegger here by interrogating Heidegger's words from "The End of Philosophy and the Task of Thinking," where he asserts that to think philosophically we must think the opening of the open region wherein everything becomes present and absent (Heidegger 1977, 384). Irigaray asks "of what" can the clearing from which "the whole emerges out of concealment and into which it enters in concealment" be and "of what" is Being? (Irigaray 1999 [1983], 3, 8) In doing so she brings matter to bear on Being. The nonsensible nature of Being is assumed, left unquestioned by Heidegger, and Parmenides, whom he invokes. They have no answer to her question, never having thought it. The "what" of Being is assumed transparent. However, transparency has a material quality in addition to its figurative meaning; it is nonvisible, fluid, and all-encompassing. Irigaray offers that air—the element that Heidegger forgets in his recollection of the Greeks—has these qualities of transparency and provides the condition for the possibility of all Being, existence as we know it. Irigaray asks Heidegger, "Is not air the whole of our habitation as mortals . . . Can man live elsewhere than in air? Neither in earth, nor in fire, nor in water is any habitation possible for him . . . No other element is as light, as free, and as much in the 'fundamental' mode of a permanent, available, 'there is.' " (Irigaray 1999 [1983], 8)

Air is the most evident, though nonapparent, to Heidegger. It is, to echo Heidegger and Aristotle before him, the most near yet furthest away. Heidegger deconstructs the metaphysics of presence, but forgets or does not *see* that air is itself the excess that permeates this metaphysics and disrupts it.[3] It is air that provides even for his Being, his thinking, his language and even his Nothing. Following this revelation that air is the condition for Being, that is, that the open expanse is of air, Irigaray precedes to lay out the implications of this discovery in the perspective of Heidegger's thought. Irigaray's discussion of air plays with early Greek thought in order to seriously contest Heidegger's neglect of sexual difference. She overlays air with woman-mother-nature, a symbolic common to her literary projects, and thereby brings sexual difference to Heidegger's thought. Air becomes symbolic for woman, mother, and nature. Irigaray draws on the character of materiality in general to explain this: "She gives—first—air, and does so irrecoverably . . . from and within her, of whoever takes air from her" (Irigaray 1999 [1983], 28). Here Irigaray refers to the transference of air in the womb from mother to child, a one-way transference that takes place in fluid. Continuing with the passage, "While this air is—first—fluid matter carried by the blood she gives, it can also be understood as voice and phenomenon. These issue from it and are the possibility—ever material—of naming-denominating, of appearing in presence" (Irigaray 1999 [1983], 28). In connecting the fluidity of air to "voice and phenomenon," Irigaray invokes language and being as essentially dependent upon air, that is, conditional upon woman-mother-nature, who remains invisible. Parmenides and Heidegger, in their theories and persons, neglect to recognize the transcendental necessity of air/woman.

Irigaray takes Heidegger at his word that *noein* (thinking) only appears in *eon* (the Being of being, or the twofoldness of Being); he does not think or say that which does not arise out of the Being of beings. Reading Parmenides' explanation of Being and its essential connection to thinking, Heidegger claims that thinking is not an outside relation to Being, but only appears in the *eon*.[4] The relation of the Being of beings to thinking lies in two directions. On the one hand, thinking is due to the Being of beings; that is, thinking is given by the twofoldness of Being. On the other, the Being of beings needs both thinking and saying: "That, however, which for its part demands *noein* and at the same time along with it *legein*, letting-lie-before, and calls them on the way to itself, is the *eon*, the Being of beings" (Heidegger 1999, 175). Thinking is not outside of *eon*, but belongs to the emergence of the Being of beings. Thinking is joined to saying because that which is thought is always lying before us (*legein*), thus "*noein* comes to appear in what is spoken" (Heidegger 1999, 178). The saying of Being is not the spoken word, but ontologically precedes the spoken word: the gathering of that which presences itself. What is spoken and thus thought only appears "in the *eon* itself" (Heidegger 1999, 179), the presencing of the Being of beings. Saying, then, occurs in/as the unconcealment of Being.

Heidegger notes that Parmenides does not speak directly to the specifics of the relationship of saying, the essence of language, and the Being of beings, leaving him to wonder, "[i]s saying at home in the twofold of Being and beings because of the house of *Being* (which also means: of the *Being of* beings), because the house of the twofold is—the house, however, having been built from the essence of language?" (Heidegger 1999, 180). Being and language are *essentially* at home with one another (and here I want to underscore the significance of essence as Heidegger posits it). In other words, the house of Being, in which we dwell and which gives shelter, is such because of the essence of language—letting the Being of being lie before us in its emergence. When this event occurs, truth or unconcealment occurs, out of concealment into the light: "Language prevails in its essence where appearing prevails, where coming-forth-before is appropriated: arrival before us into unconcealment and from out of concealment" (Heidegger 1999, 180). Language gathers Being, language is its essence.

Evaluating Heidegger's analysis, Irigaray notes that what lies outside his own propositions is the matter of air, and yet Heidegger claims an encompassing explanation of being and language. The first gift of air is the "unthinkable beginning of Being," and "its advent is prior to all saying" (Irigaray 1999 [1983], 30). That which lies beyond the Being of beings is not attended to by *noein* or *legein*, and therefore must be unthinkable and unsayable; it is Nothing, you can never think of, nor indicate Nothing (Parmenides fr. 2, lines 7–8). Nothing is outside of thought and language. Having shifted Heidegger's structures to the originary of air, Irigaray proceeds to show how language and thought appropriate air, are conditional upon it, though this conditionality remains concealed: "He assimilates this still-fluid trace of a 'presence' that penetrates into him, and forgets it in light of the truth of the matters to be treated in thought" (Irigaray 1999 [1983], 48). Heidegger's airs are not about matter, but ideas—the speculations of thinking about truth, unconcealment, the lighting, all of which supercede matter—as we learn from Parmenides. Nothing, air, is the abyss of language, thought, saying, thinking. Irigaray's point here is that Heidegger cannot think beyond his ontological schema. He cannot think air, or woman; it is the beyond of his thought, that is, sexual difference.

Irigaray's study of Heidegger's relation to Parmenidean thought paves the way for her most recent dialogue with Heidegger, where she again explores Heidegger's relation to Parmenides. In *The Forgetting of Air*, not only is there the mimetic, phenomenological strategy at work which we find in Irigaray's early writings as described above, but through this early strategy she creates a way of opening the conceptual issues that will come to the forefront in her recent discussion of relationality. By describing the proximity of Heidegger to Parmenides, by revealing his failure in his attempt to truly find presencing in its origin, Irigaray shows Heidegger to remain within the idealist tradition that begins with Parmenides. In her later work, Irigaray will continue her argument with Heidegger's position to show the death that his system of language begets. Though Heidegger finds the possibility of overcoming the metaphysics of presence in Parmenides thought in the *eon*, he doesn't go far enough in his analysis, not engaging in the acknowledgment of material elements much discussed by pre-Socratic thought of the materialist schools, and which Irigaray shows to be the animating force of language. Had he done so, the movement of Being would not have ossified into a presence associated with the word, as Irigaray will contend. The connection between language and thought that Heidegger legitimates in his reading of Parmenides, Irigaray will argue, does not open up the clearing of the presencing of being, but rather instills a homogeneous metaphysics that does not adequately describe reality. Despite Heidegger's efforts, his suppression of transcendental conditions for presencing acts to stagnate being in naming, a claim that Irigaray has laid the groundwork for in *The Forgetting of Air* but, as we will see, establishes explicitly in *The Way of Love*. It is Heidegger's insight of the verbal as embodying movement and openness that Irigaray will reinvoke in her own theory of the possibilities of a new language. However, Heidegger's hope for the verbal aspect of being is precluded by the structure of homogeneity in his conceived language. The standpoint of woman, here symbolized in air, is not merely ignored, but structurally rendered invisible in order that speaking, as Heidegger understands it, emerges. Clearly, a speaking predicated on the silence of another, the other, is not a speaking of authenticity. The political ramifications of Irigaray's reading here leads us to question the systematic exclusion of woman and search for another beginning, a beginning beyond the convergence of thought and language in the house of language that is a death. Alongside those identified as feminist standpoint thinkers, Irigaray offers a better vantage point on reality by giving voice to the oppression of women that in Heidegger's philosophical system leaves them (in)sensible, a vantage point and politics that Heidegger himself grounded in his phenomenological method but which he could not see.[5]

THE PROXIMITY OF HEIDEGGER

By the time of the publication of *The Way of Love*, then, we are prepared for Irigaray's positive philosophy to emerge out of her phenomenological background, the Heideggerian brand of phenomenology with his radicalization of that tradition. As demonstrated, we find that Irigaray follows Heidegger's path of gathering appearances in their relationality but with a perspective that is forgotten. Without this perspective, the relationality that Heidegger offers is partial at best, failing to describe the real possibilities of relations, that is, possibilities

that are based out of material realities. Irigaray's main contention
with Heidegger is with his idealism, his ability to separate Being from
the elements, to reinforce the economy of the same by centering the
masculine subject as the locus of the reception of Being. She contrasts
the language of thinking and being with the language of materialism
and the relationality of the sensible. The themes that mark Irigaray's
early writings are at play in her recent work as well: the phenomenological critique, the sensible transcendental, the use of psychoanalysis
to uncover lost mother/woman/nature. In addition, where before
Irigaray pointed to the idea of a new language as a new way of being
in the world, here she offers an explicit articulation of just what that
would entail, and with political import.

It is my reading of Irigaray that with each of these themes, Irigaray
leads us a step at a time into new aspects of the political, a politics that
is there all along and always developing. In her early work, Irigaray's
politics were present in the critique of the history of philosophy and
psychoanalysis, revealing the hidden and sometimes not so hidden prejudice and silencing of women, along with overt statements regarding the
condition of women's lives. Irigaray's early strategy was a mimetic revealing—a borrowing of the status of women given by the terms of
traditional philosophical thought and through it, an enactment of a
phenomenological project to reveal the conditions for the possibility of
the overt thought structures. In *The Way of Love*, and in her later work
in general, we find Irigaray engaging with and beyond this mimetic
strategy, pointing us toward a fuller understanding of transformative
mimesis. The transformation that the mimetic strategy invokes is not
only the overturning of thought like that which we found in *The Sex
Which Is Not One*, but is the condition for the furthering of the
transformative agenda which, at this point in Irigaray's thinking, has
resulted in a new relationality. Irigaray addresses the consequences of
her deconstruction:

> The dialectical method, such as I use it, is not at the service
> of reassumption (*Aufhebung*) of all singularity into an absolute
> objectivity to be shared by any subject. My way uses the
> negative as a path which permits, at each moment, dialogue
> between subjects in the respect of singularities, in particular
> of gender. Here, the negative is therefore insurmountable and
> the absolute can never be unique nor universally shared. The
> negative maintains real and living the *dialegomai* between

subjectivities which, beyond appearing to self and to the other, must speak to one another in order to be and to become self, in order to elaborate a culture resulting from the spiritual fecundity of subjective differences. (Pluháček and Bostic 1996, 351)

I quote Irigaray at length here not only to show her relation to Hegel (though it is actually more complex than is obvious here), but to point to her thought of a new relationality, both in the subject of her discourse, but also in the movement of her thought across the writings of her corpus. The thinking to which she brings us now is an engagement that can only occur because of the multiple types of analysis that she has earlier employed in breaking down hegemonic thought structures and which would not have been possible prior to this deconstruction of the metaphysics of presence of woman. Where we arrive with her is a different power relation, a politics of dialogue that respects difference as real and irreducible in terms of appropriation of the Other to/by the One. Her structural innovation gives rise to the possibilities of change at the historical material level, a new being in the world.

What remains intensely interesting is Irigaray's continuous dialogue with Heidegger in her political thinking. As the above quotation reveals, this dialogue is not one of mere negation. If Irigaray had merely negated Heidegger, she would have left him in her early writings. But he remains in proximity with her, in her, apart from her as she pursues this transformative politics. She engages his work such that she enters a sharing of thought, one of advancement not through a simple critique, but through a dialogue of recognition of difference. This is not to say that Irigaray does not offer a criticism of Heidegger's thought; she does, finding it phemonenologically inadequate to the task of expressing the relation of difference between two. However, this criticism does not prevent Irigaray from a fluid engagement and discussion with Heidegger. Irigaray does not try to overcome Heidegger. Rather, she lets his thoughts which help us to think beyond metaphysical language stand, thinking along with Heidegger and turning his insights to difference in order to think further, in the true sense of that term. Irigaray thinks with and out of Heidegger's thought and, due to this closeness, goes another step on the path Heidegger has laid out. She develops in conversation with Heidegger a new path upon which to find a new relation, a new politics of relationality. The sameness and difference in their thought allows us to understand this

new relationality, an understanding that would not be possible without the shared engagement. And, of course, this is not different from
her earlier engagement with Heidegger; it is a development thereof
along with and as a manifestation of the development of her own
thinking over time. Irigaray's engagement with Heidegger is so thoroughgoing in *The Way of Love* that it is impossible to fully document
the allusions to Heidegger's texts and ideas. There are too many and
they are made with such fluidity that to attempt to mark them philo-
logically would destroy their importance and subtlety. As such, I will
pull out a few threads to show the relationality at work in the dialogue between the two.[6]

The focus of both Irigaray's and Heidegger's project is language
itself. Irigaray follows Heidegger in his insight that in language a
transformative power lies. For Heidegger, the power resides in the
ability of language to disrupt the metaphysics of presence. For Irigaray,
it is manifest as the path upon which the feminine symbolic will come
to fruition such that an ethic of recognition will emerge. And while
she will ultimately contest Heidegger's success in his project, it is not
before sharing in Heidegger's insights. Irigaray demonstrates in her
relation with Heidegger the very sense of relationality that she advocates in the context of her essay. In this way, Irigaray is able to avoid
the same pitfalls of conceptual thinking that she critiques by making
her ideas actions, which work in conjunction with her speech. As
such, her ideas are open-ended and malleable, whereas conceptual
thinking, as she will point out, resigns ideas to a totalizing effect in
the containment of them with a word, in a language already set in
meaning, or, to use Heidegger's phrase, "always already" sedimented.

Language, traditionally conceived, functions to convey meaning
between subjects about objects. Heidegger attempts to open language
up beyond this function to circumvent the pitfalls that implicitly
characterize this understanding of language. If language merely acts as
a carrier of thought, then language itself is meaningless and contributes nothing to the uncovering of thought. Putting aside the question
of what thought might be without language, the problem Heidegger
finds with this conception of language is its reliance on the temporal
moment of presence. In this traditional conception of language, thought
and meaning are captured as an appearance to be carried, as if an
object, from one mind to another, which relegates thought and being
to a staid conception that can be easily quantified and replicated.
Thus, at the heart of this conception of language is a metaphysics of

presence. Heidegger wants to upset this notion of language to show that language acts to reveal being in its presencing—that is, in language we can grasp the movement of being. Heidegger relies heavily on the verbal aspect of language in his demonstration of this other way to consider language, and poetry acts as the premier example of how language itself ruptures the metaphysics of presence and allows us to grasp the presencing of being.

Irigaray takes up Heidegger's investigation of the word in his essay "Words" from *On the Way to Language* (Heidegger 1971). In discussing the force of the word for the poet and in an exploration of Stefan George's poem "Words," Heidegger elucidates the relation between word and being, word and thing:

> [I]t is the word which first holds the treasure in its presence, indeed first fetches and brings it there and preserves it. Suddenly the word shows a different, a higher ruler. It is no longer just a name-giving grasp reaching for what is present and already portrayed, it is not only a means of portraying what lies before us. On the contrary, the word first bestows presence, that is, Being in which things appear as beings. (Heidegger 1971, 146)

Irigaray finds common ground with Heidegger here. With him, she problematizes the naming function of words as mired in the representational view of language. Naming keeps thinking situated in a substantive view of the world, rather than in the linkages which bind the world, binds selves, together. For Heidegger, naming can fall into the one-sided understanding of being as presence and thus cover over the movement of being and its temporal relation to nothing. The word allows the being of the thing to come into appearance, "lets beings appear in their 'it is'" (Heidegger 1971, 155). With this, Heidegger draws the connection between saying and thing, the revelatory possibilities thereof. And though he also lays out the relation between this revelation and its inherent veiling, he does not draw the reader to that which is truly veiled in the veiling, namely, the other.

Irigaray explains that his reliance on the word places Heidegger still within a homologous system of language. Despite Heidegger's demonstration that the being that the word reveals is presencing itself, and therefore offers the possibility of eluding the metaphysical connotations of Being and being, Irigaray shows that Heidegger fails to account for the other. Presencing does not embody the open-ended movement outside of the temporality of presence, but rather enacts another presence in its covering over of the other in its otherness. The speech which speaks to more than one person necessitates a closure of meaning so that each can apprehend it in the right way (Irigaray 2002, 24). It is a type of Platonic participation in the universal, a language of idealism, and one in which the speaker speaks with itself. In other words, it is a monologism, or a saying of one, a saying which Irigaray attributes to the masculine subject. This monological saying cannot account for the other as otherness would preclude understanding within the system created: "[The closed word] is, in a way, an already realized work that does not correspond to the work of a present communication with the other. It can seduce, become the other's property, as it can be that of a people or of a tradition. It is not really shared between two" (Irigaray 2002, 25). For Irigaray scholars, it is apparent that her argument for this claim is fully laid out in conjunction with her early deconstructive project and linguistic analysis, a realization Irigaray assumes. Already we find the layering in Irigaray's thought. The themes of *The Forgetting of Air* mentioned above are also present here: Heidegger's latent idealism, his focus on thinking and being, his failure to hear the other in language. By following Irigaray's conversation with Heidegger, we come to a deeper appreciation of her movement as a thinker.

Though Heidegger presents naming as revealing the movement of being, Irigaray, who also desires movement in thought, recognizes where Heidegger does not that his naming remains situated in the closed, staid system of language. In the following passage, we find Irigaray's affirmation and correction of Heidegger. Her words bear a rhythm of back and forth with Heidegger:

> In our tradition, the highest and most disinterested intention of language would be naming the world and its objects. It is a matter of grasping them in a saying through words corresponding to the Western logos with its conceptual predominance, or of designating them while letting them be, which is nearer to the Eastern language that the Western poet sometimes approaches. Language is the tool, the *techne*, which the speaking subject uses in order to exist in a world, to dwell in it and to continue to construct it as human. (Irigaray 2002, 38)

When Irigaray remarks upon the value of naming the world and objects, she is both asserting Heidegger's belief and accusing him. Heidegger also rejects a naming that reveals the object as representational. He explains that while the poet initially finds words to be "full of being" and to "present what already is to representational thinking," (Heidegger 1971, 144) the poet does not stop with this discovery. The word allows presencing, that is, in the word we find the mystery of being: "He has allowed himself . . . to be brought face to face with the word's mystery, the be-thinging of the thing in the word" (Heidegger 1971, 151). Here Heidegger denies the will of the subject over the object in the subject's desire to represent the world, and thereby opens up the possibility for the movement of being to emerge, the "be-thinging of the thing."

Irigaray embraces Heidegger's thinking in that she too wants to think beyond the representational function of words, as Heidegger brings to our attention in presencing, in be-thinging. Irigaray, too, wants to supplant the tradition subject/object relation, but sees that Heidegger remains with the nominative function of the word. Though Heidegger radicalizes logos—"The oldest word for the rule of the word thus thought, for Saying, is *logos*: Saying which, in showing, lets beings appear in their 'it is' " (Heidegger 1971, 155)—on Irigaray's view, logos still remains tied to the object, reaffirming the masculine subject's relation to objects even in Heidegger's radicalization of that relation. Language that primarily asserts the subject's relation with objects and not other subjects assumes the sameness of subjects and thus a denial of the material difference between subjects. Though the designating of world and objects in letting be is closer to the Eastern tradition in which Irigaray finds greater possibilities for relationality, thus affirming and thinking with Heidegger, this is also where Irigaray must turn the direction of Heidegger's discourse, taking his insights and radicalization to a new level beyond dwelling in the nominative and testamentary language, which is the death of language in its precluding of openness and becoming. The word, for Heidegger, rests with the nominative while the "verb as acting on the world, the other, the subject, is not analyzed in its complexity . . . the verb disappears, fades away, is forgotten in the substantive" (Irigaray 2002, 39). Paying attention to the verb allows one to both assume subjectivity when the subject takes the active voice, and realize the work of the other in its subjectivity when the verb remains in the infinitive or is appropriated by another (Irigaray 2002, 59). As such, the verb allows us to recognize

the links that bind the world, rather than the objects of the world—
a task Heidegger set for himself but could not realize because he only
accounted for the verb in relation to the object.

What is more radical is a language which speaks between subjects who are different. Unlike the closed word, this speaking is always
open, "meaning quivers and always remains unstable" (Irigaray 2002,
28). The speaking subjects affirm a resignation of the inability to say
the whole, and an inability to appropriate the other in the dialogue.
This creates the instability and an always becoming. A distance not
only always remains in dialogue, but is necessary:

> . . . to refrain from a word granted in dialogue is to let an
> intimacy-between happen, but safeguarding a free space with-
> out violating the intimate of the one or of the other. The
> clearing of language—the vastness—is then built by two. It
> becomes a place where the intimate is possible with measure
> thanks to respect for the one or for the other. And also thanks
> to the renunciation of dominating the 'representational rule
> of the word' (cf. On the Way to Language, p. 151). (Irigaray
> 2002, 29)

Again, Irigaray is with Heidegger here, and beyond him. The language of the new relationality between subjects requires what Heidegger
could not think in his neglect of being-with, namely, the demand to
disappropriate the world in one's subjectivity. Irigaray asks that we
literally re-cognize difference which means refiguring the relation of
the subject. The difference between subjects cannot be covered over
in the assertion of the sameness of subjectivity. We must rethink
difference with regard to its materiality, and its concomitant irreduc-
ibility (Irigaray 2002, 36). This requires a listening rather than
assumptive speech, a silence that is not Heidegger's unfolding of Being,
but the unfolding of the between. Though Heidegger models possibilities for the holding of separate subjectivities in, for instance, his insistence of the Open region, it collapses into sameness on Irigaray's
reading because it is not grounded in materiality.

This step towards the third demonstrates Irigaray's movement as
a thinker, a becoming with Heidegger. It calls for her readers to necessarily grasp Irigaray's corpus in its layering and unity. Just as we
found in Irigaray's dialogue with Heidegger in The Forgetting of Air,
Irigaray calls our attention to the third, the between. The difference
in the two works is that in The Way of Love we find not so much a

grounding condition as it was laid out in her earlier work, as a coexistence emergent with two subjects. She says, "The transcendence between us, this one which is fecund in graces and in words, requires an interval, it engenders it also" (Irigaray 2002, 66). The third both creates and is created by relationality. Her thought clearly develops out of her earlier deconstructive project. Elemental air, which on her earlier analysis acted as the condition for Heidegger's language, is transformed into that which allows for respect between two: "Air is what is left common between subjects . . . it is the elemental of the universe . . . that in which we dwell and which dwells in us . . . Air is the medium of our natural and spiritual life, or our relation to ourselves, to speaking, to the other" (Irigaray 2002, 67). The between of two, here marked with air, offers a new power relation among humans whereby there are always two. Sexual difference is maintained at the level of recognition and respect for the other, instead of the phallocentric economy's act of rendering woman silent and invisible. The between holds the one apart from the other and thus prevents that very subsumption. Air allows us to think the "trilogy of the real," (Irigaray 2002, 108) that is, the necessity of the in-between of subjects, I, you, between us. If the between is transgressed, the two collapse, then the dual becomes one and monologism maintains its hegemonic hold. Given the patriarchal history of language, that one is always masculine: "And no mirror can give an account of this trilogy that remains unrepresentable" (Irigaray 2002, 111). Irigaray's earlier deconstructive work revealed the economy of the same to literally engender a mirror: the feminine acts to reflect the masculine but has no image herself. By recalling for us the mirror and its place in her mimetic strategy, Irigaray signals to us that she has, out of this strategy, come to a new place of thinking, a radicalization of Heidegger's radical thinking.

CONCLUSION

We can understand Irigaray's engagement with Heidegger as a dance. She has adopted his phenomenological method, turned it upon his discourse, and now reflects with him his discourse in her own. The distance between them remains in the discourse; Irigaray does not appropriate it nor simply reject it. She instead speaks with Heidegger in proximity: "Co-propriation in the human necessitates a dialogue in which the elements remain two—speaking oneself to the other and listening to oneself and to the other" (Irigaray 2002, 82). Any thinker who upsets the structures of thought, is in my view a political thinker, for if feminism has taught us nothing else, it is that structures of thought are already political, regulating discourse and thought, to borrow Judith Butler's terminology. Both Irigaray and Heidegger are thus nothing but political thinkers. Heidegger's radical politics was to disrupt the grand narrative of the subject/object relation by revealing the hidden structures of language. Irigaray's politics rests in nearness with Heidegger here. She offers a relationality that recognizes materiality, difference, and a speaking that does not assume. One cannot help but to see in her conversation with Heidegger his influence, her anger at him for failing her, and her turning him to more productive thought. It is out of this interlocution with him that Irigaray's politics arrives at the place for which her early work has prepared us. The language of relationality, from Heidegger to a beyond of his relationality, offers a politics that allows for a space wherein both men and women are given the space to grow and flourish, a basic feminist goal, but one which remains unrealized. Irigaray's transformative mimesis has brought us here. Recognizing difference in language is another step, in Irigaray's thinking, and in society's transformation.

NOTES

1. Irigaray says of Freud, "The fact that Freud took sexuality as the object of his discourse does not necessarily imply that he interpreted the role of sexualization in discourse itself, his own in particular" (Irigaray 1985 [1977], 152–53). It is clear that Irigaray's accusation of the entirety of the history of philosophy, including Heidegger's work, is the same: it does not take into account the sexualization of discourse, in other words, sexual difference. Rather, it universalizes this difference under the rubric of sameness, that is, maleness.

2. Portions of this section appear in nascent form in my "The Horror of Language: Irigaray and Heidegger," *Philosophy Today* 45:5 (Spring 2003).

3. One should not miss the irony here of Heidegger's inability to *see*—the preeminent sensory function that coincides with the rise of metaphysics of presence, as Heidegger himself explains in the Nietzsche lectures.

4. If we recall Parmenides' poem, its intent is to reveal the truth of being. Fr. 3 of his poem reads, "thought and being are the same." At Fr. 6 he says, "What is there to be said and thought must needs be: for it is there for being, but nothing is not." Again, at the end of Fr. 8, Parmenides reiterates this relation: "The same thing is there to be thought and is why there is thought. For you will not find thinking without what is, in all that has been said" (lines

34–36). Translations, Kirk, Raven, and Schofield, *The Presocratic Philosophers*, 2nd ed. (Cambridge: Cambridge University Press, 1983).

     5. See Nancy Hartstock's articulation of the claims of standpoint theory, including the following point: "As an engaged vision, the understanding of the oppressed, the adoption of a standpoint exposes the real relations among human beings as inhuman, points beyond the present, and carries a historically liberatory role" in the much anthologized piece "The Feminist Standpoint: Toward a Specifically Feminist Historical Materialism" from *Money, Sex and Power*, Longman Press, 1983. Though the sense of materialism differs in Irigaray's use of the term from the strictly Marxist connotation that Hartstock invokes, the overlap is substantial enough for us to recognize the parallels of the two. While Hartstock's view leaves unquestioned the very idea of humanity, Irigaray would agree that patriarchy inhumanizes woman, but from that insight goes on to show that the very idea of humanity is irredeemably flawed due to the inherently masculinist origins that prevent dialogue and recognition of difference.

     6. The space of the essay here does not allow for a full explication of the layering of thought between Irigaray and Heidegger in these two texts, *The Way of Love* and *On the Way to Language*. Clearly, Irigaray's title alone speaks to the dialogue she has with Heidegger. A fuller account would draw out the numerous intersections Irigaray creates, including Heidegger's description of renunciation and the nothing as it pertains to woman, one of the more important elements of Irigaray's critique of Heidegger from *The Forgetting of Air*, as noted above.

WORKS CITED

Beauvoir, Simone de. 1980. *The Second Sex*. Translated by H. M. Parshley. New York: Vintage Books.

Heidegger, Martin. 1971. "Words." In *On the Way to Language*. Translated by Peter D. Hertz. New York: Harper & Row.

———. 1977. "The End of Philosophy and the Task of Thinking." In *Basic Writings*. Edited by David Krell. San Francisco: HarperCollins.

———. 1999. "The Last, Undelivered Lecture (XII) from Summer Semester 1952," translated by Will McNeill. In *The Presocratics after Heidegger*, edited by David C. Jacobs. Albany, N.Y.: State University of New York Press. Published in German in *Hegel-Studien*. Band 25. Bonn: Bouvier Verlag, 1990.

Irigaray, Luce. 1985 [1977]. *This Sex Which Is Not One*. Translated by Catherine Porter. Ithaca, N.Y.: Cornell University Press.

———. 1999 [1983]. *The Forgetting of Air in Martin Heidegger*. Translated by Mary Beth Mader. Austin: The University of Texas Press.

————. 2002. *The Way of Love*. Translated by Heidi Bostic and Stephen Pluháček. London: Continuum.

Kirk, G. S., J. E. Raven, and M. Schofield, eds. 1983. *The Presocratic Philosophers*. 2nd ed. Cambridge: Cambridge University Press.

Pluháček, Stephen, and Heidi Bostic. 1996. "Thinking Life as Relation: An Interview with Luce Irigaray." *Man and World* 29, no. 4 (October).

BIBLIOGRAPHY OF WORKS
BY LUCE IRIGARAY

The following bibliography lists chronologically all the major texts of Luce Irigaray, by *both* the date of original publication or presentation *and* the first appearance in English, a reference method also used in all the essays in this book. Essays initially published individually and later assembled into books as chapters or as parts of a collection are listed by the date and, in most cases, under the title of their original presentation or publication and under the date and title of their first appearance in English. The information provided below the entries for the original essays includes, where applicable, the translated title of the work, the date of its first appearance in translation, and the titles and publication dates of works in which the untranslated essay has been reprinted. Full copyright information is provided only for Irigaray's books and those books or journals in which the essays originally appear.

The entries for works translated into English are listed under the title and date of their first appearance in English as well as the title and date of the untranslated work's original publication or presentation. Any information that is not provided under the listing for the English essay will be included in the original essay's entry. The material provided under the English entries includes the name and publication date of the work of which the English title is a translation, any other titles the essay appears as in English, and the titles and dates of the most significant works in which the essay has been reprinted.

---

*Bibliography compiled by Sara McNamara.

Translator information is provided only for the first appearance of an essay or book.

In those instances where an essay first appears as a chapter in one of Irigaray's books and is later reprinted in another collection, the essay is listed under the date of its original publication and the date of its first appearance in English. Information regarding the text(s) in which this essay has been reprinted is provided under these entries. In all cases, every entry for an essay or text should be consulted in order to obtain the full history of each publication.

1957. "Le dernier visage de Pascal." In *Revue Nouvelle*. Brussels.
1963. "Inconscient freudien et structures formelles de la poésie." In *Revue philosophique de Louvain* 61: 435–66.
1964. "Un modèle d'analyse structurale de la poésie: A propos d'un ouvrage de Levin." In *Logique et analyse* 27: 168–78.
1965. "Analyse distributionnelle en neurolinguistique: le comportement verbal des aphasiques et des déments dans les épreuves de langage répété" (with J. Dubois, P. Marcie, H. Hécaen, and R. Angelergues). In *Langage et comportement* 1: 111–34.
1965. "Transformation négative et organisation des classes lexicales" (with J. Dubois and P. Marcie). In *Cahiers de lexicologie* 7: 1–32.
1966. "Communication linguistique et spéculaire." In *Cahiers pour l'analyse* 3 (May).
   • Translated into English as: "Linguistic and Specular Communication" (2002).
   • Reprinted in: *Parler n'est jamais neutre* (1985).
1966. "Approche expérimentale de la constitution de la phrase minimale en français" (with J. Dubois). In *Langages* 3: 90–125.
   • Translated into English as: "Experimental Method in Psycholinguistics" (1966).
1966. "Les Structures linguistiques de la parenté et leurs perturbations dans les cas de démence et de schizophrénie" (with J. Dubois). In *Cahiers de lexicologie* 8: 47–69.
1966. "Experimental Method in Psycholinguistics" (with J. Dubois) (lecture delivered by Jean Dubois at the Linguistic Institute Conference on Linguistic Method, University of California, Los Angeles, 1–3 August).
   • Published in: *Method and Theory in Linguistics*, edited by Paul L. Garvin. The Hague: Mouton.
   • Translation of: "Approche expérimentale de la constitution de la phrase minimale en français" (1966).
1967. "Approche d'une grammaire d'énonciation de l'hystérique et de l'obsessionnel." In *Langages* 5 (March).
   • Translated into English as: "Towards a Grammar of Enunciation for Hysterics and Obsessives" (2002).

- Reprinted in: *Parler n'est jamais neutre* (1985).

1967. "Approche psycholinguistique du langage des déments." In *Neuropsychologia* 5 (March).

1967. "La Production de phrases chez les déments." In *Langages* 5 (March).

1967. "Négation et transformation négative dans le langage des schizophrènes." In *Langages* 5 (March).
- Translated into English as: "Negation and Negative Transformations in the Language of Schizophrenics" (2002).
- Reprinted in: *Parler n'est jamais neutre* (1985).

1968. "Du fantasme et du verbe." In *l'Arc* 34.
- Translated into English as: "On Phantasm and the Verb" (2002).
- Reprinted in: *Parler n'est jamais neutre* (1985).

1968. "Épreuve de production de phrases chez les déments et les schizophrènes." In *Revue de Psychologie Française* 13 (2): 157–65.
- Translated into English as: "Sentence Production among Schizophrenics and Senile Dementia Patients" (2002).
- Reprinted in: *Parler n'est jamais neutre* (1985).

1968. "L'inconscio premeditato." In *Sigma* 9: 23–34.

1969. "Langage de classe, langage inconscient." In *Le Centenaire du Capital*, edited by E. Balibar, L. Goldmann, and P. Macherey. Paris: Editions Mouton.
- Translated into English as: "Class Language, Unconscious Language" (2002).
- Reprinted in: *Parler n'est jamais neutre* (1985).

1969. "La psychanalyse comme pratique de l'énonciation." In *Le langage et l'homme*. Brussels: Institut Libre Marie Harps.

1969. "L'énoncé en analyse." In *Langages* 13 (March).
- Translated into English as: "The Utterance in Analysis" (2002).
- Reprinted in: *Parler n'est jamais neutre* (1985).

1969. "Le v(i)ol de la lettre." In *Tel Quel* 39 (Autumn).
- Translated into English as: "The Rape of the Letter" (2002).
- Reprinted in: *Parler n'est jamais neutre* (1985).

1970. "Le sexe fait comme signe." In *Langages* 17 (March).
- Translated into English as: "Sex as Sign" (2002).
- Reprinted in: *Parler n'est jamais neutre* (1985).

1971. "Le schizophrène ou le refus de la schize." In *Expression et signe* 1 (February).
- Translated into English as: "Schizophrenics, or the Refusal of Schiz" (2002).
- Reprinted in: *Parler n'est jamais neutre* (1985).

1973. *Le Langage des déments*. The Hague: Mouton.

1973. "Le miroir, de l'autre côté." In *Critique* 309 (February).
- Translated into English as: "The Looking Glass, from the Other Side" (1985).
- Reprinted in: *Ce sexe qui n'en est pas un* (1977).

1973. "Retour sur la théorie psychanalytique." In *Encyclopédie medico-chirurgicale, gynécologie* 3: 167 A–10.
   • Translated into English as: "Psychoanalytic Theory: Another Look" (1985).
   • Reprinted in: *Ce sexe qui n'en est pas un* (1977).
1974. *Speculum de l'autre femme*. Paris: Editions de Minuit.
   • Translated into English as: *Speculum of the Other Woman* (1985).
1974. "L'incontournable volume." In *Speculum de l'autre femme*.
   • Translated into English as: "Volume-Fluidity" (1985).
1974. "Une 'cause' encore: la castration." In *Speculum de l'autre femme*.
   • Translated into English as: "Another 'Cause'—Castration" (1985).
1974. "Toute théorie du 'sujet' aura toujours été appropriée au 'masculin.' " In *Speculum de l'autre femme*.
   • Translated into English as: "Any Theory of the 'Subject' Has Always Been Appropriated by the 'Masculine' " (1985).
1974. ". . . éternelle ironie de la communauté. . . ." In *Speculum de l'autre femme*.
   • Translated into English as: "The Eternal Irony of the Community" (1985).
1974. "L'hom(m)osexualité feminine." In *Speculum de l'autre femme*.
   • Translated into English as: "Female Hom(m)osexuality" (1985).
1974. "Le praticable de la scène." In *Speculum de l'autre femme*.
   • Translated into English as: "The Stage Setup" (1985).
1974. "La 'mécanique' des fluides." In *l'Arc* 58.
   • Translated into English as: "The 'Mechanics' of Fluids" (1985).
   • Reprinted in: *Ce sexe qui n'en est pas un* (1977).
1974. "Questions I" (these questions were raised, explicitly or implicitly, by members of the jury during a doctoral thesis defense in the Philosophy Department of the University of Vincennes, 2 October).
   • Translated into English as: "Questions I" (1985).
   • Published in: *Ce sexe qui n'en est pas un* (1977) [as part of chapter "Questions" (1977)].
1974. "Question IV" (this question was addressed to instructors by the Department of Psychoanalysis in the fall. Following this, Irigaray was suspended from teaching and told her project was not accepted).
   • Translated into English as: "Question IV" (1985).
   • Published in: *Ce sexe qui n'en est pas un* (1977) [as part of chapter "Questions" (1977)].
1975. "Questions II" (questions raised by Philippe Lacoue-Labarthe in preparation for *Dialogues*, a television program broadcast 26 February. These, abbreviated, "questions" and "answers" were exchanged in a series of letters).
   • Translated into English as: "Questions II" (1985).

- Published in: *Ce sexe qui n'en est pas un* (1977) [as part of chapter "Questions" (1977)].

1975. "La Femme, son sexe et le langage." Interview by Catherine Clément. In *La Nouvelle critique* 82 (March): 36–39.

1975. "Così fan tutti." In *Vel* 2 (August).
- Translated into English as: "Così fan tutti" (1985).
- Reprinted in: *Ce sexe qui n'en est pas un* (1977).

1975. "Des marchandises entre elles." In *La quinzaine littéraire* 215 (August).
- Translated into English as: "When the Goods Get Together" (1980).
- Reprinted in: *Ce sexe qui n'en est pas un* (1977).

1975. "Pouvoir du discours / subordination du féminin." In *Dialectiques* 8.
- Translated into English as: "The Power of Discourse and the Subordination of the Feminine" (1985).
- Reprinted in: *Ce sexe qui n'en est pas un* (1977) [as "Pouvoir du discours, subordination du féminin"].

1975. "Ce sexe qui n'en est pas un." In *Cahiers du Grif* 5.
- Translated into English as: "This Sex Which Is Not One" (1978).
- Reprinted in: *Ce sexe qui n'en est pas un* (1977).

1976. "Le marché des femmes" (originally published in Italian in *Sessualità e politica*. Milan: Feltrinelli).
- Translated into English as: "Women on the Market" (1985).
- Reprinted in: *Ce sexe qui n'en est pas un* (1977).

1976. "Femmes en exil." Interview by Svein Haugsgjerd and Fredrik Engelstad. In *Seks samtales om psykiatri*, edited by Svein Haugsgjerd and Fredrik Engelstad. Oslo: Pax.
- Translated into English as: "Women's Exile" (1977).

1976. "Quand nos lèvres se parlent." In *Cahiers du Grif* 12.
- Translated into English as: "When Our Lips Speak Together" (1980).
- Reprinted in: *Ce sexe qui n'en est pas un* (1977).

1976. " 'Françaises,' ne faites plus un effort." In *La quinzaine littéraire* 238 (August).
- Translated into English as: " 'Frenchwomen,' Stop Trying" (1985).
- Reprinted in: *Ce sexe qui n'en est pas un* (1977).

1977. *Ce sexe qui n'en est pas un*. Paris: Editions de Minuit.
- Translated into English as: *This Sex Which Is Not One* (1985).

1977. "Questions." In *Ce sexe qui n'en est pas un*.
- Translated into English as: "Questions" (1985).

1977. "Questions sur les prémisses de la théorie psychanalytique." In *Ce sexe qui n'en est pas un* [as part of chapter "Retour sur la théorie psychanalytique" (1973)].
- Translated into English as: "Questions about the Premises of Psychoanalytic Theory" (1985).

1977. "'Ce Sexe qui n'en est pas un': Les Femmes entre deux mondes." Interview by Martine Storti. In *Histoires d'elles* 0 (March): 21.

1977. "Women's Exile." Translated by Couze Venn. In *Ideology and Consciousness* 1: 62–76.
  • Translation of: "Femmes en exil" (1976).
  • Reprinted in: *The Feminist Critique of Language: A Reader* (1990).

1977. "Misère de la psychanalyse." In *Critique* 365 (October).
  • Translated into English as: "The Poverty of Psychoanalysis" (1991).
  • Reprinted in: *Parler n'est jamais neutre* (1985).

1978. "This Sex Which Is Not One." Translated by Randall Albury and Paul Foss. In *Language, Sexuality and Subversion*, edited by P. Foss and M. Morris. Sydney: Feral Publications.
  • Translation of: "Ce sexe qui n'en est pas un" (1975).
  • Reprinted in: *New French Feminisms* (1980), *This Sex Which Is Not One* (1985), *Essential Papers on the Psychology of Women: Essential Papers in Psychoanalysis* (1990), *A Reader in Feminist Knowledge* (1991), *The Women and Language Debate: A Sourcebook* (1994), *Feminism and Sexuality* (1996), *From Modernism to Postmodernism: An Anthology* (1996), *The Second Wave: A Reader in Feminist Theory* (1997), *Writing on the Body* (1997), *Feminisms: An Anthology of Literary Theory and Criticism* (1997), *Twentieth Century Continental Philosophy* (1997), *Philosophy and Sex* (1998), *Contemporary Social Theory* (1999), and *Gender Space Architecture: An Interdisciplinary Introduction* (2000).

1978. "Un art différent de sentir." Interview with Marie-Françoise Hans and Gilles Lapouge. In *Les Femmes, la pornographie et l'érotisme*, edited by Marie-Françoise Hans and Gilles Lapouge. Paris: Seuil, 43–58.

1978. "Le langage de l'homme." In *Revue Philosophique* 4 (Autumn).
  • Translated into English as: "The Language of Man (The Sexuation of Discourse)" (2002).
  • Reprinted in: *Parler n'est jamais neutre* (1985).

1979. *Et l'une ne bouge pas sans l'autre.* Paris: Editions de Minuit.
  • Translated into English as: "And the One Doesn't Stir Without the Other" (1981).

1979. "Mères et filles vues par Luce Irigaray." Interview by Martine Storti and Marie-Odile Delacour. In *Libération* (21 May).
  • Translated into English as: "Mothers and Daughters" (2000).

1979. "Etablir une généalogie des femmes." In *Maintenant* 12 (28 May).

1979. "Elle appelle toujours la nuit" (on Marguerite Duras's film *Navire Night*). In *Sorcières* 18: 26–27.

1980. *Amante marine de Friedrich Nietzsche.* Paris: Editions de Minuit.
  • Translated into English as: *Marine Lover of Friedrich Nietzsche* (1991).

1980. "Lèvres voilées." In *Amante marine de Friedrich Nietzsche.*
  • Translated into English as: "Veiled Lips" (1981).

1980. "Commodities on Their Own." Translated by Claudia Reeder. In *New French Feminisms*, edited by Elaine Marks and Isabelle de Courtivron. Brighton: Harvester.
- Translation of: "Des marchandises entre elles" (1975).
- Reprinted in: *This Sex Which Is Not One* (1985) [as "Commodities among Themselves"] and *Literary Theory: An Anthology* (1998) [as "When the Goods Get Together"].

1980. "La Femme n'est rien et c'est là sa puissance" (review of Baudrillard's *De la séduction*). In *Histoires d'elles* 21 (March): 3.

1980. "Grève de la parano." In *Histoires d'elles* 22 (April): 3.
- Reprinted in: *Paris-Féministe* 24 (1–15 April 1986): 13–15 [as "Les grêveuses"].

1980. "Le corps-à-corps avec la mère" (lecture delivered at the Fifth Conference on Mental Health, "Women and Madness," Montreal, 31 May).
- Translated into English as: "The Bodily Encounter with the Mother" (1991).
- Published in: *Le corps-à-corps avec la mère* (1981).
- Reprinted in: *Sexes et parentés* (1987).

1980. "Interview: Paris, Summer 1980." Interview by Lucienne Serrano and Elaine Hoffman Baruch.
- Published in: *Women Writers Talking*, edited by Janet Todd. New York: Holmes and Meier Publishers, 1983.
- Reprinted in: *Women Analyze Women in France, England and the United States* (1988).

1980. "La croyance même" (lecture delivered at a conference on the work of Jacques Derrida: *The Ends of Man*, Cerisy-la-Salle, 10 August).
- Translated into English as: "He Risks Who Risks Life Itself" (1991).
- Published in: *Sexes et parentés* (1987).
- Also published as: *La croyance même* (1983).

1980. "L'Autre de la nature." Conversation with Xavière Gauthier, Anne-Marie de la Vilaine, and Françoise Clédat. In *Sorcières* 20: 14–25.

1980. "Les femmes-mères: ce sous-sol muet de l'ordre." Interview by Pleine Lune. In *Le corps-à-corps avec la mère*.
- Translated into English as: "Women-Mothers, the Silent Substratum of the Social Order" (1991).

1981. *Le corps-à-corps avec la mère*. Montreal: Editions de la Pleine Lune.

1981. "And the One Doesn't Stir Without the Other." Translated by Hélène Vivienne Wenzel. In *Signs* 7:1 (Autumn): 60–67.
- Translation of: *Et l'une ne bouge pas sans l'autre* (1979).
- Reprinted in: *Refractory Girl* 23 (1982): 12–14 [as "One Does Not Move Without the Other"] and *Feminist Social Thought: A Reader* (1997).

1981. "When Our Lips Speak Together." Translated by Carolyn Burke. In *Signs* 6:1 (Fall): 69–79.

- Translation of: "Quand nos lèvres se parlent" (1976).
- Reprinted in: *This Sex Which Is Not One* (1985), *Feminist Theory and the Body: A Reader* (1999), *The Routledge Language and Cultural Theory Reader* (2000), and *The Gendered Cyborg: A Reader* (2000).

1982. *Passions élémentaires*. Paris: Editions de Minuit.
- Translated into English as: *Elemental Passions* (1992).

1982. "L'Amour du transfert." In *Etudes freudiennes* 19–20 (May).
- Translated into English as: "The Limits of Transference" (1991).
- Reprinted in: *Parler n'est jamais neutre* (1985) [as "La limite du transfert"].

1982. "Le prix de la sérénité." In *Exercices de la patience* (3–4): 155–66.

1982. "La différence sexuelle" (lecture delivered 21 September at Erasmus University, Rotterdam).
- Translated into English as: "Sexual Difference" (1987).
- Published in: *Ethique de la différence sexuelle* (1984).

1982. "L'amour sorcier (Lecture de Platon. *Le Banquet*, 'Discours de Diotime')" (lecture delivered 22 September at Erasmus University, Rotterdam).
- Translated into English as: "Sorcerer Love: A Reading of Plato, *Symposium*, 'Diotima's Speech'" (1989).
- Published in: *Ethique de la différence sexuelle* (1984).

1982. "Le lieu, l'intervalle (Lecture d'Aristote. *Physique* IV, 2, 3, 4, 5)" (lecture delivered 22 September at Erasmus University, Rotterdam).
- Translated into English as: "Place, Interval: A Reading of Aristotle, *Physics* IV" (1993).
- Published in: *Ethique de la différence sexuelle* (1984).

1982. "L'amour de soi" (lecture delivered 19 October at Erasmus University, Rotterdam).
- Translated into English as: "Love of Self" (1993).
- Published in: *Ethique de la différence sexuelle* (1984).

1982. "L'admiration (Lecture de Descartes. *Les passions de l'âme*, art. 53)" (lecture delivered 20 October at Erasmus University, Rotterdam).
- Translated into English as: "Wonder: A Reading of Descartes, *The Passions of the Soul*" (1993).
- Published in: *Ethique de la différence sexuelle* (1984).

1982. "L'enveloppe (Lecture de Spinoza. *L'éthique*, 'De Dieu')" (lecture delivered 20 October at Erasmus University, Rotterdam).
- Translated into English as: "The Envelope: A Reading of Spinoza, *Ethics*, 'Of God'" (1993).
- Published in: *Ethique de la différence sexuelle* (1984).

1982. "L'amour du même, l'amour de l'Autre" (lecture delivered 16 November at Erasmus University, Rotterdam).
- Translated into English as: "Love of Same, Love of Other" (1993).
- Published in: *Ethique de la différence sexuelle* (1984).

1982. "Ethique de la différence sexuelle" (lecture delivered 18 November at Erasmus University, Rotterdam).

- Translated into English as: "An Ethics of Sexual Difference" (1993).
- Published in: *Ethique de la différence sexuelle* (1984).

1982. "Le sujet de la science est-il sexué?" In *les Temps modernes* (November).
- Translated into English as: "Is the Subject of Science Sexed?" (1985).
- Reprinted in: *Parler n'est jamais neutre* (1985) and *Sens et place des connaissances dans la société* (1988) [as "Sujet de la science, sujet sexué?"].

1982. "L'amour de l'autre" (lecture delivered 13 December at Erasmus University, Rotterdam).
- Translated into English as: "Love of the Other" (1993).
- Published in: *Ethique de la différence sexuelle* (1984).

1982. "L'invisible de la chair (Lecture de Merleau-Ponty. *Le visible et l'invisible*, 'L'entrelacs—le chiasme')" (lecture delivered 14 December at Erasmus University, Rotterdam).
- Translated into English as: "The Invisible of the Flesh: A Reading of Merleau-Ponty, *The Visible and the Invisible*, 'The Intertwining—The Chiasm' " (1993).
- Published in: *Ethique de la différence sexuelle* (1984).

1982. "Fécondité de la caresse (Lecture de Lévinas. *Totalité et infini*, Section IV, B, 'Phénoménologie de l'éros')" (lecture delivered 14 December at Erasmus University, Rotterdam).
- Translated into English as: "The Fecundity of the Caress: A Reading of Levinas, *Totality and Infinity*, 'Phenomenology of Eros' " (1993).
- Published in: *Exercises de la patience* 5 (Spring 1983): 119–37.
- Reprinted in: *Ethique de la différence sexuelle* (1984).

1983. *La croyance même*. Paris: Editions Galilée.
- Also published as: "La croyance même" (1980).
- Reprinted (with slight alterations) in: *Sexes et parentés* (1987).

1983. *L'oubli de l'air chez Martin Heidegger*. Paris: Editions de Minuit.
- Translated into English as: *The Forgetting of Air in Martin Heidegger* (1999).

1983. "Où et comment habiter?" In *Cahiers du Grif* 24 (March): 139–43.

1983. "An Interview with Luce Irigaray." Interview by Kiki Amsberg and Aafke Steenhuis. Translated by Robert van Krieken. In *Hecate* 9 (1/2): 192–202.
- Also known as: "For Centuries We've Been Living in the Mother-Son Relation."

1980. "Veiled Lips." Translated by Sara Speidel. In *Mississippi Review* 11 (Winter/Spring): 93–131.
- Extracts from: "Lèvres voilées" (1980).
- Full translation in: *Marine Lover of Friedrich Nietzsche* (1991).

1984. *Ethique de la différence sexuelle*. Paris: Editions de Minuit.
- Translated into English as: *An Ethics of Sexual Difference* (1993).

1984. "Femmes divines" (lecture delivered at an interdisciplinary conference organized by the Women's Center on *Melusine*, Venice-Mestre, 8 June).
- Translated into English as: *Divine Women* (1986).

- Published in: *Critique* 41 (1985): 294–308
- Reprinted in: *Cross-References: Modern French Theory and the Practice of Criticism* (1986) and *Sexes et parentés* (1987).

1984. "Les femmes, le sacré, l'argent" (lecture delivered at the C.E.F.U.P. Conference at the University of Aix-Marseille on "Woman and Money," Aix-en-Provence, 17 November).
- Translated into English as: "Women, The Sacred, Money" (1986).
- Published in: *Sexes et parentés* (1987).

1985. *Parler n'est jamais neutre*. Paris: Editions de Minuit.
- Translated into English as: *To Speak Is Never Neutral* (2002).

1985. *Speculum of the Other Woman*. Translated by Gillian C. Gill. Ithaca, N.Y.: Cornell University Press.
- Translation of: *Speculum de l'autre femme* (1974).

1985. *This Sex Which Is Not One*. Translated by Catherine Porter. Ithaca, N.Y.: Cornell University Press.
- Translation of: *Ce sexe qui n'en est pas un* (1977).

1985. "The Stage Setup." In *Speculum of the Other Woman*.
- Translation of: "Le praticable de la scène" (1974).
- Reprinted in: *Mimesis, Masochism, and Mime* (1997).

1985. "Female Hom(m)osexuality." In *Speculum of the Other Woman*.
- Translation of: "L'hom(m)osexualité feminine" (1974).
- Reprinted in: *The Material Queer: A LesBiGay Cultural Studies Reader* (1996).

1985. "The Eternal Irony of the Community." In *Speculum of the Other Woman*.
- Translation of: ". . . éternelle ironie de la communauté . . ." (1974).
- Reprinted in: *Feminist Interpretations of G. W. F. Hegel* (1996).

1985. "Any Theory of the 'Subject' Has Always Been Appropriated by the 'Masculine.' " In *Speculum of the Other Woman*.
- Translation of: "Toute théorie du 'sujet' aura toujours été appropriée au 'masculin' " (1974).
- Reprinted in: *Trivia* 6 (Winter 1985): 133–46, *Art and its Significance: An Anthology of Aesthetic Theory* (1994), and *The Feminism and Visual Culture Reader* (2003).

1985. "Another 'Cause'—Castration." In *Speculum of the Other Woman*.
- Translation of: "Une 'cause' encore: la castration" (1974).
- Reprinted in: *Feminisms: An Anthology of Literary Theory and Criticism* (1991).

1985. "Volume-Fluidity." In *Speculum of the Other Woman*.
- Translation of: "L'incontournable volume" (1974).
- Reprinted in: *The Irigaray Reader* (1991) [as "Volume without Contours"].

1985. "The Looking Glass, from the Other Side." In *This Sex Which Is Not One*.
- Translation of: "Le miroir, de l'autre côté" (1973).

1985. "Psychoanalytic Theory: Another Look." In *This Sex Which Is Not One.*
   • Translation of: "Retour sur la théorie psychanalytique" (1973).
1985. "The 'Mechanics' of Fluids." In *This Sex Which Is Not One.*
   • Translation of: "La 'mécanique' des fluides" (1974).
1985. "The Power of Discourse and the Subordination of the Feminine." In *This Sex Which Is Not One.*
   • Translation of: "Pouvoir du discours / subordination du féminin" (1975).
   • Reprinted in: *The Irigaray Reader* (1991), *Feminist Theory: A Reader* (1996), *The Continental Philosophy Reader* (1996), and *Literary Theory: An Anthology* (1998).
1985. "Così fan tutti." In *This Sex Which Is Not One.*
   • Translation of: "Così fan tutti" (1975).
1985. "Women on the Market." In *This Sex Which Is Not One.*
   • Translation of: "Le marché des femmes" (1976).
   • Reprinted in: *The Logic of the Gift: Toward an Ethic of Generosity* (1997) and *French Feminism Reader* (2000).
1985. " 'Frenchwomen,' Stop Trying." In *This Sex Which Is Not One.*
   • Translation of: " 'Françaises,' ne faites plus un effort" (1976).
1985. "Questions." In *This Sex Which Is Not One.*
   • Translation of: "Questions" (1977).
   • Reprinted in: *The Irigaray Reader* (1991) [extracts] and *Feminist Philosophies: Problems, Theories, and Applications* (1992).
1985. "Questions I." In *This Sex Which Is Not One* [as part of chapter "Questions" (1985)].
   • Translation of: "Questions I" (1974).
   • Reprinted in: *French Feminism Reader* (2000) [as "This Sex Which Is Not One"].
1985. "Questions II." In *This Sex Which Is Not One* [as part of chapter "Questions" (1985)].
   • Translation of: "Questions II" (1975).
1985. "Question IV." In *This Sex Which Is Not One* [as part of chapter "Questions" (1985)].
   • Translation of: "Question IV" (1974).
1985. "Questions about the Premises of Psychoanalytic Theory." In *This Sex Which Is Not One* [as part of chapter "Psychoanalytic Theory: Another Look" (1985)].
   • Translation of: "Questions sur les prémisses de la théorie psychanalytique" (1977).
   • Reprinted in: *The Material Queer: A LesBiGay Cultural Studies Reader* (1996).
1985. "Une lacune natale." In *Le nouveau commerce* 62–63, 39–47.
   • Translated into English as: "A Natal Lacuna" (1994).

1985. "The Difference Between the Sexes." Interview by Roger-Pol Droit (originally published in French in *Le monde* (7 June)).
   • Reprinted in: *Why Different? A Culture of Two Subjects* (2000).

1985. "Is the Subject of Science Sexed?" Translated by Edith Oberle. In *Cultural Critique* 1 (Fall): 73–88.
   • Translation of: "Le sujet de la science est-il sexué?" (1982).
   • Reprinted in: *Hypatia* 2 (Fall 1987): 65–87, *Feminism and Science* (1989), and *To Speak Is Never Neutral* (2002).

1985. "Sorella donna, libera nos" (with Franca Chiaromonte). In *Rinascita* (September).
   • Translated into English as: "Women-Amongst-Themselves: Creating a Woman-to-Woman Sociality" (1991).

1985. "Créer un Entre-Femmes" (originally published in Italian in *Rinascita* (28 September)).
   • Reprinted in: *Paris-Féministe* 31–32 (September 1986): 37–41.

1985. "Le geste en psychanalyse" (lecture delivered at a conference organized by the L.A.R.P. at the French Institute: "The Transmission of Private Experience: Image, Writing, Voice," Florence, 2 November).
   • Translated into English as: "Gesture in Psychoanalysis" (1989).
   • Published in: *Sexes et parentés* (1987).

1985. "Le genre féminin" (lecture delivered at a conference at Erasmus University: "The Other and Thinking About Difference," Rotterdam, 14 November).
   • Translated into English as: "The Female Gender" (1993).
   • Published in: *Sexes et parentés* (1987).

1985–86. "Language, Persephone, and Sacrifice." Interview by Heather Jon Maroney. Translated by Heather Jon Maroney. In *Borderlines* 4 (Winter): 30–32.

1986. *Divine Women*. Translated by Stephen Muecke. Sydney: Local Consumption Occasional Papers, no. 8.
   • Translation of: "Femmes divines" (1984).
   • Also published as: "Divine Women" (1993).

1986. "The Fecundity of the Caress: A Reading of Levinas, *Totality and Infinity*, 'Phenomenology of Eros.' " Translated by Carolyn Burke. In *Face to Face with Levinas*, edited by Richard A. Cohen. Albany: State University of New York Press.
   • Translation of: "Fécondité de la caresse (Lecture de Lévinas. *Totalité et infini*, Section IV, B, 'Phénoménologie de l'éros')" (1982).
   • Reprinted in: *An Ethics of Sexual Difference* (1993) and *Feminist Interpretations of Emmanuel Levinas* (2001).

1986. "L'universel comme médiation" (lecture delivered at the Sixteenth Annual Hegel Conference at the University of Zurich, 25 March).
   • Translated into English as: "The Universal as Mediation" (1993).
   • Published in: *Sexes et parentés* (1987).

1986. "Les couleurs de la chair" (lecture deliverd at a seminar on psycho-analysis organized by the L.A.R.P., Ancona, 5 April).
  • Translated into English as: "Flesh Colors" (1993).
  • Published in: Sexes et parentés (1987).

1986. "Egales ou différentes?" (originally published in German in Die Tageszeitung, on the occasion of the death of Simone de Beauvoir, 19 April).
  • Translated into English as: "Equal or Different?" (1991).
  • Reprinted in: Paris-Féministe 61 (April), Fluttuaria 6–7 (March–June) Je, tu, nous: Pour une culture de la différence (1990).

1986. "Les trois genres" (lecture delivered at a conference organized by the Centro documentazione donna and the Libreria delle donne: Il viaggo, Florence, 11 May).
  • Translated into English as: "The Three Genders" (1991).
  • Published in: Sexes et parentés (1987).

1986. "Une chance de vivre" (lecture delivered at the festival of women of the Italian Communist Party, organized around the theme: "Life after Chernobyl," Tirrenia, 22 July).
  • Translated into English as: "A Chance for Life" (1993).
  • Published in: Sexes et parentés (1987).
  • Reprinted in: Le temps de la différence: Pour une révolution pacifique (1989).

1986. "Women, The Sacred, Money." Translated by Diana Knight and Margaret Whitford. In Paragraph 8 (October): 6–18.
  • Translation of: "Les femmes, le sacré, l'argent" (1984).
  • Reprinted in: Sexes and Genealogies (1993) and Psychoanalytic Criticism: A Reader (1996).

1986. "Le Religieux comme droit féminin" (open letter to the Pope on the occasion of his visit to France). In Paris-Féministe 34 (1–15 November): 15.

1986. "Le Christianisme, religion de l'incarnation?" (open letter to the Pope on the occasion of his visit to France). In Paris-Féministe 34 (1–15 November): 16.

1987. Sexes et parentés. Paris: Editions de Minuit.
  • Translated into English as: Sexes and Genealogies (1993).

1987. Zur Geschlechter Differenz: Interviews and Vortrage. Vienna: Wiener Frauenverlag.

1987. "La nécessité de droits sexués." In Sexes et parentés.
  • Translated into English as: "The Necessity for Sexuate Rights" (1991).

1987. "Sexual Difference." Translated by Seán Hand. In French Feminist Thought: A Reader, edited by Toril Moi. Oxford: Basil Blackwell.
  • Translation of: "La différence sexuelle" (1982).
  • Reprinted in: The Irigaray Reader (1991), An Ethics of Sexual Difference (1993), Continental Philosophy: An Anthology (1998), French Feminism

Reader (2000) [as "An Ethics of Sexual Difference"], and *Modern Literary Theory* (2001).

1987. ed. *Le sexe linguistique*. Special edition of *Langages* 85 (March). Paris: Larousse.

1987. "Présentation." In *Le sexe linguistique*.
- A revised version appears as: "L'oubli des généalogies féminines" (1987).

1987. "La placenta comme tiers." In *Le sexe linguistique*.

1987. "Le penseur neutre était une femme." In *Le sexe linguistique*.

1987. "L'ordre sexuel du discours." In *Le sexe linguistique* (1987).
- Translated into English as: "Women's Discourse and Men's Discourse" (1993).
- Reprinted in: *Je, tu, nous: pour une culture de la différence* (1990).

1987. "L'oubli des généalogies féminines" (March).
- Translated into English as: "The Neglect of Female Genealogies" (1993).
- A revision of: "Présentation" (1987).
- Published in: *Je, tu, nous: Pour une culture de la différence* (1990).

1987. "Mythes religieux et civils" (originally published in Italian in *Rinascita* (18 April)).
- Translated into English as: "Religious and Civil Myths" (1993).
- Published in: *Je, tu, nous: Pour une culture de la différence* (1990).

1987. "Egales à qui?" (review of Elisabeth Schüssler Fiorenza's book *In Memory of Her*). In *Critique* 43 (May): 420–37.
- Translated into English as: "Equal to Whom?" (1989).

1987. "A propos de l'ordre maternel" (July).
- Translated into English as: "On the Maternal Order" (1993).
- Published in: *Je, tu, nous: Pour une culture de la différence* (1990).

1987. "La culture de la différence" (September).
- Translated into English as: "The Culture of Difference" (1987).
- Published in: *Resources for Feminist Research* 16 (December).
- Reprinted in: *Je, tu, nous: Pour une culture de la différence* (1990).

1987. "Sexes et genres linguistiques" (October).
- Translated into English as: "Linguistic Sexes and Genders" (1993).
- Published in: *Je, tu, nous: Pour une culture de la différence* (1990).

1987. " 'Le sida ne passera pas par moi' " (October).
- Translated into English as: " 'I Won't Get AIDS' " (1993).
- Published in: *Paris-Féministe* 74 (December 1998): 24–27.
- Reprinted in: *Je, tu, nous: Pour une culture de la différence* (1990).

1987. "Le droit à la vie" (November).
- Translated into English as: "The Right to Life" (1993).
- Published in: *Je, tu, nous: Pour une culture de la différence* (1990).

1987. "A quand notre devenir femmes?" (originally published in *Fluttuaria*, Milan, November).
- Reprinted in: *Paris-Féministe* 74 (December 1988): 24–27.

1987. "Writing as a Woman" (as part of a study on women's writing). Interview by Alice Jardine and Anne Menke. In *Yale French Studies* 75: 244–46 [excerpts].
   • Appears in French as: "Écrire en tant que femme" (1990).
   • Full interview published in: *Shifting Scenes: Interviews on Women, Writing, and Politics in Post-68 France.* Translated by Margaret Whitford. Edited by Alice Jardine and Anne Menke. New York: Columbia University Press.
   • Reprinted in: *Displacements: Women, Tradition, Literatures in French* (1991), *Je, tu, nous: Toward a Culture of Difference* (1993), and *Feminism-Art-Theory: An Anthology* (2001).

1987. "Luce Irigaray." Interview by Raoul Mortley.
   • Published in: *French Philosophers in Conversation: Derrida, Irigaray, Levinas, Le Doeuff, Schneider, Serres.* London: Routledge, 1991.

1988. " 'Plus femmes qu'hommes' " (January).
   • Translated into English as: " 'More Women Than Men' " (1993).
   • Published in: *Je, tu, nous: Pour une culture de la différence* (1990).

1988. "C'est quoi ou qui, ta santé?" (February).
   • Translated into English as: "Your Health: What, or Who, Is It?" (1993).
   • Published in: *Je, tu, nous: Pour une culture de la différence* (1990).

1988. "Comment créer notre beauté?" (March).
   • Translated into English as: "How Can We Create Our Beauty?" (1993).
   • Published in: *Je, tu, nous: Pour une culture de la différence* (1990).

1988. "Quel âge as-tu?" (April).
   • Translated into English as: "How Old Are You?" (1993).
   • Published in: *Je, tu, nous: Pour une culture de la différence* (1990).

1988. "Comment devenir des femmes civiles?" (preparation for the panel "Women's Time," Rome, 8 April).
   • Translated into English as: "How Do We Become Civil Women?" (1994).
   • Published in: *Le Temps de la différence: Pour une révolution pacifique* (1989).

1988. "Il sesso della legge." Interview by Christina Lasagni. In *Il Diritto Delle Donne* 1 (May).
   • Translated into French as: "Pourquoi définir des droits sexués?" (1990).

1988. "Droits et devoirs civils pour les deux sexes" (lecture delivered at the Unità Festival, Florence, 10 September).
   • Translated into English as: "Civil Rights and Responsibilities for the Two Sexes" (1994).
   • Published in: *Le Temps de la différence: Pour une révolution pacifique* (1989).

1988–89. "L'ordre sexuel de la langage et du discours" (lecture delivered at the Collège International de Philosophie, Paris).

1989. "Le mystère oublié des généalogies féminines" (lectures delivered in Syracuse, 31 March, Palermo, 3 April, and Terni, 2 June).
- Translated into English as: "The Forgotten Mystery of Female Ancestry" (1994).
- Published in: *Le Temps de la différence: Pour une révolution pacifique* (1989).

1989. *Il Tempo della differenza. Dirritti e doveri per i sessi. Per una rivoluzione pacifica.* Rome: Editori Riuniti.
- Translated into French as: *Le Temps de la différence: Pour une révolution pacifique* (1989).

1989. *Le Temps de la différence: Pour une révolution pacifique.* Paris: Librairie Générale Française.
- Translation of: *Il Tempo della differenza. Dirritti e doveri per i sessi. Per una rivoluzione pacifica* (1989).
- Translated into English as: *Thinking the Difference: For a Peaceful Revolution* (1994).

1989. ed. *Il divino conceptio da noi.* Special edition of *Inchiesta* 19. Bari: Dedalo.

1989. "Gesture in Psychoanalysis." Translated by Elizabeth Guild. In *Between Feminism and Psychoanalysis*, edited by Teresa Brennan. London: Routledge.
- Translation of: "Le geste en psychanalyse" (1985).
- Reprinted in: *Sexes and Genealogies* (1993).

1989. "Le temps de la vie." In *Présences de Schopenhauer*, edited by Roger-Pol Droit. Paris: Bernard Grasset.
- Translated into English as: "The Time of Life" (2002).
- Reprinted in: *Entre orient et occident: de la singularité à la communauté* (1999).

1989. "Le coût des mots" (May).
- Translated into English as: "The Cost of Words" (1993).
- Published in: *Je, tu, nous: Pour une culture de la différence* (1990).

1989. "Equal to Whom?" Translated by Robert L. Mazzola. In *Differences* 1 (Summer): 59–76.
- Translation of: "Egales à qui?" (1987).
- Reprinted in: *The Essential Difference* (1994).

1989. "Pour Introduire: L'amour entre nous" (lecture delivered for the Italian Federation of Young Communists in July and September).
- Translated into English as: "Introducing: Love Between Us" (1991).
- Published in: *J'aime à toi* (1992).

1989. "The Language of Man (The Sexuation of Discourse)." Translated by Erin G. Carlston. In *Cultural Critique* 13 (Fall): 191–202.
- Translation of: "Le langage de l'homme" (1978).
- Reprinted in: *To Speak Is Never Neutral* (2002).

1989. "Sorcerer Love: A Reading of Plato, *Symposium*, 'Diotima's Speech.'" Translated by Eleanor H. Kuykendall. In *Hypatia* 3 (Winter): 32–44.

- Translation of: "L'amour sorcier (Lecture de Platon. *Le Banquet*, 'Discours de Diotime')" (1982).
- Reprinted in: *Revaluing French Feminism: Critical Essays on Difference, Agency, and Culture* (1992), An *Ethics of Sexual Difference* (1993), *Feminist Interpretations of Plato* (1994), *Feminism and Philosophy* (1994), and *Feminism and History of Philosophy* (2002).

1990. ed. *Sexes et genres à travers les langues: éléments de communication sexuée: français, anglais, italien.* Paris: Bernard Grasset.

1990. *Je, tu, nous: Pour une culture de la différence.* Paris: Bernard Grasset.
- Translated into English as: *Je, tu, nous: Toward a Culture of Difference* (1993).

1990. "Introduction." In *Sexes et genres à travers les langues: éléments de communication sexuée: français, anglais, italien.*

1990. "Représentation et auto-affection du feminin." In *Sexes et genres à travers les langues: éléments de communication sexuée: français, anglais, italien.*

1990. "Conclusions." In *Sexes et genres à travers les langues: éléments de communication sexuée: français, anglais, italien.*

1990. "Écrire en tant que femme." In *Je, tu, nous: Pour une culture de la différence.*
- Appears in English as: "Writing as a Woman" (1987).

1990. "Pourquoi définir des droits sexués?" In *Je, tu, nous: Pour une culture de la différence.*
- Translated into English as: "How to Define Sexuate Rights" (1991).
- Translation of: "Il sesso della legge" (1988).

1990. "The Culture of Difference." In *Pli* 3 (Spring): 44–52.
- Translation of: "La culture de la différence" (1987).
- Reprinted in: *Je, tu, nous: Toward a Culture of Difference* (1993).

1990. "A Bridge Between Two Irreducible to Each Other." Interview by Rosella Bofiglioli (originally published in Italian in *Il Manifesto* (3 July)).
- Reprinted in: *Why Different? A Culture of Two Subjects* (2000).

1990. "Questions à Emmanuel Lévinas sur la divinité de l'amour." In *Critique* 522 (November): 911–20.
- Translated into English as: "Questions to Emmanuel Levinas: On the Divinity of Love" (1991).

1991. *The Irigaray Reader.* Edited by Margaret Whitford. Cambridge, Mass.: Blackwell.

1991. *Marine Lover of Friedrich Nietzsche.* Translated by Gillian C. Gill. New York: Columbia University Press.
- Translation of: *Amante Marine de Friedrich Nietzsche* (1980).

1991. "How to Define Sexuate Rights." Translated by David Macey. In *The Irigaray Reader.*
- Translation of: "Pourquoi définir des droits sexués?" (1990).

- Reprinted in: *Je, tu, nous: Toward a Culture of Difference* (1993) [as "Why Define Sexed Rights?"].

1991. "The Bodily Encounter with the Mother." Translated by David Macey. In *The Irigaray Reader*.
- Translation of: "Le corps-à-corps avec la mère" (1980).
- Reprinted in: *Sexes and Genealogies* (1993) [as "Body Against Body: In Relation to the Mother"] and *French Feminism Reader* (2000) [as "Body Against Body: In Relation to the Mother"].

1991. "The Necessity for Sexuate Rights." Translated by David Macey. In *The Irigaray Reader*.
- Translation of: "La nécessité de droits sexués" (1987).
- Reprinted in: *Sexes and Genealogies* (1993) [as "Each Sex Must Have Its Own Rights"] and *French Feminism Reader* (2000) [as "Sexes and Genealogies: Each Sex Must Have Its Own Rights"].

1991. "He Risks Who Risks Life Itself." Translated by David Macey. In *The Irigaray Reader*.
- Translation of: "La croyance même" (1980).
- Reprinted in: *Sexes and Genealogies* (1993) [as "Belief Itself"].

1991. "The Three Genres." Translated by David Macey. In *The Irigaray Reader*.
- Translation of: "Les trois genres" (1986).
- Reprinted in: *Sexes and Genealogies* (1993) [as "The Three Genders"] and *Postmodern Literary Theory: An Anthology* (2000).

1991. "Women-Mothers, the Silent Substratum of the Social Order." Translated by David Macey. In *The Irigaray Reader*.
- Translation of: "Les femmes-mères: ce sous-sol muet de l'ordre social" (1980).

1991. "The Poverty of Psychoanalysis." Translated by David Macey and Margaret Whitford. In *The Irigaray Reader*.
- Translation of: "Misère de la psychanalyse" (1977).
- Reprinted in: *To Speak Is Never Neutral* (2002).

1991. "The Limits of Transference." Translated by David Macey and Margaret Whitford. In *The Irigaray Reader*.
- Translation of: "La limite du transfert" (1982).
- Reprinted in: *To Speak Is Never Neutral* (2002).

1991. "Women-Amongst-Themselves: Creating a Woman-to-Woman Sociality" (with Franca Chiarmonte). Translated by David Macey. In *The Irigaray Reader*.
- Translation of: "Sorrella donna, libera nos" (1985).

1991. "Equal or Different?" Translated by David Macey. In *The Irigaray Reader*.
- Translation of: "Egales ou differentes?" (1986).
- Reprinted in: *Je, tu, nous: Toward a Culture of Difference* (1993) and *Women's Studies: Essential Readings* (1993) [as "Women: Equal or Different?"].

1991. "Questions to Emmanuel Levinas: On the Divinity of Love." Translated by Margaret Whitford. In *Rereading Levinas*, edited by Robert Bernasconi and Simon Critchely. Bloomington: Indiana University Press.
  • Translation of: "Questions à Emmanuel Lévinas sur la divinité de l'amour" (1990).
  • Reprinted in: *The Irigaray Reader* (1991).
1991. "Introducing: Love Between Us." Translated by Jeffrey Lomonaco. In *Who Comes After the Subject?*, edited by Eduardo Cadava, Peter Conor, and Jean-Luc Nancy. London: Routledge.
  • Translation of: "Pour Introduire: L'amour entre nous" (1989).
  • Reprinted in: *Women: A Cultural Review* 6 (Autumn 1995): 180–90 and *I Love to You: Sketch for a Felicity Within History* (1996).
1991. "Do We Speak to Each Other in the Feminine?" Interview by Odette Brun (originally published in French in *Paris Féministe* 116 (March)).
  • Reprinted in: *Why Different? A Culture of Two Subjects* (2000).
1991. "Historical Perspectives." Interview by Chiara Valentini (originally published in Italian in *Expresso* (July)).
  • Reprinted in: *Why Different? A Culture of Two Subjects* (2000).
1990. "Ecce Mulier?" Translated by Madeleine Dobie. In *Graduate Philosophy Journal* 15(2): 144–58.
  • Reprinted in: *Nietzsche and the Feminine* (1994).
1992. *J'aime à toi: esquisse d'une félicité dans l'histoire*. Paris: Bernard Grasset.
  • Translated into English as: *I Love to You: Sketch for a Felicity Within History* (1996).
1992. *Elemental Passions*. Translated by Joanne Collie and Judith Still. New York: Routledge.
  • Translation of: *Passions élémentaires* (1982).
1992. "Je l'ai cherché et ne l'ai pas trouvé." In *J'aime à toi: esquisse d'une félicité dans l'histoire*.
  • Translated into English as: "He I Sought But Did Not Find" (1996).
1992. "L'autre: femme." In *J'aime à toi: esquisse d'une félicité dans l'histoire*.
  • Translated into English as: "The Other: Woman" (1996).
1992. "Toi qui ne seras jamais mien." In *J'aime à toi: esquisse d'une félicité dans l'histoire*.
  • Translated into English as: "You Who Will Never Be Mine" (1996).
1992. "A deux dehors demain?" In *J'aime à toi: esquisse d'une félicité dans l'histoire*.
  • Translated into English as: "Two of Us, Outside, Tomorrow?" (1996).
1992. "Comment nous parler dans l'horizon du Socialisme?" In *L'idée du socialisme a-t-elle un avenir?*, edited by J. Bidet and J. Texier. Paris: PUF.
  • Translated into English as: "How Can We Speak with Socialism as Our Horizon?" (2004).

1992. "Una cultura a due soggetti" (lecture delivered at the seminar "European and French contributions to equality of opportunity for girls and
boys," Paris, 22 May).
 • Translated into English as: "A Two-Subject Culture" (2001).
 • Published in: La democrazia comincia a due (1994).
1991. "The Question For Our Time." Interview by Elke Weber (originally
published in Italian in Taz).
 • Reprinted in: Why Different? A Culture of Two Subjects (2000).
1993. An Ethics of Sexual Difference. Translated by Carolyn Burke and Gillian
C. Gill. Ithaca, N.Y.: Cornell University Press.
 • Translation of: Ethique de la différence sexuelle (1984).
1993. Je, tu, nous: Toward a Culture of Difference. Translated by Alison Martin.
New York: Routledge.
 • Translation of: Je, tu, nous: Pour une culture de la différence (1990).
1993. Sexes and Genealogies. Translated by Gillian C. Gill. New York: Colum-
bia University Press.
 • Translation of: Sexes et parentés (1987).
1993. "Place, Interval: A Reading of Aristotle, Physics IV." In An Ethics of
Sexual Difference.
 • Translation of: "Le lieu, l'intervalle (Lecture d'Aristote. Physique IV,
2, 3, 4, 5)" (1982).
 • Reprinted in: Feminist Interpretations of Aristotle (1998).
1993. "Love of Self." In An Ethics of Sexual Difference.
 • Translation of: "L'amour de soi" (1982).
1993. "Wonder: A Reading of Descartes, The Passions of the Soul." In An
Ethics of Sexual Difference.
 • Translation of: "L'admiration (Lecture de Descartes. Les passions de
l'âme, art. 53)" (1982).
 • Reprinted in: Feminist Interpretations of René Descartes (1999).
1993. "The Envelope: A Reading of Spinoza, Ethics, 'Of God.' " In An Ethics
of Sexual Difference.
 • Translation of: "L'enveloppe (Lecture de Spinoza. L'éthique, 'De
Dieu')" (1982).
 • Reprinted in: The New Spinoza (1997).
1993. "Love of Same, Love of Other." In An Ethics of Sexual Difference.
 • Translation of: "L'amour du même, l'amour de l'Autre" (1982).
1993. "An Ethics of Sexual Difference." In An Ethics of Sexual Difference.
 • Translation of: "Ethique de la différence sexuelle" (1982).
1993. "Love of the Other." In An Ethics of Sexual Difference.
 • Translation of: "L'amour de l'autre" (1982).
1993. "The Invisible of the Flesh: A Reading of Merleau-Ponty, The Visible
and the Invisible, 'The Intertwining—The Chiasm.' " In An Ethics of
Sexual Difference.
 • Reprinted in: The Continental Aesthetics Reader (2000).

1993. "The Neglect of Female Genealogies." In *Je, tu, nous: Toward a Culture of Difference.*
  • Translation of: "L'oubli des généalogies féminines" (1987).
1993. "Religious and Civil Myths." In *Je, tu, nous: Toward a Culture of Difference.*
  • Translation of: "Mythes religieux et civils" (1987).
1993. "On the Maternal Order." In *Je, tu, nous: Toward a Culture of Difference.*
  • Translation of: "A propos de l'ordre maternel" (1987).
1993. "Linguistic Sexes and Genders." In *Je, tu, nous: Toward a Culture of Difference.*
  • Translation of: "Sexes et genres linguistiques" (1987).
  • Reprinted in: *Philosophy and Sex* (1998) and *The Feminist Critique of Language: A Reader* (1998).
1993. " 'I Won't Get AIDS.' " In *Je, tu, nous: Toward a Culture of Difference.*
  • Translation of: " 'Le sida ne passera pas par moi' " (1987).
1993. "The Right to Life." In *Je, tu, nous: Toward a Culture of Difference.*
  • Translation of: "La droit à la vie" (1987).
1993. " 'More Women Than Men.' " In *Je, tu, nous: Toward a Culture of Difference.*
  • Translation of: " 'Plus femmes qu'hommes' " (1988).
1993. "Your Health: What, or Who, Is It?" In *Je, tu, nous: Toward a Culture of Difference.*
  • Translation of: "C'est quoi ou qui, ta santé?" (1988).
1993. "How Can We Create Our Beauty?" In *Je, tu, nous: Toward a Culture of Difference.*
  • Translation of: "Comment créer notre beauté?" (1988).
  • Reprinted in: *Feminism-Art-Theory: An Anthology* (2001).
1993. "How Old Are You?" In *Je, tu, nous: Toward a Culture of Difference.*
  • Translation of: "Quel âge as-tu?" (1988).
1993. "The Cost of Words." In *Je, tu, nous: Toward a Culture of Difference.*
  • Translation of: "Le coût des mots" (1989).
1993. "Women's Discourse and Men's Discourse." In *Je, tu, nous: Toward a Culture of Difference.*
  • Translation of: "L'ordre sexuel du discours" (1987).
1993. "The Female Gender." In *Sexes and Genealogies.*
  • Translation of: "Le genre féminin" (1985).
1993. "The Universal as Mediation." In *Sexes and Genealogies.*
  • Translation of: "L'universel comme médiation" (1986).
1993. "Flesh Colors." In *Sexes and Genealogies.*
  • Translation of: "Les couleurs de la chair" (1986).
  • Reprinted in: *Luce Irigaray: Key Writings* (2004) [as "Flesh Colours"].
1993. "A Chance for Life." In *Sexes and Genealogies.*
  • Translation of: "Une chance de vivre" (1986).

• Reprinted in: *Thinking the Difference: For a Peaceful Revolution* (1994) [as "A Chance to Live"] and *The City Cultures Reader* (2000) [as "A Chance to Live"].

1993. "Divine Women." In *Sexes and Genealogies*.
   • Translation of: "Femmes divines" (1984).
   • Reprinted in: *Women, Knowledge, and Reality: Explorations in Feminist Philosophy* (1996).
   • Also published as: *Divine Women* (1986).

1993. "Transcendants l'un à l'autre." In *Homme et femme, l'insaisissable différance*, edited by Xavier Lacroix. Paris: du Cerf.
   • Translated into Italian as: "Transcendenti l'uno all'altra" (1994).
   • Reprinted in: *Etre deux* (1997).

1993. "Une culture à deux sujets." In *Apport européen et contribution française à l'égalité des chances entre les filles et les garçons*. Paris: Ministère de l'Education nationale et de la Culture.

1993. "Le lotte delle donne: Dall'uguaglianza alla differenza." In *Europa 1700–1992: Il ventesimosecolo*. Milan: Elekta.

1993. "Voglio l'amore e non la guerra" (lecture delivered as a presentation of *I Love to You*, Bologna, 4 March).
   • Translated into English as: "I Want Love, Not War" (2001).
   • Published in: *La democrazia comincia a due* (1994).

1993. "Different From You/Different Between Us." Interview by Fiorella Iannucci (originally published in Italian in *Il Messagero* (June)).
   • Reprinted in: *Why Different? A Culture of Two Subjects* (2000).

1993. "L'identité femme: Biologie ou conditionnement social?" (lecture delivered at the Colloquium "For a Democracy of Parity," Paris, 3 June).
   • Translated into Italian as: "L'identità femminile: biologia o condizionamento sociale?" (1994).
   • Published in: *Femmes: moitié de la terre, moitié du pouvoir*, edited by Gisèle Halimi. Paris: Gallimard, 1994.

1993. ed. *Genres culturels et interculturels*. Special edition of *Langages* 111 (September). Paris: Larousse.

1993. "Présentation." In *Genres culturels et interculturels*.

1993. "Importance du genre dans la constitution de la subjectivité et de l'intersubjectivité." In *Genres culturels et interculturels*.
   • Reprinted in: *Le partage de la parole* (2001).

1993. "The Civilization of the Two." Interview with Rossana Rossanda (originally published in Italian in *Il Manifesto* (17 September)).
   • Reprinted in: *Why Different? A Culture of Two Subjects* (2000) [as "The Civilization of Two"].

1993. "La schiavitù della donne" (lecture delivered at the national Festival of Unity, Bologna, 17 September).
   • Translated into English as: "Women's Enslavement" (2001).
   • Published in: *La democrazia comincia a due* (1994).

1993. "Come articolare la convivenza naturale e la convivenza civile?" (lecture delivered at the conference "European Citizenship," Bologna, 22–23 October).
  • Translated into English as: "How to Manage the Transition from Natural to Civil Coexistence" (2001).
  • Published in: *La democrazia comincia a due* (1994).
1993. "If Only Daughter and Mother Spoke to One Another." Interview by Maryse Marty (originally published in Italian in *Horizon femme* (November–December)).
  • Reprinted in: *Why Different? A Culture of Two Subjects* (2000).
1993. "Rifondare la famiglia su basi civili" (lecture delivered at the National Conference of Women of the PDS, Rome, 12 December).
  • Translated into English as: "Refounding the Family on a Civil Basis" (2001).
  • Published in: *La democrazia comincia a due* (1994).
1993. "Un Horizon future pour l'art?" In *Compara(i)son: An Internation Journal of Comparative Literature* 1: 107–16.
  • Translated into English as: "A Future Horizon for Art?" (2003).
1993–94. "Verso una cittadinanza dell'Unione europea" (with Renzo Imbeni, May 1993–January 1994).
  • Translated into English as: "Towards a Citizenship of the European Union" (2001).
  • Published in: *La democrazia comincia a due* (1994).
1994. *Essere due*. Torino: Bollati Boringhieri.
  • Translated into English as: *To Be Two* (2001).
  • Translated into French as: *Etre Deux* (1997).
1994. *Thinking the Difference: For a Peaceful Revolution*. Translated by Karin Montin. New York: Routledge.
  • Translation of: *Le Temps De La Différence: Pour une révolution pacifique* (1989).
1994. "Le nozze tra il corpo e la parola." In *Essere due* (1994).
  • Translated into English as: "The Wedding Between the Body and Language" (2001).
1994. "Transcendenti l'uno all'altra." In *Essere Due*.
  • Translation of: "Transcendants l'un à l'autre" (1993).
  • Translated into English as: "Each Transcendent to the Other" (2001).
1994. "How Do We Become Civil Women?" In *Thinking the Difference: For a Peaceful Revolution*.
  • Translation of: "Comment devenir des femmes civiles?" (1988).
1994. "Civil Rights and Responsibilities for the Two Sexes." In *Thinking the Difference: For a Peaceful Revolution*.
  • Translation of: "Droits et devoirs civils pour les deux sexes" (1988).
  • Reprinted in: *Luce Irigaray: Key Writings* (2004).

1994. "The Forgotten Mystery of Female Ancestry." In *Thinking the Differ-*
ence: For a Peaceful Revolution.
  • Translation of: "Le mystère oublié des généalogies féminines" (1989).
1994. "La voie du féminin." In *Le jardin clos de l'âme: L'imaginaire des religieuses*
dans les Pays-Bas du Sud, depuis le 13ᵉ siècle (bilingual French-Dutch
exhibition catalogue). Bruxelles: Martial et Snoeck.
  • Translated into English as: "The Way of the Feminine" (1999).
1994. "Je—Luce Irigaray." Interview by Elizabeth Hirsh and Gary Olson. In
Hypatia 10 (2) (Spring): 93–114.
  • Reprinted in: *Women, Writing and Culture* (1995).
1994. "Man-Woman in Search of Harmony." Interview by Maria Angela
Masino (originally published in Italian in *Gazzetta del Sud* (5 April)).
  • Reprinted in: *Why Different? A Culture of Two Subjects* (2000) [as
"Man and Woman in Search of Harmony"].
1994. "Different but United Through a New Alliance." Interview by Fiorella
Iannucci (originally published in Italian in *Il Messagero* (11 April)).
  • Reprinted in: *Why Different? A Culture of Two Subjects* (2000).
1994. "The Teaching of Difference." Interview by Paola Azzolini (originally
published in Italian in *L'Arena* (29 April)).
  • Reprinted in: *Why Different? A Culture of Two Subjects* (2000).
1994. "La questione dell'altro" (lecture delivered at the University of Verona,
30 April).
  • Translated into French as: "La question de l'autre" (1995).
  • Translated into English as: "The Question of the Other" (1995).
  • Published in: *La democrazia comincia a due* (1994).
1994. "Verso una filosofia dell'intersoggettività." In *Segni e compresione* 22
(May): 29–33.
1994. "A Natal Lacuna." Translated by Margaret Whitford. In *Women's Art*
Magazine 58 (May/June): 11–13.
  • Translation of: "Une lacune natale" (1985).
1994. "Dieci suggerimenti per costruire l'Unione europea" (suggestions sent
to Renzo Imbeni for the European Electoral Campaign, 7 May).
  • Translated into English as: "Ten Suggestions for the Construction of
the European Union" (2001).
  • Published in: *La democrazia comincia a due* (1994).
1994. "Politica e felicità" (lecture delivered during the European Electoral
Campaign, Reggio Emilia, 6 June).
  • Translated into English as: "Politics and Happiness" (2001).
  • Published in: *La democrazia comincia a due* (1994).
1994. "La rappresentanza delle donne" (lectured delivered on the occasion of
the European Electoral Campaign, Pesaro, 8 June).
  • Translated into English as: "The Representation of Women" (2001).
  • Published in: *La democrazia comincia a due* (1994).

1994. "Europa rapita da nuovi miti" (originally published in the newspaper *Il Quotidiano*, on the occasion of the results of the European elections, 19 June).
- Translated into English as: "Europe Captivated by New Myths" (2001).
- Reprinted in: *La democrazia comincia a due* (1994).
1994. "La democrazia è amore" (lecture delivered at the Festival of Unity, Imola, 15 July).
- Translated into English as: "Democracy is Love" (2001).
- Published in: *La democrazia comincia a due* (1994).
1994. *La democrazia comincia a due*. Torino: Bollati Boringhieri.
- Translated into English as: *Democracy Begins Between Two* (2001).
1994. "L'identità femminile: biologia o condizionamento sociale?" In *La democrazia comincia a due*.
- Translation of: "L'identitié femme: Biologie ou conditionnement social?" (1993).
- Translated into English as: "Feminine Identity: Biology or Social Conditioning?" (2001).
1994. "Homme, femme: les deux 'autres.'" In *Turbulences* 1 (October): 106–13.
1995. "Hommes et femmes: Une identité relationnelle différente." In *La Place de femmes: Les enjeux de l'identité et de l'égalité au regard des sciences socials*. Paris: La Découverte.
- Reprinted in: *Le partage de la parole*" (2001).
1995. "Pour une convivialité laïque sur le territoire de l'Union Européenne." In *Citoyenneté européen et culture*. Mons: University of Mons.
1995. "La question de l'autre." In *De l'égalité des sexes*, edited by Michel de Manassein. Paris: CNDP.
- Translation of: "La questione dell'altro" (1994).
- Translated into English as: "The Question of the Other" (1995).
1995. "The Question of the Other." Translated from the French by Noah Guynn. In *Another Look, Another Woman*. Edition of *Yale French Studies* 87 (May): 7–19.
- Translation of: "La question d'lautre" (1995).
- Reprinted in: Democracy Begins Between Two (2001) [translation of the Italian "La questione dell'altro" (1994)].
1995. "La diferencia sexual come fondamento de la democrazia." In *Duoda* 8: 121–34.
1995. "The Time of Difference." Interview with Patrick de Sagazan (originally published in Italian in *Famille rurales* (September)).
- Reprinted in: *Why Different? A Culture of Two Subjects* (2000).
1996. ed. *Le Souffle des femmes*. Paris: Action Catholique Générale Feminine.
1996. *I Love to You: Sketch for a Felicity Within History*. Translated by Alison Martin. New York: Routledge.

- Translation of: *J'aime à toi: esquisse d'une félicité dans l'histoire* (1992).

1996. "Introduction." In *Le Souffle des femmes*.

1996. "La rédemption des femmes." In *Le Souffle des femmes*.

1996. "Le divin entre nous." Conversation with Rosi Braidotti, Ied Guinée, Marion de Zanger, Renée Hablé, Camille Mortagne, Anne-Claire Mulder, and Agnès Vincenot. In *Le Souffle des femmes*.

1996. "He I Sought But Did Not Find." In *I Love to You: Sketch for a Felicity Within History*.
  - Translation of: "Je l'ai cherché et ne l'ai pas trouvé" (1992).
  - Reprinted in: *Philosophy of Language: The Big Questions* (1998).

1996. "The Other: Woman." In *I Love to You: Sketch for a Felicity Within History*.
  - Translation of: "L'autre: femme" (1992).
  - Reprinted in: *Feminisms* (1998).

1996. "You Who Will Never Be Mine." In *I Love to You: Sketch for a Felicity Within History*.
  - Translation of: "Toi qui ne seras jamais mien" (1992).
  - Reprinted in: *Luce Irigaray: Key Writings* (2004).

1996. "Two of Us, Outside, Tomorrow?" In *I Love to You: Sketch for a Felicity Within History*.
  - Translation of: "A deux dehors demain?" (1992).
  - Reprinted in: *Luce Irigaray: Key Writings* (2004) [as "Being Two Outside Tomorrow?"].

1996. "Da *L'Oblio dell'aria* a *Amo a te* e *Essere due*" (originally published as the introduction to the Italian edition of *The Forgetting of Air*. It was written to commemorate the twentieth anniversary of Martin Heidegger's death in the Spring of 1976).
  - Translated into English as: "From *The Forgetting of Air* to *To Be Two*" (2001).

1996. "Words to Nourish the Breath of Life." Interview by Ida Dominiganni (originally published in Italian in *Il Manifesto* (13 July)).
  - Reprinted in: *Why Different? A Culture of Two Subjects* (2000).

1996. "The Air of Those Who Love Each Other." Interview by Brena Niorelli (originally published in Italian in *Unitá* (30 July)).
  - Reprinted in: *Why Different? A Culture of Two Subjects* (2000).

1996. "La famille commence à deux." In *Panoramiques: La famille malgré tout 25*.
  - Translated into English as: "The Family Begins with Two" (2002).
  - Reprinted in: *Entre Orient et Occident: de la singularité à la communauté* (1999).

1996. "Thinking Life as Relation: An Interview with Luce Irigaray." Interview by Heidi Bostic and Stephen Pluháček. In *Man and World* 29: 343–60.

1996. "Questions to Luce Irigaray." Interview by Kate Ince. In *Hypatia* 11: 122–40.

1997. *Etre deux*. Paris: Bernard Grasset.
  • Translation of: *Essere Due* (1994).
1997. "Scrivo per dividere l'invisibile con l'altro." In *Scrivere, vivere, vedere*, edited by Francesca Pasini. Milan: La Tartaruga.
1997. "The Spirit of Women Blows." Interview by Monica Bungaro (originally published in Italian in *Il quotidiano de lecce* (22 May)).
  • Reprinted in: *Why Different? A Culture of Two Subjects* (2000).
1997. "Progetto di formazione alla cittadianza per ragazze e ragazze, per donne e uomini" (work undertaken at the request of the Commission for parity between boys and girls, women and men, in the Emilie Romagne Region, and presented to regional authorities 27 May).
1998. "Breath of the Orient." Interview by Helena Bellei (originally published in Italian in *Noi Donne* (June)).
  • Reprinted in: *Why Different? A Culture of Two Subjects* (2000).
1999. *Entre Orient et Occident: De la singularité à la communauté*. Paris: Bernard Grasset.
  • Translated into English as: *Between East and West: From Singularity to Community* (2002).
1999. *The Forgetting of Air in Martin Heidegger*. Translated by Mary Beth Mader. Austin: University of Texas Press.
  • Translation of: *L'oubli de l'air chez Martin Heidegger* (1983).
1999. *Le temps du souffle*. Rüsselsheim: Christel Göttert Verlag.
  • Translated into English as: "The Age of Breath" (2004).
1999. *Chi sono io? Chi sei tu? La chiave per una convivenza universale*. Casalmaggiore: Biblioteca di Casalmaggiore.
1999. "S'approcher de l'autre en tant qu'autre." In *Entre Orient et Occident: de la singularité à la communauté*.
  • Translated into English as: "Approaching the Other as Other" (2001).
1999. "The Way of the Feminine." Translated by David Macey. In *New Trends in Feminine Spirituality: The Holy Women of Liege and Their Impact*, edited by Juliette Dor, Lesley Johnson, and J. Wogan-Browne. Turnhout, Belgium: Brepols Publishers.
  • Translation of: "La voie du féminin" (1994).
1999. "Children Divided by Sex." Interview by Laura Lilli (originally published in Italian in *Repubblica* (7 June)).
  • Reprinted in: *Why Different? A Culture of Two Subjects* (2000).
2000. ed. *Why Different? A Culture of Two Subjects* (with Sylvère Lotringer). Translated by Camille Collins, Peter Carravetta, Ben Meyers, Heidi Bostic, and Stephen Pluháček. New York: Semiotext(e).
  • Translation of: *Pourquoi la différence?: Une culture à deux sujets* [not yet published as a book in French].
2000. *A deux, nous avons combien d'yeux?* Rüsselsheim: Christel Göttert Verlag.
  • Translated into English as: "Being Two, How Many Eyes Have We?" (2001).

2000. "Mothers and Daughters." In *Why Different? A Culture of Two Subjects.*
  • Translation of: "Mères et filles vues par Luce Irigaray" (1979).

2000. "Feminist Philosophy" (with Mary Daly, Sally McFague, Julia Kristeva, Pamela Anderson, and Grace Jantzen). In *Twentieth-Century Western Philosophy of Religion*, edited by Eugene Thomas Long. Boston: Kluwer Academic Publishers.

2000. "Tâches spirituelles pour notre temps." In *Religiologiques, Luce Irigaray: Le féminin et la religion*, edited by Marie-Andrée Roy. Montreal: University of Quebec.

2000. "Sostituire il desiderio per l'altro al bisogno di droghe." In *Animazione Sociale* 25 (February): 12–20.
  • Reprinted in: *Senza il bacio del Principe* (2002).

2000. "Le partage de la parole" (Zaharoff Lecture).
  • Published in: *Le partage de la parole* (2001).

2000. "Comment habiter durablement ensemble?" (lecture delivered at the International Architectural Association of London, November).
  • Translated into English as: "How Can We Live Together in a Lasting Way?" (2002).

2001. *Democracy Begins Between Two.* Translated by Kirsteen Anderson. New York: Routledge.
  • Translation of: *La democrazia comincia a due* (1994).

2001. *To Be Two.* Translated by Monique M. Rhodes and Marco F. Cocito-Monoc. New York: Routledge.
  • Translation of: *Essere due* (1994).

2001. *Le Partage de la parole.* Oxford: European Humanities Research Centre, University of Oxford.

2001. "A Two-Subject Culture." In *Democracy Begins Between Two.*
  • Translation of: "Una cultura a due soggetti" (1992).

2001. "I Want Love, Not War." In *Democracy Begins Between Two.*
  • Translation of: "Voglio l'amore e non la Guerra" (1993).

2001. "Feminine Identity: Biology or Social Conditioning?" In *Democracy Begins Between Two.*
  • Translation of: "L'identità femminile: biologia o condizionamento sociale?" (1993).

2001. "Women's Enslavement." In *Democracy Begins Between Two.*
  • Translation of: "La schiavitù delle donne" (1993).

2001. "How to Manage the Transition from Natural to Civil Coexistence." In *Democracy Begins Between Two.*
  • Translation of: "Come articolare la convivenza naturale e la convivenza civile?" (1993).
  • Reprinted in: *Luce Irigaray: Key Writings* (2004) [as "How to Ensure the Connection between Natural and Civil Coexistence"].

2001. "Rounding the Family on a Civil Basis." In *Democracy Begins Between Two.*

- Translation of: "Rifondare la famiglia su basi civili" (1993).

2001. "Towards a Citizenship of the European Union." In *Democracy Begins Between Two.*
- Translation of: "Verso una cittadinanza dell'Unione europea" (1993–94).

2001. "Ten Suggestions for the Construction of the European Union." In *Democracy Begins Between Two.*
- Translation of: "Dieci suggerimenti per construire l'Unione europea" (1994).

2001. "Politics and Happiness." In *Democracy Begins Between Two.*
- Translation of: "Politica e felicità" (1994).
- Reprinted in: *Luce Irigaray: Key Writings* (2004).

2001. "The Representation of Women." In *Democracy Begins Between Two.*
- Translation of: "La rappresentanza delle donne" (1994).

2001. "Europe Captivated by New Myths." In *Democracy Begins Between Two.*
- Translation of: "Europa rapita da nuovi miti" (1994).

2001. "Democracy is Love." In *Democracy Begins Between Two.*
- Translation of: "La democrazia è amore" (1994).

2001. "Feminine Identity: Biology or Social Conditioning?" In *Democracy Begins Between Two.*
- Translation of: "L'identità femminile: biologia o condizionamento sociale?" (1994).
- Reprinted in: *French Feminism: An Indian Anthology* (2003).

2001. "The Wedding Between the Body and Language." In *To Be Two.*
- Translation of: "Le nozze tra il corpo e la parola" (1994).
- Reprinted in: *Luce Irigaray: Key Writings* (2004).

2001. "Each Transcendent to the Other." In *To Be Two.*
- Translation of: "Transcendenti l'uno all'altra" (1994).

2001. "From *The Forgetting of Air* to *To Be Two.*" Translated from the French original by Heidi Bostic and Stephen Pluháček. In *Feminist Interpretations of Martin Heidegger*, edited by Nancy Holland and Patricia Huntington. University Park, Penn.: Pennsylvania State University Press.
- Translation of: "Da *L'Oblio dell'aria* a *Amo a te e Essere due*" (1996).

2001. "Being Two, How Many Eyes Have We?" Translated by Luce Irigaray with Catherine Busson, Jim Mooney, Heidi Bostic, and Stephen Pluháček. In *Dialogues: Around Her Work.*
- Translation of: *A deux, nous avons combien d'yeux?* (2000).

2001. "Luce Irigaray y la Construcción de una Cultura Democrática fundada en la Diferencia." Interview by Maria José Oramas. In *Periódico La Jornada, Suplemento La Triple Jornada* 5 (March): 5–7.

2001. "Why Cultivate Difference?" (lecture delivered at the University of Nottingham, 20 June).
- Published in: *Dialogues: Around Her Work* (2001).

2002. *The Way of Love.* Translated by Heidi Bostic and Stephen Pluháček. New York: Continuum.
  • Translation of: *La Voie de l'amour* [not yet published in French].
2002. *To Speak Is Never Neutral.* Translated by Gail Schwab. New York: Routledge.
  • Translation of: *Parler n'est jamais neutre* (1985).
2002. *Between East and West: From Singularity to Community.* Translated by Stephen Pluháček. New York: Columbia University Press.
  • Translation of: *Entre Orient et Occident: de la singularité à la communauté* (1999).
2002. "The Intimate Requires Separate Dwellings." In *The Way of Love.*
  • Reprinted in: *Luce Irigaray: Key Writings* (2004).
2002. "The Rape of the Letter." In *To Speak Is Never Neutral.*
  • Translation of: "Le v(i)ol de la lettre" (1969).
2002. "Linguistic and Specular Communication." In *To Speak Is Never Neutral.*
  • Translation of: "Communication linguistique et spéculaire" (1966).
2002. "Negation and Negative Transformations in the Language of Schizophrenics." In *To Speak Is Never Neutral.*
  • Translation of: "Négation et transformation négative dans le langage des schizophrènes" (1967).
2002. "Towards a Grammar of Enunciation for Hysterics and Obsessives." In *To Speak Is Never Neutral.*
  • Translation of: "Approche d'une grammaire d'énonciation de l'hystérique et de l'obsessionnel" (1967).
  • Reprinted in: *Luce Irigaray: Key Writings* (2004).
2002. "On Phantasm and the Verb." In *To Speak Is Never Neutral.*
  • Translation of: "Du fantasme et du verbe" (1968).
2002. "Sentence Production among Schizophrenics and Senile Dementia Patients." In *To Speak Is Never Neutral.*
  • Translation of: "Épreuve de production de phrases chez les déments et les schizophrènes" (1968).
2002. "The Utterance in Analysis." In *To Speak Is Never Neutral.*
  • Translation of: "L'énoncé en analyse" (1969).
2002. "Class Language, Unconscious Language." In *To Speak Is Never Neutral.*
  • Translation of: "Langage de classe, langage inconscient" (1969).
2002. "Sex as Sign." In *To Speak Is Never Neutral.*
  • Translation of: "Le sexe fait comme signe" (1970).
2002. "Schizophrenics, or the Refusal of Schiz." In *To Speak Is Never Neutral.*
  • Translation of: "Le schizophrène ou le refus de la schize" (1971).
2002. "The Family Begins with Two." In *Between East and West: From Singularity to Community.*
  • Translation of: "La famille commence à deux" (1996).

2002. "Approaching the Other as Other." In *Between East and West: From Singularity to Community.*
  • Translation of: "S'approcher de l'autre en tant qu'autre" (1999).
  • Reprinted in: *Luce Irigaray: Key Writings* (2004).

2002. "The Time of Life." In *Between East and West: From Singularity to Community.*
  • Translation of: "Le temps de la vie" (1989).

2002. "How Can We Live Together in a Lasting Way?" Translated by Alison Martin, Maria Bailey, and Luce Irigaray. In *Rethinking Architecture*, edited by Neil Leach. London: Routledge.
  • Translation of: "Comment habiter durablement ensemble?" (2000).
  • Reprinted in: *Luce Irigaray: Key Writings* (2004).

2003. "On Old and New Tablets." Translated by Heidi Bostic. Introduction to *Religion in French Feminist Thought: Critical Perspectives*, edited by Morny Joy, Kathleen O'Grady, and Judith L. Poxon. New York: Routledge.
  • Reprinted in: *Luce Irigaray: Key Writings* (2004) [as "Fulfilling Our Humanity"].

2002. *Dialogues: Around Her Work* (a collection of the lectures and responses given in the *Dialogues* conference at the AHRB Centre for Cultural Analysis, Theory, and History in Leeds, 2001). Special issue of *Paragraph* 25(3) (November).

2002. "Introduction." In *Dialogues: Around Her Work.*

2002. "Conclusions." In *Dialogues: Around Her Work.*

2003. "La transcendance de l'autre." In *Autour de l'idolâtrie: Figures actuelles de pouvoir et de domination.* Brussles: University of St. Louis.

2003. "What Other Are We Talking About?" Translated by Esther Marion. In *Yale French Studies* 104: 67–81.

2003. "A Future Horizon for Art?" Translated by Jennifer Matey. In *Continental Philosophy Review* 36(4): 353–65.
  • Translation of: "Un Horizon future pour l'art?" (1993).
  • Reprinted in: *Luce Irigaray: Key Writings* (2004).

2004. ed. *Luce Irigaray: Key Writings.* New York: Continuum.

2004. "How Can We Speak with Socialism as Our Horizon?" Translated by Joanne Collie and Judith Still. In *Luce Irigaray: Key Writings.*
  • Translation of: "Comment nous parler dans l'horizon du Socialisme?" (1992).

2004. "Animal Compassion." In *Animal Philosophy: Readings in Continental Thought*, edited by Matthew Calarco and Peter Atterton. New York: Continuum.

Forthcoming. "The Ecstasy of the Between Us." In *Intermedialities*, edited by Hank Oosterling and Krzysztof Ziarek. New York: Continuum [forthcoming].

Forthcoming. "The Path Towards the Other." In *After Beckett*, edited by Stan Gontarski and Anthony Uhlman [forthcoming].

NOTES ON CONTRIBUTORS

DEBRA BERGOFFEN

Debra Bergoffen is Professor of Philosophy and a member of the Women's Studies and Cultural Studies faculties at George Mason University. Her book, *The Philosophy of Simone de Beauvoir: Gendered Phenomenologies, Erotic Generosities* details the significance of Beauvoir's singular philosophical voice and examines its impact on contemporary philosophical theory and current feminist thought. Her latest research explores the ways in which UN Criminal Tribunal judgments in the wake of the genocides in the former Yugoslavia and Rwanda direct us to revisit our concepts of humanity, human dignity, women's rights and human rights and to reconsider the implications of just war theory.

MARIA C. CIMITILE

Maria Cimitile is Associate Professor of Philosophy and Associate Dean of the College of Liberal Arts and Sciences at Grand Valley State University. Her area of research is continental feminist thought and political theory. She is currently working on a book on psychoanalytic theory and political identity, tentatively titled *National Identity and Political Structures: A Feminist Analysis*. She has published on Irigaray, Heidegger, and the ancient Greeks.

PENELOPE DEUTSCHER

Penelope Deutscher is Associate Professor of Philosophy at Northwestern University. She is the author of *Yielding Gender: Feminism,*

Deconstruction and the History of Philosophy (Routledge, 1997), *A Politics of Impossible Difference: The Later Work of Luce Irigaray* (Cornell Univesity Press, 2001), and *How To Read Derrida* (forthcoming Granta) and co-editor (with Kelly Oliver) of *Enigmas: Essays on Sarah Kofman* and (with Françoise Collin) of *Repenser le politique: l'apport du feminisme* (Campagne première 2005).

SARA HEINÄMAA

Sara Heinämaa is Senior Lecturer of Theoretical Philosophy at the University of Helsinki, Finland. She also works as Professor of Humanist Women's Studies at the Centre for Women's Studies and Gender Research, University of Oslo, Norway. She has published several articles on phenomenology, focusing on the problems of method, embodiment, and sexuality. Her latest publications include *Toward a Phenomenology of Sexual Difference: Husserl, Merleau-Ponty, Beauvoir* (2003), and the collection *Metaphysics, Facticity, Interpretation* (2003), co-edited with Dan Zahavi and Hans Ruin.

ELAINE P. MILLER

Elaine Miller is Associate Professor of Philosophy at Miami University in Oxford, Ohio. She is the author of *The Vegetative Soul: From Philosophy of Nature to Subjectivity in the Feminine* (State University of New York Press, 2001) and articles on Kant, Hegel, Nietzsche, Beauvoir, and Irigaray.

ANN V. MURPHY

Ann V. Murphy is currently New South Global Postdoctoral Fellow in the School of Philosophy at the University of New South Wales in Sydney, Australia. Her background is in twentieth-century French philosophy, phenomenology, political philosophy, and feminist theory. Her current research focuses on the relationship between symbolic and material violence in relation to sexuality and race. She has published on Beauvoir, Irigaray, Merleau-Ponty, Foucault, and Levinas.

KELLY OLIVER

Kelly Oliver is W. Alton Jones Professor of Philosophy at Vanderbilt University, where she is also an affiliate in Women's Studies. She is the author of over fifty articles and seven books, most recently *The Colonization of Psychic Space: Toward a Psychoanalytic Social Theory* (University of Minnesota, 2004), *Noir Anxiety: Race, Sex, and Maternity in Film Noir* (University of Minnesota, 2002), and *Witnessing: Beyond Recognition* (University of Minnesota, 2001). She has edited several books, including *Recent French Feminism* (Oxford University Press, 2004) and *French Feminism Reader* (Rowman & Littlefield, 2000).

CATHERINE PEEBLES

Catherine Peebles is the Coordinator of the Humanities Program at University of New Hampshire. She is the author of *The Psyche of Feminism: Sand, Colette, Sarraute*, as well as a number of articles in her areas of interest, which include feminism and psychoanalysis, and French thought.

GAIL SCHWAB

Gail Schwab is Professor of French in the Department of Romance Languages and Literatures at Hofstra University, and Acting Associate Dean of Hofstra College of Liberal Arts and Sciences. Translator of Luce Irigaray's *Parler n'est jamais neutre*, and co-translator of *Sexes et genres a travers les langues*, in addition to several shorter pieces recently published in *Luce Irigaray: Key Writings*, she has published extensively on Irigaray in anthologies and journals. She is currently working on a book on Irigaray and language, and her most recent contribution to Irigaray studies is an article, "Mother, Sisters, and Daughters: Irigaray and the Female Genealogical Line in the Stories of the Greeks," forthcoming from State University of New York Press in a collection on *Irigaray and the Greeks*.

MARGARET WHITFORD

Margaret Whitford is Professor of Modern French Thought at Queen Mary and Westfield College, University of London. Her interests lie in modern French philosophy, the history of ideas, feminist theory, and psychoanalytic theory. Her publications include: *Merleau-Ponty's Critique of Sartre's Philosophy* (1982), *Luce Irigaray: Philosophy in the Feminine* (1991), *Feminist Perspectives in Philosophy* (ed., 1988), *The Irigaray Reader* (ed., 1991), *Engaging with Irigaray* (ed., 1994), and *Knowing the Difference: Feminist Perspectives in Epistemology* (ed., 1994).

EMILY ZAKIN

Emily Zakin is Associate Professor of Philosophy at Miami University in Ohio. She has published essays on psychoanalytic, continental, and feminist theory and is currently at work on a book project tentatively entitled *Fantasies of Origin: The Birth of the Polis and the Limits of Democracy*. She is also co-editor of two volumes, *Derrida and Feminism: Recasting the Question of Woman* (Routledge) and *Greek Tragedy, Sexual Difference and the Formation of the Polis* (forthcoming).

KRZYSZTOF ZIAREK

Krzysztof Ziarek is Professor of Comparative Literature at the State University of New York at Buffalo. He is the author of *Inflected Language: Toward a Hermeneutics of Nearness* (State University of New York Press), *The Historicity of Experience: Modernity, the Avant-Garde, and the Event* (Northwestern University Press), and *The Force of Art* (Stanford University Press). He has also published numerous essays on Coolidge, Stein, Stevens, Heidegger, Benjamin, Irigaray, and Levinas, and co-edited a collection of essays, *Future Crossings: Literature Between Philosophy and Cultural Studies*. He is currently working on aesthetics and globalization.

INDEX